African Studies Since 1945

A Tribute to Basil Davidson

African Studies Since 1945

A Tribute to Basil Davidson

Proceedings of a seminar
in honour of
Basil Davidson's
sixtieth birthday at the
Centre of African Studies
University of Edinburgh
under the chairmanship of
George Shepperson

Edited by
Christopher Fyfe

**AFRICANA
PUBLISHING
COMPANY**

IMPORT DIVISION

A Division of Holmes & Meier Publishers, Inc.
101 Fifth Avenue, New York, N.Y. 10003

Longman Group Limited
London

Associated companies, branches and
representatives throughout the world

© Centre of African Studies, Edinburgh, 1976

First published 1976

ISBN 0 582 64208 6 (paper)
              64207 8 (cased)

Printed in Great Britain by
T. & A. Constable Ltd., Edinburgh

Contents

Seminar participants included

David Abercrombie
Edinburgh University

Mary Abercrombie
Edinburgh

Arthur Abraham
Sierra Leone University

Anne Akeroyd
York University

M. E. Aldridge
Edinburgh University

Robert Baldock
York University

Helmut Bley
Hamburg University

Lalage Bown
Ahmadu Bello University

Sheila Brock
Edinburgh University

E. K. Brown
Edinburgh University

Gilian Brown
Edinburgh University

Lynne Cannon
London University

T. H. R. Cashmore
Foreign Office

T. R. M. Creighton
Edinburgh University

Duncan Clarke
St Andrews University

G. Clendenden
Edinburgh University

Robin Cohen
Birmingham University

James Currie
Heinemann

Basil Davidson
Hereford

Ian Duffield
Edinburgh University

Paul Edwards
Edinburgh University

A. Erwin
York University

J. D. Fage
Birmingham University

Ruth First
Durham University

Erica Flegg
Edinburgh University

O. W. Furley
Lanchester Polytechnic

Christopher Fyfe
Edinburgh University

M. R. Grant
Heriot-Watt University

Imanuel Geiss
Bremen University

Frances Harding
Edinburgh University

Judith Head
Durham University

Ian Henderson
Lanchester Polytechnic

Christopher Hill
York University

Polly Hill
Cambridge University

C. M. G. Himsworth
Edinburgh University

J. A. Hocking
Moray House

Rosemary Hutton
Edinburgh University

David Idah
Moray House

Ahmadu Jalingo
Edinburgh University

K. A. B. Jones-Quartey
Ghana University

I. D. M. Joseph
York University

John B. Kabera
Birmingham University

Mara Kalnins
Malawi University

Victor Kiernan
Edinburgh University

Kenneth King
Edinburgh University

A. H. M. Kirk-Greene
Oxford University

Robin Law
Stirling University

J. Lenga-Kroma
Edinburgh University

M. Lewally-Taylor
Edinburgh University

Godfrey Lienhardt
Oxford University

Kenneth Little
Edinburgh University

John McCracken
Stirling University

John Macdonald
Edinburgh University

Madu Mailafiya
Edinburgh University

Shula Marks
London University

Joseph C. Miller
Virginia University

Patricia Miller
Edinburgh University

Peter Mitchell
Birmingham University

Joseph Mullen
Edinburgh University

S. A. Omole
Moray House

Henry Ord
Edinburgh University

Carol Page
Edinburgh University

A. Pallinder-Law
Glasgow University

Faith Pullin
Edinburgh University

Charles Raab
Edinburgh University

T. O. Ranger
Manchester University

C. J. Rea
Longman

M. Robinson
Birmingham University

Peter Robson
St Andrews University

Andrew Ross
Edinburgh University

Neville Rubin
London University

Michael Ryan
St Andrews University

Dianne Sabharwa
Birmingham University

M. S. M. Salim
Edinburgh University

T. V. Sathyamurthy
York University

Thurstan Shaw
Cambridge

George Shepperson
Edinburgh University

N. J. Small
Edinburgh University

John Suckling
York University

Bing Taylor
Longman

Bankole Timothy
London

Rosina Visram
Edinburgh University

Peter Warwick
York University

Peter Wass
Edinburgh University

J. Whybrow
Edinburgh University

Gavin Williams
Durham University

Roy Willis
Edinburgh University

Harry Wilson
York University

Christopher Fyfe

Introduction

On 8 November 1974 a group of academics assembled at the University of Edinburgh under the auspices of the Centre of African Studies for a two-day seminar to discuss how African Studies have changed since the end of the Second World War. Their underlying purpose was to honour Basil Davidson, whose sixtieth birthday was the following day. That same day an African representative of MPLA flew into Luanda to receive, after ten years of fighting, official recognition by the Portuguese government of Angola. These fortuitously synchronic events linked two of Basil Davidson's abiding concerns—his untiring championship of the liberation struggles against the former Portuguese regime in Africa, witnessed not only in his writings but in his long visit to the Angolan war theatre in 1970, and his pioneer work as an interpreter of the African past, which has been a constant stimulus and inspiration to scholars and the general reading public.

His career as an Africanist has consistently combined an immediate concern for those struggling against oppression with sympathetic understanding of their history. His interest in Africa was first roused when he became secretary to the League for Colonial Freedom. He then visited South Africa as a journalist, and published *Report on Southern Africa* in 1952. Two years later he toured Angola, retracing the steps of another courageous enemy of oppression, Henry Nevinson (see p. 12). From the embittered African present he turned to the neglected African past. In 1959 he published *Old Africa Rediscovered*, one of the seminal works which ushered in the heroic period, the 'golden age', as Terence Ranger calls it (p. 17), of African historiography. *Black Mother* followed, a moving, scholarly account of the Atlantic slave trade.

Unlike most of the historians and social scientists who were then turning to Africa, he wrote for a wide audience. His books have been translated into seventeen languages. He has also written school textbooks: a Nigerian secondary school headmaster, David Idah, who attended the seminar, paid tribute to the stimulus of his work. Inevitably his early books were slighted by those who, unable themselves to command the attention of any but specialists in their own narrow realms, will ever justify their narrowness by decrying popularisation. But in presenting his work to a wide audience he has never sacrificed accuracy to popularity, and in so doing he has inspired a whole generation in Africa, Europe and America to see African history in a new way. Nor has he forgotten the visual appeal in history. The original edition of his *Africa in History* (the best general introduction to African history) was beautified by superb photographs, taken by Werner Forman, but chosen by himself with a scholarly and aesthetic discrimination which enriches the text.

The artistic and poetic awareness of 'a poet who writes in prose' (as one reviewer described him), also sustained *The Africans*, published in 1970. Again, a deceptively popular presentation masked deep and original insights. Always the pioneer, he here anticipated the 'need to give further thought to African cosmologies as a means of understanding the relationship between belief and action' which A. G. Hopkins calls for (p. 37).

Meanwhile he was writing books and articles to publicise the struggle against the Portuguese government in Africa. Here his writings had a dual purpose. He sought to inform an apathetic European and American public about events that most journalists ignored. More important, he showed that the leaders of the liberation movements, notably his close personal friends Agostino Neto and the late Amilcar Cabral, were striving to do more than merely displace colonial rule —that they had learnt the lessons Fanon had preached, and were seeking to supplant the oppressive colonial structures with new structures. He developed this theme in *Can Africa Survive?*, published in 1974, based on lectures given in 1972 as visiting professor at the University of Edinburgh.

In his own work, therefore, we see already raised some of the themes elaborated in the papers and discussions at the seminar. This was stressed by the chairman, Professor George Shepperson, himself a distinguished pioneer in the study of African and Afro-American history. The participants were deliberately chosen to represent the disciplines he has been particularly concerned with. Hence the absence of papers on the physical and medical sciences. The seminar was also restricted in time (to a day and a half), and by limited finances which made it impossible to bring participants from overseas. Only one African, K. A. B. Jones-Quartey, Emeritus Professor of Adult Education at the University of Ghana, was able to present his paper personally. Hence it turned out (and why not?) to be largely a tribute paid by British scholars to a distinguished British scholar. Inevitably, however, as was pointed out more than once during the proceedings, the approach tended to be more Eurocentric than was perhaps appropriate for a celebration to honour the proponent of an Afro-centred focus in the study of Africa.

African Studies, as Lalage Bown put it during the discussion, have grown since the Second World War from a cottage industry to a multi-national enterprise. In the process they have had to struggle out of a paternalistic prison. When in 1938 Lord Hailey included in his *An African Survey* a chapter on 'The Future of African Studies', he envisioned European scholars and technicians working to develop Africa for the ultimate benefit of its peoples. No one, thirty-six years later, would have openly subscribed to such a formulation. Yet in the flood of books, articles and reports that have appeared since then on African subjects, there has persisted, and (as our seminar proceedings showed) to some extent still persists, an unspoken assumption that the serious and important decisions must always be made outside Africa.

Regularly during the proceedings it was suggested that African Studies were in a state of crisis. Kenneth King sounds a warning note in his paper on education (p. 77). He explains how educational planners and aid-givers, disillusioned by the new African bourgeoisie, have lost faith in the system that bred them. They turn from the expensive plans of the 'Ashby decade' to inexpensive self-help projects—often painfully reminiscent of the colonial period, when, as he described in his *Pan-Africanism and Education*, Africans were to be given 'appropriate', which usually meant inferior, education.

Terence Ranger senses a crisis in African historiography (p. 17), noting the disillusionment expressed by young African scholars who are questioning the value of studying African history. His answer is to emphasise more relevant approaches. This seemed inadequate to some of the participants—seemed even a 'Whig interpretation' of African history to Gavin Williams who demanded a more explicitly radical framework of analysis. Ann Seidman's contribution (pp. 49-65), setting out the conflicting contemporary interpretations and solutions of African economic problems, was seen as a similar sign of crisis among the economists.

Godfrey Lienhardt, however, denied during the discussion that there was any crisis in social anthropology. Some of his audience were sceptical, remembering recent published self-criticism by members of his profession, and the disrepute which his discipline tends to attract in Africa where it is often branded with the stigma of colonialism. But Roy Willis pointed out that though the name 'social anthropology' may be avoided in Africa, it is increasingly studied under the label 'African Studies'. As Thurstan Shaw put it, African scholars, hitherto rightly suspicious of the 'guinea-pig syndrome' which placed them at the lower end of the microscope, are now looking through the other end. Indeed an Anthropological Association of Nigeria has been founded, inspired and largely officered by Nigerians.

In archaeology Thurstan Shaw sees no crisis (pp. 156-68). The success story of West African archaeology, for which he has been largely responsible in his years as head of the Department of Archaeology at the University of Ibadan, proves that constant questioning of methodology is not a sign of crisis but of vitality, witnessed by the steadily increasing number of African archaeologists. Similarly John Hunwick, in his paper on Islamic Studies (p. 149), points to the growing number of African scholars in his field. A. H. M. Kirk-Greene reminds us of a flourishing new branch of African Studies, public administration (pp. 125-35), which he has himself pioneered. Nor would Polly Hill admit that the new discipline of economic anthropology which she is pioneering is in a state of crisis. But she was alarmed at the insistent demands made on her for theory before the empirical data to construct it were yet available.

Paul Edwards's paper on African literature (pp. 91-5) reveals uncertainty rather than crisis—whether for instance the published African literature of the past two decades is really relevant to contemporary African society. He is inclined to see drama as a more fruitful form than fiction. This was confirmed during the discussion, by reference to the original and immensely popular dramatic productions in Nigeria, given live and on TV and radio, which display exuberance and vitality, not crisis and uncertainty.

Even the crisis in educational planning is primarily a crisis for Americans and Europeans. In Nigeria, as Lalage Bown observed, millions are being spent on extending the existing educational system to include universal primary education.

Perhaps in their readiness to diagnose crisis, Africanists, Whig or radical, are showing themselves the heirs of the Hailey tradition, interpreting as a crisis in African Studies their own failure to solve (as they somehow feel it their responsibility to solve) Africa's problems.

Another question raised by Lalage Bown, and considered explicitly or implicitly in several papers, was whether African Studies should exist in isolation from studies of Asia and Europe. There was general agreement that Africa cannot be isolated meaningfully, and that in any discipline it can serve as a base from which wider comparisons can be made. Even apart from obvious comparative studies by historians and social scientists, it can be rewarding, as Paul Edwards mentions (p. 91), to compare certain types of African literature with the literature of mediaeval Iceland. But probably most of the participants would still have echoed Terence Ranger's forthright declaration, 'I am determined to remain an Africanist'. No one, however, questioned the use of the term, or quoted the words Conor Cruise O'Brien put into the mouth of the sinister financier in his *Murderous Angels*; 'An Africanist is a specialist whom we employ in order to get the better of Africans'.

Several of the papers raise the difficulties of communication. In the discussion of publishing, arising out of Julian Rea's paper (pp. 96-105), James Currie of Heinemann commented on the balkanisation of African book distribution. Local export regulations make it easier to market a book produced in Lagos in Moscow than in Accra. Hence African governments are giving an advantage to the big international publishing firms, and penalising their own publishing houses. In this way African authors, who may in any case prefer an expatriate publisher for financial or prestige reasons, are further discouraged from publishing their books locally. Nor is it easy to find out what books are being published in Africa, let alone to buy them. Agneta Pallinder-Law of Glasgow University Library regretted the absence of an African equivalent of *Books in Print*—a deficiency since remedied by the inauguration of Hans Zell's *African Book Publishing Record* in 1975.

To these technical obstructions may be added direct official pressures. K. A. B. Jones-Quartey describes (pp. 119-20) how the *Legon Observer*, almost the only serious, critical news-journal in independent Africa, has been deliberately silenced by the authorities in Ghana.

Turning from independent to dependent Africa, Shula Marks's paper describes the changes that have taken place in South African historiography (pp. 186-99). She shows how the complacent liberal tradition, so long unchallenged, and still voiced in the *Oxford History of South Africa*, has been undermined by a radical revaluation of Davidsonian type. But the revaluation has been the work of exiles. Within South Africa critical historiography is barely stirring. Within what was Portuguese Africa too, historiography has tended to be equally uncritical. The important work has come from outside. Allen Isaacman and Gerald Bender have supplied a comprehensive historiographical guide to Mozambique and Angola as an American tribute to Basil Davidson (pp. 220-48).

The impending liberation of Portuguese Africa gave an added cause for rejoicing to the participants in this 1974 seminar in honour of Basil Davidson. It also seemed to justify the 'unquenchable optimism' which, Terence Ranger recalled, he has always displayed. Too often European and American scholars, burdened with the sense of the crisis within their own society, dismiss as facile or ridiculous the optimism that fires many utterances, and inspires many policies, within Africa. Basil Davidson, with his courage, goodness and wisdom, reminds us that optimism is not ridiculous, and that we must not lose hope in Africa or in ourselves.

Thomas Hodgkin

Where the Paths Began

This is meant as some kind of brief commentary on the writings of Basil Davidson, *Opera omnia Basilensia et quaedam alia*, but also as a partly personal, semi-autobiographical account of what I believe to have been our presuppositions at the time, twenty-five years ago, when we both started writing about African questions. Writing about presuppositions is always a tricky business, even when they are one's own. To write about what one supposes to have been common, or shared, presuppositions presents greater problems—and if I misrepresent Basil's ideas and opinions I hope I shall be forgiven. 'Lord, Lord, how subject we old men are to this vice of lying', as Falstaff remarked of himself and Justice Shallow. Like Shallow I will be prating of the wildness of our youth and the feats which we have done about Great Turnstile Street. But any actual lies in the remarks which follow will be wholly unintended.

It must be almost exactly a quarter of a century ago that I first met Basil, early in 1950. The first letter that I have from him on the file originally labelled 'Crisis in Africa' and relabelled 'U.D.C. General File', which I thoughtfully carried off when I left the Oxford Delegacy for Extra-Mural Studies in May 1952, is dated 24 March 1950. This must have been not long after the memorable lunch to which Kingsley Martin and Dorothy Woodman invited us both, to throw us together and encourage our cooperation in the African field—a kindly and productive thought. Our cooperation was thought of as lying particularly within the framework of the Union of Democratic Control, of which Basil was then General Secretary and Kingsley Martin Chairman, and which (I wrote in a letter at the time) was meaning 'to begin to work on African problems in the way they worked on Chinese problems in the past'. The first fruit of this cooperation was a conference on 'the Crisis in Africa' organised by the UDC—meaning in practice Basil and Audrey Jupp, with some help from myself—at a curious conventlike retreat, tended by soft-footed nuns, at Hayward's Heath during the weekend of 22-23 October 1950. This conference had a certain historical importance. It brought together an interesting collection of people. Peter Ady, Henry Collins, Ayo Ogunsheye, Adenekan Ademola, Fenner Brockway, Obahiagbon, A. A. Amponsah, Lord Boyd Orr, Ritchie Calder, Harold Davies, Bankole Timothy, P. P. Chella, Catherine Marshall, Tom Driberg, Charles Njonjo, Musazi, Michael Carritt, Okoi Arikpo, Guy Routh, F. Le Gros Clarke Tony McLean, Leonard Barnes and Hastings Banda are among those whose names appear on the roll call. It helped to emphasise the essential relatedness of African problems, the common interests of African liberation movements and the need for combined operations between these movements and British

Socialists. At the same time it provided a point of departure for the UDC's future work.

How did we ourselves think about Africa at this historical moment? We were both, naturally, very ignorant. We approached the subject from different backgrounds of experience, yet with much that was common in our standpoints. Basil's interest in 'the national and colonial question' had developed, or at least flowered, while he lived and worked as a liaison officer with the Jugoslav partisans during the years 1943 and 1944. It was, I think, in Bosnia and the Voivodina particularly that he became aware of certain universal truths which have informed all his later work. To state them crudely: that it is of the nature of imperialism to generate movements of national liberation—the more brutal and repressive the imperialism, the more violent the methods of the liberation movement; that liberation movements to be effective must be based on the people, meaning in an agrarian society above all the peasantry; that revolution, with its vision of a future transformed society, transforms the consciousness and characters of the individual participants. It is nice, too, to find in the early account of his experience of the Jugoslav revolution, *Partisan Picture*,[1] forms of expression, ways of presenting contemporary history, which recur in his more recent studies of African revolutions, in Guiné and Angola[2]: the delineation of fascinating men and women; the use of popular songs and ballads to help to explain what revolutions are about ('The corn is ripe and Voivodina, our Voivodina, will be a Republic'); a particular interest in revolutionary organisation and language (the 'famous verb, *konspirati*, which meant far more than "to conspire"—it meant security in all its aspects'); dramatic conversation as a method of bringing into sharp relief the issues which divide and unite people in a revolutionary situation (see especially the moving chapter 'How to be a Partisan').

My own interest had been shaped much more by experience of the Arab world, and particularly Palestine, during the years 1933 to 1936. It was possibly richer as regards involvement in the actual working of the colonial apparatus, but far poorer as regards any kind of inner understanding of a national revolutionary movement. For me the most important universal truths (again crudely stated) were perhaps—that colonial systems depend for their continuing existence on inter-communal conflict, which they at the same time create, stimulate and deplore; that such conflicts can only be overcome within the context of a revolutionary movement that is based upon a supra-national, Marxist-Leninist ideology (hence in any colonial society the most rational people are almost always to be found in gaol); that imperialism, while it oppresses and exploits the colonised, also corrupts the colonisers, generating in the minds of the alien ruling class a set of racist myths with which they seek to justify their domination. Simple and familiar truths, but sufficient to wake me from my dogmatic slumbers. I had also more recently gone on three African journeys, connected with the development of extra-mural studies—to the Gold Coast (Ghana) and Nigeria in 1947 and again in December 1949/January 1950, and to the Sudan in 1948. This last Gold Coast journey had been at the time of the general strike, an interesting historical moment, when I first tried to learn something about the history of the national movement and the antecedents of the Convention People's Party through discussion with a group of Ghanaians at the Commenda New Year School. What I then learned I wrote up in a series of articles for the journal, *West Africa*, under the name of Kwesi Robinson (Sunday's child, plus patronymic).

So, with these different backgrounds but converging interests, we both believed that African national movements would have an increasing impact on human history and that to understand them as adequately as possible was an important task. One of the purposes of the Hayward's Heath conference was to equip ourselves, and others like us, better for this work. (If the list of participants—particularly the African participants—in the conference looks unbelievably respectable, remember that some of the respectables were radicals then. Besides, whom we could invite was limited by whom we knew—and some stayed away.) And, while we wanted to understand these various movements in all their specificity, their historically determined differences, we assumed that they were essentially comparable—as regards their roots, the factors stimulating their development, their dominant ideas, objectives and programmes, forms of organisation, etcetera—with national movements which had emerged in other types of colonial situation, under the Habsburgs and Ottomans in eastern Europe, under Ottomans, British and French in the Arab world, under British, French and Dutch in India and south-east Asia. This belief in the basic comparability, in spite of all diversity, of national movements in the colonial and former colonial world was for us a necessary tool of enquiry: all the more because of the current tendency to emphasise the uniqueness, the oddity, the mysteriousness, the absolute otherness of sub-Saharan Africa, on the principle enunciated by Hegel in his 1830-31 Jena lectures and repeated constantly since:

> The peculiarly African character is difficult to comprehend, for the very reason that in reference to it we must quite give up the principle which naturally accompanies all *our* ideas—the category of Universality. In Negro life the characteristic point is the fact that consciousness has not yet attained to the realization of any substantial objective existence—as, for example, God, or Law—in which the interest of man's volition is involved and in which he realizes his own being.... The Negro ... exhibits the natural man in his completely wild and untamed state. We must lay aside all thought of reverence and morality—all that we call feeling—if we would rightly comprehend him; there is nothing harmonious with humanity to be found in this type of character....
>
> At this point we leave Africa, not to mention it again. For it is no historical part of the World; it has no movement or development to exhibit.... What we properly understand by Africa is the Unhistorical, Undeveloped Spirit, still involved in the conditions of mere nature, which had to be presented here only as on the threshold of the World's history.[3]

This Hegelian idea—of the essentially unknowable, unhistorical, undeveloping, tradition-bound, character of African societies—built into the structure of racist ideologies, remains a serious force, expressing itself at both an academic and a popular level.

Part of the difficulty in trying to understand African national movements at that moment of history was the lack of a useful literature. It seems surprising now, when the study of African politics has become such a tremendous growth industry, supported by such a wealth of journals, in the USA especially. But in 1950 it was not like that. In a sense a literature of African politics scarcely existed because African politics was scarcely supposed to exist—not in French Africa, outside the Quatre Communes, before 1945; not much in British Africa either; and not at all, of course, in Belgian, Portuguese or Spanish Africa. Literature mirrored reality—in the sense that it reflected the interests of the imperial powers which controlled the greater part of the African continent. What literature there was that had a bearing on African politics was concerned in the main with the kinds of problems that found their way onto the desks of European administrators—chiefs and indirect rule, local government, land and labour, urbanisation, 'native education' and the like. The classic expression of this colonial administrator's view of Africa was Hailey's *African Survey* (1938), whose genesis, by Rhodes out of Rockefeller, has been illuminatingly described by Professor Hargreaves.[4] (The 1956 revised edition, unlike the first, at least recognised the existence of African politics—but by then it was difficult not to.)

On processes of political change in general, and anti-colonial movements in particular, what sort of a literature was there? The social anthropologists of course were interested in everything that was happening in the African societies which they studied, but most of those who had published by 1950 had done their fieldwork in the 1930s in societies in which the development of anti-colonial movements had not been particularly marked, or detectable, even for those for whom the concept of social change was important. (Jomo Kenyatta's historically important *Facing Mount Kenya* (1938), with Malinowski's introduction, was a special case.) This was why the work of Georges Balandier, when it began to appear round about 1950, was so exciting, since he seemed to be almost the only social anthropologist, or sociologist, who was particularly interested in asking questions about the colonial situation (a category which he described and elaborated) and its impact on peasant societies, the Fang and the Bakongo especially. His account of the development among the Bakongo of the messianic movement Kimbanguism-Gounzism-Matswanism over the period, roughly, from 1920 to 1950, as a vehicle of anti-colonial ideas and an effective form of popular organisation, threw new light on this whole phase in the history of African national movements.[5]

A very different and much earlier work, Raymond Buell's *The Native Problem in Africa* (1928), once one had discovered it, was a rich mine of information for the obscure first quarter of the twentieth century. No one else had brought together so much useful material about early strikes, parties and proto-parties, riots, rebellions, breakaway churches—the kind of evidence that the colonial administrator-historians largely ignored because they had a concept of history which made it appear trivial and unimportant. (So it is not surprising that the 'patron of African Studies', Thomas Jesse Jones, should have felt in 1929 that

'R. L Buell's pioneer survey departed so far from the viewpoint of men actually dealing with African problems as to "border closely on propaganda'"[6] As always, government reports on explosive political happenings—the Aba riots of 1929, the Copperbelt disturbances of 1935, the Nigerian general strike of 1945, the Gold Coast disturbances of 1948—and even more, when one could get at them, the minutes of evidence, contained useful political material, however distorted in its manner of presentation. (Reports on 'subversive' activities were useful too, like the Tomlinson-Lethem report on Islamic Propaganda in Northern Nigeria (1929)—but that was a much later discovery.)

What was most valuable—a much richer and more varied source than in one's ignorance one had expected—was the whole body of nationalist literature, books, pamphlets, party documents, song, hymn and prayer books, broadsheets, manifestos, newspaper articles, etcetera, the writings not only of the contemporary generation of political leaders but also of many less familiar, obscurer people, the local cadres of parties, unions, churches; and not only of this but of earlier generations—of the generation of Casely Hayford, Herbert Macaulay, Blaise Diagne, Lamine Senghor, Harry Thuku, John Chilembwe and 'Abd al-Krim. Gradually one became aware of yet earlier ancestors, of the nationalist tradition of the nineteenth century—of James Africanus Horton, James Johnson, James Mensah Sarbah, Edward Blyden. This field—the work of the theoreticians, expounders and agitators of African nationalism—has been increasingly thoroughly cultivated in recent years. But in 1950 one had to fight for precious material. Danquah would tell stories of the inter-war period—of the National Congress of British West Africa, the Youth League and the cocoa hold-up. Zik would explain about the ways in which his ideas had been influenced by Garveyism. Eyo Ita would give one copies of his self-published pamphlets on the concept of 'One Nigeria'. But to have access to this rich body of material, both documents and oral tradition, it was necessary to live at a low level, travelling hard—by train, bus, lorry, horse or camel—avoiding (as a rule) the fortresses and bungalows of the colonial administration (who tended in any case to avoid us), moving along the party networks or the extra-mural networks. This indeed was one of our presuppositions, even if a rather self-evident one—that to learn anything about African politics one must spend as much time as possible with those who were actually making African politics. And, as always in the context of anti-colonial struggle, the cadres were enormously generous, as regards time, hospitality, conversation, documents, ideas. Luck was important too. I remember travelling on a three-day journey from Bamako to Nara (on the way to Kumbi Saleh and Walata) in November 1952, on the eve of the general strike in support of the Code du Travail, in a post-car, and finding quite by accident that my companion in the front seat was Fajallah Keita, organising secretary of the Union Soudanaise-RDA. So for three days we talked and met party representatives along the route. And for both Basil and myself Claude Gérard, that devoted Frenchwoman, who edited *Afrique-Informations* and starved in her Paris flat, provided a marvellous means of access to the Rassemblement Démocratique Africain with all its contradictions and complexities.

We were conscious also of belonging ourselves to a tradition—the radical anti-colonial tradition—which had a symbiotic kind of relationship with that other tradition of African nationalism, and which meant that our presuppositions were necessarily different from, and in general opposed to, the presuppositions of the imperial administrator-scholars (though the work of the best of them, particularly the French in the Islamic-historical field, Maurice Delafosse, Charles Monteil, Paul Marty and others, remains interesting and valuable).[7] For most of this school imperialism, whatever its 'mistakes' or 'excesses', was on balance a progressive, civilising force, a necessary precondition of the development of African societies, technical, cultural and moral. For us it was essentially retrogressive, destructive of African civilisation (which did not require colonial conquest in order to develop in interesting and fruitful ways), corrupting and brutalising our own. This was a very large, important, unbridgeable opposition.

Who were the ancestors—the earlier representatives of the anti-colonial school to whom we looked back and from whom particularly we had learned? In the generation immediately preceding us, Leonard Barnes, a frequent lecturer at WEA Schools in the 1930s, lucid, modest and courageous, probably influenced my thinking about Africa more than anyone. Later he introduced me to Edward Roux's *Time Longer than Rope* (1948), from which I first began to learn something about the ICU and the history of the anti-colonial movement in South Africa. Norman Leys was important as a source for Kenya and helped me to understand more clearly how the presence of *colons* necessarily generates the institutions of the colour bar.[8] George Padmore, regrettably, I did not meet until after 1945 and the Manchester Pan-African Congress, though I had come across some of his earlier writings, and *Britain's Third Empire* (1949)—a book which Padmore says arose out of that congress—was valuable, partly because it was one of the few works which gave some account of the history of African national movements. C. L. R. James, on the other hand, I had met during the 1930s and, though we were ideologically somewhat opposed, I had been much excited by his small important book, *Black Jacobins* (1931). Among the more orthodox Marxists Palme Dutt was naturally pre-eminent. His *India Today* (1949) seemed admirable, partly on account of its universality, its bearing on the general problems of colonial peoples and national liberation movements, though aspects of his analysis were worrying in their rigidity, particularly his attitude to Gandhi and the bourgeois nationalists. But Reginald Bridgeman, International Secretary of the League Against Imperialism, probably did more than anyone during the brief period while we worked together (from 1936 to 1938, approximately) to help me to understand the common characteristics of the colonial situation and the interdependence, common interests of, need for brotherly relations between, those whom we then called the colonial and semi-colonial peoples but who have since become the peoples of the *Tiers Monde*.

Among ancestors of an earlier generation Basil's work with the Union of Democratic Control had made him aware of the importance of E. D. Morel, one of the union's founders, just after the outbreak of the First World War, and its first secretary. I on the other hand knew little about him beyond *Red Rubber* (1906) and his campaign against the atrocities in 'the Congo Slave State'—not having yet come across his later writings, *Africa, and the Peace of Europe* (1917), *The Black Man's Burden* (1920), in which he moved on to a critique of all forms of imperialism, including British.[9] It was Basil also who first interested me in the writings of Henry Nevinson, having the splendid idea of celebrating the fiftieth anniversary of Nevinson's journey through Angola in 1904—the outcome of which was his great book, *A Modern Slavery* (1906)—by making his own Angolan journey to report on the system of forced plantation labour which had replaced outright slavery. The book which grew out of this journey, *The African Awakening* (1955), dealing mainly with what was then the Belgian Congo (Zaïre) and Angola, derives its significance partly from the fact that Basil must have been the first British (or indeed European) radical for many years to slip into Angola and write objectively about social conditions there—'telling the truth about things as they happen, or at least . . . trying to tell it'.[10] And his account there of Affonso I, Nzinga Mbemba, sixteenth-century ruler of the Kingdom of the Kongo, must be one of his earliest excursions into the field of pre-colonial African history. More important, the book marks the beginning of his twenty-year involvement with the liberation movements in the former Portuguese African territories, so fruitful in its consequences—friendships, writings, experiences, achievements.

Of course, this anti-colonial tradition within the colonising states can be traced back much further than the late nineteenth and early twentieth centuries —back to the Abbé Gregoire and his *De la Littérature des Nègres* (1808) at the time of the French Revolution, and beyond.[11] But in 1950 we knew little about its earlier history: this kind of knowledge came, and is still coming, slowly. What we did know was that those who talked as though anti-colonial attitudes in Britain and the West were a relatively recent—post-1918, and even more post-1945—development, and argued that in the period of imperial expansion and success we, the petty-bourgeois intelligentsia, the *lettrés*, were all imperialists, were talking nonsense. There was an ancient and honourable tradition of patriotic anti-imperialism. Another point that seemed, and seems, to be sometimes misunderstood was that on the basic issue—what practical steps should we, the people of Britain, take in regard to the colonial question?—the real conflict was not so much between Marxists and non-Marxists (however much we might disagree on matters of theory and analysis) as between those who, from whatever philosophical standpoint, sought the end of empire—who were opposed to the colonial relationship as such—and those who wished to modify, reform and 'humanise' it. The test of seriousness was willingness to attack, or seek to overthrow, one's own imperialism. This meant that one must, naturally and necessarily, support the demands of national movements for total independence, even if this seemed likely to lead immediately to what we thought of then as the dictatorship of the national bourgeoisie—what Fanon later called 'false decolonisation' —though we were hopeful, over-hopeful no doubt, of the possibility of other kinds of outcome.

In 1950 we had hardly even begun to think seriously about the history of pre-colonial Africa. It was, I suppose, an intelligible kind of logic that pushed us both, by somewhat different paths, in this direction: natural curiosity and dissatisfaction with our own ignorance; recognition of the need to understand the past in order to throw light on the problems of the present (inter-ethnic contradictions in Nigeria, for example, or Khatmiyya-Ansar rivalries in the Sudan); desire to know more about the historical realities lying behind the racist myths of the imperialists and the romantic counter-myths of the cultural nationalists. (It is a terrible reflection of the extent to which my own thinking had been dominated by the Hegelian notion of the essential 'darkness' of the African past that I can remember so clearly the moment in February 1947, when I first learned, talking in Ghana to an Achimota master, about the kingdoms of the western Sudan, and, asking where I could read about them, was recommended Bovill's *Caravans of the Old Sahara*—whatever its weaknesses a remarkable work, which became my constant companion). Our situation was thus quite different from that of professional European historians, described by Professor Fage—translated to African universities, obliged to turn 'the Expansion of Europe' inside out for the benefit of African students.[12] We had never been trained as professional historians, knew little of 'the Expansion of Europe'. In so far as we enjoyed the stimulus of trying to teach the African history which we were at the same time trying to learn, it was not, initially, in university lecture rooms, but informally, in WEA classes, Extension courses, Day, Weekend, Summer and New Year Schools, in Britain and Africa, where we enjoyed what Tawney called the friendly battering of students who knew more about the subject, often, than we did. We assumed that the historical questions which interested or would interest everyone, were intrinsically interesting; that the civilisations of pre-colonial Africa were as well worth studying as European, Asian or any other civilisations, possessed their own kind of internal development, and could be studied by methods which were not essentially unlike those used to study the histories of other human societies. This seems a simple proposition, but it has practical implications.

One such implication is the relevance of all kinds of evidence. Basil seems to me particularly committed to the Collingwoodian principle that everything is evidence that helps one to answer a historical question.[13] So his interest in finding out what the archaeologists, the classical historians, the Arabists, the Sinologists, the anthropologists, the linguists, the ethno-botanists, the musicologists, the art historians, the astronomers, the theologians and the rest have to say about the problems which he regards as important has been a special virtue. And no doubt he started his historical writing at a happy time—not long after the first SOAS Conference on African History and Archaeology in 1953, itself a historically important event—when the various specialists were themselves making exciting discoveries, many of them, and, as he modestly put it, 'glad to have someone to talk to'. But to use the new evidence which was becoming available at this time it was not, of course, enough to listen, or to understand, or even to frame intelligent questions. It was necessary also to have a unifying mind. And this capacity of Basil's for unification and synthesis was valuable in another way. It led him to take a particular interest in the interrelations of

African societies, both with one another and with the world beyond Africa. A dominant characteristic of the colonial period had been its compartmentalism, academic preoccupations again mirroring political realities. As 'Berbérologie' was a French science, so Congology was a Belgian, Nigeriology a British. Colonial administrations, wishing to keep 'their' natives free from corruption by subversive movements in adjacent—and distant—territories presented isolation, self-sufficiency, as permanent characteristics of African society. Gradually one began to learn the error of this view.

It was Théodore Monod, director of IFAN in Dakar, that most gifted and uncolonial polymath of the late colonial period, who first in 1952 helped me to see that West Africa could only be understood in its relations with the Maghrib. Some years later Ivor Wilks's *Northern Factor in Ashanti History* opened the way to many discoveries regarding the ties of trade and scholarship linking Ashanti and its northern neighbours with the western, and central, Sudan—the extractive industries of the forest with the distributing centres of the upper Niger. Mohammed Al-Hajj and others threw new light on the reciprocal relationship between western, central and eastern Sudan from the late eighteenth century—the movement of men and millenarian ideas along the hajj route. The ancient connections of the east African coastal towns with the trading system of the Indian Ocean—with India, south-east Asia and above all with China—and with the interior were illumined by Gervase Mathew, Greville Freeman-Grenville and Joseph Needham. On the other side of the continent the Atlantic system in the epoch of the slave trade and slave revolts, and later in the epoch of Ethiopianism, Black Zionism and the birth of liberation movements—the period of the fertilising influence of the West Indies and North America—we learned about from Aimé Césaire and others of the Présence Africaine group, from W. E. Burghardt Du Bois, from Pierre Verger, Melville Herskovits, George Shepperson and, later, Walter Rodney.[14] So one important thing about Basil's historical writing, from *Old Africa Rediscovered* on, was this synthesising quality, breaking down old barriers between academic disciplines and territorial academic interests, noticing historical connections that had not been observed before, showing that, in spite of Hegel, sub-Saharan African history really was an integral and interesting part of world history.

But that revolutionary leap forward was taken some time ago. It seems difficult now to leave the subject without saying something about the kind of questions which Terence Ranger raises in his contribution to this book,[15] and which, in a different form, have been discussed in earlier articles by Christopher Wrigley,[16] Professor Ayandele[17] and others. How far were we wrong, wrong not about detailed interpretations—obviously we were often wrong about them—but wrong about fundamentals, mistaken in our presuppositions, or in our methods of using them? In particular, how far were we excessively concerned with the histories of states, dynasties, bureaucracies, ruling classes, towns, merchants, trading networks, learning and literature, Islamic institutions, etcetera—too little interested in the histories of stateless societies, oppressed classes and castes (and women), the organisation of agriculture and food production, the living conditions of the people, their songs and dances, bandits and outlaws, peasant insurrections and slave revolts? In other words, did we produce a kind of history which in some sense was in direct conflict with our ideas of what history ought to be about?

The answer seems to me to be mixed. Yes, certainly, writing at a time when the second edition of *Nigerian Perspectives* is about to be published, I can see what large areas of the history of the Nigerian peoples (as contrasted with dynasties and ruling elites)—economic, social, intellectual, but also political—it would have been good to have known much more about. (Basil, in *The Africans* (1969), moved more into this newer field.) I can also see some of the reasons for what, for the sake of brevity, one can call state-centred history: the nature of the evidence—chronicles, correspondence, praise-poems, documents generally, tend to mirror the lives of ruling families; concern to establish a working chronology (dynasties have more and better dates than 'the short and simple annals of the poor'); desire to explode the colonial stereotype, with its confused, and confusing, categories of 'tribal', 'primitive', 'stagnant' and the like; and in my case, I must admit, a particular affection for, interest in, the Arabic sources and the universal civilisation which they reflected—and continue to reflect. But to explain the error is not to justify it. There are two points, though, that need to be made. First, in so far as we tended to write 'about Africa's past in terms of the construction and expansion of governmental systems', it was not because we saw it, in Wrigley's words, 'as moving always to its grand climacteric, the emergence of the New Independent States of the later twentieth century.'[18] We were not particularly committed to the bourgeois, territorial, post-colonial state—which seemed a transitional category—nor anxious to provide it with historical respectability. If we were guilty of the sin of 'historicism' (though I prefer Marx to Popper on this point), the end of the historical process to which we looked, and still look, forward—a new beginning in fact as much as an end—was not the bourgeois territorial state but the world socialist commonwealth and the withering away of the state.

Second, I confess that I am worried by Terence Ranger's notion of a 'unusable African past'. Even with the qualifications which he introduces there seems a certain gritty pragmatism about it. True, the purpose of understanding society should be to change it, and in this sense knowledge of the past must be 'usable'. But Ranger seems to contrast (most existing?) 'African historiography', which 'has been important in Africa for reasons of pride *because it could not possibly have been useful for anything else*' (his italics), with another kind of (improved) African historiography, 'for men who want to know what to do at the local level— how best to grow food, or how best to mobilise support for a guerilla movement . . . '[19] This seems to me a mistaken antithesis. The intelligent guerilla, the intelligent revolutionary, must inherit, interpret, enjoy and use the whole of history, not serviceable bits of it. 'All places that the eye of heaven visits / Are to a wise man ports and happy havens.' The history of cookery and medicine and dress and dance and games and astrology and military strategy and mining—and court ritual and diplomacy and eunuchs and concubines—and everything else— all help to illumine a past which the intelligent revolutionary, or guerilla, needs neither to take pride in (apart from those aspects which are intrinsically worthy of pride) nor to dismiss as irrelevant, but simply to understand as adequately as possible. It is partly surely because he has had this catholic, comprehensive view of what history is about that Basil has made such a serious contribution.

Notes

1   Basil Davidson, *Partisan Picture*, London, 1946.
2   Basil Davidson, *The Liberation of Guiné*, Penguin African Library, 1969; *In the Eye of the Storm*, Penguin African Library, 1975.
3   G. W. F. Hegel, *The Philosophy of History*, New York, 1944, pp. 93 and 99.
4   J. D. Hargreaves, *History: African and Contemporary*, ASAUK Presidential Address given at the London symposium, September 1973.
5   Balandier's major work on this theme, *Sociologie actuelle de l'Afrique noire*, was first published in Paris in 1955; English translation, London, 1970.
6   Hargreaves, *op. cit.*, p. 6.
7   See J. D. Fage, 'Continuity and Change in the Writing of West African History', *African Affairs*, lxx, 280, July 1971, p. 242, and Peter Duignan and L. H. Gann, *Colonialism in Africa, 1870-1960*, vol. v, *A Bibliographical Guide to Colonialism in Sub-Saharan Africa*, Cambridge, 1973, *passim*.
8   Norman Leys, *Kenya*, London, 1924; *A Last Chance in Kenya*, 1931.
9   On E. D. Morel see particularly the useful study by Andrew Rothstein in *British Foreign Policy and its Critics, 1830-1950*, London, 1969. See also Michael Wolfers, *Black Man's Burden Revisited*, London, 1974, prologue.
10   Basil Davidson, Introduction to Henry W. Nevinson, *A Modern Slavery*, Sourcebooks in Negro History, New York, 1968, p. ix.
11   See Imanuel Geiss, *The Pan-African Movement*, London, 1974, and Philip Curtin, *The Image of Africa*, Madison, 1965.
12   Fage, *op. cit.*, pp. 236-8.
13   R. S. Collingwood, *The Idea of History*, Oxford, 1946, v, §3.
14   Basil Davidson's *Black Mother*, London, 1961, paperback 1970, has of course become a classic for the period of the slave trade.
15   T. O. Ranger, 'Towards a Usable African past', pp. 17-30 below.
16   Christopher Wrigley, 'Historicism in Africa', *African Affairs*, lxx, 279, January 1971.
17   E. A. Ayandele, 'How truly Nigerian is our Nigerian History?', *African Notes*, University of Ibadan, v, 2, 1968-69.
18   Wrigley, *op. cit.*, p. 118.
19   Ranger, *op. cit.*, p. 24.

T. O. Ranger

Towards a Usable African Past

Introduction

There is a widespread sense that African historiography is in a state of crisis. When it was known that I was returning to Britain to teach, I received a number of letters bewailing the state of British African Studies in general and of African history in particular; it was said that the old excitement and commitment had gone; we had passed from an age of gold, or at least of silver, into an age of lead, or at best of iron. In the United States the obvious economic crisis—the falling away of job opportunities for graduates in African history; the severe cut-back in graduate research grants; the collapse of much Africanist publishing— appears to merge with an intellectual crisis, as the various constituencies for African history seem to be losing interest in it and as universities become more interested in methodology and less interested in regional studies.

Within Africa, it is true, this sense of crisis is much less obvious. At the Edinburgh conference, for instance, participants from Nigeria made it clear that in their view the achievements of Nigerian academic historians—as represented by the Ibadan history series—were still very much a source of legitimate pride, and the kind of topics they had explored were still very relevant to the intellectual concerns of the Nigerian nation. And yet, as I shall seek to document later, there *is* a widespread disenchantment with African historiography inside Africa itself; a widespread feeling of its artificiality and distance from real issues.

The invitation to contribute a paper on African historical writing in English since the end of the Second World War gave me an opportunity to explore this sense of crisis; to look back into the golden age; to remember its excitements and achievements and to see clearly for the first time the price that was paid for them. It also allowed me to focus more sharply my own feeling that if there is a crisis for African history arising out of the collapse of the consensus of the golden age, it is a crisis of opportunity, and that out of the dispute about the methodologies, content and relevance of African history there is emerging work which responds very satisfactorily to the challenges of the present.

The 'Golden Age' : achievements and costs

In the last fifteen or twenty years there has been a revolution in the study of African history, The emergence of *The Journal of African History* as the combined manifesto, charter, programme and shop-window for the field; the growth of the American graduate schools of African history; the enormous increase in African publishing; above all, the successful development of schools of historical studies within Africa itself—all this constitutes a remarkable achievement. Anyone who served, even as a foot soldier, in the armies that fought and won these battles can remember the sense of solidarity and excitement. I can remember myself my admiration for the coherence and vigour of the strategy for research embodied in the first issues of the *Journal*; my gratitude for the first synthesising works which made undergraduate teaching possible; my even greater gratitude for the essential demonstrations of the respectability of oral history or of historical linguistics. I can remember the exhilaration of being part of the small but active historiographical communities which developed in east and central Africa. And I can remember the sense that historians of Africa everywhere were engaged in the same task of *demonstration* of the possibility and viability of the field.

Looking back at all this, my emotions of admiration and excitement and gratitude to the pioneers still persist. These *were* times to have lived through and to bore students by recalling. But thinking back over it—re-reading the whole run of the *Journal*; re-reading the pioneer works in oral history, in historical linguistics and historical archaeology; reviewing what was produced in Dar es Salaam, or Nairobi or Ibadan—I can see more clearly what the *costs* were. For achievements of African historirgraphy, though crucially important and obtainable in no other way, were nevertheless bought at the price of ignoring two major weaknesses.

One weakness was created by our need for 'culture heroes' and by the consequent pressures on the development of methodology. The other weakness was created by the fact that we were catering for interests that were too easily satisfied and too little demanding. In combination they have been responsible for a certain 'flabbiness' in African historiography.

I have written about the boldness of the strategy of the *Journal of African History*. It made it plain from its first issues that a combination of techniques was needed to attack the African past, and it summoned up the oral historian, the historical linguist, the archaeologist, the banana geneticist, and many more. Some of these have not yet responded to the summons. But much more importantly, some 'culture heroes' *did* respond. One of these, for example, was Jan Vansina whose two articles on Kuba oral history appeared in the first and second issues of the *Journal*.[1] Vansina was so essential to us all that if he had not existed we should have had to have invented him—as we did try to invent other oral historians. Fortunately for us, Vansina did very much exist, with all his experience and skill. The work that he was producing then was admirable as well as essential. But the point is that the pressures of our need for him as a 'culture hero' really prevented that work from coming to its full fruition. He was under pressure to move rapidly from the very cautious assessments of the value of oral tradition in his book[2] to the much bolder claims of his articles in the *Journal*. The book required an intense scrutiny and debate from within the field of African historiography; it required to be taken as a starting point rather than as a stopping point. But it was impossible for this to happen. We needed that book too much, and it rapidly suffered the fate of canonisation, so that before long an oral historian could remark in a footnote that Vansina's classic work had settled all problems of methodology and that all that needed to be done was to go out and collect![3] Moreover, Vansina was under other pressures. His articles had sounded the clarion call for other oral historians, but very few responded in those early days. Vansina had to give us enough work for several oral historians and heroically to over-extend himself. In his further writing he departed from his own principles of work by collating traditions collected by others, relating to societies in which he had not worked and with whose languages he was not familiar, taking this risk because it was necessary to make further demonstrations of the potentialities of oral history and necessary to provide at least some framework for the history of the savanna.[4]

The same sort of fate awaited other pioneers; linguists like Guthrie or archaeologists like Roger Summers were made the focus of a flattering but in many ways distorting interest on the part of the historian. And in Africa itself, of course, the role of the 'culture hero' was an equally burdensome one. The first African academic historians—the Dikes, the Ajayis, the Ogots—were even more essential; once again if they had not existed they would have had to have been invented—as some African academics were 'invented' in those early days; once again it was fortunate that Dike and Ajayi and Ogot, and others, *did* exist with all their energies and abilities. Still, it was not to be expected that they would be challenged by the sort of criticism valuable for growth; the very considerable growing they have done has come from the demands they have made upon themselves. To take one example, Alan Ogot was essential not only as the first emphatic demonstration of Kenyan historical gifts, but also because his dissertation was the first to be based almost exclusively on oral traditional material. Ogot himself would now say that a good deal of it was inadequately based, just as Vansina would now write a very different version of *Oral Tradition*. But when Ogot's book was published it was not possible for there to be a rigorous discussion of exactly *how* best to go about basing historical reconstructions exclusively on oral material for fear of compromising his demonstration that it could be done at all.[5]

The same sort of thing happened to those of us whose work was based on material in African territorial archives and on written material of African provenance. Such work was hailed warmly as showing that the tyranny of the metropolitan archives could be broken, and as demonstrating that 'the African Voice' could be documented. We were not rigorously enough pressed to analyse the nature of the material collected in territorial archives; to explore how one could use material of police provenance in the same thorough way that historians of Europe had done; or to think hard about the different significance of written material produced by a newly literate few within a society in which most people were still not literate.

In a sense then the African historians had too easily satisfied a constituency in their own colleagues. As in all young fields, African historians tended to think that new methods and above all new data would fill in the outlines of the past by themselves. But they also had too easily satisfied a constituency outside. In Europe and America there was a demand to know something—anything— about the new African nations; within Africa itself there was a demand for some—

almost any—past. Our very real sense of excitement, of importance even, was partly the result of the very ready and flattering interest shown. When our customers were so satisfied with what we gave them, there was not much incentive to examine more closely how related to African realities it really was.

I hope I am not striking in all this the sour note of the middle-aged Puritan, regretting the excesses of his youth. I glory in those 'excesses', for it seems to me that the shared enthusiasm for African history of teachers and students, writers and readers, academics and bureaucrats and guerillas has made African history an enormously worthwhile activity and has attracted into African historiography the numbers and the talents that it now requires to develop. But it certainly does need to develop and for this it needs a harsher climate.

Fortunately, at least from this perspective, the harsher climate is with us. And it reveals itself particularly in regard to the two sources of weakness, of 'flabbiness'. The old eager acceptance of new statements of methodology has given way to intense questioning and debate. The old readily satisfied market for African history has given way to the complaints of customers who are much harder to please.

Methodologies in flux

Two developments have combined towards a radical rethinking of methodologies. In the first place, the 'culture heroes' of the golden age have produced their crops of graduate students, and these students, returned from their own field experience, are qualified to debate issues of methodology in a way nobody was before. In the second place, other disciplines, and particularly anthropology, have become much more concerned with historical interpretation so that their criticisms of methodology have become pertinent rather than antagonistic. All this is very clear so far as oral history is concerned. There have always been anthropological critics of Vansina's treatment of oral history. At first, however, the hostility of such critics towards the whole idea of history made them not only unpersuasive but also ineffective. More recently an anthropologist like Wyatt McGaffey, who is himself seeking to understand how one can use Kongolese oral tradition to reconstruct the past, has written enormously more penetrating and effective criticism.[6] Oral historians increasingly tend to make themselves almost equally effective as anthropologists—as in the cases of Steven Feierman and Joseph Miller. And Vansina himself, in his splendid recent book on the Tio, has shown how a historian's approach, coupled with a careful use of oral and other evidence, can produce very superior anthropology.[7]

Meanwhile the work of Vansina's students, and others of the second generation of oral historians, have revealed some of the mistakes of interpretation and assumption which underlay the work of the first generation. We have been rightly cautioned against an over-literal interpretation of tradition; against the 'fallacy of misplaced concreteness'; against the inevitable foreshortening of oral tradition, which runs mythical time, heroic time and commonplace time into one narrative, which personalises principles of development into single rulers, which reaches back into the past to validate recent dynasties as founding culture heroes.

We have been warned against over-elaboration and over-systematisation; advised to categorise oral material in the terms of each society in which it is collected. All this calls into question the reconstructions of pre-colonial history which were accepted only a short while ago.[8]

The situation is a little different so far as historical linguistics are concerned. In this field Christopher Ehret has emerged as a rather belated 'culture hero', effectively discrediting the uses made by historians of Guthrie's data, but having himself to play the same sort of universal role which Vansina had to assume in oral history fifteen years ago. In this more sceptical era Ehret's work has been received with more caution than Vansina's, but we shall have to wait for the fieldwork of his students before we can obtain significant modifications of his methods or conclusions.[9]

The situation is different yet again in relation to archaeology—though the end result is the same one of caution and of the abandonment of previous reconstruction. As Professor Thurstan Shaw makes plain (pp. 156-68), archaeologists of Africa do not feel that their discipline is in any sort of crisis, but are instead hopeful that the increasing amount of excavation and survey, the application of new methods, the emphasis on the relationship of sites to their total environment, will produce ever more reliable interpretations. Nevertheless, historians have good reason to be cautious about historical generalisations by archaelogists and about their own use of archaeological material. The rapidly changing patterns of interpretation of central African archaeology, for instance, are enough to induce caution: it would be a rash historian who today accepted the conclusions of Garlake and Huffman with the same simple-minded trust as I myself accepted the conclusions of Summers and Robinson.[10] And in any case, if we are in a state of uncertainty about the conclusions to be drawn from historical linguistics and oral history, this cannot but affect the interpretation of the archaeology of the last two or three thousand years.[11]

I shall argue later that this new questioning of methodology is already proving immensely fruitful. But it has resulted in a sort of temporary crisis in the sense that none of the available generalising works about African history can now be accepted as even broadly reliable.

The changing audience

The unreliable character of the available generalisations about the African past is especially ironic just at this moment. The general studies already produced have really sufficed to meet most of the extra-academic demands for information about Africa in the United States and in Britain. Even in some African countries there has been a feeling after the appearance of the first 'national' history that now a past has been established one can move on to more practical concerns. African historians are left with two more demanding audiences. One is demanding in the negative sense; the other in the positive. The first is the audience constituted by historians of Europe, America and the rest of the world, and the challenge which they present is that they still require to be shown good reasons why they should be interested in African historiography at all. The second is the audience constituted by younger students and intellectuals within Africa and the challenge which they present is that they find present African historiographical interpretations 'useless' to them, and demand something more pertinent.

Writing in 1972, after returning to Britain from Tanzania, John Iliffe remarked that 'the general neglect of the European side of African history has meant that the work of the last decade, whatever its impact on the African public, has had very little impact on the public in Europe'. He went on to admit that 'it is debatable whether those responsible for advancing the study of African history should also concern themselves with attitudes and interests within Europe', but concluded that 'a historian of Tanganyika based in Europe does need to think seriously about the needs of a European public, now that the necessity to establish the existence of African history as a subject is passing.'[12]

I share his view that a historian of Africa, working in the universities of America or Europe, has a major responsibility to integrate the methods and findings of African historiography with those of the historiography of Europe and Africa. Some participants in Edinburgh felt that this view was apologetic and defensive; that I believed that African historiography could only in some sense 'come of age' if it were 'recognised' by other historians. This is not my view at all. African historiography has at least as much to teach as to learn at the level of research and writing. At the level of teaching it is extremely important to ensure that knowledge of the African past becomes available to every student of history. But we have a long way to go before we achieve this sort of integration. The influence of Africanist scholarship is certainly evident in many recent studies of popular religion or popular recreation in sixteenth- and seventeenth-century Europe—but it is the influence of African anthropology not of African history.[13]

The major responsibility of the African historian, however, is to what John Iliffe calls 'the African public'. Because of this I think we have to pay particular attention to the complaints made by many young Africans. They see African historiography as having contributed exclusively to cultural nationalism. The African past has been important as a source of pride and sometimes as a legitimising charter for the present regimes. But, the young radicals object, the poor and hungry cannot *eat* past cultural achievements, and in any case contemporary regimes merely manipulate a version of the past and in practice often display a commitment to modernist transformation which disregards African realities. Thus Armah has bitterly described the 'con-game' played by academics anxious for reputation on the one hand and by the ruling élites on the other. Stanislaus Adotevi has attacked the way in which the hovels of the poor are metaphorically garlanded with the laurels of a hypothetical golden age. William Ochieng has launched an outspoken attack on what he calls African history from 'a narrowly nationalistic viewpoint'.[14]

Ochieng's article requires some citation here, since it is addressed to the whole achievement of African historiography since the war. 'Building on the foundation which had been laid by Vansina, Ogot, Davidson, Oliver and Fage', he writes, 'the majority of African historians have largely demonstrated in thought, if not in fact, that Africa is a dynamic entity, with a glorious past and a promising future'. Ochieng dismisses this view as mere romance. Professor

Trevor Roper, he says, was able to see that the emperor of African historiography had no clothes, and to ask the crucial questions—'how are we to account for Africa's age-long stagnation?' and in view of it, how are we to argue that African history has any universal significance? 'For his candour', writes Ochieng, 'Trevor-Roper has become the butt of innumerable emotional insults by nationalist African historians, who see his viewpoint as motivated by purely racial prejudice.' Ochieng insists that the problem of African poverty is not only a real problem but the central problem of African historiography, and if we are to tackle it 'we must bring to the discussion a freshness and detachment of mind which far exceeds our racial attitudes and standards. For many of the ideas, concepts and models which have so far been employed for the analysis of our past are no longer pertinent or useful; it will not, for example, be enough just to glorify the African past by lifting shoulder high a few of her glittering achievements like the Zimbabwe architecture, the primitive peasant empires of the Sudan, and the Makonde sculptures . . . mere flashes within a background of utter stagnation'.[15]

Few of us, I imagine, would accept Ochieng's summary of the message of African historiography as entirely accurate, or accept his reiterated emphasis upon 'utter stagnation' as the new problem which faces African historians. Clearly his article is designed to shock by embracing the unthinkable. But it seems to me to be necessary to ask why Ochieng, along with many others, feels the need to shock us out of our current approaches to African history. It seems to me that there is an essential truth in what they are saying: African historiography has been important in Africa for reasons of pride *because it could not possibly have been useful for anything else.*

There are many reasons for this. One of them has been the largely political emphasis of most African historical writing and a consequent emphasis on state structures rather than on local realities. Another has been the neglect until recently of economic or agricultural or conceptual history. Another has been the question of scale in African historiography. I can best illustrate this by means of contrast. In the United States there is much discussion of how best to develop Amerindian historiography. American Indian students are very interested in this, but they are reluctant to challenge the authority of the tribal elders as custodians of the past. The result is that Amerindian historiography, as seen by Indians themselves, remains fragmented and localised; it is very difficult to use it to create a sense of pride in an America-wide movement of Indian cultural nationalism. On the other hand, it retains its relationship to the reality of specific Indian situations and to the specific concepts of the past which distinguish one group from another. A very different situation prevails in Africa. Lip-service has been paid to the elders, who 'hold the Chair of Oral History' in the village. But in general their evidence has been taken and processed by academic historians— both African and non-African—in such a way as to make possible the construction of much wider patterns and much larger generalisations. The academic history which results has been an important agency for expanding the consciousness of students, but it bears little relationship to the sense of past or present reality of the men and women who produced the evidence. Few of us, including African academics, have any other securely grounded criteria of African reality; thus our general reconstructions have tended to drift without an anchor in daily experience. Almost anything *might* be true once we have departed from the known boundaries of the microcosmic society. This holds good not only for generalising political analyses, but for many of the recent generalising economic analyses as well. For men who want to know what to do at the local level—how best to grow food, or how best to mobilise support for a guerilla movement, or for that matter how to resist being mobilised—African historiography has not been much use.

Responses to the new situation

The 'crisis' which I have outlined has affected other disciplines in much the same way as it has affected African historiography. In her paper in this book Ann Seidman shows how the need 'to help expose the causes and suggest effective solutions to the pervasive problems of underdevelopment which still oppress the vast majority of Africans' have obliged 'political economists' to sharpen 'their theoretical tools'. Colin Leys has recently remarked that 'during the 1960s empirical studies of African politics passed through a frequently unrewarding phase. The perspective which informed many if not most of them was that of regimes in power . . . at the level of empirical inquiry what this orientation was apt to produce were studies of the *mechanisms* of rule—party organisation, development administration, managed elections, etc—from which the stuff of politics—conflict, struggle, and above all, the historical significance of the issues at stake had largely been excluded.' Leys argues that because of the failure of 'development' policies, there has been 'a revival of concern with politics proper' and a move towards 'valuable empirical research on the social formations bequeathed by colonialism, (and) the nature of the political struggles taking place within them'[16]

Colin Leys emphasises the need for political scientists to establish 'the historical significance of the issues at stake'; Ann Seidman emphasises that political economists must make 'inter-disciplinary analysis' of the 'historical roots and consequences' of underdevelopment. In short, faced with the problem of African poverty, scholars of other disciplines are increasingly turning to historical explanation, as well as to 'valuable empirical research' on social formations. Here there is obviously a context in which historians could make a most important contribution.

I believe that the turmoil of debate about methodology is already reaching some conclusions which will help historians to make such a contribution. I also believe that work is already being done which responds very strikingly to the demands of the present.

The lessons we are learning from the debate about oral history—and not least from Vansina's own rethinking[17]—are that we must interpret the evidence within the assumptions of the society which produces it. Much oral material is public fantasy but a fantasy which is part of a real and concrete local situation. Moreover, we are learning that we need not only concentrate on those who 'own' formal political tradition, but that we can make use of oral material to reconstruct agricultural change, or the development of specialisations of trade and manufacture, or the experience of women.[18] The new emphases in archaeology stress the study of a total environment and the need to understand man's relationship with an eco-system. Historical linguistics has so far proved most convincing when applied to the history of the introduction of sheep or cattle or to other instances of economic change.[19] In all these ways methodological developments enable us to focus on the problem of poverty; of development and decline in the rural areas.

We need a further reconsideration of methodology, especially on the part of those who use archival material. Work has begun, for instance in the analysis of the impact of literacy on the traditions of Bakongo expression,[20] which will allow us to understand much better than we do at the moment the particularity of many African documents. Once again it will be a matter of opening ourselves up not to what these seem to us to mean but to what they mean to the author and his audience.

This all sounds like a retreat from the general to the small-scale; a retreat from historical interpretation on a useful scale into ethnography. But it seems to me that the answers to the problem of poverty will have to be given simultaneously on a much smaller scale than the nation-state and on a much larger scale. An instance of this comes from Tanzania. Since the decentralisation of administration, the university research bureaus have received a whole series of specific requests for research in relation to the specific problems of the regions; research which can be much more 'useful' than wider attempts at national generalisation. But this has been combined with a developing appreciation of the total economic system in which Tanzania is situated.

The most recent historical fruits of this double approach have been the first set of M.A. theses produced by graduate students in Dar es Salaam,[21] which combined a thorough study of regional economic change with an attempt to integrate this in a general theory of underdevelopment. Rather differently, there is the emphasis placed by John Iliffe on the significance of studies of the particular in a country which is striving towards heroic generalisation. Ordinary men, writes Iliffe, are more complex than heroes, and it is ordinary men who experience and to some extent make the problem of poverty.[22]

Now, of course, the new sophistication in oral history; the new approaches in archaeology; a rigorous use of historical linguistics; a penetrating use of African archival material—all this can be, and is being, used to transform and enrich studies of the sort that have hitherto dominated African historiography. African historians will not stop writing about the origin of states, or the formation of nations, of African cultural initiatives. But at the same time it is plain that many historians are turning to other questions.

There is, for example, the growing number of studies of the emergence, flourishing and decline of an African peasantry in colonial southern, central and eastern Africa.[23] Parallel with this, and not yet interacting sufficiently with it, is the growing number of studies of African agricultural change. These are studies which call for new skills on the part of historians—the ability to take soil samples or to map an eco-system or to make a calendar for the agricultural year; studies which are pre-eminently down to earth. Already they are suggesting that we need to revise many of our assumptions about African collective agricultural systems in the pre-colonial period.[24] There are studies being made of the growth of cattle systems and of the role of cattle management in the control of the eco-system. There are studies being made of internal specialisation and exchange and of innovations in diet which in combination are often more important than the effects of external trade. There are especially important studies being made of the changing division of labour between men and women, which is turning out to be crucial to an understanding of recent African economic history.[25]

Studies like these not only offer some hope of pragmatic responses to the need to know more about African poverty. They also offer an answer to the problem of the significance of African history. For in this respect only African history is fully relevant. Agronomists tell us that the application of the technology of the temperate zones to tropical agriculture has been disastrous, whether the technology has been British or American or Chinese or Japanese. No one knows how to grow large quantities of food in tropical soils without ecological damage. In many ways we have to start all over again—and part of that starting is the business of agricultural history, the recovery of the insights into and the relationship with the eco-system of communal cultivators and herders over the last centuries.

But an answer to the problem of poverty is not to be found by means of an exclusive concentration upon production history. The study of changing concepts is also very relevant. African history needs to make a connection not only with the material way of life of the people but also with their modes of thought. Conceptual history is no longer a business of 'Bantu philosophy'— great schemes of Pan-African metaphysics—but of the difficult study of the evolution of ideas of causation in each region over the past decades. The sort of work which the young historian, Robert Papstein, and the young anthropologist, van Binsbergen, are producing on the conceptual history of western Zambia, for example, is not only fascinating but relevant to the whole question of poverty and how to transform it.[26] Of course, it is relevant in a different way. It would be hard to dispute that more food needs to be grown, though there is plenty of room for dispute over how and at what cost. But no one can simply say that people need more ideas or 'better' ideas. The history of ideas should not be simply an aid to developers, to enable them better to manipulate populations. My criterion of 'usefulness' is not as crude as that; it means history that can be 'used' in many different ways by different people, but used because it connects with what is their experience of life.

There seems to be reason to hope for a new 'social' history of Africa which takes into account both 'modes of production' and techniques of production; social differentiation and the shifting roles of the sexes; the relationship of societies to their environment; the formulation of explanations and their interaction with conduct. Such a social history, as it is carried into an exploration of the African experience in the twentieth century, would need to extend to the experience of the migrant labourer, as he moved along regional networks; the experience of the urban worker; the creation of a popular culture appropriate for dealing with a new world. And fortunately historical studies of this sort are under way as well.[27]

It was objected at the conference that in saying all this I was providing an easy way out for African historians who felt a sense of inadequacy or crisis. When I recommended the work of Colin Bundy on 'peasantisation', it was said, or the work of Charles van Onselen on the experience of the migrant labourer, I neglected to point out that both of them were really writing about capitalism. It was objected that I seemed to be saying that all would be well if only historians began to write about farmers or labourers or women; whereas no sound work could be done on any of these subjects without an effectively 'radical', indeed Marxist, approach. Obviously there has been and will be bad work done on the problem of African poverty—both bad non-Marxist work and bad Marxist work. Obviously there are some historians to whom the topic will be so uncongenial that they will not wish to work on it at all. But at this point to maintain that only studies from within one approach can be fruitful implies that we already essentially know the nature of African poverty and what is to be done about it. This seems to me to be untrue.

African history and European history

These developments within African historiography are bound to affect its relationship to the historiography of Europe in two ways. In the first place, students of Africa will begin to want to remake their models of European history in order that they can better understand the widest dimensions of the problem of African poverty. An admirable example of this is the work of Immanuel Wallerstein, who has written a four-volume study of the rise of agrarian capitalism in Eastern Europe and the development of a system of world trade in order to answer questions posed to him by his study of Africa.[28] And in the second place, there will be an obvious interaction between this new African historiography and major currents within the historiography of Europe.

It may well be that Manchester is atypical in this respect, but I sense there three developments in the approach to the history of Europe. One is a movement away from chronological narratives of territorial history and towards a comparative and thematic approach. An example of this is the rise of 'peasant studies', which has the effect among other things of opening up different regions of Europe for study, and of allowing the Africanist to compare and contrast his material not only with the classical Europe of the old dominant historiographical tradition—England, France, Germany—but also with Central and Eastern Europe. In discussion of comparative peasant experience, or comparative nationalism, or comparative urbanisation, or of millennial movements, an Africanist can have a good deal to say.

Within the study of Western Europe itself, it seems to me that there is a growing emphasis on topics like internal colonisation and the destruction of provincial cultures; popular religion and popular culture; the spread of literacy and of the schools; and so on. . . .

Even in terms of period the Africanist is dealing with many of the same themes. Peasants in the French regions were beginning to see the point of sending their sons to school to learn standard French not very long before cultivators in Senegal. The church campaign to reach the children of the English towns coincided with the establishment of mission schools for freed slave children in Zanzibar. The forms which urban migrants in nineteenth-century Western Europe found, to survive and to construct new modes of living, were paralleled in the associations, churches and dance societies of Central Africa a hundred years later.

Europeanists are increasingly looking towards anthropology and sociology for insights into questions of this kind. And here, too, the Africanist is in a position of strength. The historian of Africa has been obliged to come to terms with the data and interpretations of anthropologists and sociologists; he has been obliged to develop his own field methodology which in some ways parallels and in other ways contrasts with their fieldwork experiences. The African historian both knows his debt to the social sciences and knows their limitations for diachronic reconstruction. He might be able to bring a healthy scepticism to the study of topics where Europeanists tend to be all too respectful of anthropology—like the study of witchcraft, for instance. The African historian certainly ought to ensure that historians of witchcraft, or popular religion, or popular recreation in Europe are familiar with and cite the works of historians of Africa as well as of anthropologists.

Finally, there is the central question of the direct encounter between Europe and Africa. This encounter, within the more general confrontation of Europe and the rest of the world, is more and more obviously the most important theme in the history of the last hundred years. In Manchester at any rate, courses in world history or in the history of the relationship of Britain and the world have increasingly come to revolve around it. And here the Africanist must seek not only better to comprehend what Europe has done and gained and believed in the encounter but also how it has been conceptualised and what it has meant for Africa and the world.

What is most hopeful about all this is that the ways in which African historiography is relating to European are identical with the ways in which it is becoming more relevant to Africa. The development of this single thrust will be the dominant theme of the next decade of African historical studies.

Notes

1   Jan Vansina, 'Recording the oral history of the Bakuba', *Journal of African History* (*JAH*), i, 1 and 2, 1960, pp. 45-54, 257-70.

2   Jan Vansina, *De la Tradition Orale*, Tervuren, 1961.

3   E. J. Alagoa, 'Oral Tradition among the Ibo of the Niger Delta', *JAH*, viii, 3, 1966.

4   Jan Vansina, 'The Foundation of the Kingdom of Kasanje', *JAH*, iv, 3, 1963; *Kingdoms of the Savanna*, Madison, 1966.

5   B. A. Ogot, *History of the Southern Luo*, 1, Nairobi, 1967.

6   Wyatt McGaffey, 'Oral tradition in central Africa', *International Journal of African Historical Studies*, vii, 3, 1975.

7   Jan Vansina, *The Tio Kingdom of the Middle Congo, 1880-1892*, London, 1973.

8   J. C. Miller, 'The Imbangala and the Chronology of Early Central African History', *JAH*, xiii, 4, 1972; J. S. Boston, 'Oral tradition and the History of the Igala', *JAH*, x, 1 1969; E. J. Alagoa, 'The Development of Institutions in the States of the Eastern Niger Delta', *JAH*, xii, 2, 1971; Kennell Jackson, 'An ethnohistorical study of the oral traditions of the Akamba of Kenya', UCLA doctoral dissertation, 1972; Wyatt MacGaffey, *Custom and Government in the Lower Congo*, Berkeley, 1970.

9   Christopher Ehret, *Southern Nilotic History*, Evanston, 1971; *Ethiopians and East Africans*, Nairobi, 1974; 'Bantu origins and history; critique and interpretation', *The Transafrican Journal of History (TAJH)*, ii, 1, 1972, 'Patterns of Bantu and Central Sudanic Settlement in Central and Southern Africa, ca. 1000 BC-500 AD', *TAJH*, iii, 1 and 2, 1973.

10 Roger Summers and K. Robinson, *Zimbabwe Excavations, 1958*, Occasional Papers of the National Museums of Rhodesia, no. 23A, December 1961; Summers, *Zimbabwe. A Rhodesian Mystery*, Johannesburg, 1963; P. S. Garlake, *Great Zimbabwe*, London, 1973; T. N. Huffman, 'The rise and fall of Zimbabwe', *JAH*, iii, 3, 1972

11 For attempts to correlate archaeology and historical linguistics, see: T. N. Huffman, 'The linguistic Affinities of the Iron Age in Southern Africa', and J. E. G. Sutton, 'The Peopling of Eastern Africa: some archaeological and linguistic correlations', UCLA language and history colloquium, November 1973.

12 John Iliffe, 'The recent historiography of 19th and 20th century Tanganyika', School of Oriental and African Studies, London, February 1972.

13 For example: Keith Thomas, *Religion and the Decline of Magic*, London, 1971; A. D. J. Macfarlane, *Witchcraft in Tudor and Stuart England*, London, 1970; Mary Douglas, editor, *Witchcraft. Confessions and Accusations*, London, 1970.

14 S. Adotevi, 'Discours', O. A. U. Pan-African Cultural Festival, Algiers, July 1969; William Ochieng, 'Undercivilisation in Black Africa', *Kenya Historical Review*, 2. 1, 1974.

15 Ochieng, *op. cit.*

16 Colin Leys, 'Foreword', in Geoff Lamb, *Peasant Politics*, Lewes, 1974.

17 Jan Vansina, 'Traditions of Genesis', *JAH*, xv, 2, 1974.

18 Margaret Hay, 'Economic Change in Luoland', Wisconsin doctoral thesis, 1972; John McKenzie, 'The Njanja Iron industry: the decline of a pre-colonial enterprise', University of Rhodesia seminar, 1974.

19 C. Ehret, 'Cattle-keeping and milking in eastern and southern African history', *JAH*, viii, 1, 1967; 'Sheep and Central Sudanic Peoples in Southern Africa, *JAH*, ix, 2, 1968; 'Agricultural history in Central and Southern Africa, ca. 1000 BC to ca. 500 AD', U.C.L.A. seminar, 1973.

20 Wyatt MacGaffey and J. Jenzen, 'Literacy and Truth', in *Anthology of Kongo Religion*, Lawrence, Kansas, 1974.

21 J. R. Mlahagwa, 'Agricultural change in the Uluguru Mountains during the colonial period'; S. K. S. Bakengesa, 'A historical survey of the coffee industry in Bukoba district, 1932-54'; G. Manyanda, 'A history of the growth of the commercial cotton cultivation in Ndagalu, Kwimba district'; C. K. Magoti, 'The development and impact of the money economy on Musoma district, 1939-60'; A. Tambala, ' A history of the Tanga sisal labour force, 1936-64'; L. Sago, 'A history of labour migration in Kasulu district, 1928-60'; M.A. theses, Dar es Salaam, June 1974.

22 John Iliffe, Introduction, *Modern Tanzanians*, Nairobi, 1973. Iliffe writes: 'This is a book about people, not about heroes ... Few of these men—and indeed few men of any time or nation—can meet at every point the high standards of morality

and selflessness which are taught in contemporary Tanzania. But precisely for this reason, the men who form the subject of this book must become a real part of the history of Tanzania as it is taught and studied. Ordinary people like these may sometimes be less admirable than heroes, but they are much more complicated than heroes. They need understanding rather than adulation, and understanding is more difficult than adulation. The fact that much African history lacks human personalities means that it is often taught in stereotypes ... these categories have some value but they are categories and not realities. Real people do not fit the categories for people are more complicated than ideas. If the history which is taught and studied lacks this sense of human complexity, the understanding it brings will be partial and the action it inspires will be inhumane.'

23 Giovanni Arrighi, 'Labour supplies in Historical Perspective: a study of the proletarianisation of the African peasantry in Rhodesia', *Journal of Development Studies*, 6, 1970; Colin Bundy, 'The emergence and decline of a South African peasantry', *African Affairs*, lxxi, 285, 1972; Martin Channock, 'The Political Economy of independent agriculture in colonial Malawi', *Journal of Social Science*, 1, 1972; Ian Phimister, 'Peasant production and Underdevelopment in Southern Rhodesia, 1890-1914'; Robin Palmer, 'The Agricultural History of Rhodesia', both forthcoming in Palmer, ed. *The Roots of Rural Poverty*.

24 Margaret Hay, *op. cit*; Helge Kjekshus, 'Ecology control and economic development', Dar es Salaam, seminar, 1974; David Beach, 'The Shona economy: branches of production', University of Rhodesia seminar, 1974.

25 Jacques Depelchin, 'From pre-capitalism to Imperialism: a history of social and economic formations in Uvira, Zaire, 1850-1972', doctoral thesis in progress for Stanford; Ester Boserup, *Women's Role in Economic Development*, London, 1970; M. Z. Rosaldo and L. Lamphere, *Woman, Culture and Society*, Stanford, 1974; Maud Mutemba, 'Women in agricultural change: a case study of the Lenje of Zambia'; Sheri Young, 'Fertility and Famine: Women's agricultural history in Southern Mozambique', UCLA colloquia papers, Spring 1974.

26 Bim van Binsbergen, 'Religious change in Central Western Zambia: towards a synthesis', in T. O. Ranger, editor, *The Problem of Evil in Eastern Africa*, forthcoming; J. M. Schoeffeleers, 'The Prophets of Nsanje'; Peter Rigby, 'Prophets, diviners and prophetism: the recent history of Kiganda religion'; B. A. Ogot, 'A community of their own: a study of the search for a new order by the Maria Legio of Africa Church', all delivered to the Limuru conference on the Religious History of Eastern Africa, August 1974; Sholto Cross, 'The Watch Tower movement in south central Africa, 1908-1945', Oxford doctoral thesis, 1973.

27 Charles van Onselen, 'Worker consciousness in Black Miners: Southern Rhodesia, 1900-1920', *JAH*, xiv, 2, 1973; 'African Mine Labour in Southern Rhodesia, 1900-1933', Oxford doctoral dissertation, 1974; Sylvia A. N. Mabaso, 'The urbanisation of William Mubita and Isaac Banda', *Zambian Land and Labour Studies*, 1, September 1973, Lusaka.

28 I. Wallerstein, *The Modern World System. Capitalist Agriculture and the Origins of the European World Economy in the Sixteenth Century*, 4 volumes, New York, 1974; see also Walter Rodney, *How Europe underdeveloped Africa*, London, 1972; Samir Amin, 'Underdevelopment and Dependence', *Journal of Modern African Studies*, x, 4, 1972.

A. G. Hopkins

Clio-Antics: A Horoscope for African Economic History

Historiographical surveys have their peculiar pitfalls.[1] The immediate temptation is to present an inventory in the format of a company report, in which the author details the output of the academic labour force, comments on successful and unsuccessful branches and calls for greater effort in the future. The tediousness which can so easily accompany this approach is avoided only at the cost of introducing a degree of selectivity that is bound to leave some readers dissatisfied—though still awake. The present analysis departs from custom by casting a horoscope for African economic history, looking into the future rather than surveying the past. Of course, the past cannot be ignored in an exercise of this kind, for there is a sense in which, as Anatole France very nearly put it, 'all our futures lie behind us'. Thus, the date of birth of the subject is important because it reveals the disposition of the heavens at the time, and so helps to chart the trajectory of subsequent developments. Admittedly, the procedure used for discerning the future cannot meet the strictest canons of historical scholarship. The technique employed here is based on reading a selection of academic palms, on gauging the atmosphere at some current (1974) conferences in North America, and on shuffling the bibliographical cards of recent publications. If the result is Clio-antics rather than Clio-metrics, speculation about the future rather than measurement of the past, let it be said that at least the sequence makes sense: the hunches nearly always come first. Furthermore, the exercise may have practical value for research which is in the mind, but not yet undertaken.

The first clear signal received with respect to the study of Africa is that history is back in fashion. In the 1950s and 1960s historians of Third World countries tended to be regarded by other social scientists as labourers shovelling data for the Higher Learning. Financial rewards, high status and an element of missionary zeal inspired the problem-solvers in the theoretical and applied social sciences. These were the men who had the tools and could finish the job. This was the moment of optimism, when economists seemed capable of planning prosperity for the underdeveloped world, when sociologists and social psychologists felt certain they could convert Weberian Traditional Man into a Marshallian maximiser, and when systems analysis seemed to have reached the point where political scientists knew what inputs, throughputs and outputs were needed to maintain stability in a decolonised world. History, too, partly by accident, partly by design, had a role to play in legitimating the new nation states. Hence the stress laid on the creativity of African cultures, the prominence given to famous African leaders, and the emphasis placed on the importance and, by sleight of mind, the desirability of large unitary states. The shortcomings of this style of history appear obvious today, though it is by no means easy to see what alternatives were open at the time.

The problem-solvers have now lost some of their funds, much of their status and virtually all their *élan*. In the face of the enduring and in some cases deepening problems of the Third World, optimism has been replaced by pessimism. Development plans achieved far less than had been expected. The sociology of development lost a good deal of its initial impetus as it became clear that the dichotomy between traditional and modern societies was, in many respects, misleading; and political stability (and fidelity) seemed as unpredictable as they were when Plato and Aristotle first analysed the problems of order and change. Economists, political scientists and sociologists have entered a phase of self-criticism which can be taken to signify either the final collapse of the old doctrines or a period of constructive reformulation—depending on the observer's viewpoint. Presidential addresses to established disciplinary associations now lament the abstraction from reality which resulted from years spent in pursuit of High Theory and call for more empirical work, and sometimes for more history.[2] However, since Western capitalism has so far failed to solve the problems of the Third World and is itself experiencing a profound crisis, it is not surprising that the main drive behind the current revival of history comes from a radical pessimism which draws its inspiration, though not always its teaching, from Marx. 'Relevance' is still the test of the new history *vérité*, as it was in the early 1960s, but now the purpose of history is to locate the roots of underdevelopment rather than to legitimate post-colonial states. Today, economists, political sociologists and political historians are turning to economic history for an explanation of the present and for a guide to the future.[3] Dredging the data of distant centuries has now acquired not merely respectability in the eyes of non-historians, but also the urgency of a normative science.

The new history has a clear focus and commitment. It is centred on the dependency thesis, and in particular on the concept of 'the development of underdevelopment'. Dependency 'theory' had its origin and has been developed in Latin America in the period following the Second World War, when disappointment with the limited success of various national development plans led to increasingly radical criticism of conventional policy recommendations. As disenchantment set in with the moderate policy sponsored by the United Nations,[4] new inspiration was drawn from the action programme of Fidel Castro in Cuba. Criticism of orthodox analysis culminated during the 1960s in the influential publications of Andre Gunder Frank, who rejected the diffusionist model of international trade as an agency of economic growth, and argued that capitalism had retarded the independent development of the Third World.[5] Frank's thesis was presented in terms of the concept of 'the development of underdevelopment', which held that while Latin America may have been *un*developed before the impact of the West, it only became *under*developed as a result of being locked into the international trading system. According to Frank, many so-called causes of underdevelopment are in reality no more than symptoms or products of the functioning of international capitalism. Underdevelopment results from dependence, that is from a situation in which the economies of one group of countries are conditioned by the economies of another group.[6] The evolution of the whole is both combined and unequal: the fortunes of the dependent countries are decided by the dominant industrial powers, and the expansion of the capitalist centre is assisted by the transfer of surplus value from the periphery. One of the principal tasks of history is to study how dependency arose, and one of the chief policy recommendations of dependency theorists is that international trading links must be severed or at least greatly reduced if Third World countries are ever to stand a chance of achieving independent industrialisation.

Economic historians can be expected to sympathise with an interpretation of the past which stresses the importance of their own sub-discipline. There is no doubt that the dependency thesis has been beneficial in resurrecting lines of enquiry that had been accorded low status during the heyday of modernisation theory, and in stressing the connections between regional and global history. However, the new approach is producing an orthodoxy some way in advance of the evidence needed to validate it. This can be seen clearly in the widespread and often unreflective deployment of terms such as 'dependency', 'political economy' and 'the development of underdevelopment', and in the tendency to classify those who are slow to adopt the new terminology as supporters of an outmoded neoclassical or 'bourgeois' orthodoxy. This trend is now observable in African Studies, where Frank's thesis has been taken up and applied without full awareness of the intricacies of the debate which it has generated in Latin American circles. A particularly influential expression of Frank's general approach can be found in Walter Rodney's stimulating study, *How Europe Underdeveloped Africa*.[7] Claims to exclusiveness may stimulate a dialogue from which both parties emerge wiser than they were beforehand, but exclusiveness itself has all the deficiencies of a doctrine formulated to rule out not only alternative lines of future enquiry, but also past categories of hard-won information.

At first sight, it might seem from the combative use of terminology, and from the concern to distinguish the new offering from the old, that we are witnessing, in Kuhnian terminology, the transition from normal to revolutionary science.[8] Kuhn's now celebrated argument, expressed briefly and therefore incompletely, is that normal science, that is the everyday activity of a body of scholars within a particular discipline, takes place within a paradigm or framework of values and research priorities which derive, typically, from a major scientific breakthrough, and which define the concepts, methods and problems that are studied. Sooner or later there arises a problem that cannot be handled within the established paradigm. This failure brings about a crisis in normal science. The existing paradigm comes under criticism, passes through various stages of reaction, and is eventually made redundant by a piece of research which solves the problem from a non-paradigmatic base. The transition from normal to revolutionary science takes place, and eventually a new paradigm is established. It is tempting to view the shift from modernisation theory to 'underdevelopment studies' in terms of the collapse of one paradigm and the creation of another. However, this interpretation would be facile. In history and the social sciences it is rare for one school of thought to comprehend the totality of a subject or even a speciality within a subject. It is more realistic to think of the existence of competing schools which act on and against each other, and experience changes in popularity over time. Furthermore, a paradigm is based on a substantive scientific achievement which solves a fundamental problem, and then leads to far-reaching changes in methodology and research priorities. At present the dependency thesis can claim a new terminology and a shift of focus, but these do not constitute a novel paradigm. To say that the new history is different does not make it so. It is possible that a new paradigm will arise in the future. But failure to appreciate the ways in which the old and the new are still entwined does not advance the cause of innovation, and the use of an imprecise terminology, by obscuring fundamental assumptions, may actually harm the purpose it is supposed to serve.

One of the greatest difficulties in applying the dependency thesis to the African past lies in what might be termed the pre-dependence period. Dependency theorists are critical of the emphasis placed on 'trade and politics' in the historical research undertaken on Africa in the 1950s and 1960s, but are themselves committed to a similar stress on international trading relations, albeit with different conclusions in mind. Rodney's model, for example, is derived from Frank, who claims that capitalism penetrated Latin America from an early date following the growth of commercial ties with Europe.[9] It is important for students of Africa to realise that Frank's interpretation of Latin American history has been contested vigorously, on empirical grounds by historians, who claim that feudal and semi-feudal relations persisted in spite of the creation of international trading links,[10] and on theoretical grounds by Marxists, who argue that the motor of history must be found in an internal dialectic located in a mode of production.[11] It is hard to see how dependency theorists can make sizable concessions to the classical Marxist viewpoint, even if they were willing to do so, without virtually giving their case away. At the same time, adherence to the Frank-Rodney line leaves little room for an independent, internal approach to African history in the period before the impact of the West. It would seem that there are only two ways in which this dilemma can be handled. The first is to try to eliminate the distinction between pre-dependent and dependent Africa by pushing the impact of the West back in time as far as possible, and by focusing on other types of dependency, such as that associated with Arab and Indian connections at even earlier dates. There would thus be a case, though surely not an illuminating one, for saying that all African history is the history of dependency. The result, a new diffusionism, would have the appeal of a grand and coherent generalisation, but it would also exclude a great deal of indigenous history in the pre-colonial period. The other possibility is simply to interpret internal developments in terms which have no necessary and logical connection with the dependency thesis. To do this is, on present evidence, either to embrace romanticism or to attempt a Marxist analysis without fully appreciating the extent to which Marxism and the dependency thesis are incompatible. Both possibilities represent a needless retreat from the research of the 1960s, which began to reveal the variety, complexity and, let it be said, the independent character of the African past.

Interpreting internal developments in terms of dependency 'theory' probably has its fullest justification in dealing with the twentieth century, when external influences reached their peak. One likely result, given the size and importance of the rural sector, will be the proliferation of 'peasant' studies, in which the expansion of export crops, and official policy towards land and labour, are linked to the growth of economic and social differentiation in rural areas and to the emergence of incipient class relationships.[12] Studies of this kind, merging with a stream of research from other parts of the world,[13] are potentially illuminating, for the dimensions of social change in Africa's rural economies have still to be charted. There is a danger, however, that misleading analytical categories will be created for verifying in Africa a sequence of change derived from the history of other continents.[14] A great deal of energy could easily be spent, for instance, in search of the quintessential peasant. Whether or not African cultivators can be called peasants cannot be discussed in the space available here, but it is worth observing that African agrarian production does not lend itself readily to classifications inspired by studies of Europe or Latin America. Landlords are not widely recognisable as a group or class; important constituents of the rural economy, notably pastoralists, are not encompassed by peasant analysis; and the concept of rent cannot be defined readily except perhaps with respect to external transfers of 'surplus' value. Even this usage is far from straightforward.[15] It is hard to see how the term 'peasant' can achieve wide currency in African studies without its meaning becoming diluted, in which case the result will simply be a label covering heterogeneity rather than a concept offering fresh insight into the dynamics of rural socio-economic organisation.[16]

In the pre-dependence period (which will vary according to which part of Africa is being considered, and what definition is given to the concept of dependence), it is difficult to see what positive contribution dependency theory can make. The main thrust of research on pre-colonial economic history is likely to come from a more classical Marxist concern with relations of production, as exemplified in the increasingly influential work of French anthropologists, notably Godelier, Meillassoux and Terray.[17] The importance of this perspective lies in the attempt to lay bare the structures of pre-capitalist societies (using the term 'pre-capitalist' to refer to pre-industrial societies, and not simply to societies without developed internal exchange relations). It is too early to say how successful this venture in historical economic anthropology will be. Advantages which can be hoped for include an end to the substantivist-formalist debate, since it should be clear that production for use and production for exchange were both common in pre-colonial Africa, and a fuller understanding of cohesion, division and the nature of power in African societies. The main goal, however, is to discover an internal dialectic in the African past, and in this quest Marxist and non-Marxist scholars alike are still just entering the maze of history. The efforts made in the 1960s to fit Africa into Germanic and Asiatic modes of production now look heavy-handed. The present mood of Marxist thinking on this subject can be depicted as one of revisionism following an initial phase of unreflective orthodoxy. Thus there has been an attempt to distinguish an African mode of production based on long-distance trade.[18] This classification, though illuminating, appears to strain orthodoxy to the limit, since it is hard to see how a mode of production can be based on commerce. The concern to remedy the deficiencies of concepts which are either formulated inappropriately or misapplied when related to Africa, is now leading to a particularism that threatens to produce as many modes as cases. Meillassoux has defined one kind of domestic mode of production and Sahlins another, while Terray, re-working Meillassoux's data, has found two modes of production among the Gourou alone.[19] As the list lengthens, contributors and observers alike may be forgiven for wondering whether they are gazing at forms or norms, at modes or mirages.

Non-Marxist research trends are already moving towards the study of production, though for pragmatic rather than for theoretical reasons. An outline of the history of Africa's external and internal trade was charted in the 1960s and early 1970s, and it is now recognised that the rural economy remains the principal area of scholarly ignorance. There are good reasons for pursuing lines of enquiry which have not been selected because of the high ranking accorded them in Marxist theory or neo-classical economics, but which might (for that very reason) contribute to an understanding of the structure of underdevelopment in pre-colonial Africa. Ecology, polity and cosmology are worth noting to illustrate the type of research that can span and inform Marxist and non-Marxist approaches, and to indicate the importance of research topics which fall outside the orbit of dependency theory. For a pioneering survey of these themes on a continent-wide scale, it is hard to improve on Basil Davidson's *The Africans: an Entry into Cultural History* (1969).

Historians can gain by turning, in the spirit of Febvre,[20] to the study of geography, though to ecology rather than to the older varieties of human and regional geography. The ecological approach makes it possible to delineate the parameters within which man and physical resources interact, and to explore the great variety of types of interaction. Ford's remarkable study of the tsetse fly must surely become one of the principal starting points for research into African ecological history.[21] Ford shows how the spread of agriculture led to the creation of cleared and settled lands separated by virgin territory, where fauna and their disease-bearing parasites lived; how maintaining a certain density of population, cultivation and livestock was necessary for containing the natural eco-system; and how this ecological balance was upset by European conquest and by migration. An obvious extension of Ford's general thesis would be to consider how far migrations and conquests in the pre-colonial period led to ecological change involving a retreat from agriculture and also, possibly, to political conflict. This approach could be complemented by investigating patterns of drought and famine in the Sahel, where migration can be seen as a result rather than as a cause of ecological change.[22] These themes in ecological history have a continent-wide application, and relate to pastoral as well as to agricultural societies. They also have close connections with such important questions as the causes and consequences of the relative scarcities of land and labour in Africa, and the possibility of identifying regional economies as a means of building on micro-studies, without relying on formal political divisions.

Next, economic historians need to give further thought to African cosmologies as a means of understanding the relationships between belief and action.[23] Open societies have a capacity for dealing with anomalous developments by advancing explanations which modify the existing belief system, whereas closed societies regard anomalies as threats to core values and fend them off by rituals aimed at preventing disfunctional change, and by taboos, like prohibitions on enumerating certain categories of objects.[24] Notions of space and time express attitudes towards objects and persons in the external environment, and illustrate the connection between the conceptual order and the ecological order. Hunters and gatherers tend to establish a relationship of kinship, and hence respect, with the forest, 'borrowing' from it rather than regarding it simply as an object to be exploited. Agriculturalists are more likely to see the forest as a threat to their way of life, and forge human alliances to guard against its hostile advance. Repetitive 'ecological time' is charted by the oscillation of the seasons, whereas linear time marks stages of birth, growth, maturity, decline and death; its irreversible trend is measured ultimately by a religious chronometer which extends into the hereafter. Different cultures stress different stages of linear time, and these varying emphases provide information about societal values and goals.[25] At what point in man's relationship with his natural environment, his ancestors, his contemporaries and his descendants does he need to devise a notation which measures space and time precisely and permanently? This question deserves more attention than it has received so far, especially since it raises a problem, that of non-literacy, which historians of Africa have not yet met head-on. The causes of the limited development of written notation in Africa may well remain elusive, but the consequences surely merit further study, especially with reference to the development of technology and the creation of large organisations.[26]

Lastly, further thought needs to be given to the connection between economy and polity, not so much at the level of trade and politics, which has been fairly well covered already, but with reference to the larger problem of how far the state is an expression of the structure of underdevelopment and how far it is a determining factor in it. A key issue here is the extent to which African state systems experienced the kind of generative antagonisms which have been motors of cumulative change in some other parts of the world. Varying degrees of openness in political systems are clearly relevant to this issue, and so are questions of economic specialisation and social differentiation, which may, indeed, have a bearing on value systems and their transformation.[27] At first sight it seems unlikely that the landlord-peasant and noble-bourgeois contrasts, central to the history of mediaeval and early modern Europe, were replicated in sub-Saharan Africa. Conflicts existed, but those between pastoralists and agriculturalists or between masters and slaves do not appear to have had the same potential for cumulative change, and those which pitted lineage against lineage were essentially conflicts of personnel within corporate structures. The historian who looks for secular change might find himself studying instead the non-dialectic of the relatively stable equilibrium. This is an unorthodox hypothesis, but one which, if tested, will undoubtedly provide a better understanding of the role of the polity in the economy.

Dependency 'theory' appears to achieve its best fit when applied to the eighteenth, nineteenth and twentieth centuries, which cover the high point of the Atlantic slave trade, the era of imperialism, colonial rule and neo-colonialism. As far as the selection of research subjects is concerned, the chief effect of the dependency thesis will be to reinforce trends already in sight or becoming established. It is likely that more quantitative research will be carried out on the overseas slave trade, following the lead given by Curtin.[28] Studies will be made of import and export prices, of the incidence of mortality on the Atlantic crossing, of domestic output forgone as a result of forcible emigration, and of the social losses which the traffic involved. Qualitative research, testing, for instance, propositions about the decline and survival of traditional crafts, should also be pursued. The problem of the causes and the timing of partition will remain a focus of research, and further impetus will be given to economic theories of imperialism, emphasising capital flows,[29] commercial pressure groups, the quest for markets, and the demand for raw materials. Perhaps the most important feature of the late 1970s will be the revival of colonial history. The incentive to understand the role of the colonial powers in 'underdeveloping' Africa, combined with the availability of official records covering the greater part of the colonial period, will lead to the quantification of data relating to the overseas trade sector to provide both periodisation and measures of gains and losses; to institutional studies of policy-making machinery[30] and of the expatriate firms;[31] and to a revival of biographies of pro-consuls, a type of history that has been out of favour for some years.[32]

More significant than the selection of research topics (since none is entirely new) are the interpretative assumptions which dependency theorists bring to the study of history. The dependency thesis argues that European capitalism penetrated Africa from the time of the overseas slave trade, that external exchange relations distorted the indigenous economy by fostering sectors which catered solely for foreign demand, and that as a result of the creation of asymmetrical exchange relationships 'surplus' value was transferred from the periphery to the centre. The process of excavation continued, even after colonies achieved formal independence, as a consequence of the monopoly power of large multi-national corporations acting in concert with tame national bourgeois governments. International trade is thus seen as a zero-sum game, in which the gains of one party are the losses of the other. The notion that international trade can help to generate industrialisation in poor countries is regarded as little more than a fantasy based on false optimism. This interpretation is commonly accompanied by an attack on neo-classical economics (or, more vaguely, on bourgeois economics), which is criticised for emphasising the market-oriented behaviour of rational men in a world abstracted from the politics of reality.

The presumed dichotomy between dependency 'theory' and bourgeois economics raises important conceptual and empirical problems. There is a degree of false novelty about the very notion of dependency which suggests that many dependency theorists have failed to do justice to the complexity of the tradition they are attacking. Neither the concept nor the undoubted fact of dependence is new: both have been recognised in standard neo-classical texts of theory and economic history for some time, and have closely related terms, such as 'open' and 'export' economies.[33] What is new is that in the last few years, and for the first time, the term dependence has achieved widespread currency outside the ranks of economists, especially among historians, political scientists and sociologists. But whereas specialists in international trade theory defined dependence in fairly narrow terms, dependency theorists use the word more generally to encompass historical, political and social as well as economic dimensions of underdevelopment. Their usage also embodies a theory of causation and prediction. The apparent universality of the theory is undoubtedly one of its principal attractions. Unfortunately, the broader the usage the greater is the danger of tautology. At the level of global generalisation, dependency theory must be right because it is impossible to envisage its antonym, independence, except in a state of autarky, which, historically, is an exceptional (and often unenviable) condition. Even where autarky exists at the level of the nation state, relations of dependency will be found within the polity on a regional basis and as a result of social differentiation. To counter the charge that dependency theory is tautological, it is necessary to give the concept empirical anchorage. However, once the attempt is made to apply the theory to the history of world capitalism, it becomes apparent that dependency was not a uniform state, but one that differed spatially, temporally and analytically. Latin America's dependence on Spain in the sixteenth century was not the same as its dependence on the USA in the twentieth. Nigeria and New Zealand were both dependent on Great Britain in the first three-quarters of the twentieth century, but this observation reveals little about the constitutional standing and economic structure of the two countries. Moreover, the degree of dependence varied greatly, whether measured by the ratio of export production to total output, by the volume of foreign capital as a proportion of total investment, or by any combination of these and other conventional yardsticks. If the aim of the dependency thesis was merely to point non-specialists in the direction of the problem of international economic inequalities, these qualifications could be regarded as necessary and even functional in leading to the identification of sub-systems of the general phenomenon. However, dependency 'theory' purports to be an explanation rather than a signpost. Qualifications of this magnitude suggest that it is more accurate to regard it as a label covering a bundle of assorted symptoms.

Difficulties inherent in the formulation of the concept are reflected in two of its central propositions. The first, which can be called the excavation thesis, holds that international trade caused underdevelopment. The second, which follows from it, is that a country which has been underdeveloped cannot industrialise until its international trading links have been severed.

The first problem originates in the specification of international trade theory, which is sometimes oversimplified to the extent of being presented as little more than Ricardo's doctrine of comparative costs and the associated notion that international trade brings benefits to all parties concerned.[34] But the theory of comparative costs is hedged with stringent conditions. The pursuit of comparative advantage ought to lead to the optimum allocation of the resources of the trading partners concerned, but this outcome is to be expected only where monopoly power and other market imperfections are absent, where externalities affecting production and consumption are disregarded, and where factor endowments are assumed to be fixed (because in its original formulation the theory was static rather than dynamic). Next, the theory does not claim that international trade will inevitably equalise real wages or real *per capita* incomes among trading partners, but rather that under the conditions specified the real income of each country would be higher with trade than without it.[35] Classical economists, Marx included, were optimistic that international trade would spread industrialisation. But they thought that free trade and related conditions would apply, and they were not well informed about the internal developmental problems of non-European countries. Furthermore, it seems reasonable to suggest that critics of 'the' theory of international trade have an obligation to treat current versions of the theory, which deal with the problems of long-run growth, differential bargaining power, the 'widening gap', the role of protective tariffs, and international economic reform, otherwise thay are likely to find themselves advancing criticisms of Ricardo (or even Samuelson) which have already been made and incorporated within the 'orthodox' tradition. Plainly, conventional international trade theory, which undoubtedly has numerous deficiencies, takes more account of limitations to comparative advantage than some dependency theorists seem to appreciate.

The dependency thesis has given an important stimulus to the study of unequal exchange, a concept also found within orthodox theory. The conventional argument is that, given certain conditions, international trade increases welfare, not that it increases welfare equally for all parties. Conventional theory approaches the question of differential returns by making a two-fold distinction: between private and social gains and losses, which makes it possible to say, for example, that the Atlantic slave trade was privately profitable but involved great social losses; and between absolute and relative gains and losses, which makes it possible to observe that the gains of both parties increased but that one rose proportionately more than the other. These distinctions are of the utmost importance because they permit conventional theory to analyse the differential effects of international trade with respect to types of trade and types of region. International trade is treated as a non zero-sum game in which the outcomes range from Ricardo's 'first best' solution to the disastrous results of the Atlantic slave trade, in which social costs far outweighed private gains.

The dependency thesis, in contrast, is committed to the view that the gains of one party are the losses of the other. Attempts to substantiate this thesis have produced some stimulating and valuable work, but so far no consensus on the definition or measurement of unequal exchange has emerged. Emmanuel, for example, has argued that unequal exchange results from the differential wage rates prevailing in countries involved in international trade: instead of differences in productivity causing variations in wages, as the classical economists supposed, it is wages that set levels of productivity.[36] Emmanuel's work has had a considerable influence on dependency theorists, not least because it is a bargaining theory which focuses on exchange relations. However, dependency theorists who adopt Emmanuel's viewpoint need to be aware that it is open to criticism from two sides. It departs from the traditional Marxist approach in not being rooted fully in relations of production, and it has uncomfortably close connections (for a thesis which claims to be novel) with the literature on imperfect competition which was a product of late neo-classical and post-Keynesian thinking.[37] Amin, on the other hand, holds that unequal exchange occurs only where the difference between international wage levels is greater than the difference in productivities.[38] This argument is closer to the central Marxist tradition because it is based on the assumption that it is the rate of capital accumulation which ultimately determines the distribution of wages and profits. However, Amin's thesis has its own difficulties. His formula uses the double factoral terms of trade (which, incidentally, are a late neo-classical refinement associated particularly with Pigou), not merely to measure changes in productivity, but to show that differences in productivity and welfare are the *result* of transfers of income. But the double factoral terms of trade are only a measure of association: they do not establish a causal relationship between changing productivity levels. They cannot be used to show, for example, that productivity in French exporting industries increased *because* productivity in Senegalese exporting industries was retarded.[39] Productivity gains in France do not necessarily preclude productivity and welfare gains in Senegal. What matters for Senegal is whether it obtains more goods per unit of 'exported factor-inputs' (that is, whether its single factoral terms improve), not whether imports contain more or less foreign inputs than they did previously.

The difficulties in the view that international trade must be a zero-sum game become even more apparent when industrialisation is considered. The development of underdevelopment thesis permits no compromise: it states that international trade excavates the wealth of the poor countries and prevents them from industrialising. Africanists who are attracted to this interpretation, and are inclined to associate it, however vaguely, with Marxism, should pause to consider the following objections. It is hard to accept that dependence must be the determining factor in economic development (or rather non-development) when at least some of the countries which have been dependent in the past, such as the USA, Canada, Australia, New Zealand and, briefly, Japan, developed independently subsequently. These examples, it might be admitted, constitute a qualification with respect to the universal applicability of the dependency thesis, but it could still be said that they represent special cases some way removed from the typical examples to be found in Latin America, Africa and most of Asia. This reply does little to preserve Frank's position. A fundamental objection has been made by Cardoso, who, like Frank, is strongly critical of a good deal of 'metropolitan Marxism'.[40] Cardoso's thesis, well known to Latin American specialists, but not yet fully assimilated by Africanists, is summarised by the notion of dependent development. The argument, persuasively presented, is that imperialism *has* generated a degree of industrialisation in Latin America, though this development remains under expatriate control.[41] Even with this qualification, it is clear that Cardoso's view, if accepted, substantially modifies Frank's argument. Cardoso's critique is by no means the only major attack on the development of underdevelopment thesis. The classic Marxist view, restated recently in an arresting article by Warren,[42] holds that eventually capitalism will spread to the underdeveloped world through the agency of imperialism, which will eliminate feudalism, introduce industrial capitalism, and ultimately generate proletarian revolutions. Warren argues not only that there is more industrialisation in the so-called periphery than most dependency theorists have been prepared to admit, but that this development is associated with a very real degree of economic and political independence, as the examples of Nigeria and Iran illustrate. To speak of connections between the developed and the underdeveloped worlds in terms of centre-periphery relations is to ignore that some peripheries have become centres in their own right.[43]

History is back in fashion, but historians have reason to view the rising status of their discipline with a degree of caution. Refugees from the social sciences and converts from political to economic history seek not merely sanctuary in the past but solutions to contemporary problems. There is a danger that history will be treated as the black box containing the reasons why Rostow's plane collapsed on the runway.[44] Reification, in which socio-political institutions become real entities instead of mere surrogates, combined with a relentless teleological commitment can always 'explain' the present, and doubtless the future too. Althusser's dictum that 'a pure science only exists on condition that it continually frees itself from the ideology which occupies it, haunts it, or lies in wait for it',[45] is probably too high-minded for historians and social scientists to uphold. Nevertheless, the concept of a usable past presumably still requires that historical propositions should be tested for conceptual logic and empirical validity. This exercise is neither theological nor antiquarian, but, given the desire to use history for purposes of current policy, of practical importance. A misreading of history (from whatever ideological standpoint) can lead to policy recommendations the welfare effects of which are quite contrary to the intentions of their advocates.

It seems clear that the dependency thesis is becoming influential in African Studies, particularly in African history, because of the apparent universality of its message, the clarity and simplicity of its diagnosis and prescription, and the appealing way in which it expresses the generally gloomy mood of the moment. However, the new orthodoxy does not possess paradigmatic qualities, despite energetic shadow-boxing with a novel terminology. It is best regarded as a school of thought representing the pessimism of radical nationalism and claiming an association with Marxism which turns out, on inspection, to be extremely tenuous.[46] Much of its popular appeal is based on its tautological characteristics. *Dependentistas* may have views on pre-dependent Africa, but these are not derived from the 'theory' itself, which is silent, by definition, on the period before subordination to external powers began. This omission is scarcely relevant for Latin America, where the thesis originated, because the Europeans very nearly obliterated the indigenous population in large parts of that continent shortly after their arrival. But in Africa, even allowing for the destructive effects of the external slave trade, it is hard to envisage an enlightening theory of history that does not incorporate indigenous and—to use the term in its conventional sense—pre-contact history. The gap will be filled partly by the application of Marxist economic anthropology to history. This exercise should be productive, but it carries its own idiosyncratic problems. The particularism which will result from detailed research into modes of production is likely to produce a diversity which some Marxists will see as a departure from the specifications laid down by historical materialism. If so, the result may be not a new synthesis but a reversion to an older orthodoxy. The suggestion made here (though only incidentally as a safeguard against the possible closure of important Marxist lines of enquiry), is that there is good reason to pursue research themes relating to ecology, polity and cosmology which are either ignored by dependency 'theory' or thought by orthodox Marxists to be of secondary importance. As for the period of European contact, it has been argued that the concept of dependence is less novel than some of its advocates believe, and that the embellishments added to existing terms (such as 'open' or 'export' economies) have made the theory very nearly inoperative, first because it has been over-generalised, and second because it has been tied to an inflexible interpretation of international trade theory which is frequently inapplicable and presents important and still unresolved problems of proof.

In failing to establish a separate identity for itself, dependency 'theory' draws attention to the difficulty of defining the conventional wisdom it seeks to oppose. As long as terms such as 'neo-classical' and 'bourgeois' economics are used without elucidation, it is possible to convey the impression that dependency theory, despite its internal weaknesses, stands in opposition to a clearly defined body of doctrine. But the descent from high level generalisation leads to some awkward dilemmas. Is it, in fact, neo-classicism, with its stress on exchange relationships, which is under attack, and classicism, with its emphasis on social relations of production, which is being praised? Marxists can answer in the affirmative with more consistency than can dependency theorists, whose own approach stresses exchange relations, and also uses the tools developed by neo-classical economists to analyse those relationships. If, despite this obstacle, an intellectual connection with the classical tradition of political economy is claimed, if not established, then further problems arise. Is Adam Smith to be rejected because of his stress on self-regulating markets or admitted because of the value he placed on the social context of economic relationships,[47] and because it is now accepted that he was less hostile to government intervention in the economy than some of his successors, notably Ricardo? And is Ricardo himself to be included because of his important influence on Marx and, more recently, Sraffa,[48] or outlawed because of his doctrine of comparative costs, his advocacy of minimal government and his belief in rational economic man? Merely to pose these questions, which are only a small sample of those that could be asked, suggests that dependency theory lacks a paradigmatic base and is still closely connected to the tradition it attacks.

It is hard to see that the dependency thesis has added a new dimension to the criticisms of international trade theory advanced by Prebisch and his associates shortly after the Second World War.[49] At that time, development economics was just emerging as a separate specialism. Its first practitioners discovered that much of the emphasis and analysis of existing theory was imperfectly attuned to the problems of the non-industrial world. For the past thirty years there have been debates among development economists about such questions as differentiation in the structure of underdevelopment (notably the distinction between 'peasant' and 'enclave' economies), long-run movements in the terms of trade, tariff protection for infant industries and the means of redistributing world income.[50] Undeniably some formulations of international trade theory have been too optimistic. But the dependency thesis, at least in its Frankian versions, opposes one exaggeration with another: it asks too much of the evidence in explaining underdevelopment solely in terms of the European presence, in presenting international trade as a zero-sum game, and in denying the possibility that more than token industrialisation can result from a relationship of dependency. Dependency and its consequences are not identical. The results of international trade range from those which lend support to the original hypothesis to those which substantiate a more pessimistic view. What is required is not a theory of dependence, but a theory of interdependence which leaves scope for a variety of outcomes. It makes little sense to group oil-producing and industrialising states like Iran and Nigeria with resource-deficient countries like Chad, or with large but currently immiserised states like India. It would seem to follow that 'first-best' solutions must vary spatially and through time: comparative costs may be a sensible doctrine in one period; tariff barriers in another. It is at this point that a fruitful connection between history and policy can be made, for the major research achievement of the 1960s was to reveal the diversity of the African past, the uneven consequences of the European presence, and the likelihood—if a modest prediction is allowed—of a varied future.

Notes

1   I should like to express my gratitude to the Institute for Advanced Study, Princeton, for its support during the time this essay was being prepared. I am grateful, too, to Fernando Henrique Cardoso, Ray Dumett, Albert Hirschman, Robin Law, Sidney Mintz and Guillermo O'Donnell for commenting on an earlier draft. This acknowledgement in no way implies that any of these scholars agrees with the views expressed here.

2   Examples from economics are Kenneth E. Boulding, 'Economics as a Moral Science', *American Economic Review*, lix, 1969, pp. 1-12; Wassily Leontief, Theoretical Assumptions and Non-observed Facts', *American Economic Review*, lxi, 1971, pp. 1-7; E. H. Phelps-Brown, 'The Underdevelopment of Economics', *Economic Journal*, lxxxii, 1972, pp. 1-10.

3   Samir Amin, 'Underdevelopment and Dependence in Black Africa—Origins and Contemporary Forms', *Journal of Modern African Studies*, x, 1972, pp. 503-24; Immanuel Wallerstein, *The Modern World System: Capitalist Agriculture and the Origins of the European World Economy in the Sixteenth Century*, London, 1974; Ralph A. Austen, 'Economic History', *African Studies Review*, xiv, 1971, pp. 425-38. See also Edward A. Alpers, 'Re-thinking African Economic History: a Contribution to the Roots of Underdevelopment', *Ufahamu*, iii, 1973, pp. 97-129, for a view opposed to that presented here.

4   See Stanley G. Stein and Shane G. Hunt, 'Principal Currents in the Economic Historiography of Latin America', *Journal of Economic History*, xxxi, 1971, pp. 222-53.

5   See especially, *Latin America: Underdevelopment or Revolution*, New York, 1969, pp. 3-17.

6   For an elaboration of the concept of dependence, see Theotonio dos Santos, 'The Structure of Dependence', *American Economic Review*, lx, 1970, pp. 231-6.

7   London, 1972. The argument is also found in Basil Davidson's latest book, *Can Africa Survive?*, London, 1974, but is treated there selectively and with restraint.

8   T. S. Kuhn, *The Structure of Scientific Revolutions*, 2nd ed., Chicago, 1970. One of the best of numerous attempts to consider the relationship between Kuhn's theory and the social sciences is David A. Hollinger's article 'T. S. Kuhn's Theory of Science and its Implications for History', *American Historical Review*, lxxviii, 1973, pp. 370-93.

9   The political implications of this viewpoint hardly need stressing: if underdevelopment still had a pre-capitalist basis then the orthodox Marxist strategy would be to promote the next historical stage, namely capitalism, by supporting a national bourgeoisie, whereas if capitalism has permeated traditional societies as a result of international trade, then history is, in a manner of speaking, one step ahead of itself, and the national bourgeoisie becomes a target rather than an ally.

10   For example, Ernest Laclau, 'Feudalism and Capitalism in Latin America', *New Left Review*, 67, 1971, pp. 19-38.

11   For example, Raúl A. Fernandez and José F. Ocampo, 'The Latin American Revolution: a Theory of Imperialism not Dependence', *Latin American Perspectives*, i, 1974, pp. 30-61. Frank has responded to the charge that his analysis is insufficiently class-based, but evidently without satisfying his critics. See Andre Gunder Frank, *Lumpenbourgeoisie and Lumpendevelopment*, New York, 1972.

12   The other obvious result, the study of the urban wage labour force, has already occurred: with 'peasant' studies academics are spreading into the hinterland, having occupied the large coastal towns first of all.

13   Peasant studies are, of course, very much in vogue at present. The *Peasant Studies Newsletter* began publication in 1972, and the *Journal of Peasant Studies* in 1973.

14   For a somewhat broad definition of terms, see John Saul and Roger Woods, 'African Peasantries', in Teodor Shanin, ed., *Peasants and Peasant Societies*, London, 1971, p. 105. For an example of the way in which the term 'peasant' can be controlled (even though not completely defined) and put to use for a specific purpose and in a specific context, see Ken Post, 'Peasantisation and Rural Political Movements in Western Africa', *Archives Européennes de Sociologie*, xiii, 1972, pp. 223-54.

15   Eric R. Wolf, *Peasants*, Englewood Cliffs, 1966, is helpful on this question. Nevertheless, a major problem remains: the production of a 'fund of rent' may well distinguish peasants from 'primitive cultivators', but it may also be a characteristic of cultivators who are neither peasants nor primitives.

16   Thus Donald, reviewing William Derman's book on Guinea, *Serfs, Peasants and Socialists*, Los Angeles, 1973, first observes that Derman's usage of the term 'peasant 'is so broad that it includes large numbers of the inhabitants of most west African countries, and then goes on to approve this usage on the grounds that it ensures that observers will realise that these societies are stratified. It seems legitimate to wonder whether this is the best means of achieving this desired (and desirable) state of knowledge. See Leland Donald, 'Serfs and Peasants: West Africa', *Reviews in Anthropology*, i, 1974, pp. 371-8. Two scholars who studied peasants long before they achieved their current academic popularity

have sounded warnings which Africanists would do well to heed: Sidney W. Mintz, 'A Note on the Definition of Peasantries', *Journal of Peasant Studies*, i, 1973, pp. 91-106, and Rodney Hilton, 'Medieval Peasants—Any Lessons?', *Journal of Peasant Studies*, i, 1974, pp, 207-19.

17   Maurice Godelier, *Rationality and Irrationality in Economics*, London, 1972; Claude Meillassoux, 'From Reproduction to Production: a Marxist Approach to Economic Anthropology', *Economy and Society*, i, 1972, pp. 93-105; Emmanuel Terray, *Le marxisme devant les sociétés primitives: deux études*, Paris, 1969.

18   Catherine Coquery-Vidrovitch, 'Recherches sur un mode de production africain', *La Pensée*, 144, 1969, pp. 61-78. Translated into English and reprinted in Martin A. Klein and G. Wesley Johnson, eds., *Perspectives on the African Past*, Boston, 1972, pp. 33-51. Much the same point was made by E. W. Bovill in *Caravans of the Old Sahara*, Oxford, 1933.

19   Claude Meillassoux, 'From Reproduction to Production: a Marxist Approach to Economic Anthropology', *Economy and Society*, i, 1972, pp. 93-105; Marshall Sahlins, *Stone Age Economics*, London, 1974, pp. 41-148; Emmanuel Terray, *Le marxisme devant les sociétés primitives: deux études*, Paris, 1969. See also the excellent study by S. I. Mudenge, 'The Role of Foreign Trade in the Rozvi Empire: a Reappraisal', *Journal of African History*, xv, 1974, pp. 373-91.

20   Lucien Febvre, *La terre et l'évolution humaine*, Paris, 1922.

21   John Ford, *The Role of the Trypanosomiases in African Ecology: a Study of the Tsetse Fly Problem*, Oxford, 1971. John Iliffe, St. John's College, Cambridge, is already pursuing some of the topics noted here. See also N. T. J. Bailey, *The Mathematical Theory of Epidemics*, London, 1957, and for a comparative study B. M. Bhatia, *Famines in India*, Oxford, 1968.

22   Historians already working on these questions include Humphrey Fisher (S. O. A. S.), Paul Lovejoy (York University, Toronto), and Steven Baier (Boston University). Important papers on drought were published in *Savanna*, ii, 1973.

23   See Robin Horton and Ruth Finnegan, eds. *Modes of Thought*, London, 1973, and Horton's earlier pioneering articles 'African Traditional Thought and Western Science', *Africa*, xxxvii, 1967, pp. 50-71, 155-87.

24   Examples are given in Claudia Zaslavsky's unusual and informative book, *Africa Counts*, Boston, 1973. Of course, no system is entirely closed, and the real issue is the degree of openness. For a psychologist's perspective on this question see Gordon W. Allport, 'The Open System in Personality Theory', *Jour. of Abnormal and Social Psychology*, lxi, 1960, pp. 302-10.

25   See Leonard W. Doob, *Patterning of Time*, New Haven, 1971.

26   The starting point for this subject is Jack Goody, ed., *Literacy in Traditional Societies*, London, 1968.

27   This suggestion is explored by Mary Douglas in *Purity and Danger*, London, 1966.

28   Philip D. Curtin, *The Atlantic Slave Trade, a Census*, Madison, 1969.

29   Reviving a theme first explored by S. H. Frankel, *Capital Investment in Africa*, Oxford, 1938.

30   Recent studies include E. A. Brett, *Colonialism and Underdevelopment in East Africa: the Politics of Economic Change, 1919-39*, London, 1973 and Richard D. Wolff, *The Economics of Colonialism: Britain and Kenya 1870-1930*, New Haven, 1974. Brett adopts a modified Frankian approach; Wolff acknowledges Marxist inspiration, but does not deploy an easily recognisable Marxist thesis.

31   Important work on the large French commercial firms, C.F.A.O. and S.C.O.A., is being undertaken by Catherine Coquery-Vidrovitch. A thorough and detailed study of European mining firms can be found in Peter Greenhalgh's recently completed Ph.D. thesis, *An Economic History of the Ghanaian Diamond Industry, 1919-1973*, Birmingham University, 1974.

32 The new biographies will probably be influenced by the recent rise of psycho-history, on which, currently, there are almost as many articles as on dependency or on the notion of paradigms. For a recent guide see Benjamin B. Wolman, ed., *The Psychoanalytic Interpretation of History*, New York, 1971. One awaits with caution results which, it is hoped, can be acclaimed. Rhodes is an obvious candidate for a new-style biography, and it can be anticipated that Lugard will be treated again and with more hostility than Miss Perham was able to command. More interesting will be the appearance of biographies of lesser-known colonial civil servants such as Sir Percy Girouard, whose career is currently being studied by Michael Mason, Concordia University, Montreal.

33 See, for example, Gerald M. Meier, *The International Economics of Development*, New York, 1968, and G. F. C. Simkin, *The Fluctuations of a Dependent Economy*, Oxford, 1959. My own book, *An Economic History of West Africa*, London, 1973: reprinted with corrections 1975, stresses and perhaps exaggerates connections between the international economy and West African domestic developments, but does so without using Frankian terminology.

34 This question has been debated recently by Rweyemamu and Stein. See G. F. Rweyemamu, 'International Trade and the Developing Countries', *Journal of Modern African Studies*, vii, 1969, and Leslie Stein, 'Developing Countries and International Trade—an Alternative View', *ibid.*, viii, 1970, pp. 605-16. In his reply, Rweyemamu chose not to challenge Stein's statement of 'conventional' theory, but stressed the need for 'historical 'explanations of underdevelopment ('The Causes of Poverty in the Periphery', *ibid.*, ix, 1971, pp. 453-5). Collectors might like to compare this exchange with the one between Schatz and Stolper in Nigerian Institute of Social and Economic Research, *Conference Proceedings, March 1962*, Ibadan, 1963, pp. 179-96.

35 I refer here to the formulation by Ricardo. Much later, Samuelson presented a theoretical case showing the conditions under which real incomes might be equalised.

36 Arghiri Emmanuel, *L'échange inégal*, Paris, 1969, translated as *Unequal Exchange*, New York, 1972.

37 The major studies are E. H. Chamberlin, *The Theory of Monopolistic Competition*, Cambridge, Mass., 1933, and Joan Robinson, *The Economics of Imperfect Competition*, London, 1933.

38 Samir Amin, *L'accumulation à l'échelle mondiale*, Paris, 1970 and *Le développement inégal*, Paris, 1973. It is impossible to do justice to Amin's voluminous publications in the space of this article. All that can be done here is to hint at the complexity of the problem of defining and measuring surplus value. A useful starting point is the recent survey by J. M. Currie, J. A. Murphy and A. Schmitz, 'The Concept of Economic Surplus', *Economic Journal*, lxxxi, 1971, pp. 741-99.

39 Samir Amin, *L'Afrique de l'Ouest bloquée: l'économie politique de la colonisation, 1880-1970*, Paris, 1971, ch. I. Translated as *Neo-Colonialism in West Africa*, Harmondsworth, 1973.

40 Fernando H. Cardoso, 'Dependency in Latin America', *New Left Review*, 74, 1972, pp. 83-95.

41 Indeed, students of what is called the 'new dependency' are particularly concerned to explore the internal political and social consequences of industrialisation.

42 Bill Warren, 'Imperialism and Capitalist Industrialisation', *New Left Review*, 81, 1973. Warren's article has been criticised rather sympathetically, on my reading, by Arghiri Emmanuel, and in a somewhat strident manner by Philip McMichael, James Petras and Robert Rhodes, all in *New Left Review*, 85, 1974, pp. 61-104.

43 The attempt to describe the middle ground has given rise to notions such as 'peripheral centres' and 'semi-peripheries', but these efforts to take account of the diversity of real-world experiences also weaken the strength of the original dichotomous classification.

44   I refer here, of course, to W. W. Rostow, *The Stages of Growth: a Non-Communist Manifesto*, Cambridge, 1960.

45   L. Althusser, *For Marx*, London, 1969, p. 70.

46   Those who have used Frank's terminology under the impression that they are thereby adopting a Marxist viewpoint should consider his own careful disclaimer: 'I have *never* had the temerity myself to claim to be a Marxist; and nowhere in my published—or unpublished—writings can or will anyone find such a personal claim'. See Andre Gunder Frank, 'Dependence is Dead, Long Live Dependence and the Class Struggle', *Latin American Perspectives*, i. 1974, p. 96.

47   Robert Boyden Lamb, 'Adam Smith's Social System: Sympathy not Self-Interest', *Journal of the History of Ideas*, xxxv, 1974, pp. 671-82.

48   Piero Sraffa, *Production of Commodities by Means of Commodities*, Cambridge, 1960. The significance of Sraffa's erudite and complex book is that he appears to have solved Ricardo's problem of defining an invariable standard of value. This achievement has important implications for neo-classical capital theory, and it has also been interpreted as rehabilitating the labour theory of value. Sraffa's invariable measure, however, depends on very special circumstances (a given supply of homogeneous labour, industries producing single commodies by single techniques, profit maximisation assumed on the part of producers, a distinction between 'basic' and 'non-basic' goods, permitting the latter, which excludes labour, to become the 'standard commodity', etc.), and is not easily related to the real world. Any non-expert who has puzzled over Sraffa's book must surely greet with unusual interest the observations of Frederick F. Clairmonte, who, having reviewed two books on Fanon and decided that Fanon was of little relevance to present-day Algeria, went on to conclude: 'Rather, it is not surprising, as I discovered recently in Algeria, to find students attempting to master one of the great revolutionary works of our time by the Cambridge University theorist, Piero Sraffa, *Production of Commodities by Means of Commodities* (1960). And that is a partial measure of the socio-political and economic transition taking place within Algeria.' *Journal of Modern African Studies*, xii, 1974, p. 157.

49   Most of the ideas and at least some of the terms used by dependency theorists today can be traced to the Argentinian economist, Raúl Prebisch, who deployed them with skill and subtlety. See especially United Nations Commission for Latin America, *The Economic Development of Latin America and its Principal Problems*, New York, 1949. It was Prebisch, too, who coined the terms 'centre' and 'periphery'—over twenty-five years ago. On the subsequent history of the terms see Aníbal Pinto and Jan Kňakal, 'The Centre-Periphery System Twenty Years Later', *Social and Economic Studies*, xxii, 1973, pp. 34-89.

50   For example, Gerald M. Meier, *The International Economics of Development*, New York, 1968. See also unconventional studies, such as Albert O. Hirschman's *The Strategy of Economic Development*, New Haven, 1958 and Gunnar Myrdal's *Economic Theory and Underdeveloped Regions*, London, 1954.

Ann Seidman

Changing Theories of Political Economy in Africa

The decade of the sixties failed to realise the hopes expressed by African leaders and embodied by the United Nations in the slogan, 'Development Decade'.[1] The vast majority of Africans remain impoverished, their life expectancy less than forty years, their *per capita* incomes among the lowest in the world. Increasing numbers have crowded into sprawling urban shanty-towns, joining the hundreds of thousands of jobless seeking wage employment in the so-called 'modern productive' sector.

Africa's mines and farms still produce rich mineral and agricultural raw materials primarily for export to the factories of Europe, America and, increasingly now, Japan. Most manufactured goods are still imported, mainly for the top ten per cent of the population who get half to two-thirds of the nations' cash incomes.[2] In widespread rural areas, millions of African farmers, using little more than hoes and cutlasses, still struggle against the vagaries of weather— searing drought in recent years—to scratch a bare subsistence from lateritic soils.

In seeking to explain why the 'Development Decade' failed to materialise, economists have, over the last two decades, pursued increasingly divergent theoretical paths. It seemed particularly appropriate to explore these divergent trends at a seminar dedicated to Basil Davidson, who contributed to the revolution in historical analysis which helped build an essential foundation for the national liberation struggles of the fifties. Political economists have now begun to face up to the necessity of sharpening their theoretical tools in the same way, to help expose the causes and suggest effective solutions to the pervasive problems of underdevelopment which still oppress the vast majority of Africans.

Initially, most economists suggested solutions based on models and tools shaped primarily in western Europe and the United States. Colonialism, they argued—whether or not they were critical of the accompanying social and political discrimination against Africans—did open the continent to the benefits of world trade. It provided the capital and skills needed to dig out vast mines, carve out commercial plantations, and stimulate peasant production of cash crops for export. Thus it introduced an 'engine for growth'. As W. A. Lewis, an early adviser to the national Government of Ghana under President Nkrumah, put it,[3]

... at low levels of economic activity, production for the foreign market is usually the turning point which sets a country on the road to economic growth. He added[4]:

> Foreigners bring new skills, new tastes, capital and expanding markets. They may also bring exploitation, but if in one's zeal to prevent the

exploitation one keeps them out altogether, the country is deprived
equally of their stimulus.

In time, the argument went, the competitive efforts of expanding private
enterprise, increasingly domestic as well as foreign, could be expected to stimulate
the spread of modern productive techniques and employment opportunities
throughout the newly independent African economies.

These economists rejected Boeke's pessimistic explanation of the causes of
the pervasive dualism characteristic of colonial economies. He had argued[5] that
the imported social system of capitalism required its own 'philosophy of life, an
attitude toward life', which clashed with the negative attitudes and 'original
organic social bonds', the limited wants and purchasing power, of the majority
of peasants in underdeveloped rural areas. His arguments had found wide
support, as they explained the causes of persistent underdevelopment by the non-
entrepreneurial attitudes[6] and institutions[7] characteristic of the Africans
themselves. Increasing numbers of economists maintained that once colonial
restrictions were lifted and new opportunities provided, Africans would respond
like 'economic men'[8] to the market incentives which capitalism could provide.

Numerous books and articles[9] provided evidence that Africans had historically
spread trading networks over vast areas of the continent prior to the coming of
colonialism. The imposition of colonial capitalism had undermined much of
this pre-existing commercial activity, but African traders still played an
important role, especially in West African intra-African trade. Indeed, the
optimistic conclusion appeared to follow: Africans would develop their continent
along the capitalist path[10] if only their newly independent national governments
gave them the chance.

United Nations experts described[11] the assumed essential preconditions:
resources and a climate attractive to foreign investors; the formulation of
conducive government policies; and, in some cases, the production of cash crops
as a profitable alternative to wage employment. W. A. Lewis listed[12] negative
government policies which could be expected to hamper the spread of domestic
and foreign private initiative.

Economics faculties in the first African universities therefore taught that the
new African states should maintain order and provide the necessary social and
economic infrastructure. Competition among private firms and individuals, to
maximise their profits, would provide the necessary stimulus to ensure a
multiplier-like spread of development to the productive sectors. Given the
shortage of capital and entrepreneurial and technical skills, initially most private
investment would be foreign, but as local funds and technical know-how were
accumulated, domestic entrepreneurs would come forth.

The first African national economic plans were shaped by this economic
philosophy.[13] Western experts, whether from the former colonial power, the
World Bank, or the USA, wrestled with inadequate data[14] and scanty government
funds to produce complex input-output tables and linear programming models.
The new plans incorporated ministry programmes for the expenditure of
government revenues and borrowed funds to build the economic and social
infrastructure perceived as the foundation of the hoped-for expansion of private

investment. New tax and fiscal measures were introduced to cover mounting costs. The targets set for the productive sectors—the expansion of exports, the anticipated growth of import substitution industries, the spread of cash cropping to remote rural areas—were to be met primarily by private investors. An array of government incentives including tax holidays, provision of external economies and protective tariffs, were fashioned to create the appropriate 'hospitable investment climate'. At the same time, policies encouraging African entrepreneurs especially in trade and small industries, became the cornerstone of new development plans in several countries, especially Kenya, Nigeria, and Ivory Coast, and, after the 1966 coup, in Ghana.

As the decade of the sixties unfolded, it became increasingly apparent that the anticipated spread of productive opportunities was not taking place. The typical pattern appeared to be 'growth without development'.[15] Exports of crude minerals and cash crops doubled, tripled and even quadrupled.[16] Manufacturing sectors remained capital-intensive, producing the wrong kinds of output, located in the export enclave, and externally dependent.[17] Agricultural production for domestic markets lagged. Prices of foodstuffs consumed in the cities rose and foodstuff imports multiplied.[18] The drain of rural dwellers into urban squatter-compounds continued. Unemployment mounted to over 20 per cent of the labour force in the major cities.[19]

Controversy arose. S. Schatz[20] maintained that his Nigerian research showed that the problem was not lack of investible funds, but the lack of viable projects which would-be African entrepreneurs could mount. I. Diaku argued in reply[21] (expressing appreciation to S. Aluko and W. A. Lewis), 'it is not viable projects *per se* that are in short supply in Nigeria, but the factors preventing the detection of viable projects and these factors are in themselves broader aspects of capital shortage'.

Several other Nigerian economists, following a study of the ownership and control structure of business enterprise in their country,[22] concluded that foreign shareholders still dominated share holdings and boards of directors in publicly held firms. They warned: 'A policy of indigenizing ownership, except carefully formulated, may not necessarily lead to indigenization of control at the same time.'

J. D. Esseks,[23] exploring the consequences of the post-1966 policy of stimulating African entrepreneurs in Ghana, maintained that, because they had limited economic capacity, they received little support, and hence did not grow. Therefore the private sector could not expand sufficiently to absorb those who failed to obtain places in the 'élite' circles of government.

In Kenya, the efforts to facilitate African entry into private sector enterprises were also frustrated. A few wealthy African civil servants and politicians successfully acquired Government credit to buy large farms, about a fifth of the former 'White Highlands'. Their farms never equalled in size the remaining settler and corporation farms, which continued to own three-fifths of the former 'White Highlands'. Governmental efforts to Africanise trade through licensing and credit were gradually reduced, leaving the dominant wholesale and import-export sectors much as before, though a very few large-scale African traders now participated. African shareholdings and directorships in large industrial trading and financial firms in Kenya, as in Nigeria, primarily constituted 'window-dressing'. In all, the Kenya efforts to Africanise appeared to have contributed only to an illusion of change.[24] As Sir Michael Blundell had prophesied at independence, when military efforts to suppress the Kenyan liberation movement proved too expensive, such policies served 'to make our position safe by other means'.[25]

In view of the increasingly evident failure of small African businessmen to compete with the dominant foreign firms, increasing numbers of African governments began to acquire shares in the larger import-export, internal wholesale trading, and manufacturing firms. This approach, too, received theoretical sanction by well-known development economists, G. M. Meier wrote[26]: 'It still may be the absence of a capitalist class with the necessary ability and motivation to undertake long-term productive investment' which hinders the spread of development. 'We must confront the problem of how a class of private capitalists is to emerge, or we must rely at the outset on the presence of foreign capitalists or a class of state capitalists.'

Foreign firms, themselves, did not resent government participation as much as they would have a decade or two earlier. A leading international business survey reported[27]: 'A large number of Western investors in Africa consider joint ventures attractive, or at least the surest way to gain acceptance by the host country. . . . Minority local participation will ensure that managerial control lies with the foreign investor, and at the same time satisfy many of the requirements of "national interest".'

In short, the dominant trend among economists in the first years of independence tended to foster policies directed towards 'freeing' would-be African entrepreneurs from the fetters imposed by colonialism, and creating a 'hospitable climate' for foreign investors, bolstered if necessary by state capitalism. But the consequences appeared to be mounting unemployment in crowded urban slums in the heart of externally dependent enclaves, while rural areas stagnated.

2

During the sixties, a new trend emerged among economists. They began to recognise that orthodox Western models and concepts were ill-designed to explain, far less solve, the pressing problems of underdevelopment. Africans gradually replaced foreign experts in many new universities and planning commissions, bringing greater familiarity with the underlying characteristics of the problems to be solved. There was also a growing conflict of interest between the emergent social classes, and more contacts with socialist as well as capitalist developed nations.

The authors of this new trend directed their attention to the historical growth of political, social and economic institutions. Returning to the classical title 'political economy', they insisted that the problems of development could not be crammed into disciplinary boxes neatly labelled 'economics', 'sociology' or 'political science'.

The political economists rejected the Boeke explanation of inherited dualism. But their critique was not focused on the entrepreneurial potential of individual Africans. They maintained that the political-economic institutions dominating the export-oriented capitalist enclave had undermined the pre-existing trade and production relationships,[28] forcing increasing numbers of Africans to join the growing migratory labour force which worked the mines and plantations producing for export.[29]

As Meillassoux put it, rejecting outright the Boeke-type of interpretation of dualism as a static concept of two isolated sectors:

> In other words . . . [historical analysis] demonstrates the irrelevance of the notion of a 'dual economy' made of two distinct sectors, traditional and modern, foreign to each other.

He underscored the essential dialectical interrelationship, the interpenetration and interdependence, of the two sectors.[30]

> Capitalism acts in two different ways. On one hand, it elicits a sector of production built up in its own image through the presence of capital and its corollaries—private control of the means of production and wage earning. On the other hand it feeds off the precapitalist sectors through the mechanism of primitive accumulation (cf. Marx, I, viii; R. Luxembourg)—with the contradictory results of both perpetuating and destroying them at the same time. The introduction of capitalism had the dual effect of maintaining a dependent African commercial sector and of competing eventually with traditional trade.[31]

The externally dependent capitalist export enclaves carved out in the African colonies had undermined the developing trading and productive activities of the pre-colonial peoples. The mines and plantations, the cash crop farming areas and great trading companies, depended critically on the cheap labour power provided by the millions of migratory labourers, who were, historically, forced[32] to join the labour reserves required to keep African wages among the lowest in the world. The destruction of rural handicrafts and trade, the undermining of traditional institutions and agricultural activities by the loss of essential labour, left increasing numbers of rural dwellers with no choice but to seek wage employment at whatever wages they could get.

In South Africa, the institutionalisation of underdeveloped rural areas as cheap labour reserves for the capitalist sector has been rigidified by the racist *apartheid* Bantustanisation. The South African government relies on direct control of labour as a foundation for its Keynsian-prescribed policies to ensure one of the most rapid rates of economic growth in Africa.[33]

In a less formally institutionalised way, the continued underdevelopment of vast rural areas in independent Africa still provides a reservoir of underemployed rural dwellers. They drift into the commercialised areas seeking wage employment providing a ready cheap supply of labour in the export enclave.

Samir Amin has characterised[34] the eastern and southern parts of the continent as 'Africa of the Labour Reservers'. Although he terms West Africa a 'colonial trade economy', analysis of the labour migration flows that furnish the sharecrop and hired labour which produce the bulk of the cocoa, coffee and rubber, as well as mineral exports, suggests a similar phenomenon there. The difference is that in the capitalist economy of eastern and southern Africa, where the white settler population usurped for itself the outright ownership of the major share of the means of production in the export enclave, the role of the mass of Africans in providing cheap labour has become especially evident. In West Africa, the fact that African capitalist farmers (as Polly Hill terms them) hire migrant labour for bare subsistence wages or a small share of the crop (typically a third or less), has been obscured by a mythology of the sturdy African peasant using only family labour. There can be little doubt that the low pay of the hundreds of thousands of migrant labourers who produce a major share of the export crops has been a crucial factor permitting the foreign trading companies to reap vast profits from their indirect domination of key productive sectors and through their control of overseas trade.

Now that more and more Africans participate in control of the means of production, the facts can no longer even appear to be explained merely by the colour of the ruling groups. It has become evident that a primary feature of the externally dependent dualism typical of most African economies is the continued expansion of the so-called 'modern productive' sectors at the expense of the mass of Africans.

The foreign trading and, in some countries, mining firms, with the associated banking system, still dominate the 'commanding heights' of the export enclaves. This is now disguised to some extent by Africanisation of top level local posts. These firms continue to reap a major share of the investible surpluses produced by low-cost labour, either directly, in the form of profits, interest and the high salaries paid to their management personnel; or indirectly, through control over the terms of trade. J. Rweyemamu, Professor of Economics at the University of Dar es Salaam, has pointed out[35] that it is this domination which has historically been the fundamental cause of poverty in the periphery. These economic relations, created in the colonial era, have perpetuated the role of African economies as satellites of the developed capitalist economies of Europe. Samir Amin has underlined[36] the critical role of the institutions controlling the export enclave in perpetuating the underdevelopment of the 'neo-colonies' of independent Africa.

The political economists argue that, in the context of the externally dependent enclave dominated by foreign firms, a domestic capitalist class will necessarily remain linked to and dependent on the very institutions which must be changed fundamentally if more integrated self-reliant national development is to be attained.[37] The establishment of predominantly state-capitalist machinery, even under the rubric of 'socialism', will be unlikely to restructure the political economy which has brought it into being. The African civil servants and politicians who took over the top offices from the former colonialists are more likely to use a considerable share of increased tax revenues to expand the administrative bureaucracy, pay higher salaries, construct prestigious infrastructure and provide other 'fringe' benefits.[38] They may use their positions to facilitate their own—or relatives'—expansion in profitable private business ventures within the inherited economic structure.

Political economists contend that a precondition for restructuring the inherited set-up is the formulation of an alliance of the low income urban wage workers and unemployed with the rural mass of small peasants, sharecroppers and hired labourers. New political channels must be forged to ensure that this basic alliance assumes a critical position in the decision-making structure of the state. Given this kind of backing, the government must extend control over the 'commanding heights'—the banks and financial system, the export-import and internal wholesale trading institutions, and basic industry—to implement physical and financial plans for attainment of more balanced, integrated industrial and agricultural growth. Education and manpower planning must be designed to facilitate the appropriate kinds of productive employment activities.

In the longer run, this basic alliance should press for the gradual socialisation of the means of production throughout the economy, directly through the state, or indirectly through the establishment of various forms of collective ownership. Such a long-run transition would probably take twenty years or more, as the necessary skills and understanding, as well as productive employment opportunities, spread to all sectors of an increasingly integrated, less externally dependent, economy.

There has not been complete agreement on the nature of the changes that should be made to implement this perspective. Amin[39] has argued that rural capitalism and an African commercial bourgeoisie need to be encouraged as a basis for national development and displacement of the foreign firms.[40] R. H. Green, for years an adviser to the Tanzanian Treasury, has objected, claiming that Tanzania's approach is more realistic.[41]

> While recognizing the potential value, under certain circumstances, of external capitalists as partners in specific aspects of development within a socialist frame, it finds a substantial African capitalist class—especially one linked with the public-service or parastatal sector—inconsistent with a gradual and peaceful transformation to socialism, and therefore proposes to insulate the African private and public sectors from each other and to channel development support to public-sector or joint ventures, including co-operatives.

Clearly a new trend in political economic theory in Africa has been fostered. It is to be hoped that it contributes more effectively to policies directed to restructuring the institutions dominating African economies, as a necessary precondition for the spread of productive employment opportunities, the reduction of external dependence, and improved levels of living for the broad masses of the African people.

3

Four additional areas of debate will be considered briefly.

Industrial strategy

Almost without exception, African development plans initially incorporated import substitution industrialisation programmes. The planners, following the approach developed earlier in Latin America, assumed that foreign investors could be attracted by the appropriate mix of tax incentives and tariff protection to build domestic factories to produce goods previously imported. The manufacturing sectors which emerged in the early post-independence years, however, tended to be oriented increasingly to the last-stage assembly and processing of imported parts and materials.[42] Their output was largely directed to meeting the needs of the limited high income group, which had previously imported the main share of its consumer goods, and a few broadly consumed but technologically simple items like textiles, beer and cigarettes. For instance, beverages and cigarettes constituted from 15 per cent of the manufacturing value added in Kenya[43] to about 30 per cent in Ghana[44] and about 40 per cent in Zambia.[45] Built mainly near the existing urban markets in the export enclaves, these manufacturing sectors further aggravated the lopsided dualism imposed during the colonial era. The foreign investors, whether investing alone or in partnership with African governments, tended to import relatively capital-intensive technologies already incorporated in the machines and equipment produced in their home countries—despite the fact that in Africa urban unemployment is chronic and growing.

Mounting evidence has led most political economists to reject the market criteria and continued foreign dependence implicit in import-substitution industrialisation programmes. Many have begun to propose the formulation of long-term industrial strategies. They argue that implementation of these strategies would require increasing state control of the 'commanding heights', and have begun to debate the detailed institutional changes required to implement them. But as yet these have been incorporated in few, if any, African development plans, so there has been little opportunity to observe their consequences.

Rural development policies

Most economists, regardless of other disagreements, have agreed in recent years that agriculture and industry should, where possible, be developed side by side.[46] Each is needed to provide the other with essential inputs and markets. This is all the more essential in Africa, where most people still live in the underdeveloped rural areas. Some years before independence most economists argued that traditional land tenures must give way to private land holding.[47] since African peasants have no incentive to invest and improve their productivity as long as land remains communally-held. In West Africa, traditional land tenures had already been greatly altered by changing custom and court decisions as cash cropping for export spread.[48]

In the estate-dominated territories of East and Central Africa, this approach led to the formulation of two sets of policies, sometimes viewed by their authors as complementary, sometimes as conflicting: (1) that caution should be used in breaking up existing commercial estates which produce most of the marketed crops of countries like Kenya and Zambia; and (2) measures should be introduced to individualise land ownership in the remaining rural areas to stimulate the initiative of the more 'progressive' 'emergent' African farmers.

56

To implement the second set of policies, marketing cooperatives[49] have been spread widely to facilitate the sale of small farmer crops, and sometimes to provide farm inputs and credit. State marketing boards have been introduced to provide fixed producer prices, and sometimes to replace, sometimes to supplement the marketing cooperatives in collecting crops and providing farm inputs. Rural credit agencies have been attempted, although their repayment record has been dismal. Economists studying in Western universities, especially in the United States, have sought to devise mathematical techniques to identify the new crops and methods which, given existing internal and external markets, would be most likely to maximise peasant participation in the monetised capitalist economy.[50]

Most political economists, critically examining the available evidence of expanding cash crop production, maintain that the stratification taking place in rural areas as a result of these policies is likely to have undesirable political and social consequences. They argue, with President Nyerere,[51] that a class of increasingly powerful African land owners, profiting from the low wages paid to their hired labour, has begun to emerge. Heavy investment in farms by the salariat and politicians has aggravated this tendency. If consolidated, this class will inevitably block the increase of rural incomes and spread of rural markets. It already tends to manipulate cooperatives and state machinery to its own advantage. In the longer run, it is likely to seek to thwart efforts to implement a transition to a socialised political economy.

Some political economists support the formation of producer cooperatives, if possible building on the foundations of cooperation alleged to have existed in traditional societies. Tanzania's *ujamaa* programme is frequently proposed as a prototype. Others question whether such forms of cooperation can be translated into modern producer cooperation. Agricultural productivity, they suggest, may be more effectively expanded through stimulating small-scale private production of cash crops until essential skills and capital, and ideological leadership, emerge to tackle producer cooperation at a later stage in the transition to socialism. They tend to agree, however, that an alliance of workers and peasants should be mobilised to control the state, and through it the 'commanding heights', so as to direct available investible surpluses and trade policies to the implementation of an industrial strategy to restructure the economy.

Samir Amin, originally the best-known of this latter group of theorists, has recently shifted his position to maintain[52] that, 'in Tanzania and other countries, a correct ideology and correct organization structures mean that Ujamaa, for example, represent a step towards a socialist transformation . . . [if they] ensure the development of the fundamental alliance between the exploited proletariat and the peasantry.' Amin relates the issue of agricultural development policy directly to the long-term perspective:

> Any development of production based on profit (particularly agrarian capitalism) which puts this alliance into question will prove negative in the long run, even if in the short run it facilitates a rapid growth of production.
>
> This is the crux of the matter. In my opinion, the transition in Africa, as well as in the Third World generally, demands that the main effort

be concentrated on increasing productivity in those sectors in which the great masses of people find themselves; and this increase will immediately bring about an improvement in their living conditions. But agrarian capitalism makes either of these developments impossible, and therefore the socialist road is historically necessary. In this perspective, the role of the 'modern' sector, after having been completely taken over, must be to aid in this immediate task . . .

On this point, I have progressed in the last few years . . .

National incomes policy

A controversy continues over the appropriate incomes policy to be adopted. Western oriented economists tend to maintain that the primary issue should be to hold the line on wages, apparently in line with the Lewis argument.[53] H. A. Turner, sent to several African countries by the International Labour Organisation, has argued for wage restraint as the key feature of any national incomes policy. He has patched together orthodox theory and statistical correlations which, he argues, show that rising wages constitute an underlying cause of growing unemployment in urban areas.[54]

Even some of Turner's critics insist that rising urban wages contribute to the widening rural-urban gap and the rush of rural dwellers into urban slums. The argument that all urban wage earners constitute a relative 'aristocracy of labour'[55] overlooks that ten per cent or less of salary and wage earners capture almost half the total wage bill in the form of high salaries, commonly supplemented by extravagant housing and car allowances.[56] The notion of an 'aristocracy of labour' was given wide currency in Africa by G. Arrighi,[57] but one of his close collaborators has agreed that the term has been misused to imply that all urban workers are in sympathy with the *status quo*, whereas the problem in reality is that of the buying off of the highest paid salariat.[58]

Amin asserts[59]:

> It is incorrect to view the class of wage-earners as a uniform mass of 'privileged' persons benefiting even in small measure from the system. They *do* benefit—but only at the outset of the transition from the initial state of the imposition of capitalist productive relations, especially for export, and the second state characterised by massive implantation of direct capitalist relations through import substitution.

Increasing numbers of studies[60] demonstrate that the lower two-thirds of urban wage earners are still obtaining wages that barely cover subsistence. Wage freeze policies, especially when imposed in the face of rising prices, chronic in most of Africa, have tended to undermine actual living standards and alienate low income wage earners from governments. This undoubtedly helped to turn the workers against the Nkrumah administration in Ghana, where wages remained frozen after 1961 despite an 80 per cent rise in local food prices by 1965.

Focusing the discussion of national incomes policies on wages has diverted attention from the fact that in most countries a major share of investible surpluses is still drained out of the continent as profits, interest, and expatriate salaries of foreign firms. It is difficult to obtain accurate information on the amounts. Estimates of investible surpluses produced in Zambia[61] in the 1970s ran as high as 700 to 900 million dollars, about a third of which was shipped out of the country. In 1971 alone, more money was shipped out of Zambia than the value of the total manufacturing industry assets of INDECO, the government's parastatal holding company for manufacturing—the largest in independent sub-Saharan Africa. About 60 million dollars was officially reported under the heading 'errors and omissions'.

At the same time governments have spent most of their increased tax revenue on prestigious infrastructural projects and expanding the civil service with more high-salaried administrative posts. As a result, GDP growth has tended to stagnate as productive sectors have lagged, while government current and capital deficits have led to increased internal and external borrowing. The former has tended to aggravate inflationary pressures. The latter, especially with the high interest rates reflecting in part the current international monetary crisis, has tended to augment the future balance of payments burdens. In Zambia, the post-independence government taxes actually captured about two-thirds of the investible surpluses produced in the country at their peak in 1970.[62] Taxes *per capita* totalled about 100 dollars, compared with about 15 dollars to 20 dollars *per capita* in East Africa.[63] The failure to invest a significant share of these revenues in increasingly productive employment opportunities in the context of a balanced industrial and agricultural development strategy was a serious factor contributing to the decline of the GDP when the world copper price fell in 1971-72 and again in 1975.

The newer trend among political economists has been to advocate overall incomes policies as an integral feature of long-term financial plans to capture investible surpluses and direct them to essential productive sectors. This would justify government ownership and coordinated direction of the banks and financial institutions, and facilitate coordination of planned expansion of credit and the money supply, controlled prices, and government tax and spending policies, to finance the integrated growth of industry and agriculture.

African economic integration

Numerous arguments have been advanced as to the advantages—indeed necessity—of economic integration to achieve the large markets, combined resources and capital needed to build basic industries in Africa. The inherited pattern of tiny balkanised states, with populations averaging less than those of large European cities, and Gross Domestic Products considerably smaller than those of large multi-national firms, renders each incapable, separately, of building the industries needed to produce iron and steel, chemicals, machinery and equipment, the essential backbone of a self-reliant industrial economy. Without integration with its neighbours, each independent African government may only plan relatively small, labour-intensive consumer goods and agricultural processing industries; it will inevitably remain dependent on imported machines, equipment, skills and technologies.[64]

The more orthodox economists have emphasised the creation of broader protected markets to attract foreign capital and skills to build basic industries. Yet evidence from East and West Africa—not to mention the still-to-be-liberated southern third of the continent—suggests that the consequences of this type of integration is the concentration of private investment (foreign or domestic) in the limited more developed centres, further aggravating disparities of production and incomes throughout the 'integrated' region.[65] In the East African Common Market, often touted as the African integration success story, the introduction of differing monetary systems and 'transfer taxes'[66] appear to constitute steps towards an eventual breakup.

Political economists have begun to suggest a different approach. Their analysis of the historical consequences of imperialist growth tends to argue that integration can only lead to more even development if achieved by joint action of states, exercising firm control of their national commanding heights, to plan and implement a long-term industrial allocation policy, capable of setting off chains of growth in each country, leading to balanced growth throughout the resulting integrated region. The political precondition for the implementation of this approach is the institutionalisation of the effective participation of workers and peasants in governmental decision-making machinery. As this precondition can hardly be said to have been achieved anywhere in Africa, there has, as yet, been no opportunity to examine the consequences of this approach.[67]

4

To sum up, two divergent theoretical trends have emerged among economists in Africa over the last two decades. Early post-independence economic advisers, university teachers and textbooks tended to base their analyses on models formulated in the developed capitalist countries. They held that, once the constraining shackles of colonialism were removed, African entrepreneurs would emerge and achieve parallel development in Africa. To facilitate this process, African governments should provide the necessary infrastructure, if necessary, perhaps in partnership with foreign firms.

It has become increasingly apparent that these policies have tended to produce 'growth without development', leaving most Africans no better off, perhaps worse off. The Western theories and models assume as given precisely that institutional structure which has hampered the spread of productive employment opportunities.

A new group, re-adopting the classical rubric of 'political economy', began to expose the harsh reality, maintaining that the continued domination of the 'commanding heights' of the export enclave by foreign firms perpetuates the lopsided, externally dependent dualism that condemns the masses of Africans to a bare subsistence existence, a reservoir of cheap labour for the so-called modern sector, whether or not an illusion of African participation is created by involving a few wealthy Africans or some form of joint state-private capitalism.

They urge an alliance of the impoverished rural dwellers and the urban low-wage earners and unemployed to direct African governments to take effective control of the 'commanding heights' as a precondition for implementation of long-term plans to restructure the national political economy, and to initiate the long transition to socialism.

In the context of these two divergent trends in theory, four main issues emerged:

1. The early economic advisers to African governments incorporated proposals for import-substitution manufacturing industries. Political economists recommend, instead, the formulation and implementation of a long-term industrial strategy which explicitly incorporates essential physical projects in a step-by-step process to restructure the inherited dual economy.

2. The Western-oriented theorists propose individualisation of ownership of communally held land to provide subsistence farmers with incentives to invest and expand agricultural production. Many political economists, fearing that further stratification in the rural areas would serve primarily to strengthen the African classes committed to the *status quo*, urge consideration of various forms of producer cooperation to increase agricultural output and broaden rural markets as a necessary corollary to the proposed long-term industrial strategy.

3. Orthodox theorists propose incomes policies which focus on holding the line on wages to attract private investors to productive sectors. Political economists argue that primary attention should be given instead to coordinated tax and pricing policies, with direct state control of the banking system and financial institutions. This control, they maintain, is essential to capture investible surpluses already being produced in the African economies and direct them to balanced industrial and agricultural development.

4. Orthodox prescriptions for economic integration among African governments centre on the creation of common markets and customs unions to attract foreign investors. Analysis of the uneven development fostered by these policies leads political economists to emphasise the necessity for joint state planning for industrial allocation, backed by sufficient state control of the 'commanding heights' to ensure implementation of plans.

In short, during the last two decades a growing conflict has emerged among economists in Africa which permeates every aspect of economic analysis. The real test must be: Which set of theories best explains and offers the most effective solutions for the crucial problems of underdevelopment on the continent? Which theories are most likely to contribute most effectively to the spread of productive employment opportunities, better food and clothes, enough schools and hospitals, to improve the levels of living for the vast majority of Africans?

Notes

1   E. C. Edozien, 'The Development Decade in Africa, a Preliminary Appraisal', *Nigerian Journal of Economic and Social Studies*, xiv, 1, March 1972, pp. 77-92. It might be noted that the author was primarily concerned with the growth of the

GDP and capital formation, rather than an analysis of the spread of productivity and increased levels of living of the broad masses of the population.

2 Cf. UN Economic Commission for Africa, *Economic Bulletin for Africa*, ii, 2, June 1962, p. 26, for statistics re Zaïre (then Congo).

3 W. A. Lewis, *The Theory of Economic Growth*, Allen and Unwin, fifth impression, 1961, p. 274.

4 *Ibid.*, pp. 411-12.

5 J. H. Boeke, *Economics and Economic Policy of Dual Societies*, New York, 1953, pp. 5-6.

6 Cf. D. McLelland, *Achieving Society*, Van Nostrand, 1961, esp. chs. 2, 3.

7 B. F. Hoselitz, 'Unity and Diversity in Economic Structure' in *Economics and the Idea of Mankind*, ed. Hoselitz, Columbia University Press, 1965, esp. pp. 88-9.

8 W. O. Jones, 'Economic Man in Africa', *Food Research Institute Studies*, May 1960.

9 For a compilation of articles on this issue, see C. Meillassoux, ed., *The Development of Indigenous Trade and Markets in West Africa*, Oxford, 1971.

10 Cf. P. Hill, explicitly characterised Ghana's cocoa farmers as 'capitalist' in *Migrant Cocoa Farmers of Southern Ghana. A Study in Rural Capitalism*, Cambridge University Press, 1963.

11 UN Department of Economic Affairs, *Structure and Growth of Selected African Economies*, New York, 1958, pp. 1-5.

12 Lewis, *The Theory of Economic Growth, op. cit.*, pp. 411-12.

13 See A. Seidman, *Planning in Subsaharan Africa*, New York: Praeger Publishers; and Dar es Salaam; Tanzanian Publishing House, 1974, esp. ch. 4 for the limitations in theory and practice of the first round of post-independence plans.

14 W. F. Stolper, *Planning without Facts: Lessons in Resource Allocation from Nigeria's Development*, Harvard University Press, 1966.

15 R. W. Clower, G. Dalton, M. Harwitz, A. A. Walters, *Growth without Development. An Economic Survey of Liberia*, Northwestern University, 1966.

16 *FAO Annual Yearbook*, 1969.

17 E.g. A. Seidman, 'The Distorted Growth of Import Substitution Industry: The Zambian Case', *Journal of Modern African Studies*, xii, 4, 1974, pp. 601-31; see also, A. Seidman, *Comparative Development Strategies in East Africa*, Nairobi: East African Publishing House, 1972, ch. VI.

18 Cf. Consumer goods price indices and data re imports for African countries in *UN Statistical Yearbooks*.

19 Cf. *Manpower and Unemployment Research in Africa, A Newsletter*, Montreal: McGill University, Centre for Developing Area Studies, 1972, for data relating to unemployment. In Zambia, it has been estimated that unemployment in 1973 was about 20 per cent of the urban labour force, and expected to double by the end of the Second National Development Plan—1976. (T. Chelleswami, *Employment, A Survey View*, Lusaka, 1973, typescript.)

20 S. Schatz, *Development Bank Lending in Nigeria: The Federal Loans Board*, Ibadan: Oxford University Press, 1964.

21 I. Diaku, 'A Capital Surplus Illusion—The Nigerian Case Revisited', *Nigerian Journal of Economic and Social Studies*, xiv, 1, March 1972.

22 O. Teriba, E. C. Edozien and M. O. Kayode, 'Some Aspects of Ownership and Control Structure of Business Enterprise in a Developing Economy: The Nigerian Case', *Nigerian Journal of Economic and Social Studies*, xiv, 1, March 1972.

23 J. D. Esseks, 'Government and Indigenous Private Enterprise', *Journal of Modern African Studies*, ix, 1, May 1971.

24 Cf. G. Bucknell, *State Trading in Kenya*, Ph.D. Thesis, University of Wisconsin, 1971. As C. M. Kamau (in 'Localising Capitalism: The Kenya Experience' in D. P. Ghai, ed., *Economic Independence in Africa*, Nairobi: East African Literature

Bureau, 1973, p. 170) concludes: 'It is clear . . . that Kenyanisation and the growth of the economy are causing greater income differentiation among the Africans.'

25 M. Blundell, *So Rough a Wind. The Kenya Memoirs of Sir Michael Blundell*, Weidenfeld and Nicolson, 1964, p. 203.

26 G. Meier, *Leading Issues in Economic Development. Studies in International Poverty*, Oxford University Press, 1970, 2nd edition, p. 162.

27 *Prospects for Business in Developing Africa*, Geneva: Business International, S.A., p. 55.

28 Meillassoux, ed., *op. cit.*, p. 85.

29 E.g. S. Amin, 'Under-Populated Africa', *Manpower and Unemployment Research in Africa. A Newsletter*, Montreal: McGill University, Centre for Developing Area Studies, vol. 5, no. 2, November 1972, pp. 5-17; and S. A. Aluko, 'Population Growth and the Level of Incomes: a Survey', *Journal of Modern African Studies*, ix, 4, December 1971, esp. pp. 574-5. The political economists in Africa reject the proposals for population control, urged by agencies like the United States AID and the World Bank as essential to the solution of unemployment in Africa. Given that large areas of Africa are underpopulated, they assert, this proposal serves primarily to divert attention from the critical issues.

30 E.g. W. Rodney, *How Europe Underdeveloped Africa*, Dar es Salaam: Tanzania Publishing House, 1973. Recent studies in Southern Africa include Q. N. Parsons, 'The Economic History of Khama's Country in Southern Africa', *African Social Research*, Lusaka, No. 18, December 1974; C. P. Luchembe, 'Rural Stagnation: A Case Study of the Lamba-Lima of Ndola Rural District', History Seminar No. 17 and L. Van Horn, 'The Agricultural History of Barotseland', History Seminar No. 14, Lusaka: University of Zambia History Department, 1973-74, mimeo.

31 Meillassoux, ed., *op. cit.*, p. 76.

32 H. Johnston, Trade and General Conditions Report, Nyasaland, 1895-96. Sir Harry Johnston, one of the early architects of British colonial policy, maintained that development in Africa could be achieved, 'if the European can be induced by proper security to invest his money in Africa . . . and if native labour can be obtained . . . The native must be prepared to guarantee a fairly handsome return for money hazardously invested.' This required, 'A gentle insistence that that Native should contribute his fair share to the revenue of his country by paying his tax is all that is necessary on our part to ensure his taking a share in life's labour which no human being should avoid.'

33 R. Horwitz, *The Political Economy of South Africa*, Weidenfeld and Nicolson, 1967, pp. 400-1.

34 S. Amin, 'Underdevelopment and Dependence', *Journal of Modern African Studies*, x, iv, p. 504.

35 J. Rweyemamu, 'International Trade and the Developing Countries', *Journal of Modern African Studies*, vii, 2, 1969, pp. 203-19; and reply, *ibid.*, ix, 2, 1971, pp. 453-5.

36 S. Amin, in Meillassoux, *op. cit.*; see also 'Underdevelopment and Dependence', *op. cit.*

37 This point is well formulated by B. Van Arkadie, 'Development of the State Sector and Economic Independence', in D. P. Ghai, ed., *Economic Independence in Africa*, East African Literature Bureau, esp. pp. 108-12. It is also theoretically analysed by J. S. Saul, in 'The Political Aspects of Economic Independence', in the same book, pp. 123-52.

38 Cf. S. Amin, *Neo-Colonialism in West Africa*, Penguin African Library, 1973 and *The Maghreb and the Modern World*, Penguin African Library, 1972.

39 S. Amin and C. Coquery-Vidrovitch, *Histoire Economique du Congo, 1880-1968*, Dakar, 1969.

40   It appears that he has changed his argument in recent years. See below, p. 57.

41   R. H. Green, 'Review of *Histoire Economique du Congo*, 1880-1968', in
      Journal of Modern African Studies, viii, 2, 1970, p. 322.

42   Seidman, *Comparative Development Strategies in East Africa, op. cit.*, ch. VI, and,
      'The Distorted Growth . . .' *op. cit.*; R. Szereszweski, 'The Performance of the
      Economy, 1955-1963' in W. Birmingham, I. Neustadt and E. N. Omaboe, *A Study
      of Contemporary Ghana*, vol. I, *The Economy of Ghana*, Allen and Unwin 1966;
      ch. 3.

43   Republic of Kenya, *Census of Industrial Production, 1963*, Nairobi, Ministry of
      Economic Planning and Development, Statistics Division, 1965.

44   Republic of Ghana, *Two Year Development Plan, 1968-70*, Accra, Government
      Printer, 1968, pp. 50-2.

45   Government of Zambia, Central Statistical Office, *Monthly Digest of Statistics*,
      ix, 12, December 1973, Table 54, p. 54.

46   Cf. R. B. Sutcliffe, *Industry and Underdevelopment*, London, Addison-Wesley
      Publishing Company, 1971.

47   E.g. M. P. K. Sorrenson, *Land Reform in Kikuyu Country: a Study in
      Government Policy*, Oxford University Press, 1967.

48   E.g. S. K. B. Asante, 'Interests in Land in the Customary Law of Ghana—A New
      Appraisal', *Yale Law Journal*, xxiv, 1965, pp. 848-85.

49   For summary of experience and data re marketing cooperatives, see Seidman,
      Planning for Development in Suburban Africa, op. cit., ch. 11, Part A.

50   E.g. S. O. Olayide and S. O. Oluwade, 'Optimum Combination of Farm
      Enterprises in Western Nigeria: A Linear Programming Analysis', *Nigerian
      Journal of Economic and Social Studies*, xiv, 1, March 1972, pp. 63-76; and T. M.
      Kasapu, 'Some Aspects of Comparative Economic Efficiency Analysis among
      Small Scale Commercial Maize Farmers in Monze and Petauke Districts using a
      Cobb-Douglas Function', Lusaka, University of Zambia, Economics Seminar,
      1974.

51   J. Nyerere, *Socialism and Rural Development*, Dar es Salaam, 1967, p. 7.

52   S. Amin, 'Transitional Phases in Sub-Saharan Africa', *Monthly Review*, October
      1973, pp. 56-7.

53   W. A. Lewis, 'Economic Development with Unlimited Supplies of Labour',
      Manchester School, May 1954, pp. 139-91: and, 'Unlimited Labour; Further
      Notes', *ibid.*, January 1958, pp. 1-32.

54   International Labour Office, United Nations Development Programme,
      Technical Assistance Sector, *Report to the United Republic of Tanzania on Wages,
      Incomes and Prices Policy*, Dar es Salaam: Government Printer, 1957, Government
      Paper No. 3; and, H. A. Turner, *Report to Government of Zambia on Incomes,
      Wages and Prices in Zambia*, Lusaka: Government Printer, 1968.

55   E.g. J. Fry, 'Prices, Incomes, Employment and Labour Productivity', Lusaka,
      University of Zambia, Economics Seminar, 1973, pp. 25-7.

56   E.g. for Zambian case, see A. Seidman, 'A Note: the Haves and Have-Nots in
      Zambia—or, What happens to the investible surpluses in Zambia', Lusaka,
      University of Zambia, 1973, mimeo.

57   G. Arrighi, 'International Corporations, Labor Aristocracies, and Economic
      Development in Tropical Africa', in R. I. Rhodes, ed., *Imperialism and
      Underdevelopment: A Reader*, New York, Monthly Review Press, 1970, pp. 220-67.

58   J. Saul, statement reported from Toronto International Studies Programme,
      University of Toronto, 5-8 April 1972, *Journal of Modern African Studies*, ii, 3,
      p. 457.

59   Amin, 'Transitional Phases in Sub-Saharan Africa', *op. cit.*, pp. 52-5.

60   Central Statistical Office, 'Consumer Price Index—Low Income Group: New
      Series', Lusaka, 1970, mimeo, together with charts obtained from Central
      Statistical Office showing income and expenditure patterns of low income group

derived from that study; and Central Statistical Bureau, *Household Budget Survey of Wage Earners in Dar es Salaam*, Dar es Salaam, May 1967.

61 Seidman, 'A Note: the Haves and Have-Nots in Zambia', *op. cit.*, p. 11.
62 Central Statistical Office, *Monthly Digest of Statistics*, Lusaka, 1973, xix, 12, December 1973, pp. 29-30.
63 Seidman, *Comparative Development Strategies*, *op. cit.*, p. 263.
64 See R. H. Green and A. Seidman, *Unity or Poverty? The Economics of Pan-Africanism*, Penguin African Library, 1968, for details of this argument.
65 E.g. for summary of recent East African Common Market experience see Seidman, *Comparative Development Strategies*, *op. cit.*, ch. x.
66 Essentially another name for 'tariffs'.
67 On the need for more research, see R. H. Green, 'Economic Independence and Economic Co-operation', in Ghai, *Economic Independence in Africa*, *op. cit.*, pp. 80-2.

Michael Dei-Anang

Foreign Policy of the Independent African States

'Africa is like a zebra. It has black and white stripes', observed the Black Bishop of Ovamboland, 'You cannot eliminate one or the other without killing the beast itself.' The truth of this has been borne out by the problems incurred in granting independence to a collection of heterogeneous African states which naturally had fundamental differences of outlook.

In colonial times neglect of education for the indigenous people was widespread, but the new states have striven hard to amend this. Independence came to many African countries when they had few people with technical or managerial skills and only a few graduates.

The twentieth-century African might well accuse those who handed over their sovereignty in the words of an imaginary Red Indian chief created by Dr Johnson (1759): 'Either they promised protection which they never afforded, or instruction which they never imparted. We hoped to be secured by their favour from some other evil, or to learn the arts of Europe, by which we might be able to secure ourselves. . . . Their treaties are only to deceive and their traffic only to defraud us.'

Ndabaningi Sithole, the African nationalist from Zimbabwe, has declared: 'Politically, the white man dominates the African; economically he exploits him; socially he degrades his human status. . . . It is these things that the African hates, and not the white man himself.'

Any nation, country, or society that has been subjected to foreign government —whether good or bad—must look forward to its independence. There is a saying: 'it is preferable to sleep under one torn blanket of your own, than to be smothered in a dozen provided by other people.'

Self-rule brings responsibility, not only at home but also in the complicated problems resulting from involvement in global affairs. In the constantly changing world conditions of today, with rapid means of transport and communication, and dependence for existence on international trade, it is hard for any country to remain isolated or unaffected by the actions of others. The independent African states, sharing a common ideology of African nationalism, have evolved a common viewpoint on foreign affairs. A policy, as far as possible, not to become drawn into the machinations of other parts of the world has been generally accepted. This recalls the attitude of the United States after their independence in the eighteenth century.

Although sympathetic to the French revolution, Jefferson, then Secretary of State, kept the new nation from joining in the wars that engulfed the Old World.

66

He warned against the 'entangling alliances' with Europe and in spite of the seizure of American trading vessels by the British and French, the United States remained at peace.

Movement towards self-government has been slow and often hindered rather than helped by British policy. In 1850 an African member of the legislative council of the Gold Coast was nominated. Six years later, three municipal councils were established; this became recognised as the first indication that representative government for the whole country was now inevitable, unless prevented by force.

The voice of nationalism began to be heard during the First World War. A National Congress of British West Africa was formed and other similar organisations came into being. A scheme for the whole of this territory was postulated at Freetown in 1920.

Joseph Ephraim Casely Hayford, a Gold Coast lawyer and journalist, stated: 'We have passed the childhood stage and much as we appreciate the concern of our guardians, the time has come for us to take an intelligent active part in the guiding of our national destiny; and that is the primary fact that has called into being the National Congress of British West Africa.'

The European concept that you have first to become a nation before you can attain freedom was relentlessly drummed into the Africans, who realising this could not be ignored, began pressing their claim for freedom in a limited national structure. There was an hiatus during the 1920s and 1930s. Then during the Second World War, perhaps somewhat unexpectedly, anti-German propaganda provided a boost for African nationalism.

In *Democracy and the Party System*, Julius Nyerere tells of a British officer trying to persuade the Africans to fight against Hitler.

> 'Away with Hitler! Down with him,' the British officer said.
> 'What's wrong with Hitler?' asked the African.
> 'He wants to rule the whole world,' said the British officer.
> 'What's wrong with that?'
> 'He is German, you see,' said the British officer, trying to appeal to the African's tribal consciousness.
> 'What's wrong with his being German?'
> 'You see,' said the British officer, trying to explain in terms that he believed would be conceivable to the African mind, 'it is not good for one tribe to rule another. Each tribe must rule itself. That's only fair. A German must rule Germans, an Italian, Italians, and a Frenchman, French people.'

During the stages of acquiring independence, hostility to foreign inter-ference naturally developed. Africans quickly became sensitive to overt or covert attempts to provide foreign aid.

Simply pumping funds or goods into indigenous societies will not necessarily result in economic progress; without the necessary component of technical skills the danger of misuse of funds and even corruption is real; there is always a danger of graft. Misappropriation has been largely reduced by directing aid into such projects as dams or factories and making it available in the form of goods or services required for their construction. An influx of funds from abroad increases the danger of foreign involvement in African affairs, and the risk of external control. Trade, not aid, is a far more forceful lever for independent growth and development.

Even in the better administered unilateral schemes of technical assistance far too large a part of the funds is wasted on needless trips and conferences; this waste becomes enormous in international organisations. If technical aid is to be effective it must also have a proportion of moral education. People are inclined to pick up vices more easily than virtues, so that it is highly important for the countries supplying aid to be represented by persons likely to be a good example to the persons with whom they will associate. Corruption is not a one-way process.

Africans rightly fear that commercial penetration by trading companies (such as the British and Dutch East India Companies in the past) may lead to a similar domination by the foreign countries they represent today.

Most of the independent African states need financial and technical assistance if they are to survive and prosper. But the present global economic crisis and inflation means that foreign aid is bound to be limited, and may well be reduced. Speaking at the UN Economic Commission for Africa as long ago as 1967, the late Tom Mboya of Kenya said:

> The present status of aid today holds no promise for the future.
> Optimistically, it means gently rising *per capita* incomes to achieve for
> the very poor countries perhaps $200 per annum by the end of the
> century; it means rising debts and perennial balance of payments
> problems; it means continuously falling terms of trade and continued
> barriers to the sale of industrial products; it means no escape from
> the abyss of primary production.

Mboya and others advocated a 'Marshall Plan for Africa': 'a massive inflow of capital over perhaps 30 years and an equally massive inflow of technical assistance personnel over 10 to 15 years.'

Opposed to this were Nyerere and the socialists who foresaw that there was no hope for any such aid; even if it could be made available, they argued that it was undesirable because it would, in one way or another, lead to a new, indirect form of outside control.

Another matter needing urgent attention is the evolution of a continental policy on raw material supply to the developed nations. A unified agreement on the regulation of commodities essential to their existence, might well prove a means of checking too overbearing an attitude by foreign powers.

Most of the African territories gained their independence during the 1960s, an era when strained relations among the Great Powers produced a 'Cold War', particularly between the USA and the Soviet Union. The original concept of African nationalists had been to 'join the family of independent nations'.

Differences between the dominant nations were soon realised by Africans when they were urged to support the 'West' against the 'East'. Apart from some of the Arab states in the north, there was little Communist influence to claim support for the policies of the 'East'. What line should Africans adopt? Would their freshly achieved independence be thwarted if another kind of association with the rich nations was developed?

A number of the African states opted to keep out of the issues of dissension between the Big Powers. These were mainly the 'bloc alliances' known as the Casablanca Powers—so named after the capitals such as Casablanca, Monrovia and Brazzaville, where they were formed.

This meant a refusal to participate in any part of the Western defence scheme such as was envisaged in the North Atlantic Organisation or to commit themselves to the Communist bloc. The late Sir Abubakar Tafawa Balewa, Federal Prime Minister of Nigeria, insisted that 'neutralism meant freedom to choose'.

Following the lead of India, a policy of 'neutralism and non-alignment' was agreed. Kwame Nkrumah and others defined their attitude by a declaration of *Positive Neutrality*. Progress towards 'Third World' unity on the question of foreign policy was demonstrated by the establishment of links with Asia and Latin America. The first was the Bandung conference in 1955, which I had the privilege of attending as one of my country's delegates. Six years later, in September 1961, some African states attended the first serious non-aligned conference in Belgrade, Yugoslavia. The attempt then was to foster the establishment of a neutral force between the super powers of East and West. But there was significant difference in the manner in which neutralism was regarded by various states. Some looked upon it as a means of opposition to neo-colonialism.

Neo-colonialism or economic imperialism, as it appears in Latin America, is basically a process of economic penetration begun by uncoordinated traders, but liable to assume undue powers when it becomes concentrated in a few hands. In *La Planification Economique*, the Guinea leader, Sékou Touré, wrote:

> Given the general absence of an investing class, as well as the fact that foreign companies are primarily out for higher profits than they can earn at home (such being their *raison d'être*), the promotion of African independence within the capitalist system must result in surrendering the rate and course of growth to the decisive arbitration of the stronger partner.

Kwame Nkrumah was more forthright in describing neo-colonialism as 'the process of handing independence over to the African people with one hand, only to take it away with the other hand'. He also defined it as: 'clientèle sovereignty, or fake independence; namely, the practice of granting a sort of independence by the metropolitan power, with the concealed intention of making the liberated country a client-state and controlling it effectively by means other than political ones'.

In *Africa Must Unite* (1963) he expanded his views.

> The greatest danger at present facing Africa is neo-colonialism and its major instrument, 'balkanisation'. The latter term is particularly appropriate to describe the breaking up of Africa into small weak states, since it arose from the action of the great powers when they divided up the European part of the old Turkish Empire and created a number of dependent and competing states in the Balkan peninsula.

The effect was to produce a political tinderbox which any spark could set ablaze.

Some links with the former colonial powers still remained, although they varied through the type of close association with the francophone states to the more free 'commonwealth' arrangements. This may possibly be explained by the tendency for relations between the French-speaking states and their former masters to be franker and less guarded than in the case of the former British colonies. Alternatively, it might be attributed to traditional British 'stand-offishness'; although the British have, by and large, probably been the best colonisers and the most correct in personal relations, this characteristic prevented them from making friends among their subjects to the same extent as other colonial powers.

Africans tended to think that they had some reasonable right to expect some foreign aid from the developed countries in redress for the centuries of exploitation they had endured. The present approach, however, is to foster relations based on trade rather than aid. In 1963, the United Africa Company (a dependant of Unilever) opened a plant in Ghana to manufacture soap, tooth-paste and related products thus establishing a new relation with foreign investors. In the past, palm-oil had been bought in Africa, and returned as soap made in Europe; now the finished product, the whole process from its raw materials, was completed in its country of origin.

One of the chief impediments to economic progress in Africa is a shortage of competent businessmen. Petty traders are numerous in West Africa, but medium-scale trade is mainly in the hands of Lebanese and Indians; in East Africa with the recent exception of Uganda, Indians have had almost complete control. Increasing government interest in trading tends to make business profits basically dependent on the good will of officials; changes of ministry staff can therefore seriously affect the progress of business.

Many men and women of African descent, forced by circumstances to live under white American cultures, have looked hopefully back across the great distance that divides them from their native land, in the continuous hope that a free Africa may one day liberate Negroes overseas. This aspect of Pan-Africanism was based on ideals of Black rights and 'Africa for the Africans', which were first forcibly expressed at the original Pan-African Congress in 1900. In the New World all Africans had lost their differences of language, culture, and ethnic loyalties which they valued, to be united in disfranchisement; all Africans were considered as belonging to one territorial unit. This was how it was outlined by W. E. B. DuBois at that first congress:

> The problem of the 20th century, in the year of its birth, and with
> colonial conquest in full assault, is the problem of the colour line—
> the relation of the darker to the lighter areas of man in Asia and Africa,
> in America and the islands of the sea.

Not much attention was paid at first to Pan-Africanists, but they went on steadily and persistently expounding their views.

In 1919 another congress was held in Paris, attended by fifty-seven delegates; resolutions were passed calling for a code of law for the international protection of the inhabitants of Africa. During the years before the Second World War their libertarian ideas became more generally and openly supported by young nationalists in Africa.

A fifth congress was held in Manchester in 1945; the delegates included a number of Africans whose names were later to become celebrated in the history of their countries and of Africa—Kenyatta (Kenya), Nkrumah (Gold Coast), Akintola (Nigeria) and Johnson (Sierra Leone).

A challenge was made demanding for Africa 'autonomy and independence, so far, and no further, than it is possible in this One World for groups and people to rule themselves subject to inevitable world unity and federation.'

Hopes were raised by the likelihood of independence being granted to India, in the late 1940s. For the first time reference was made to the possibility of adopting other than peaceful methods to secure their demands. 'We are determined to be free, and if the Western World is still determined to rule mankind by force, then Africans, *as a last resort*, may have to appeal to force in the effort to achieve freedom. . . .'

Following Ghana's independence, President Nkrumah, aware of the need for the unity of action, made loans of millions of pounds sterling to other nationalist states. In December 1958, sixty-two organisations assembled in Accra for an All-African People's Conference. In 1960 no fewer than sixteen African colonies gained at least a measure of political sovereignty. Some differences of outlook and opinion still formed a stumbling block to a united Africa.

Representatives from twenty-six African student unions in Europe and America met in London in 1963 and emphasised the need for partnership of the African countries. Wide support for the students' opinions was revealed at the African Unity Conference held in Addis Ababa in May, which was attended by thirty-two independent African countries.

A charter was drawn up and the Organisation of African Unity was formed. Under this, Heads of State or government were to meet at least once a year; a council of ministers not less than twice a year; there was to be a secretariat established in Addis Ababa and a commission set up for mediation, conciliation and arbitration.

The main driving power behind the Addis conference, Nkrumah of Ghana, declared 'Africa must unite or perish', and argued that 'it should be possible to devise some constitutional structure which secured these objectives and yet preserves the sovereignty of each country joining the Union.'

Desirable as it may seem in anticipation, independence has brought responsibilities and problems. What kind of government is likely to prove most successful to the African states, still considerably influenced by their varying traditional, cultural and 'family' customs?

In his book *Pan-Africanism or Communism*, George Padmore has shown that neither economic principle is valid for Africa, where there is not—and cannot be—a consensus of opinion on these issues, until there is a continental outlook politically and economically within a unitary African government.

Political advance is of little avail unless it can be followed up by social and economic reconstruction. Money is essential, but where is it to come from without capitalists? Kojo Botsio, one-time Foreign Minister of Ghana, observed in 1960:

> You cannot mobilise capital from our traders or businessmen, they will not do it. We have in fact helped our Ghanaian businessmen over the last few years with loans for their capitalist development. Very large sums too. And nearly all of it has been wasted.

Benefits from capitalism can apparently be achieved by only two alternatives: either a long, slow period in which a few gain wealth before passing its benefits to the many; or else, an era of commercial training under countries of the Western world followed by a massive injection of investment funds.

To the African peasant it makes little difference whether the monopolistic power which reduces what he gets for his product is in the hands of foreigners or indigenous rulers; in the latter case he may possibly expect some return in the form of expenditure on roads, education and medical care.

Nationalist organisations in Africa may have differed in form or content. But they were all inspired by the same passion—to challenge and oppose foreign rule. One example of such an organisation was that of TANU in East Africa. There in Tanzania President Julius Nyerere has used his knowledge of strong family and kinship ties to build up a powerful nationalist body with socialist leanings. Family and kinship groupings are still very influential in Tanzania. Writing in 1962, Julius Nyerere explained:

> The function and objective of African Socialism is the Extended Family. The true African Socialist does not look on one class of men as his brethren and another as his natural enemies. . . . He regards *all* men as his brethren—as members of his ever-extending family. That is why the first article of TANU's creed is *Binadamu wote ni ndugu zangu, na Afrika ni moja.* If this had been originally put in English, it could have been: I believe in Human Brotherhood and the Unity of Africa.
>
> Ujamaa or Familyhood, describes our Socialism. It is opposed to Capitalism, which seeks to build a happy society on the basis of the exploitation of man by man; and it is equally opposed to the doctrinaire socialism which seeks to build its happy society on a philosophy of inevitable conflict between man and man . . .

The question of Africa's relations with the Big Powers is, unfortunately, often strategic and overshadowed by the struggle for world domination; economic power is used to secure political advantage, rather than the other way round. The concern of the US government is not that they may have to pay more for tin or rubber, but rather that important sources of such materials would be denied them altogether if they fell into the hands of the USSR, whose power would thereby be increased both relatively and absolutely.

Attempts to manipulate African governments are very real and are carried on as much by the communist as the capitalist nations. The chief cause is desire for supremacy in politics rather than the object of profit, although this, obviously, is also an incentive which cannot be ignored.

The USSR and China, nervously apprehensive of each other's movements, are seeking to secure some measure of linkage with the Independent African States. Chinese interest can be seen in the construction of the Tanzanian railway, over one-third of which, built by Chinese labour, has been handed over ahead of schedule. The status of China has certainly been raised by this achievement, while her prominence in the state is also noticeable in her training and equipment of Nyerere's army.

A sudden military coup in Portugal in April, resulting in establishment of rule by the Army, faced a number of African countries with a new predicament. Mozambique was most affected. In the London *Daily Telegraph* of 14 June 1974, Ian Colvin wrote:

> A settlement in Guinea-Bissau could release badly needed troops which could be used to police Mozambique until there can be a referendum and constitutional arrangements confirming ethnic realities and economic needs.
>
> The political centre of Mozambique today is the Army headquarters town, Nampula. There it is realized that the large Macua tribe, three million strong, which for 12 years successfully defied penetration by the Frelimo, cannot be disregarded, nor can the possibility of civil war be ignored. This does not mean that Portugal is seeking to evade a transfer of power to the people of Mozambique, or that it places confidence in any small European group.
>
> This resilent attitude towards the emergence of an independent Mozambique, is of course, suspect to the Liberation Committee in Dar es Salaam, to the Organization of African Unity in its summit meeting in Mogadiscio and to the communist powers. . . .

Since Ian Colvin wrote this report, General Spinola's military regime in Portugal itself has yielded power to a more radical leadership. The ultimate result has been the total collapse of Portuguese colonialism in Africa.

The United Nations Organisation provides for all countries a much-needed forum for discussion. Each African state as it acquired its independence was given international status and accepted as a member of the United Nations with equal voting rights with other nations; they were thus enabled to declare their views to the world and could take part in important issues.

On its inception the OAU stated its desire to strengthen and support the United Nations Organisation and invited African governments to instruct their representatives, without prejudice to their membership in, and collaboration with, the African-Asian group, to constitute a more effective African group to bring about closer cooperation and better coordination in matters of common concern. There is no doubt that the presence of African countries is playing an increasingly important role in UNO affairs.

During his term of office as Secretary-General of UNO, U Thant did much to support the OAU. His position did much to enhance the image of the Third World.

A noteworthy step forward towards greater cooperation was the decision of the forty-three Independent African States to negotiate 'as one unit' with the European Economic Community in Brussels.

In Resolution II of the Charter of Unity at Addis Ababa the Independent African States unanimously emphasised the urgent need to intensify efforts to put an end to the South African Government's policy of apartheid and racial discrimination.

A number of measures were set out, but at this stage it is hard to see what further pressures can be brought to bear that might induce some change of attitude, short of direct military intervention.

The purposes of the OAU, outlined at the Addis Ababa gathering in May 1963, were:

> To promote the unity and solidarity of the African states;
> To coordinate and intensify their cooperation and efforts to achieve a better life for the peoples of Africa;
> To defend their sovereignty, their territorial integrity, and independence;
> To eradicate all forms of colonialism from Africa;
> To promote international cooperation, having due regard to the Charter of the United Nations and the Universal Declaration of Human Rights.

In order to attain these goals, member states were to harmonise their general policies, especially in: political and diplomatic matters; transport and communication; education and culture; health, sanitation and nutritional organisation; scientific and technical advancement and problems of defence and security.

What of the future? Ten years of independence have brought the African countries face to face with the hard realities of nationhood—economic troubles, population growth, trade difficulties and vital problems of educational and technical progress. The need for a realistic approach to problems and a united continental policy are becoming more fully appreciated.

African leaders are aware that public opinion is gathering force in a demand for progress, and that they can no longer afford to ignore the feelings of the populace. Most of the problems of transition to independence have been tolerant and pacific, although there has, inevitably, been a case here and there of unhappy 'growing pains' which will probably be overcome in due course.

A matter of considerable concern is how to educate and improve the status of millions of rural Africans. How can a way be found to excite their interest in a fresh outlook on work, better organisation, new ways of cooperation and more modern methods of production?

The basis of the whole problem of emancipation of the African countries seems to lie in unification at two levels. One of intra-territorial states whose frontiers were fashioned by Europe and include within themselves a far larger number of pre-colonial states; the other, an inter-territorial combination of these states within the boundaries of Africa itself. Emancipation to succeed must have not only a definite policy from the united leaders, but also the willing support of the majority of the peoples.

There is still a long way to go on the road to full recognition of the rights of all African peoples, but the end is in sight. By adherence to its ideals and a determined and united effort, the OAU will surely attain its objectives of freedom, equality and justice. The whole of civilisation of which African life and culture constitute a part will be gravely endangered unless we learn to think and act as brothers.

I conclude with a quotation from one of my poems in which Africans are seen as weighing the merits and demerits of her past against the confusion and complexities of the modern world, and wondering which course to follow:

Forward! To what?
The slums, where man is dumped upon man;
Where penury
And misery
Have made their hapless homes,
And all is dark and dreary?
Forward! To what?
The factory
To grind hard hours
In an inhuman mill,
In one long ceaseless spell?

Forward, to dusty tools
And sordid gains,
Proved harbingers
Of mortal strife?

Or forward
To the crafty laws
Of Adam Smith
That turn the markets upside down
And steel men's hearts
To hoard or burn
The food supplies of half the world
E'en when the other half must starve?

Or backward?
Backward to the primal source
Of ethic qualities:
Man's love of fellow man
And fear of God,
Emanating from a chainless soul,
Full and frank and free?

Sail cautiously, O Fatherland,
Along thy course well-tried;
But whither bound, O Africa?
Oh, whither bound?

(from *Africa Speaks*)

Further reading

Awolowo, Chief Obafemi, *Awo*, C.U.P., London, 1960.

Dei-Anang, Michael, *The Administration of Ghana's Foreign Relations, 1957-1965*, University of London, The Athlone Press, 1975.

——, *Exploitation of Man by Man*, R. D. Publishing House, New Jersey, 1976.

Mazrui, Ali A., 'The U.N. and some African Political Attitudes', in *International Organization*, xviii, 1964, pp. 499-520.

Nyerere, Julius K., *Uhuru na Ujamaa*, O.U.P., Dar es Salaam, 1968.

——, *Freedom and Development*, O.U.P., New York, 1974.

Nkrumah, Kwame, *Africa Must Unite*, Panaf Books, London, 1963.

——, *Neo-Colonialism: The Last Stage of Imperialism*, International Publishers, New York, 1965.

Odinga, Oginga, *Not Yet Uhuru*, London, 1967.

Onésimo, Silveira, *Africa South of the Sahara*, Rabén & Sjögren, Stockholm, 1976.

Wallerstein, Immanuel, *Africa: The Politics of Unity*, New York, 1967.

——, 'The Early Years of the OAU: The Search for Organizational Pre-eminence', in *International Organization*, xx, 1966, pp. 774-787.

Kenneth King

Educational Perspectives on Africa

In the field of educational studies, one of the most surprising phenomena of the 1970s has been the widespread mood of disillusionment with Africa's formal school systems. It must be emphasised at the outset, however, that this feeling of crisis is particularly conspicuous at the international level, among the range of external bodies that concern themselves with development. These span the UN Specialised Agencies, the World Bank, individual country donors, the private foundations and university institutes concerned with the Third World. What is alarming is not so much their criticism of the schools (most school systems after all are under attack from time to time) but the rapidity with which opinion has coalesced on the failure of the African school, and the tendency for the voices raised to be non-African.

There is, in fact, as we shall shortly see, a very great deal of new insight associated with this disenchantment, but the mass of this advisory literature on education is almost bound to be perceived politically as much as pedagogically from inside Africa. It is perhaps difficult for Western readers to grasp this point, for although school systems in the West are often attacked by sections of their own nationals, they are not used to being the subject of widespread international concern. It might be easier to appreciate this difference if within a space of three years a country like Scotland were visited by some fifteen high-level education missions, or survey teams, drawn from the ILO, UNICEF, UNESCO, and from some of the richer Third World countries. If Scotland's educated unemployed and urban school problems became the subject of numerous investigations by Saudi Arabian, Nigerian and Chinese research teams, and these in turn formed the themes of the major international conferences, and were written up in the most prestigious scholarly journals (not to mention Ph.D. dissertations), and if Scots analysis did not participate in these activities, then it would be rather similar to what has been going on in some African countries in the last year or two.

Of course, there is rather a long tradition of the poorer parts of the world, and indeed the poorer parts of the rich countries, being advised on what form of education they should embrace. The most notable example of this was perhaps in the United States of America a century ago. After Emancipation the first frail structure of higher education for Blacks was just beginning to be erected in the Southern States with significant financial aid from the White North, when the tide turned. Quite suddenly, the major aid agencies and philanthropic funds in the North changed their priorities away from Black colleges towards low-level agricultural and artisan training.[1]

The context of the 1970s is a far cry from the racial politics of the post-Reconstruction era in America. The contemporary attack on the African school is part of a much wider Western disillusion with the direction in which African states appear to be moving. This centres on what is seen as a series of galloping inequalities emerging in many states, with the education system viewed as one of the major allocators of these very uneven income opportunities. In retrospect, many analysts see that the pattern of immediate post-independence Western aid —to create industrial estates, promote African entrepreneurship, or revolutionise agriculture through miracle strains—has often merely confirmed the same trend towards rural and urban inequality. Hence the switch of priority away from the so-called modern sector of the economy towards ways of aiding the mass of peasants and workers on very small incomes—the group whom the ILO have termed the 'working poor'.

As far as education specifically is concerned, there are really two groups of approaches that have been taken towards Africa's formal schools: (1) Reform from within and (2) Reform from outside the school system. As the latter has had the most publicity in these last few years, we will start with it.

Reform from outside formal schools

This approach begins with the premise that the formal Ministry-of-Education school system is not delivering the goods in a large number of Third World countries. In states where education enrolment is relatively low, the school budget is already perilously high; and even in those few states which *seem* to be enrolling more than 50 per cent of the age group, it is suggested that a more rigorous analysis of over-age children, repeaters, drop-outs and of skills actually acquired in primary schools can have the effect of slashing the apparently quite promising Ministry figures to a fraction of what was claimed:

> The conclusion to be drawn . . . is that in a country with an over-all primary school participation rate of, say, 50 per cent, the chances are that in some of the poorer rural areas as many as 90 per cent or more of all young people (especially girls) are reaching maturity without knowing how to read or write.[2]

This deflation of official statistics is designed to drive home the point that despite the heady expansion at Independence, the often vast outlays of money on teachers and the local forms of self-help, African countries are not getting a fair return for their sacrifice. They should, therefore, it is argued, consider whether what most children are failing effectively to get through the schools can be provided by alternative methods. Some of the main avenues currently being explored are termed *non-formal*—in the sense of their being various sorts of organised programme obtained outside the mainstream of ordinary schools. Descriptions and recommendations for non-formal education often point to the following ingredients:

A skill to live by

This the conventional primary school notoriously fails to provide. Children enter too early, or drop out too soon. And anyway the expense of the traditional primary school is heavy enough without contemplating schemes for effective vocationalisation. Hence, the interest of the non-formal enthusiasts has been directed towards indigenous learning systems, local apprenticeship arrangements, on-the-job training, and particularly to innovative methods of acquiring skill in situations that are not too institutionalised. Paradoxically, this has meant a reawakening of outside interest in those institutions such as Koranic schools, Coptic church schools, tribal lore acquisition (as among pastoral peoples) which caught the attention of some of the colonial 'indirect rulers' fifty years ago.[3]

The parallel is not as close as it seems. In earlier decades, the fascination with African systems of learning flowed from an anxiety about the potential social disruption of the Western school on local communities; it was hoped that here and there modern schools could be sensitively grafted on to existing structures so that (as the refrain went) the best of the old and the new might prevail. By contrast, now, the interest derives from a realisation that despite the investment in formal vocational training, the very great majority of all skilled people in urban and rural areas get their expertise outside any systematic setting. If this is true, it is obviously important to know something about local skill acquisition, especially if the skills gained there are more realistically adjusted to rural technology and productivity than current courses in formal technical schools.[4] This current interest in traditional and non-formal systems should not, Julius Nyerere has warned, be regarded as a possible substitute for formal schools:

> ... it is quite clear that in Africa at any rate the problem of integrating education with the society cannot be solved by abandoning a formal education structure.
>
> We cannot go back to an exclusive dependence on the traditional system of what I previously called 'learning by living and doing'. We cannot go back because modern knowledge is not dispersed in our societies.[5]

Basic communication skills

Here, too, the non-formal education analyst would claim that the ordinary rural primary school has been weighed and found wanting. It is so caught up with certification (very often in English and French) for the few that it fails in its obligations to the majority. Instead of the extended sequential system of seven or more years in primary school, non-formal proponents believe that the very notion of a complete primary cycle could be dropped in favour of short tailor-made units or packages. Certainly the more successful adult literacy campaigns would testify to the fact that communication skills can be picked up in much less orthodox ways than seven years of continuous classroom attendance. The trouble, however, with the literacy package has been that its impact has in general been more uneven and patchy than anything alleged of the ordinary primary school. Here and there literary work has caught fire, as for instance in some of the mass education campaigns in the Gold Coast in the early fifties, or with some of the more politically conscious literacy drives associated with Tanzania since 1970, or for a brief period with Paulo Friere in north-east Brazil. All too often, however, the popular response has not been there, and it has been difficult, even with UNESCO-backed functional literacy projects to be clear about their impact after almost a decade of experimentation.

In fact, the fate of so many adult literacy drives both in the colonial and Independence periods highlights one of the real obstacles to promoting such non-formal programmes as alternatives to seven-year primary schools. This is that the state of adult and out-of-school education is not really independent from the educational mainstream; indeed, the very *underdevelopment* of, say, literacy work is intimately connected with the *development* and expansion of the formal system, in rather the same way that the lack of development in rural areas can be associated with a concentration of resources in the urban sector.

Community orientation

It is alleged also in studies of non-formal education that African primary schools, as they presently operate, tap almost nothing of the knowledge that exists in the community around them. The assumption is that only teachers can teach, and that *a fortiori* a qualified and certified teacher must be more effective than an unqualified one. This view disqualifies most members of the community from contributing to the school as resource people, reservoirs of local history, craftsmen and in other roles. Lacking any local flavour or community participation, primary schools operate as merely a network of more or less effective examination centres, each releasing two or three fortunate children a year into the next level of the national grid. Accordingly, new structures need to be worked out which can be put to more effective use by all members of the community. Non-formal educators have been scanning the continent for places where institutions appear to have been designed in this spirit.

Few living examples of such integrated community learning have so far been documented—perhaps not surprisingly. Consequently, community education proposals are now, as in the colonial period, much more common on paper than in practice. For instance, the influential sector review of Ethiopian education (before the coup) proposed that after four years of minimum basic education the majority of students would either start work or go into 'community practicums' which would combine various elements of non-formal education such as apprenticeship training adjusted to local conditions. Unlike schools, many of the teachers would be craftsmen or local extension experts in the fields of public health, home economics, adult literacy or agriculture. Similarly, in Tanzania where since 1970 adults have already been making use of primary schools for literacy work in the afternoons, the concept of a community education centre has been introduced. This will take the integration of school and community a great deal further by building into the same unit: classrooms, day care centre, practical room, dispensary, rural library, kitchen and dinning/assembly hall. This project to convert all of Tanzania's primary schools into community education centres has already attracted the support of external aid, with the World Bank sponsoring a pilot group of eight centres to become operational in 1976.[6]

Even when projects such as these have become operational, it looks as if community education will continue to be an affair of isolated institutions rather than an expanding alternative to the formal school. This was certainly true of the colonial period where only a handful of institutions such as Kenya's Jeanes School, or Sudan's Bakht-er-Ruda embodied the spirit of community-conscious education, and as a consequence these were visited and publicised on a scale that almost exaggerated their significance to the territory they served.[7] Similarly today a tiny number of innovative projects are almost better known in educational and aid circles *outside* their countries than they are inside. The tendency, for instance, in educational thinking about Kenya is therefore to refer to Village Polytechnics as a critical innovation, in much the same way as Swaneng Hill is inevitably associated with any discussion of Botswana.[8]

Non-formal education as extension

There is nothing particularly surprising about this fascination with 'model' institutions. Indeed the same concentration upon a handful of really innovative experiments characterises many of the Western systems of education. However, it is not quite fair to the non-formal education movement to suggest that it is just interested in spotlighting the occasional out-of-school project that operates on community conscious lines, and offers skill or knowledge in less conventional modes than the formal system. It has admittedly served such a documentary role, but it is also concerned with a more systematic approach to all out-of-school provision. It is interested to examine whether the many currently uncoordinated little centres of innovation can be drawn together and can become the germ of a new approach. Equally, however, non-formal surveys usually lay claim to the *training* functions of government departments such as Health, Agriculture, Trade and Industry, and may suggest that although the officials involved there in extension work, traders' courses, population education and so forth are not accustomed to think of themselves as being adult educators, they are nevertheless involved in non-formal education.

It is, of course, the inclusion of these on-going extension activities of government within the concept of non-formal education that makes it possible to argue that there is already in most African countries the basis of a learning system that is not related to the formal school. There certainly are large numbers of people who come into contact with the state's extension services, and who get access to skill improvement or to agricultural advice in a wide variety of ways. And it is clearly a valuable aspect of the non-formal education movement that, in a year or two, a very great deal more will be known about the rather grey area of extension education. It is hoped, too, that the publicity may encourage greater allocation of resources to some of these activities at the field level. The difficulty, however, with relabelling extension work as non-formal education is that it confers conceptual unity upon what is in reality a deeply fragmented field. The same sort of thing may be going on in the Ministry of Agriculture, Health or

Veterinary Services in the training of field workers, for instance, but the sum of these activities can only very loosely be called a *system* of non-formal education in the same way that schools, colleges and universities constitute a system. Perhaps in recognition of this, many surveys of non-formal education regard it of paramount importance that there be *integration* of activities that seem conceptually to be under the same umbrella.[9] It should be recognised, however, that departmental divisions are probably as deeply entrenched in the developing countries as they are in the West, and it is not on the face of it likely that any very significant degree of cooperation will be achieved in the training and extension outreach of differing ministries without a considerable effort. Indeed, possibly most countries have evidence of how protracted and often unsatisfactory it can be to try to establish a project whose sponsors insist that it be an integrated scheme with an inter-ministerial committee.

Non-formal education as provision for the poor

We return to what is a fundamental consideration of non-formal education— the issue of inequity in African states. Its promoters are anxious to design provision for the educationally disqualified, those whom the traditional formal school has, for all its expense, roughly discarded after a brief and pointless spell in the lower classes. It wants to offer a relevant second chance package to this large group, and equally wishes to offer a different kind of first chance provision to the 30 to 50 per cent of young people who are still not entering schools at all. Parallel in a way to the thinking in the West that the urban poor cannot be helped by ordinary schools, non-formal education is implicitly suggesting that Africa's poor need different approaches, if they are to be compensated, and not just inferior versions of the monolithic educational system. This is naturally an exceedingly sensitive topic, and may well be expected to raise controversy in much the same way as have the Educational Priority Areas in Britain, and the Headstart Programmes in the United States. It has to be remembered in addition that the colonial period is only fifteen years away for most African states and there is still a rather vivid awarenss of how the present education system was assembled in face of frequent colonial schemes for special, 'appropriate' or 'relevant' education for Africa. There is nothing, therefore, particularly novel presumably in Africans' hearing advice in the 1970s on how the mass of their poorer countrymen cannot benefit from traditional Western education and why they should embrace a different model of educational provision. This colonial legacy is almost certainly not regarded sufficiently by some writing on non-formal education, as we shall see. But first we must consider reform from within the school.

Reform from within formal schools

Apart from the advisory literature that has been promoting non-formal education, a good deal of thought has been given in recent years to ways of reforming African school systems from within. The spectrum of bodies has been quite wide, and, amongst the external agencies, includes some of those that have also been working on alternatives to school. Their anxiety flows from the same features as the non-formal educators: the apparent inequity of function, the inappropriateness of what little is learnt, and the problematic linkage of school to job. Unlike the non-formal analysts, they see much more room for manoeuvre, even using the existing structures. Some of their most characteristic concerns at the moment are designed to regulate the overheated machinery by a number of controls and checks:

Certificate escalation

Much more rapidly than in an industrialised country, the relentless pressure to expand formal education in Africa raises the qualifications necessary to land a job in the modern sector. Indeed, it seems as if, in some areas, almost twice as much schooling is required to get the same job in 1975 as was needed in 1955 or 1960. Would-be manipulators of this situation desire to break this spiral upwards of certification, and look for ways in which schools can have the insidious pressure of the labour market taken off them. They would also want selection for jobs to be got over sooner rather than later, since it is this which keeps students for years longer in the system than there will be jobs afterwards to justify. In fact, research and policy recommendations along these lines are very recent, so that little practically has come of them at this stage.[10] It is, nevertheless, worth noting that measures to prevent the overproduction of qualified people were a feature of colonial education, particularly the rather rigid manpower approach of the Francophone territories. The whole tendency in Anglophone Africa has been away from a system of early decisive selection at, say, Standard II or IV towards one of open competition at higher and higher levels. By contrast, a good proportion of Francophone states have maintained the earlier manpower planning approach, and they are greatly assisted in this by the *concours* system in which the major vocations and professions organise their own selection rather than leaving it to the schools. As an individual country, Tanzania is almost alone in planning to abandon the reliance on each educational level to determine entry to the next, and is considering for 1975/76 a variant of Chinese selection for entry to university: secondary school leavers will first have to become absorbed in the labour market, and later, on the basis of their performance in ordinary work, they will be recommended to enter higher education.[11]

The relevancy question

Another area suggested for manoeuvre is that very large numbers of those not finally selected for jobs or higher education leave school with no marketable skill whatsoever. This has been true of the primary school leaver in many countries since Independence, but increasingly applies to the products of the expanding secondary school systems. To meet the situation, a wide variety of suggestions has been made for work-oriented courses, or diversified curricula. Indeed, the area in general remains one in which recommendations for 'practical' inputs come in thick and fast from every convention or education mission in the 1970s as in earlier decades. There is the same hiatus today as then between advocacy and practice. However, a slightly different emphasis is sometimes apparent in the proposals for schools to prepare their leavers for self-employment and petty entrepreneurship. This arises quite naturally from the now widespread recognition that the schools produce more aspirants than there are wage and salary jobs in the economy. But there has been scant attention in such advisory literature to whether ordinary primary schools *could* replicate the training and work conditions of the petty self-employed in African economies; nor has it been noticed that although, unlike the colonial period, most upper primary schools are now completely *non-vocational*, thousands of primary leavers do become self-employed very rapidly by force of circumstance. Thus, given the situation that the last year or two of primary school is regarded principally as a national lottery for all those who would gamble on secondary school entry, there seems little that can be done to alter its main institutional message for the benefit of the eventually self-employed, short of a major political reassessment of social and economic values. And even where, as in Tanzania, there has been a firm commitment to relevancy, the President has admitted seven years after *Education for Self-Reliance* that the battle is by no means won:

> Yet even so, I think we must admit that we have not done all that is necessary. We have been too timid—too unliberated—to effect the required radical transformation of the system we inherited. We have important changes. . . . But we are still mentally committed to 'international standards' in education . . .
>
> So the first problem we have to solve is that of building sufficient self-confidence to refuse what we regard as the world's best (whatever that may mean), and to choose instead the most appropriate for our conditions.[12]

The examination as the judo-trick

As well as being concerned with certification and the labour market, reformers today have identified the examination as the main cause of the internal defects of schools. From it are seen to stem cramming, irrelevancy, repeating of classes, poor teaching, and inequitable access to further education. Its backwash affects many classes earlier than the examination year. And, as a recent ILO report for Kenya affirms, it is with the examination that reform must begin: 'It is only after the root cause of the disease affecting the present function of schools (i.e. the existing examination structure) has been eliminated that a change in the content of education begins to make sense.'[13] Analysts are anxious to see if, for instance, by switching from the traditional achievement tests to various forms of aptitude testing the role of rote learning could be diminished, and the backwash through the schools reduced. Recommendations along these lines have been made by the World Bank and the ILO for several countries but, as in other matters, it looks as if Tanzania will be almost alone if it proceeds to implement the 1974 TANU policy of discarding the traditional primary school leaving examination, in favour of general day-to-day performance.

Quotas for equity

A key motive with the reformers as with the non-formal advisers is how education systems can be prevented from intensifying what is seen as a growing inequity between group and group, region and region, town and country. At present, certain areas in most African countries are felt to get far more than their 'fair share' of secondary or university places by reason of the headstart they had in Western education, or the surplus from cash crop agriculture that could over the years be ploughed into school buildings and school fees. To control such imbalances, it is often suggested that expedients like quota systems could be introduced, and that planning units in Ministries of Education could monitor more effectively where new schools or streams should be established. One of the difficulties, however, of the quota approach to inequity is that the currently ruling groups would as likely as not be penalising themselves if they implemented quota education. Equally, as reference to the interesting scheme in the Kenya ILO mission report will make clear, quotas can be extraordinarily complicated procedures to operate.[14]

Basic education versus high level manpower

A number of the most recent international conferences have stressed the priority of the basic education cycle.[15] Again, the argument has to do fundamentally with élitism; many outside planners and experts conceive that over-investment has taken place in secondary and higher education for the few as opposed to insuring a really secure grounding for all. Indeed, basic educationists would argue that where there are still pockets, districts, states, and even whole countries in which primary participation has not yet reached 30 to 50 per cent of the school age group, it is plainly inequitable to continue what they see now as the obsession with high level manpower. On the other hand, basic education does not just presumably mean 'more of the same', as tends to happen in some of the current universal free primary schemes; it presupposes also a measure of thoroughgoing reform in content and structure. As a recent World Bank working paper has pointed out, the poorer countries cannot afford a great deal more of the same conventional primary schooling. They may, instead, have to examine whether they should try to extend a 'minimum package' of basic skills to the majority instead of maintaining a six- or seven-year primary pattern for only half the available children.[16]

This current interest in basic education points up how far the pendulum has swung away from the high level manpower preoccupations of the period 1960 to 1965. The emphasis has not only come to rest on the primary level, but even there it is being recognised that there is considerable inequity. Conventional primary schools will not deliver the goods, as people too readily assume. 'This assumption', the World Bank stated in 1974, 'is unrealistic for low-income countries which face a choice between a standard (primary) system serving only 30-40 per cent of the children, and an alternative which aims at providing some kind of education for all.'[17]

These then are some of the themes common to the crisis literature on the African school. A very wide range of education and development agencies would subscribe to this kind of analysis, the most influential being the UN Specialised Agencies, the World Bank, the Ministry of Overseas Development and private foundations such as the International Council for Educational Development. In addition, a great deal of descriptive and bibliographic material has been rapidly generated on the subject of non-formal, 'incidental', basic, or mass education in the last year or two.[18] And undoubtedly one advantage of this spotlight on non-formal education will be that some financial and institutional support will begin to flow to this hitherto rather neglected sector of Third World countries. There are, however, just a few points to be made on the history of non-formal education in Africa.

Non-formal education in African time perspective

The Africa-India contrast

It should be remembered that for perhaps the major part of the colonial period in many African countries, the education and training systems were deliberately designed to be the opposite of the system that had emerged in India. Long before the 1920s, it was being recognised that Indian education had departed from the British standard, and that equivalency of matriculation and degree work with Britain was no longer possible except in a handful of colleges. Similarly in terms of unit costs, it was acknowledged that Indian primary and secondary students were educated at a fraction of what was common in African territories. By contrast, secondary education as it emerged ever so cautiously in Africa was relatively high cost, and of extremely high quality. Then, as now, there was a good deal of discussion at the international level about the inappropriateness of this embryonic system and the need for adaptation to some more indigenous standard. However, the financial and political restrictions upon the expansion of secondary education made it almost inevitable that the one or two such institutions in any territory would be highly selective and highly regarded: Alliance High School (Kenya); École William Ponty (Senegal); Tabora Secondary (Tanganyika); King's College Budo (Uganda); Achimota (Gold Coast). Even though a form of 'adaptation' and 'relevance' was attempted in a few of these, notably Achimota, the high quality of staff and of buildings was more important than their attempts at syllabus Africanisation. Furthermore, until the end of the Second World War, there really was no money to implement the recommendations about community and mass education that had been made in the inter-war years. The exceptions would be the Jeanes Schools of East and

Central Africa which might be classified as the first significant non-formal initiatives to be made possible by external aid—from the Carnegie Corporation of New York.

After the war, the exceedingly slender education pyramids began to be crowned with tiny university colleges, intimately linked to the standards and curricula of London University, again in very marked contrast to the situation in the Indian subcontinent at that time. The mood was assimilative but still characterised by extreme caution. At the same period—just thirty years ago— money also became available for experiments in mass education and literacy work. Support was forthcoming from UNESCO, which had itself just been born, and for a time, particularly in West Africa, there was a groundswell of popular interest. Unfortunately there has not so far been any thoroughgoing research into this first major wave of 'fundamental' education—as it was then called; but it might well be instructive to examine the fate of so much of this early post-war enthusiasm. In many cases it must have appeared to local African leadership that non-formal education was being recommended before their primary and secondary sectors had even begun to expand, and as such, non-formal education seemed politically unacceptable, compared with the kind of education that people associated with the preparation for Independence.

The era of full assimilation to metropolitan standards

Part of the reason for the relative decline in literacy interest was that from the early 1950s the formal school machinery was beginning to gather speed. Thousands of illiterate parents clearly believed that they should invest in education for their children rather than themselves. And as the 1960s grew nearer with the expectation of Independence, it became obvious that the educational superstructure for all its high standards was totally inadequate. Quite suddenly the gradualism of the early advisory literature was abandoned, and, for a brief decade, overseas planners and educators urged the expansion of the top layers of the pyramid as fast as was compatible with standards. Eric Ashby, for instance, could state with pride in the *Report of the Commission on Post-School Certificate and Higher Education in Nigeria* that 'our proposals remain massive, expensive and unconventional'.[19]

As the African ministers of education plotted their targets for universal primary, and substantial percentages for secondary and higher, education, their projections were worked over by a new group of expatriate manpower planners. These concentrated their attention also predominantly on middle and high level manpower, and the shortfalls for the necessary professional and technical cadres were translated directly into secondary and university graduates. In Africa itself, governments, politicians and local committees acted in the faith that education would somehow produce development, while, outside, a good number of economists tried to prove it. Within a decade a whole literature on returns to educational investment was generated. Even in the field of literacy, the mood was infectious, and UNESCO decided to try and measure scientifically any positive correlation there might be between literacy and development. Although a good deal of attention was paid outside Africa to creating a science of educational planning, metropolitan governments and the USA did not wait for the outcome of the human capital debate to send out their volunteers, teachers, lecturers and advisers to help man the expanded system. It was, of course, only possible for the tens of thousands of expatriates to move easily from the schoolrooms of France and Britain to their counterparts in Africa because equivalency had been ridgidly maintained. And similarly African secondary students with their baccalauréat or 'A' levels could be absorbed in very large numbers in the metropolitan countries, and by extension in the United States, much more rapidly since they had been rigorously graded and certificated in their home systems.

External disenchantment: education and equity

And then, just as suddenly, the era of optimism and assimilation of African systems to European was over as far as the international literature was concerned. This change in mood is partly attributable to a world-wide critique of education, ranging from the deschooling literature at one pole to the reformist International Commission on Educational Development at the other.[20] But the themes that we have been examining in non-formal education are more than just Africa's version of the world educational crisis; they are also the result of critics associating African education with a wider misguided development strategy which has been followed in the majority of poor countries. Thus the attack on high-level manpower and hierarchically structured formal school systems derives from the broader contemporary attack on policies that concentrated resources in the tiny modern sector of Third World countries. This allegation has been put perhaps most forcefully in the World Bank Sector Working Paper of 1974:

> Education systems have been irrelevant to the needs of developing countries during the last two decades because education policies were often keeping company with overall development strategies which were themselves irrelevant to the societies and conditions of the developing countries.[21]

Non-formal education and the colonial heritage

Even granted for the moment that there are substantial grounds for this kind of criticism, the key question must remain what the local African policy-makers and administrators are to make of this international consensus. The chairman of the recent International Commission on Educational Development has stated confidently that 'They [Third World countries] *have now become aware* that these models (often obsolete, even for the people by and for whom they were devised) are adapted neither to their needs nor to their problems' (my emphasis).[22] This may be true of a handful of policymakers, the most notable being Julius Nyerere. But it is difficult to believe that many of the first generation of Africa's educational statesmen are engaged in the kind of agonising reappraisal we have noted for the assistance agencies. They are presumably too occupied in the day-to-day organisation of schools, colleges, faculties, ministries or inspectorates to have picked up much of this mood of disillusion with formal education that has been sweeping the advisory literature. And it may be perhaps further assumed that the rapidity with which this disenchantment has jelled among groups of predominantly non-African experts is itself rather questionable.

Regardless of how acute the new advice is, the conversion to the cause and education of the poorest segments of newly independent countries has been precipitate. After all, the ink is not long dry on the vast Western literature that stressed quite the opposite message about education in the Third World. How many books and articles were written in the 1960s concerning 'Education and Elite Formation'; 'Education and Political Development'; 'Education and Nation Building'; 'Education and National Development'; 'Education and Economic Development'? By contrast with these themes the new wisdom and the new approaches are contained in a work whose very title is significant: *Education and Development Reconsidered*.[23] It is the outcome of the reflections of all the most influential donors involved in the support of education in the Third World, and many of its papers urge the redirection of assistance away from conventional education towards innovative reform and experimentation with basic education.

There is bound to be some political objection to these new priorities even in states that have been free of colonialism for ten to fifteen years. But it is worth remembering in this seminar which celebrates Basil Davidson that several of the countries to which he has given his especial attention are only emerging from Portuguese rule at a time when the agencies have apparently turned their backs on formal education. It is to be doubted that their short-term needs for skill and professional talent can be rapidly made good by non-formal education.

Notes

1 See K. J. King, *Pan-Africanism and Education*, Oxford University Press, 1971, ch. 1.
2 P. Coombs, *New Paths to Learning for Rural Children and Youth*, International Council for Educational Development, New York, 1973, p. 29.
3 World Bank: *Education. Sector Working Paper*, Washington, December 1974, p. 30.
4 K. J. King, *The African Artisan*, Centre of African Studies, Edinburgh, 1975, mimeo, ch. 2.
5 J. Nyerere, speech to IDS/Dag Hammarskjold Seminar on Education and Training and Alternatives in Education in African Countries, June 1974.
6 World Bank, *op. cit.*, p. 26; see also 'Project Proposal for Vocationalization/ Practicalization of Primary Schools', Ministry of National Education, April 1973, mimeo.
7 King, *Pan-Africanism*, ch. 6, 'The Jeanes School'; W. L. Griffiths, 'Education for Citizenship in Sudan Schools 'in Colonial Office, *Education for Citizenship in Africa*, Colonial No. 216, HMSO, 1948.
8 The village polytechnics have been written up in numerous contexts; see particularly J. Anderson, *The Village Polytechnic Movement*, Institute for Development Studies, Nairobi, Evaluation Report No. 1, August 1970; also David Court, 'Dilemmas of Development. The Village Polytechnic Movement as a Shadow System of Education in Kenya', in D. Court and D. Ghai, *Education,*

Society and Development, Oxford University Press, Nairobi, 1974, ch. 10. On Swaneng Hill and the Brigades in Botswana, the most comprehensive of many shorter accounts is Patrick van Rensburg, *Report from Swaneng Hill. Education and Employment in an African Country*, Dag Hammarskjold Foundation, Uppsala, Sweden, 1974.

9   The most incisive analysis of the case for integration is P. H. Coombs, *Attacking Rural Poverty. How Nonformal Education Can Help*, Johns Hopkins University Press, Baltimore, 1974.

10 There is a recently launched research programme at the Institute of Development Studies, Sussex, along these lines: 'Qualifications and Selection in the Educational Systems of Developing Countries', mimeo, March 1974.

11 See article in *Africa*, 42, February 1975, p. 33.

12 J. Nyerere, *op. cit.*

13 ILO, *Employment, Incomes and Equality: a Strategy for Increasing Productive Employment in Kenya*, Geneva, 1972, p. 244. See also Richard Jolly, 'The Judo Trick' in Champion Ward (editor), *Education and Development Reconsidered*, Praeger, New York, 1974, pp. 58-71.

14 ILO, *op. cit.*, pp. 245-7.

15 UNESCO-UNICEF Co-operation Programme: Seminar on Basic Education in Eastern Africa, 19-23 August 1974, Nairobi, and papers presented.

16 World Bank, *op. cit.*, pp. 27-30.

17 *Ibid.*, pp. 30-1.

18 One of the earliest descriptions of non-formal provision is J. Sheffield and V. P. Diejomaoh, *Non-formal Education in African Development*, African-American Institute, New York, 1972; for a useful pointer to the work done on non-formal education in America, and particularly in Michigan State University, see Cole S. Brembeck, 'Studies in Non-formal Education: A Review Article' in *Teachers College Record*, forthcoming 1975; and also Brembeck (editor), *New Strategies in Educational Development*, D. C. Heath, Lexington, Mass., 1973.

19 Nigeria, Federal Ministry of Education, *Investment in Education*, Lagos, 1960, p. 3.

20 UNESCO, International Commission on the Development of Education, *Learning to Be. The World of Education Today and Tomorrow*, Paris, 1972.

21 World Bank, *op. cit.*, p. 3.

22 UNESCO, *Learning to Be*, pp. xix, xx.

23 C. Ward (editor), *op. cit.*

Paul Edwards

West African Literature and English Studies

When I went to Ghana in 1954 one of my first teaching jobs was 'The Pardoner's Tale' in Middle English. Something rather like a circle was completed this year (1974/75) with an invitation to Ibadan as external examiner of a Ph.D. thesis on the *Cursor Mundi*. But there has been a change. When I went to Ghana nobody seemed very surprised about Chaucer, whereas in 1975 people seem to think the *Cursor Mundi* a very curious creature to find in the African academic market. Still, many a good read comes from the most unlikely places. I toyed with the idea of giving a lecture in Ibadan entitled 'To Africa on an Iceberg', on the place of mediaeval Icelandic saga in modern Nigerian fiction. As for that once exotic beast, African literature in English, it's a satisfied cat on every bookshelf nowadays.

Coming back to the Chaucer class, after the initial culture-shock, my first response was to raise my voice against that lovable old pantomime villain, the Traditional English Syllabus. 'Relevance,' I said, 'what we want is relevance.' But it came as another shock to discover that once students had the hidden but ubiquitous copy of Coghill, 'The Pardoner's Tale' was turning out to be quite a success with them. They liked the way the moral stood on its head and pulled faces at them, and they knew that Pardoner better than I did.

So with my fairy queen, Relevance, a bit raddled under the greasepaint but a good old trouper for all that, I began, like many other teachers of English in Africa, to look around for works of literature which might aid, or at least not positively damage, the work of language teaching: and to recognise that whatever I was teaching, it was not only langauge—not language in the sense of the English Language examination, I mean. African Literature did not exist, either for myself or my students, as a thing that you could study. In fact in 1954 it did not exist for anybody; there were those French chaps up and down the coast, but they were really politicians, and some old fellows from Freetown and Cape Coast mouldering away in manuscript or entombed in bibliotechnical dust; no, they were not up to the standard of our Shakespeare, Milton, Wordsworth, Dickens, T. S. Eliot, our gifts to Africa.

True, there was a daft side to our condescension, but it also made sense at times—'The Pardoner's Tale' was an illustration of this. I started to recognise such things as African politics in *Julius Caesar* and African dilemmas in Wordsworth's 'Michael', often as a consequence of the kind of questions pupils asked about them. They scratched their heads over the opening of Arnold's 'Scholar Gipsy' and wanted to know what a shepherd was doing there, where were his sheep, where (a great question) did he get his chop. And this sent me back to Arnold, to find that he was asking not entirely dissimilar perplexed questions himself about the poem in a letter to Clough. It was not enough to talk about the literary pastoral tradition, not at this point anyway: the problem had to be faced, not simply of my students' unawareness of the conventions, but of my own bondage to these conventions. My students helped me by pointing out obstacles that I had never imagined. My favourite was the case of Madeline's fruit. After I had expanded at some length about that superb laying of quince and plum and gourd beside her bed in 'The Eve of St Agnes', one student asked whether he should do the same when he went to bed with an English girl, and what kind of fruit would I recommend. (He finished up with the United Nations.) How straight should we keep our faces when confronted by such overwhelming questions? Well, Keats is still there and looks quite undamaged.

As to African literature, it was beginning to exist but only just. There seemed to be hardly anything that I could handle in the classroom. There was Tutuola's *Palm Wine Drinkard*, but the students were upset by what they saw as its deficiencies of language and its excesses of imagination. Tutuola, I was told, had had the bad judgment to try to write a novel before emerging from the bush of his ghosts. But at the same time, the English of one of the set books for the year was haunting me from the bush of ghostly English Literature. I was finding Gray's 'The Bard' a problem, to put it mildly.

Ruin seize thee, ruthless king,
Confusion on thy banners wait

was not the kind of language one wants to hear used in the classroom. I liked Gray, and thought the *Ode on a Distant Prospect of Eton* and that cat in the goldfish bowl lovely poems, but it was 'The Bard' that had been set and if the class didn't know a hawk from a hauberk there were always visual aids. It was hard going, a lot worse than Tutuola and not half as natural. So we battled over the syllabus, did out best to honour the good fairy Relevance, taught the Great Tradition and dosed our sixth-formers with Leavis which, to their credit, they took like men.

Then, all of a sudden, African literature broke out. It was not until the early 1960s that the French and West Indian writers and critics became at all widely known in Commonwealth West Africa, but quite suddenly not only were they with us, so were their predecessors of the eighteenth and nineteenth centuries, and so were all those new men writing in English. The ground trembled a little under our feet, the bandwagon began to roll, a new generation of Ph.D. candidates began to tune up and in no time at all African literature was top of the pops. This is not the whole picture, of course, a lot of hard and useful work was done, a number of remarkable artists emerged, but the whole thing did get rather bandwagony and still is, I think. But if a book is good, we should not worry too much about it being read because it is also fashionable. Still, it ought to be acknowledged that African literature in the sixties produced some of the most forgettable writing and criticism that we are still being asked to remember.

On the positive side, though, there was the arrival on the scene of that fairly small band of capable, discerning, occasionally brilliant writers who are beginning to make the study of African literature a more serious affair, ironically, I suspect, at the very time that it may be becoming just a bit less fashionable. Everyone knows who they are, and I won't give a list because someone is bound to complain about being left out.

The earlier declarations of intent by African artists were usually very explicitly political—for example at the Congress of Negro writers held in Paris in 1956, Ben Enwonwu said that

> The present generation of African artists therefore have to face their political problems and try to look at art through politics; the kind of picture that the political aspect of African art shows is one of strife and pity.

But there has been a persistent current of debate about who is the enemy and what is political: there was a tendency among both Black and White commentators on African literature to enthuse over the art of a writer when they were really enthusing over his politics, or lack of them. From White critics there were regular thundering salvos of prejudice or whispers of sentimental endearment. But African writers, having expressed their irritation with both, have also shown themselves willing to examine each other's work increasingly critically. John Pepper Clark, for instance, takes up this question of poet and politics in the case of Dennis Brutus, to the fact of whose suffering we may respond very strongly and simply. But that there is more to a poet than his political stance Clark is quite sure:

> In *Sirens, Knuckles, Boots*, a volume of poetry published by Mbari in Nigeria, Dennis Brutus, actually then on the run from Verwoerd's police who later shot him down, succeeds to a considerable extent in transforming life direct into art. Poetry here is servant to politics. Something of the troubadour that he proclaims himself to be, Brutus cuts a tough figure of great bravura, with quite a brutal Elizabethan hold on words, and a strong smell for all the right sentiments to stir the would-be crusader safe in his liberal seat somewhere in Europe and America. Reading the work of Dennis Brutus, much of it remodelled rhetoric, one comes back to that old excuse by Mphahlele that certain situations like those in South Africa really are too paralysing for words. Perhaps—for what does one do to a dog holding up a mauled paw? A child in a fit of convulsion? Dennis Brutus in his book is a man battering his head against the bars of a cage in which he and his kind are undoubtedly held down by a devilish gaoler. The sight is terrible enough, but one gets the feeling sometimes, a wicked one no doubt, that a little less shouting and more silence and mime might not only make for manly dignity but also command attempts at rescue and action. That is the ram's one lesson to man when trussed up by man. In this way, what is truly tragic will not become mere melodrama—overdrawn, posturing, and tear-jerking. (John Pepper Clark, *The Example of Shakespeare*, Longman, 1970, p. 50)

One of the most serious problems and irritants for the African writer in the sixties was not so much the prejudiced rejection as the uninformed praise of his work, and the kind of critical judgment that Clark is making here whether or not one agrees with him about Brutus' poems it seems to me that his critical point is sound is vital to the well-being of African literature.

In the case of Achebe, one of the healthiest features of his discussion of his own work is his modesty. He does not see himself as the 'great novelist', but he does show a powerful sense of his literary responsibility: he sees himself, sometimes perhaps too simply, as an educator—in one sense, of the European who has been taught contempt for Africa: in another, of the African who has learned to be contemptuous of himself. Besides this, he is a teacher of that widespread colonial legacy, an African language, English: he has contributed immeasurably to the creation of what seemed incredible twenty years ago, an African reading public. Between 1966 and 1974, nearly a quarter of a million copies of *Things Fall Apart* were sold by Heinemann, most of them in Africa, and around a hundred thousand each of *Arrow of God* and *A Man of the People*. Achebe is not, I think, a great writer, but he is at his best a very good one, nor does he claim to be more. And to have replaced Marie Corelli and Bertha Clay on West African bookshelves, on such a scale, is a pretty meritorious performance.

Having mentioned great-writerhood, I will pursue it a little further. Achebe himself and a good many other African writers have remarked on the poor quality of a great deal of the African writing published, the condescension or ignorance of the critic who praises such writing, or the cupidity of the publisher. But the problem might be simply that some books are being taken too seriously, that a man who is in fact a fairly good writer of fiction for the kind of people who read his kind of fiction is being placed in the ranks of the literary artists, and even being persuaded by catchpenny criticism that he *is* a literary artist. Now there are lots of works of literature which we might enjoy without necessarily insisting on their being enshrined—maybe too much enshrining has been going on. My question is, are we supposed to look at *African Literature* (all of it) altogether seriously? If we insist on someone being the George Eliot of Nigerian literature, who will be the Marie Corelli or Bertha Clay? Are not the aims of the authors we read in African literature in fact often more modest than the critical attention they are given (I am not saying that they should not be given critical attention; only that a scalpel should not be taken to cut a sausage)? Is it possible that the 'fashionableness' of African affairs in the 1960s turned up the thermostat in the African literary hothouse? It seems to me that once you have the idea of a tradition or school of writing that has to be garlanded with all the paraphernalia of close literary examination you might lose your perspective and tilt your wig.

Perhaps it would be better not to insist too much on fiction in West Africa being understood in traditional Western literary terms, but rather as a growing body of local narrative which need not necessarily pretend to the status of literary art to have its own value. In any case, while the novel is a convenient thing in that we can open and close it and carry it around with us, much more deeply rooted in African society might be the song, the dance and the drama. The problem is one of accessibility, and watching things on film or television is

94

not quite the same as being on the spot, since dance-drama is public and active, whereas the novel invites the private and the reflective. I have a feeling that too much stress may have been placed on the Western style fiction and poetry, that we have not yet seen what Basil Davidson calls 'Art for life's sake' and that the finest African achievements in literary art either pretend to be invisible when they see a publisher or maybe wander straight past him without anybody ever noticing.

Julian Rea

Aspects of African Publishing 1945-74

Between 1945 and the late 1950s, in common with manufacturing industry, African publishing for schools and universities was controlled and directed from outside. University and commercial presses were not represented in middle Africa until the mid-1950s, and such book publishing as existed was conducted as a side line of mission and government printing presses and by the variously called literature bureaux. Publishing for schools was carried out by British and French houses and supplied through the Crown Agents, other metropolitan purchasing houses, or the mission bookshops.

In British Africa in the immediate post-war period, with a small number of exceptions, primary boooks were either those used in Britain or those developed in India and the Far East such as the English courses of West and French. Later, African primary syllabuses were prepared by expatriate-controlled Ministries of Education and publishers' contracts made with expatriate education staff in the schools and Ministries, either on occasional visits by European publishers or during home leaves. Inspectorate staff at this stage apparently saw little contradiction in drawing substantial royalties from courses written by themselves to match their own syllabuses and recommended for use by their own committees. Perhaps because such staff were not part of the local culture and also because, as expatriates, their postings were frequently changed, the educational dangers of this system were, at that time, less than they might have been. But it did establish a precedent which has sometimes not allowed for effective evaluation of materials and which, when coupled with single list recommendation, has in some cases resulted in a pattern familiar in other parts of the world, in which more factors than the quality and suitability of the materials themselves have affected selection and purchase of books. In secondary education in British Africa the majority of books used were those designed for metropolitan syllabuses on which examinations were conducted with only minor changes by the overseas departments of the UK examining boards. In French Africa the examinations were identical with those in France.

The majority of books were therefore the same as those used in European schools. Only in areas such as national history, geography and civics were specialist books produced. These were published and supplied in the same way as the primary texts. Predictably, since almost all these books were written by serving colonial officers, alone or in conjunction with European authors to whom they supplied the local knowledge, the political and moral standards adopted in the books reflected current colonial attitudes and, of course, nowhere more obviously than in history and civics. As late as 1959 it was possible for an expatriate-authored school history of Nigeria to deal with the Akassa raid in the following terms:

> In 1895 the Brass tribe had to be punished for an attack on the Royal Niger Company's factory at Akassa, which was followed by a cannibal feast consisting of the Company's African employees who had been captured. . . . The raid was provoked by the action of the Company in requiring all trade with the Niger to pass through its control post at Akassa on the River Nun, whereas formerly tribes living on the other outlets of the Niger had all benefited by the trade. But the circumstances of the raid required punishment.

This book, published by Longman, went on to sell, altogether, something over 50,000 copies and was still selling modestly when it was put out of print a few years ago.

It is easy to find examples of this kind in colonial books. It is also easy to dismiss all school books produced at this time as being of the same family and to forget those, such as McWilliam's *Development of Education in Ghana*, which were largely factual and unbiased and some of which, in new editions, are still in use. At this stage the number of African authors could be counted in units, which, considering the later success and high social status of so many African schoolmasters, is not only evidence of the failure of expatriate publishers to persevere with potentially talented authors but more particularly of the effectiveness of the system in repressing the self-confidence of naturally intelligent and articulate people. The one area in which African authors felt able to write freely was in African languages. Here, because so few expatriates were fluent, it was generally accepted that the field should be left to African nationals. Much, though not all, of the publishing was done by the missions or through the African language boards and bureaux. Outside Africa little is known of the work done by the Gaskiya Corporation, the Bureau of Ghana Languages, the East African Literature Bureau and all the others and it would be difficult to make a complete list of the hundreds of titles each produced under its own imprint, as they were run as civil service departments and not as publishing houses. But the lesson of this is clear in retrospect: except for the Oxford English course, now revised beyond recognition, hardly a single primary text in English of the colonial period remains in use, whereas the works of Fagunwa, Odunjo, Nwana and dozens of others first published in the forties and fifties remain the basis of African language teaching throughout the continent, with total sales running into millions of copies.

When we turn to the field of academic African Studies, the situation is not quite analogous. While school books were written and produced for the African market, African Studies materials were produced for a market almost the whole of which was outside Africa. The books produced to serve this market, though more sophisticated and based on much more rigorous research, link directly with the Golden Bough, the missionary accounts and the travellers' tales, in that the objectives were to transmit selected information to an outside audience either to further, generally, the study of man, to better appreciate the possibilities of primary production in Africa or simply to fill gaps in geographical knowledge. In a period when African Studies were conducted (except in a few Southern African centres, the then Rhodes-Livingstone Institute, Makerere and Achimota) from wholly European or American bases, publications tended to be directed automatically towards similarly based researchers and the growing university enrolments, particularly in social anthropology.

Whatever ambivalences now prevail in Africa over the role of social anthropology in African academic history, an immense amount of invaluable recording work was done and many books of enduring significance were published. In this the International African Institute played a vital part. Under the directorship of the late Daryll Forde, through the medium of the Oxford University Press and with financial support from the Colonial Office, a range of books was published, many of which have become anthropological classics. They remain the basis of the majority of contemporary university social anthropology curricula in the Commonwealth, are widely used in the United States and, in translation, throughout the world. Fortes' and Evans-Pritchard's *African Political Systems*, first published in 1940, Radcliffe-Brown's *African Systems of Kinship and Marriage* and to a lesser extent Forde's *African Worlds*, continue to provide readings in the basic theoretical models of the subject. Alongside these symposia, numbers of the great field classics, including Fortes on the Tallensi and Evans-Pritchard's later books on the Nuer together with dozens of others, appeared under the IAI imprint. The booklets in the ethnographic survey carried out by the IAI from a mixture of primary and secondary sources are sometimes overlooked, but these provide invaluable source material for current research and are to some extent interdisciplinary.

If the most prolific and concentrated publishing in this period was in social anthropology it should not be implied that the bookshelves were barren of important work in other subjects. The linguists under Professor Tucker at SOAS published regularly, Harrison-Church produced the first edition of *West Africa*, Alimen her survey of African prehistory, Bauer his controversial *West African Trade*, and in history the first products of the move away from imperial history towards a genuine African history came with K. O. Dike's *Trade and Politics in the Niger Delta*, published in 1956, and from Hodgkin, Fyfe, Fage and others. But such pioneering works, unless classified as imperial history, had no comfortable niche in a publisher's ongoing series and no subsidy from either government or foundation. A few publishers, particularly Oxford, were ready to take on books based on original historical research, but only subject to more stringent market evaluation than for books in subsidised series.

The fate of the serious novelists and poets was more extreme. In most cases there was no option but to self-publish, and this inevitably restricted the writing to what could be sold in a very narrow local market. Though Tutuola, really a Yoruba novelist using English as his medium, benefited from a fashion for the bizarre, R. E. G. Armattoe published himself, Cyprian Ekwensi made do with school and local imprints and even Chinua Achebe's *Things Fall Apart*, one of the few African novels accepted and modestly praised on publication in hardback in London, was only saved from oblivion by Heinemann's decision to launch the

African Writers' Series. In this area the Francophone countries were much better served. Assimilation, whatever its other faults, at least assumed that the assimilé should have an accepted voice. Through *Présence Africaine* and through ordinary French trade houses a collection of prose and poetry appeared, years in advance, and with a degree of philosophical and stylistic sophistication, which the English-speaking writers as a whole have yet, in their own way, fully to match.

The above implies that it was a hard struggle for Africans to get relevant material published and that publishing was the exclusive preserve of the colonial countries and their agencies. While this is largely true of the educational field and for those who wished to publish for an international audience, it would have been surprising if, in West Africa particularly, entrepreneurial skills had not been applied to those parts of the domestic market which were not serviced from overseas. There were, in the fields of political pamphleteering and popular literature, two such fields. These were most energetically pursued by numerous small publishing houses, often ephemeral offshoots of bookshops or small printing presses or the work of a single writer marketing his products through an army of small boys working on tiny commissions. Neither the number of titles nor the volume in which they were printed, in Accra, Ibadan or above all in Onitsha, can at this stage ever be known, but anyone who crossed the Niger on the old ferry at Onitsha will know that the former probably runs into thousands and the latter most certainly into millions. Alongside *Rosemary and the Taxi Driver* and *The Husband and Wife who Beat Themselves* (their deviance was more grammatical than sexual), there was a range of educational support material including model answers, question and answer, revision notes and examination hints, often of dubious quality but which at their best have provided foundations for presses such as Onibonoje, now one of Nigeria's larger indigenous educational houses. It has been argued whether these presses could eventually have expanded to provide the materials for post-colonial educational expansion but were deprived of their major market by the powerful incursion of the foreign presses, or whether the instability of small-scale West African businesses at that time would, of itself, have precluded growth and development.

National independence parties all over Africa had at the centre of their political platforms some form of accelerated development plan for education. Throughout the continent, well before the actual date of independence, the colonial authorities were encouraged and cajoled by the newly elected representative bodies to spend accumulated funds on education. Primary school enrolments doubled and redoubled in very short periods. The old secondary schools and university colleges were expanded and new ones planned to meet the increased (through grossly underestimated) manpower projections for the new states. European publishers, accustomed to looking to the USA, the white Commonwealth, India and Egypt as their principal export markets, were jolted into a realisation of the market potential as the books designed and priced for modest print runs were demanded in hundreds of thousands. For the few British houses traditionally serving the African market this was a period of rapidly rising sales, high profit margins and low operating costs, resulting from the colonial method of book supply. Some houses responded to this creatively and immediately, while others, slower to appreciate what was happening, were happy to enjoy the immediate benefits while failing to plan for the future. Longmans, Green, together with Oxford University Press were the quickest to respond. In 1957, outside Capetown, Longman's presence was confined to single sales representatives in Ibadan and Nairobi, while by 1962 there were nine locally registered companies and seven distribution points. Local manufacture was established on a substantial scale in Nigeria and Kenya and senior African staff employed in all centres. The OUP pattern was similar, though for structural reasons Oxford houses were designated branches and not companies. Other companies gradually followed suit, though Macmillan, later on the scene than the others, preferred a different approach.

In financial terms this involved investment in low cost office and warehouse buildings, employment of local staff and payment of local corporation tax on easily remittable profits. What is often forgotten is the huge investment in new publications which took place at this time. Alongside the growth in enrolments came the rewriting of almost all syllabuses at both primary and secondary levels and the demand for rapid production of more appropriate educational books and materials. Whatever view is taken of the role played by the metropolitan publishing houses in English-speaking Africa, it would have been impossible to produce the new materials which came onto the market in the 1960s anything like so quickly and efficiently by any other means, and if the price was an increase in the earnings of some foreign houses and a small addition to the foreign exchange bill, it was a cheap one for the service rendered.

In publishing terms this was a period of great excitement. There was, in effect, a clean sheet. New curricula demanded new books, and new books, new authors. For the first time African writers were not merely encouraged but begged to prepare new materials. In many cases the results were a surprise both to the houses undertaking publication and to an educational establishment trained to think of white authors as the key to examination success. Of course, the new thinking was greatly assisted by those Europeans who understood and identified with African scholarly and educational objectives and brought their skills to bear in forwarding them. Among these the historians particularly must be mentioned, and among the historians particularly Basil Davidson. *Old Africa Rediscovered* was the timely catalyst that liberated cautious African history publishers from their preoccupation with small-scale studies and their imperial constrictions, and cleared the path for the writing of general history for schools and colleges. It should also be said that at the time of its publication a less meticulously researched and less thoroughly documented book from a well-known journalist could as easily have retarded this process as much as it was in fact advanced by *Old Africa Rediscovered*. From this base grew the *Growth of African Civilization* series (Basil Davidson's own title) which contains two of his own books and which has in recent years carried hundreds of thousands of students through their certificate examinations.

The development of new school materials went far beyond the behavioural sciences. New curricula resulted in books concentrating on functional English and the special problems of African students. In maths, parallel experiments in new maths teaching in Ghana and Nigeria put African-developed course materials on the market at much the same time as they became available in the UK, and in other subjects similar developments were followed by new and better materials. In school publishing we have now reached the point at which books developed and written in Africa are beginning to be adapted for use in the metropolitan countries, a refreshing change from the one-way traffic of the past.

At a scholarly level and in creative writing it would be difficult without omission to single out individual titles from the work of the last decade. The growth and development of African universities and the interest in African studies and literature in Europe, America and elsewhere has made possible the publication of a range of books and journals which could not have been contemplated fifteen years ago. However, the greater part of this publishing, unlike that of school materials, continues to be done outside Africa. The reasons for this are, to some extent, the same as those already mentioned for an earlier period—a high proportion of purchasers are elsewhere—but there are also more fundamental reasons, relating to the complex commercial infrastructure of African nations, to the uneven development of African university presses and to continued managerial problems in the university bookshops.

University vice-chancellors are naturally interested in obtaining the best possible standards of production and distribution for the products of their universities' researchers, and the writers themselves in obtaining the best editorial services and effective and regular payment of royalties. Also, the majority of African scholars are, as yet, concerned to demonstrate academic parity with the older universities and the imprint of an international house thus has an added significance. This will change, but only with time and only in part, since contributors to international scholarship will always be attracted to publishers marketing effectively across national and continental frontiers.

Leaving aside, for reasons already given, the many individual titles of this period, I would like to concentrate briefly on three publishing developments which are of particular significance. The first of these is *Black Orpheus*, which, although a magazine, is, I think legitimately to be considered a part of book publishing. Founded in 1957 in Ibadan, *Black Orpheus*, along with Mbari and Mbari Publications, was a part of Ulli Beier's overall scheme which set out to unravel and redirect the work of many young artists whose vision either remained inward to their own culture or was occluded by the wrong kind of exposure to Western aesthetics. In retrospect, the scheme, though ephemeral, was brilliantly successful in bridging this gap, and *Black Orpheus*, the literate voice of the process, will be regarded as a landmark in African publishing history and increasingly become a collectors' piece. The covers and special display typeface were designed by Suzanne Wenger and screen printed by Tayo Aiyegbusi. The content was rich in early work not only of the West African poets and playwrights but also of writers from all over the continent, many of whom, like Rabearivelo, La Guma, Aghostino Neto and Honwana, are now focal points in African literary history.

The weakness of *Black Orpheus* was two-fold. Firstly, it had no sound commercial base. Founded with help from the Western State Ministry of

Education, it was later funded and distributed by Longman Nigeria on a non-profit-making basis which it could never outgrow without advertisements as long as it maintained the lavish production methods which, in great part, gave it its individuality. Secondly, and more importantly, it depended too heavily on the particular commitment of Ulli Beier. His insistence on his own, possibly esoteric, standards brought him into conflict with some of his African co-editors and contributors, and it may be that *Black Orpheus* had served its purpose when it ceased regular publication in 1970. However, in its time it made a contribution to the development of the African creative process which will increasingly be recognised as unique.

If *Black Orpheus* was a commercial failure but a qualitative success it looked, at its inception, as if the Heinemann African Writers' Series might be exactly the opposite. In fact it has demonstrated the long-term importance of good commercial thinking in forwarding a new literary movement. The decision to launch the Series was taken in 1959 by Van Milne and Alan Hill, directors of Heinemann Educational Books. partly to ensure, so trade lore maintains, the continued publication of Achebe's *Things Fall Apart*, then available expensively and only in hardback from William Heinemann. In its early stages the series looked undiscriminating but, owing to the demand for African writing and to some useful examination settings, the series was firmly established and over the years has been able to apply increasingly rigorous editorial standards to the work included. Now, with over 150 titles in print, it is the established mouthpiece of African writers in English (and latterly in translation), fully justifying what must have been a rather hazardous decision for an educational house, and the Series' early quantitative approach. It has also brought Heinemann into the major league of British publishers operating in Africa.

The third publishing development was in African history. If social anthropology was the dominant subject in academic publishing of the forties and fifties, history has, in the last fifteen years, taken over that role. Though sensitive to the publishing done by OUP, Cambridge and Heinemann and to the work of Nelson and Ibadan University Press, of East African Publishing House and some smaller houses such as Cass and Hurst, I believe Longman, and particularly the Ibadan History Series, can claim some pre-eminence in this field. Originally conceived by Kenneth Dike, the series was planned to provide a forum for younger Nigerian historians in the Ibadan History Department. It has been that, but it has also become, latterly under the editorship of Professor Jacob Ajayi, the permanent record of the Ibadan approach to African history, with books from historians only indirectly connected with the school itself. Now approaching its twentieth volume, the IHS has also exerted its influence on many other publications, most notably the two-volume *History of West Africa* edited by Ajayi and Crowder, and the forthcoming *Atlas of African History*.

So much for the product of the publisher's work and its relation to educational and literary trends and developments. I now summarise recent developments in African publishing houses and consider these in relation to the future.

The need for a healthy publishing industry in Africa, serving the needs of the growing school and university populations and the growing number of general readers, is self-evident. What is not always so self-evident, although the recent Ife conference on African publishing began seriously to discuss this, is the range of alternative approaches to this problem and the requirements for the skills necessary to make any constructive change of direction or even to continue to develop along current lines.

Publishing is, contrary to appearances, a complex industry. Because there is no technically sophisticated and expensive machinery involved and because many educationists have at one time or another edited and produced some kind of printed material it often appears, superficially, that the publisher's principal resource is merely adequate finance. In Africa especially, where the familiar names are those of the internationally successful few, it is often assumed that publishing is a straightforward and high-yielding investment. In fact it is not. The majority of book publishers, worldwide, find it very difficult to turn in regular net profits, let alone to generate the cash surpluses necessary to finance major new publishing programmes. New ventures in educational publishing in Europe and America are relatively rare and except with the backing of people more interested in education than return on capital, most unlikely to succeed. There is no mystery about this. School books bear high initial expenses, and to fit into the traditional price structure these initial expenses must be amortised either by writing them off and taking a loss on the first printing or by accepting reduced profits on the first two or three printings. Thus a young educational house working in an open market situation must accept, and have means of coping with, the fact that the profitability, and even more significantly the cash profile, would be regarded by most investors or development banks as a poor risk. With academic publishing the position is even more complex and uncertain. Publishing for a limited market the publisher is obliged, to achieve economic print runs, to lock up his resources in stock over long periods with the danger of heavy write-off and returns from booksellers if his judgment has been faulty. A new educational publisher in Africa has, therefore, not only to possess the traditional skills in selection, production, marketing and distribution but also to be able to forecast, plan and manage a testing financial situation, in all probability against a background of impatience and lack of comprehension from his backers, whether private or public. In addition he has to compete with established international houses which employ experienced African staff and can call upon supportive skills from headquarters.

In this situation it is hardly surprising that the temptation to exert political influence and restrict the free market has proved strong, most of all in those countries committed to or moving towards state control of the industrial sector.

Two points mentioned earlier can now be expanded in relation to the efforts of some new states to set up state publishing companies: firstly the question of single list recommendation, and secondly the approach taken by Macmillan in gaining a foothold in the African educational market. Since much information on the Macmillan role has already been published in the *Sunday Times*, in a special article on Tanzania in *Africa*, of June 1973 and in the 'Essah' report prepared for the first military government in Ghana, I do not need to go into detail on the facts. In any case the Macmillan management of the time has now changed and is pursuing different policies. What it does demonstrate, however, is the kind of commercial opportunism, coupled with managerial indifference in serving local needs, which brings the so-called multinationals into general disrepute in Africa. Certainly, in publishing, in the aftermath of Macmillan's involvement in state enterprises many other companies have found the most straightforward business propositions treated with excessive caution and even suspicion.

Briefly, when the Nkrumah government in Ghana turned towards state ownership of industry, a high priority, since Nkrumah was acutely conscious of his need for information control, was a state publishing complex through which the book requirements of the nation could be locally edited, printed and distributed. An agreement was consequently signed with Macmillan under which they became a partner in the Ghana Publishing Corporation with a brief to provide management and training. Later similar agreements were made in Uganda, Tanzania and Zambia.

All these agreements have now expired or been terminated and, generally, in those countries book supplies are limited, they are frequently still brought in from abroad and paid for in foreign exchange, there is little or no choice for schools, there are fewer bookshops, and publishing skills lag behind those countries which opted for a more open system. The question here is not only that of the service provided by the overseas partner, but equally importantly whether, at the present stage of development, state control, as opposed to state or national participation, is a realistic means of achieving this kind of national objective without damaging children's educational prospects.

Macmillan's problems, which in some measure would have been the same for any other house embarking on the same programme, were, firstly, to provide the necessary managerial skills to develop their African partnerships and which they did not possess at their own headquarters; secondly, to work through what were, inevitably, civil service procedures, with boards many of whose members were not only ignorant of publishing but often of any kind of business, and, thirdly, to use inadequately equipped and inefficient presses. The obvious commercial advantage of having effective control of main course textbook publishing was thus dissipated by failure in effective list-building, inadequate editorial control, late delivery and inefficient distribution. To counter this, huge purchases had to be made from abroad, for some of which, at least, the parent company made little, if any, price concession. At the same time other publishers, both foreign and local, finding themselves excluded from the market, ceased developing new materials, bookshops were unable to continue in the face of state monopoly over the most lucrative part of their business, and all but a few authors, drawing substantial royalties from their connection with the state house and its partners, found it a waste of time to continue writing.

How then should a developing nation in Africa attempt to solve these problems? So far the Nigerian solution seems the most likely to succeed. Here local and expatriate companies are expected to compete with each other and state supported enterprises have not, so far, been granted monopolies. The foreign publishers have been treated in exactly the same way as other foreign companies and have all recently issued 40 per cent of their share capital to Nigerian citizens. Local authorship is encouraged but not prescribed and local printing expected where possible but again, while facilities remain unable to serve the whole of the rapidly expanding market, not prescribed. Nigeria has the largest number of publishers, the greatest choice of books, by far the largest number of local authors and the most efficient book distribution system in the whole of Africa. But Nigeria can never be the model for the rest of Africa. In terms of market size, Sierra Leone and Malaŵi cannot sustain local and foreign companies operating in open competition for the same sections of the market, and they, together with Uganda, Liberia and the smaller French-speaking countries, must make compromises which can encourage local publishing while at the same time ensuring adequate breadth of choice in the schools, dynamic attitudes to the production of new materials and bookshops that can afford to hold the range of books necessary to to the country's development.

Perhaps Kenya, a middle-sized market, can show the way. By allowing foreign and local private houses a share of the market alongside the products of a government foundation acting for the state curriculum body, educational variety is achieved and an adequate supply of imports serving the needs of higher education and the general reader assured. Had East African Publishing House under John Nottingham showed a little less enthusiasm for pioneering in the academic and general market and more skills in the area of financial management mentioned above, the situation might have been even closer to the model outlined.

Some such solution is in the best interests of all African countries and of scholarship in general. The list of African publishers recently collected by Hans Zell's *African Publishing Record* is impressive. It is also growing in number and skills year by year. But with international copyright threatened under the Paris revisions to the Berne and Universal Copyright Conventions, with national governments anxiously husbanding their foreign exchange reserves and with economic nationalism ready to overrule commonsense on educational and scholarly needs, a model needs to be established which can apply not only in those countries already established but also in the new Portuguese-speaking nations and ultimately in Zimbabwe and the independent states of southern Africa.

K. A. B. Jones-Quartey

The West African Press Since the Second World War— A Bibliographical Review

Establishment, progress and problems : the 1950s

There have been many studies on the African press, both sectionally and in 'whole', since the 1950s. In this review we deal with texts written in English only, though some of the last papers to be drawn upon for the Francophone areas are translations from the French.

A good starting point in the putting together of an overall picture of the West African press since the Second World War is to be found in the 1956 revision of the work of the late Lord Hailey and his associates, *An African Survey*, which covered as far as possible facts and figures to 1955.[1] George H. T. Kimble's reference work *Tropical Africa*, published in 1960, extends the period coverage by four or five significant development years.[2]

The findings recorded in these two surveys are augmented by the following: the report of Arno G. Huth to the International Cooperation Administration of Washington D.C., entitled *Communications Media in Tropical Africa*;[3] the *Report on the Press in West Africa*, prepared in 1959/60 by an *ad hoc* body called the Committee on Inter-African Relations and circulated in 1960/61 to a limited readership by the Ibadan University Department of Adult Education and Extra-Mural Studies;[4] *Muffled Drums* and *Mass Communication in Africa—An Annotated Bibliography*, both by William A. Hachten and both published in 1971 ;[5] and, lastly, some of the specialist papers presented at a seminar on the West African mass media at the University of Ghana, Legon, in July 1971, which form the contents of a book now being produced by a Nigerian publishing company.[6]

An African Survey opens its examination of the 'General Position of the Press' of the 'Colonial Dependencies' with the observation that 'the existence of an indigenous African press presupposes a relatively high degree of literacy, and [that] while circulation increases with literacy the newspaper is itself a great stimulus to its [own] expansion'.[7] It adds the well-known claim that figures quoted for the number of copies printed for any particular newspaper or press in Africa do not need to be the 'true indication of the extent of their circulation', since many literate buyers read out the news and comments in the paper to many more who are illiterate. It then mentions the 'salient problems' the African press constantly faces: the 'provision of an adequate news service'; the 'attainment of a reasonable standard of journalism and reporting'; the 'use of efficient machinery and technical staff', and the 'burdensome question of distribution'. Finally, it declares that the key to the solution of any or all of these problems lies with *the money*, and that financing in turn implies political influence and the control of press policy, and whether the financial backing comes from internal or external sources.

This survey found that the professional system of training essential to a high standard of journalism was not then available in Africa. No general courses in journalism, but only some training in typography, could be had in the colonial dependencies, and in Francophone Africa only the then Belgian Congo (now Zaïre) had any form of training at all. In French-ruled Senegal all the pressmen, mostly white Frenchmen, were members of the Union of Journalists of French West Africa, a branch of the National Union of French Journalists, with headquarters, of course, in Paris. For Anglophone Africa some training in journalism was then being provided *in London*. Eight scholarship awards were made in 1951 to working African journalists for such overseas training, but in 1954 only one was actually in Britain for the course.[8]

Then follows a significant passage in *Survey* which we must here quote in full, as demonstrating to perfection the typical attitudinal conception of moral/ managerial commitment towards the colonial 'wards' on the part of the metropolitan fathers and mentors:

> The recognition of the value of the Native newspaper, and especially of that printed in the vernacular, in consolidating and extending literacy and in fostering interest in general development and progress, has led to the issue by Public Relations Offices and Departments of Information, of the 'official' news-sheets and papers now current in all African Colonies. In meeting the need for the creation of a reliable press, Colonial Governments are presented with three possibilities. They may choose (1) to establish an official newspaper; (2) to encourage a European-sponsored or directed journal; or (3) to grant technical and financial aid towards developing a privately owned Native paper. But in most cases the favourite solution has been to rely upon the Public Relations Office or its French, Belgian, and Portuguese equivalent, and the official newspapers produced from this source often attain large circulations.[9]

No further comment on that passage from the present writer is necessary.

The report goes on to list some of the 'typical official newspapers' established on the strength of these conceptions and attitudes, such as *Hygiène et alimentation* (French Cameroons, 10,000 copies), *La Voix du Congolais* (Belgian Congo), '. . . published weekly and intended primarily for *évolués*', and *Nos Images*, 'which has a wide circulation among the less literate mass of the population . . .'[10]

An African Survey also deals with news service, which, during and after the war years, was again an important aspect of the West African mass media establishment. British West Africa was almost wholly dependent upon the government-controlled Central Office of Information (COI) in London, acting through Regional Information and Public Relations Officers in the British overseas territories. News and information were sent out daily to overseas re-users, by cable, wireless and airmail through the London Press Service. The French-controlled territories used the Paris-based *Service de l'Information* and *Agence France Presse*, while in the Belgian Congo the newspapers were issued with the texts of the broadcasts of *Radio Congo Belge*, with the also-official Section de l'Information supplying a regular photographic service.

Hailey's *Survey* also considered the underlying intractability of the financial incapacity of most, if not all, colonial press establishments and operations, the consequential lowness of standards, and, not least, that awful business involving the theory and practice of press freedom, as well as the first appearance of the phenomenon of 'official newspapers', owned and run by governments.

On all of these realities George Kimble's *Tropical Africa* offers supporting material. His own account is prefaced with the observation that most tropical African newspapers run in the 1950s for the benefit of Africans were published in Commonwealth West Africa, and that 'it was here that the African intellectual, and his progeny the nationalist, first emerged; and for such, journalism provided one of the very few professional opportunities . . .'[11]

Here, said Kimble, at their best the newspapers stood comparison with those of 'almost any medium-sized American town', being 'competently printed, well illustrated and thoughtfully edited . . .'. The only trouble was that there were few such newspapers. Indeed it was only after 1947 when Cecil King's *Daily Mirror* Group, of London, took an investment interest in developing a West African newspaper market, that a modern, expansive look came into journalism in this region. Within a decade the differences were to be seen clearly, e.g. in the combined weekly circulation aggregate of approximately 150,000 copies, with a Sunday figure of another 100,000, from the three daily newspapers established by the Mirror Group, in Sierra Leone (*Daily Mail*), the then Gold Coast (*Daily Graphic*), and Nigeria (*Daily Times*). The others—the 'great majority of the newspapers', adds *Tropical Africa*—were 'inadequately staffed, indifferently written and edited, and poorly printed on presses of antique design'.[12]

Some other relevant and interesting figures may now be given here. According to Hailey, quoting from various sources, there were in 1954 some 12 'established newspapers' in Ghana and 'at least' 25 in Nigeria, with Dr Nnamdi Azikiwe's *West African Pilot* selling at about 17,000 copies daily, and Ghana's *Graphic* and Nigeria's *Daily Times* registering 'circulations of between 44,000 and 55,000'.[13] Kimble, using United Nations *Statistical Yearbook* figures for 1957-59, gives the table shown on the facing page for daily newspapers.

Kimble states that in spite of all its shortcomings, 'the African press of Commonwealth West Africa is still a long way ahead of the African press in other sections'. The present author may add that not only was Sierra Leone the first *African* country to see the light of newspaper journalism, in 1801, as well as see the first person of African descent to venture into this field as an owner-editor (1855), but that the then Gold Coast was in its turn the first country in the whole continent to produce a native-born African proprietor-editor, in the

Country	Year	No. of Dailies	Circulation*
Gambia	1955	1	1,000
Ghana	1957	5	101,000
Nigeria	1957	13	224,000
Sierra Leone	1953	4	7,000
Liberia	1957	1	1,000
Francophone West Africa	1957	7	32,000

* The per-thousand of population distribution from these circulation totals are given as 5, 21, 7, 3, 1 and 2 respectively.[14]

person of Charles Bannerman, of James Town, Accra, who started a hand-written paper, the *Accra Herald*, later converted into the printed *West African Herald*, in September 1857.[15]

At about the same period of Professor Kimble's enquiries, another research project on the press in West Africa was being carried out through a Study Group composed of Father J. de Benoist, a Roman Catholic priest then working in Dakar, Senegal, a former editor of *Afrique Nouvelle*; M. Patrice Diouff, a journalist of Dakar; the Nigerian veteran journalist and press historian, Increase Coker; and the present writer, then and for long afterwards, of the Institute of Adult Education at the University of Ghana.[16]

The Study Group was the creation of the Committee on Inter-African Relations (previously called the Continuation Committee), itself the creation of a seminar on 'Representative Government and National Progress' held at Ibadan University, Nigeria, in March 1959, under the auspices of the International Association (formerly Congress) for Cultural Freedom, of Paris. The Study Group prepared the material and the way for a follow-up seminar on 'Press and Progress in West Africa', which took place at the University of Dakar the following year, 1960, under the same sponsorship as the Ibadan seminar but also in collaboration with the University of Dakar and the University Colleges of Ibadan and Ghana, and with the International Press Institute, of Zürich also giving of its experience to the group.

The Committee on Inter-African Relations was headed by a Nigerian, Ayo Ogunsheye, later Professor of Adult Education and Director of the Institute of Adult Education and Extra-Mural Studies at the University of Ibadan. The other members were: M. François Amorin, a Togolese lawyer, Secretary; M. Alexandre Adande, ethnographer and at the time outgoing Minister of Agriculture of Dahomey; M. Denis Levy, the French Professor of Public Law at the University of Dakar; and myself. The papers the Study Group presented were later published as *The Press of West Africa*, edited by the author, who was its chairman. The seminar at Dakar in June 1960 was, like its parent the Ibadan Seminar of March 1959, attended by pressmen, politicians, academics and public men and women of both language groups from the whole area covered.[17]

It is important to emphasise the composition of both these seminars, because until then there had been practically no contact between English-speaking and

French-speaking West Africans on this kind of plane and in this particular specialist area. The point is strongly made by Hachten in *Muffled Drums*:

> Significantly, most of the content of radio, newspapers, television, and movies in Africa is disseminated in the languages of the colonizers—French, English and Portuguese. . . . Furthermore, the barrier between French and English speakers in tropical Africa is a much greater one than in Western Europe. Comparatively few Africans speak or read both languages. . . . The French-English split among educated Africans also has become a formidable cultural barrier. . . . There is, consequently, little contact between anglophonic and francophonic journalists . . .[18]

However, when Hachten proceeds from there to record as 'pioneer' the International Press Institute's 'effort to overcome this barrier by holding a bilingual regional meeting in Dakar, Senegal, in April 1968, for French- and English-speaking journalists to discuss common professional problems',[19] he shows he has missed out something of the history—as already proved above. But the real point here is that this *rapprochement* in 1959, 1960 and 1963 (and perhaps on an undiscovered one or two occasions previously), was one of the significant and widely welcome post-war developments in West Africa. Anglophone/Francophone relations here, developing from Kwame Nkrumah's political moves immediately after Ghana's independence in 1957, have gone on to show possibilities and give promises of future cooperation which were unimaginable before 1960.

The seminar participants noted that during the period under review there was a steady decline in the number of newspapers owned and run by the small man—what one of the reporters called the 'editor-printer'—because he could no longer compete with the 'big men'.

At the same time there has been 'a remarkable growth of newspapers run by public agencies or political groups' and momentously, foreign capital had invaded the admittedly primitive business of West African journalism, French and English language, in a big way[20]—accounting, obviously, for some of the reduction in the number of participants. This challenge, and the superior technical and other standards of the newcomers, had had a stimulating and progressive effect on those 'native-son' enterprises which had survived the invasion, particularly in Nigeria. In some countries circulation figures had jumped up phenomenally, mostly among the foreign-owned and the African language papers.

The table opposite, from *The Press in West Africa* demonstrates this last point and shows what the foreign-owned papers were.[21] It gives the 1955/56 figures taken from *The Press in Africa* by the American Helen Kitchen, published in 1956, as contrasted with those of 1959 supplied from the Study Group papers:

Other points made were: (1) that the indigenous press in Francophone West Africa was 'relatively under-developed' compared with the Anglophone, a point made perhaps only obliquely by other studies; (2) that with the exception of Togoland, African language newspapers were 'almost non-existent' in the French areas, the great increase noted before being achieved in the English speaking

Type	Title of Newspaper	Circulation 1955/56	1959
Daily	*Abidjan-Matin*	3,500–5,000	8–10,000
Daily	*Paris-Dakar*	13,000	20,000
Daily	*Evening News* (Accra)	10,000	60,000
Daily	*Daily Graphic* (Accra)	50,000	75,000
Daily	*Ashanti Pioneer*	15,000	25,000
Daily	*Daily Times* (Lagos)	63,000	99,000
Daily	*West African Pilot* (Lagos)	10,500	40,000
Daily	*Daily Service* (Lagos)	9,500	35,000
Weekly	*Les Echos de l'Afrique Noir* (Dakar)	8,000	15,000
Weekly	*Sunday Mirror* (Accra)	40,000	63,000
Weekly	*Sunday Times* (Lagos)	63,000	127,000
Weekly	*Irohin Yoruba* (Lagos)	25,000	54,000
Bi-weekly	*Liberian Age* (Monrovia)	1,500	3,000

areas almost exclusively; and (3) that Nigeria was far and away ahead of the other countries of the British connection and of politically independent Liberia, in all-round development, in liveliness and, it may be added, in variety and versatility.

The symposium also noted an obvious point already made in Hailey and Kimble, and later by Huth, Hachten and others, the crippling effect of the absence of capital in the indigenous African press, 'It is this which largely condemns most newspapers to the use of obsolete and unreliable plants, makes it well-nigh impossible for them to build up effective machinery for distribution, and difficult to attract staff of better quality.' But this is *effect*. Looking for *cause*, or causes, the symposium found it difficult at first to see 'why so little African capital has been invested in the press', especially in 'relatively wealthy countries like the Ivory Coast and Ghana'. Later it concluded that there were many factors, among them the smallness of internal markets, unequal competition from the foreign-owned sectors, and the absence of African banks, except in Nigeria, which could supply loan capital to African business entrepreneurs in this field.

Other disabilities noted include taxes crippling to small business; inadequate public utilities, like poor transport and road systems; prohibitive postal tariffs and cable rates; the depressed state of the journalist himself; and, looming large, 'the proliferation of newspapers financed out of public funds'—in short, government ownership and influence in this vital field, a subject which includes the problem of the 'freedom of the press' and to which we shall soon return.

Arno Huth's *Communications Media in Tropical Africa* was prepared in 1960. Under the main heading of 'Communications Media—Progress and Problems', he begins by observing that the press is the oldest of the mass media in tropical Africa, but that until recently it had played a rather limited role. Nevertheless he also concedes that the newspapers were conspicuous in their contribution to the struggle for independence, during which many of them acquired both recognition and status. He goes on to say that 'today' [1960] the influence of the press 'is growing rapidly', especially wherever the élite assume leadership in the modernisation process.[22]

Huth found that the circulation of daily newspapers in all of Africa, north and south, amounted to only 1 per cent of the world's total, whereas South America, by no means an advanced technological and industrial area, accounted for 4 per cent, and Asia 22 per cent. Moreover, in sub-Sahara Africa, he found the ratio to be even lower, about one-third of 1 per cent. He found that one group of fifteen countries and territories, with a combined population of twelve million, had no daily papers at all of any kind, not even a government bulletin! And except in Ghana and Rhodesia there was in 1960 less than one copy of a daily newspaper for every 100 persons in Africa, as compared with 3·5 in Asia and 7·9 in South America.

The whole continent in 1960 boasted only 220-250 dailies, the combined circulation of which numbered less than three million. In the sub-Sahara region only 125 of these dailies were in operation circulating 900,000 copies, together with 330 out of 835 non-daily publications and 680 out of 1,382 periodicals.

Huth comments on the wide variety of press activities in Ethiopia, Rhodesia, Nigeria and Senegal, which centre only on a few major cities. Others, like Guinea, Niger, Togo and Upper Volta, met the demand for news by mere mimeographed (cyclostyled) bulletins published daily either by the government or by *Agence France-Presse*, and distributed in lots of 600 to 1,200 copies each. In Mauritania there were no papers at all in 1960, except a four-page monthly news sheet prepared by the government and printed in Dakar. Most of these bulletins contained nothing but excerpts from agency despatches, government releases, and statements by the Prime Minister and members of the Cabinet.

Huth is one more commentator who mentions the steadily growing number of papers owned and operated by African governments or political parties by the end of the decade, as well as the many still controlled even then by non-Africans —colonial governments, religious groups, foreign industrial enterprises and, especially, British concerns. He too, naturally, mentions the *Daily Mirror* group of London and adds the similar experience of the French-speaking countries; all the latter showed massive French ownership of what press there was. In addition, the Francophone areas exhibited a phenomenon strange to the Anglophone countries, namely, professional journalists working there who were White French in origin.

Huth also discusses the use of African languages (some 58 of them) in many of the countries covered; the strictly local character of most African papers, with few correspondents elsewhere in the country and none abroad; the very serious obstacle of the shortage of professional African journalists and their poor command of English; and *the absence of any book publishing*.[23]

The 1960s and freedom of the press

We now turn to one of William A. Hachten's two publications for the beginning of our review of the decade between 1960 and 1970.

Muffled Drums is in two parts: 'Overview of News Communications in Africa' and 'Case Studies of News Media Systems'. Among the author's most interesting discussions for us in this review are those dealing with government involvement in the media, 'an African press for the Africans' (of Nigeria and Ghana), and what Hachten describes as the 'lingering influence of France [in e.g.] Ivory Coast and Senegal'.

On the looming role of African governments in the operation of the media, the author states that once Independence had been achieved the pressures began to grow for the Africanisation of the news media. Questions were quickly raised among the newly free leaders about ownership and control. One was whether they should permit the European ownership of newspapers to continue after Independence; another was what should be done by a new African government to mass media systems that were so thoroughly Europeanised in influence and content.

Hachten found in 1970 that the first decade after Independence had evinced a clear answer to these questions, namely: the new African governments' assumption themselves of a large degree of ownership and control of all the media. The patterns of control thus established were bound to affect the African news media for many decades to come. He cites the growing government involvement, the decline of independent newspapers and the sharp increase in the number of government-owned official ones; the rapid and extensive expansion of now completely national ministries of information; the nationalisation of radio and TV broadcasting; and the establishment of regional news agencies.[24] These trends, among others, are to be noted particularly here as differentiating the nature of the mass media of the sixties from that of the fifties. They were to be identified with one-party ideology and its rejection of political dissent and even of divergent views, with local mistrust of foreign media ownership, and with lack of economic opportunities and facilities.

As for Francophone Africa, it had never had much of an independent press anyway; and now the one big French family newspaper-chain owners, the de Breteuils, had been reduced from their holdings of five dailies in five towns to a mere two, in Senegal and Cameroun: *Dakar-Matin* (which ceased in 1970 and made way for a new national paper, *Le Soleil du Sénégal*) and *La Presse du Cameroun*.

In the English-speaking countries both Nigeria and Ghana had major commercial/popular newspapers owned and run under their Information departments or ministries. This government ownership and intervention, not to talk of control, had started with the first independent governments: in Ghana under the CPP and in Nigeria from 1961. The *Morning Post* and the *Sunday Post* of Lagos, the *Daily Sketch* in the then Western Region, *New Nigeria* in the north, in the east *Nigerian Outlook* (which was renamed *Biafran Sun* during the civil war), in Ghana the *Daily Graphic* and the *Ghanaian Times*, are outstanding examples of predominant government operation and control of the press. In addition there are of course the radio and TV services, which are, and cannot be otherwise than, government-financed and directed.

The radical changes between the 1950s and 1960s are particularly indicated by the installation and proliferation of national news agencies. We are reminded in this book that until the mid-1950s the only national news agency in the whole of Africa was the South African Press Association, which was non-governmental and was established in 1938 to 'supply domestic and foreign news' to the press of South Africa, the then Northern and Southern Rhodesia, and the Portuguese territories.[25]

In 1956 what Hachten states was the first government-controlled African news service, the Middle East News Agency, started in Cairo. Ghana was next with its 'GNA' in 1957, when the country became independent, and by 1969 there were no fewer than twenty-seven official and semi-official African news services in operation on the continent, including such outsiders as the US Information Agency and the other news-and-information services of the various embassies. Nigeria, though, and Tanzania, for different reasons, remained without national news agencies during this period, but Nigeria had plans to introduce one at a suitable date.

Hachten's discussion of the indigenisation of the African press features Nigeria and Ghana. This is rather logical and inescapable, for these are the two countries in all of Africa where most progress has been maintained in mass media history and development; in the case of Nigeria from the 1860s to the present time, especially in printed journalism though actual literary quality here is painfully mixed; and in the case of Ghana pioneering and editorial excellence were held together from 1857 until the departure of J. B. Danquah in 1934 and Nnamdi Azikiwe in 1937 from the scene.[26] These are the two countries in which the press, as in Sierra Leone, but more massively and more spectacularly so, fought for and helped to achieve political freedom, especially during the last ten years before Ghana's Independence in 1957. This is also where modernisation, for better or for worse, wears a somewhat less improbable face than elsewhere in Anglophone West Africa, and where at the same time traditional cultures are in earnest promotion, not least, as the author demonstrates, through the media, particularly in Nigeria.

If this picture differs considerably from that of Ivory Coast or Senegal, especially in historical and humanistic terms, the reasons lie deeply anchored in the differences in colonial policies between the French and the British; nor need this reviewer rehearse here the well-aired and well-established analyses on French cultural assimilationism and British cultural aloofness—except to remind the neutral observer how as a result a few local people, in the one case, learnt more in a better way, and in the other many learnt less in a worse way! But in the end 'British' West Africa came out far better prepared to promote the printed word and receive the new electronic and machine technology than the 'French' areas. 'No other black African nation came close to Nigeria in media facilities and audiences', with her '17 working [radio] transmitters that broadcast to 690,625 sets, reaching 8 to 10 million people' in many indigenous languages, by 1967; together with her 18 daily newspapers, 15 weeklies, and 22 periodicals; 5 television programming stations and 4 relay stations operating 180 hours weekly through (a partly estimated) 63,000-odd sets. In Ivory Coast, on the contrary, there were by 1965 only about 1·7 radio sets and 0·4 daily newspapers circulated per 100 Ivoriens, almost entirely in French.[27]

The 1970s

Among the latest studies and commentaries on this subject will be the seminar/ symposium papers mentioned above, due for publication as *The Communication Media in West Africa*. It will be made up of the collection of the papers presented at an All-West Africa Mass Media Seminar, held at the University of Ghana, Legon, in July 1971, under the joint-promotion of the Africa Advisory Committee of the International Association for Culture Freedom, and the Institute of Adult Education, University of Ghana.[28] They were written on commission by journalists, mass media practitioners, government information ministry/ department officers, and academics of both language connections, English and French, representing nine countries, but all African.

This seminar was designed as a follow-up to the Dakar occasion of 1960. The results tend to show: (*a*) oscillating physical development but with an overall upward trend in technology and technicality; but (*b*) a record of recurrent violence of change in the political state, affecting the mass media and subjecting them to editorial and intellectual instability and uncertainty. In Ghana and Sierra Leone the press is now for the most part timorous and sycophantic, in Nigeria rebellious, on and off, in Francophone West Africa acquiescent and subdued politically.

All students of the subject, not the least articulate of whom are the Africans themselves, concede that the decade of the 1960s is far and away the decade in which the mass media in west Africa—as in the 'Third World' generally—were converted partly into hopeful instruments of social change and improvement through programmed communication, and partly into captive tools of one-party or military government propaganda; the decade in which press freedom became a real problem for government, political party, military junta and journalist alike.

Under (*a*) above there are substantial areas of agreement between this group of African historians and observers of the Anglophone sector and most of the non-African authors we have been reviewing. Findings on facts, figures, dates and incidents agree with or approxiamte one another on the English-speaking countries. Where an author like Hachten goes slightly wrong, on, say, the early history of the Sierra Leone and Ghana presses,[29] it would be perhaps because he stopped too soon in his reading of Christopher Fyfe on Sierra Leone, or missed some later, corrective material on Ghana by Jones-Quartey.

Not so, though, in respect of Francophone Africa. Here one has to adopt an attitude of serious doubt as to the validity of any of the evidence produced by rival claimants to veracity in almost any case presented. For instance, le Père de Benoist, in *The Press in West Africa*; William Hachten, in *Muffled Drums*, and Abdou Cissé, a Senegalese freelance journalist and correspondent, in his paper for the 1971 Legon Seminar entitled 'An Historical Sketch of the French-African Press,' all differ wildly from one another, on the chronologies of Senegal and

Ivory Coast—to name just two of many—and on the records of individual papers, the circumstances of particular times, places, performances, and so on.[30]

All the contributors more or less paint the same basic picture: of financial poverty in the mass media in West Africa, except, qualifiedly, in Nigeria, Ivory Coast or Senegal; of the disappearance of the small press and the now almost complete domination of the scene by the big government newspapers and presses; of the improvement of facilities for permanent local training professionally, though only in Nigeria and Ghana[31]; of low literary and professional standards in the written press, except in Nigeria, where, even so, standards are wildly mixed, or in Senegal or Ivory Coast, where French cultural and intellectual norms have a stranglehold on the native Africans . . .

Better to turn from these now to our last topic: freedom of the press. The basic point is the freedom of the press to criticise government policy and government action. Not surprisingly, the commentators don't always agree on any one solution to the problem—not even the 'third-worlders' themselves. Why should they? Few great human questions involving emotions and personal interests ever did or ever could evoke the same answer.

The writers and editors of *The Press in West Africa* asked: 'How free is the press in West Africa?' After examining the question from the point of view of laws affecting the press, they went on to say that to carry out such a critical examination of the law, and express some fear of danger in some of it, was 'not to deny that the new governments have a heavy responsibility in maintaining public security and protecting the public against quack and irresponsible journalists'. But, they added, 'what needs to be stressed is that in pursuing such legitimate objectives, public authorities should do nothing to retard or undermine, however unwittingly, such an important institution of public opinion as the press . . .'[32]

A mild stand. Observing how editors can get into trouble with their governments on the question of what or what not to publish, 'as happened in Ghana in December 1967, when four editors on the three government dailies were summarily dismissed after criticising a government contract . . .', Hachten asks: 'At what point does honest, well-meaning press criticism become destructive of the process of orderly national development?'[33] A preliminary answer could be: it all depends on who is asking!

One also-preliminary as well as summary position was clear from the evidence produced by much of the research and the discussion at Legon: the majority of those in control of 'Third World' media today, with their assistants, lieutenants, representatives and employees, believe, or believe they believe, or are made to believe they believe, in the theory and practice of political 'centralism' (or 'democratic centralism'), and in the unification of all the ideas, methods and means employable towards the goals of national development. Since political challenge at whatever level always strikes these people as being of an anti-goal orientation, criticism of independence-era government strategies and tactics assumes in their slightly astigmatic vision this character of challenge, sabotage, and destructiveness. *And press criticism, especially, is to the new rulers and their staffs the prime exemplar of national sabotage of this kind; it is not usually accepted as 'honest [and] well meaning'.*

Some of the papers presented at Legon in 1971 by government information personnel and press officers made, or approximated, this point:

> It is the job of the Government information officer to respond to developing trends, anticipate Government concern and provide useful information. . . . The press or news release remains an important element in the dissemination of information, but to limit action to a press release routine is to fall short of the Government's responsibility to itself and all the community,

said Sam Epelle, Federal Director of Information, Republic of Nigeria; to which Moctar Kébé, at the time Chief of Press Service, Ministry of Foreign Affairs, Senegal, added:

> How can one ask young states faced with the tasks of national edification to tolerate the publication of articles capable of undermining their delicate structures. . . . Just think awhile of the catastrophic consequences of an irresponsible and whimsical press in those countries where instructions from the government are communicated by means of the press only. . . .

Yet it was obvious there was conflict here somewhere, even between and among individual government servants, as there obviously is also between and among systems of belief and practice in the fragile and explosive area of press freedom.

A Senegalese phenomenon of unique nature was here brought to notice. As analysed to the seminar, this consisted of two virtually conflicting rules. One rule expected faithful communication to the public of government news and views by official pressmen and information directors. The other part allowed these same media men, as free citizens and members of the country's journalists' organisation, to leave their offices after work, mount any available platform in town and criticise or even condemn what they had themselves put out earlier in the day for their minister, even perhaps for the President himself. Thus it was possible for the press chief of the Foreign Office, M. Kébé, for instance, to write what we have just quoted above, and yet in an earlier passage also to say:

> The 'politically involved' journalist has the onus of printing the 'official truth', and penalties ranging from imprisonment to banishment for five years or more are imposed on anybody who publishes 'false news', intentionally or otherwise, or who 'discredits' the political institutions or their operations. The opposing party press, constantly watched, is often forced to stop all activities, and it is clearly to be noted that many newspapers, tolerated not long ago by the former colonialists, have disappeared with the attainment of independence in several states. This is the era for 'official' statements in the press, and also for praise to the men in power [at any particular moment].
> It is quite clear that such presses are unable to mobilize the masses and to ensure development. In fact, how can one rely on the sincerity of people engaged in the act of intoxication and propaganda? . . .

a suspicious, tortured bit of ambivalence which may or may not have applied to M. Kébé's own Senegal paradigm. (It is to be noted here that the third member of the Senegal team to the Legon Seminar, the radical freelance, Abdou Cissé, was for years, before and since, in constant trouble with the Senghor regime, and was not able to travel outside his country from soon after the 1971 seminar.) M. Ibrahim Dem, chief of staff in the Senegal President's office at the time, supported M. Kébé generally, and in his own paper re-emphasised the journalistic dualism under description.

In Nigeria, as Increase Coker's paper said, '. . . ownership and control are decisive factors in determining performance, contents and physical quality in this field'. Of the three main groups of newspapers in the country in 1970 (indigenously owned and controlled, originally capitalised and financed from abroad, and government owned and controlled), the 'last named group are the more dominant in the development of the press since independence'. With this majority share ownership, so to speak, came also during the sixties what he describes as 'the changing attitude of governments towards freedom of the press and other media'.

He agreed with the point made by the 1960 Dakar Study Group, namely that in principle the new governments started out with the legitimate intention of protecting both authority and public, in this case 'against the excesses of the media', and that there followed in fact many successful government court actions against independent newspapers for such excesses. But, later, 'political action took various forms. One was to convert the media into instruments of blackmail and national disunity; another was to ban, molest and even physically rough-handle opposing media', though the military governments, he said, were not themselves to blame for the more violent attacks on media people.

Eustace Palmer, of the Department of English at Fourah Bay College, University of Sierra Leone, told a similar story:

> In the pre-independence days there was almost unrestricted freedom of the press, to judge from Wallace-Johnson's outspoken articles and the *Daily Mail*'s independence. Prosecutions of journalists for libel or sedition were mercifully rare. With the intensification of party political activity just before and immediately after independence, however, there was a change in the climate . . .

not so much in any moves by the government against the press as in its attempts to acquire and control it. They culminated in the purchase of the country's biggest paper, the *Daily Mail*, and the establishment of a new one, *Unity*.

The period 1965-67 saw 'the beginning of acrimony between the government and journalists of the anti-government press; prosecutions and libel actions became much more frequent'. *Unity* and the *Daily Mail* actually closed their columns to any correspondents with an independent view. One opposition paper, *We Yone*, however, was allowed to carry on with 'the most scathing denunciation and exposure of government policies', to the extent of the government being forced to change its mind on at least two major occasions as a result of the debate it conducted. Yet by 1971

> the three papers being published are all pro-government; the editor

of one of the largest is also the manager of the other, an unhealthy arrangement which does not make for competition.

Perhaps the most spectacular case of all is that of Ghana, related by K. E. Senanu, another lecturer in English turned press historian for this exercise. He dwells on the theme of a press groping in search of its own image and of proper direction. But this is in the post-Nkrumah/CPP regime; *during* that regime the press 'certainly had a self-conscious image and self-assurance', in Senanu's studied finding. 'The editors, well-paid and cultivated by Nkrumah, were aware of the influence they wielded with the mass of Nkrumah's followers . . .' But was this solid mahogany or just brilliant veneer? Senanu's judgment is that this identity of the CPP press was

> essentially borrowed from the regime. Its self-assurance was that of a man who was constantly receiving narcotic shots in the arm. Its expansive image was of one who has an access of power to dominate rather than to serve responsibly.

Yet he admits:

> It may not have been a popular press. But it was an influential and intimidating one. Not in its own right but as an arm of Nkrumah's political machinery. What the Ghana Press said on continental African politics and, generally, on world affairs, was certainly listened to widely and perhaps even respected in certain circles abroad.

After the 1966 coup, untypically in West Africa, the pattern of press ownership changed, the emphasis shifting from government-owned papers to private and independent ownership. But, however that might have been for the years immediately after 1966, the dominating power of the successor governments was always one to reckon with, even if unevenly and often capriciously exerted or restrained.

Immediately after the coup, a group of Ghanaian academics at the University of Ghana established a fortnightly they called the *Legon Observer*, which others promptly described as one of the best things to have come out of the turmoil of the Nkrumah crash. The *Observer* was without doubt of a predominantly critical character. Officially unattached and beholden to no person or party or government, civilian or military, it was guilty of the occasional rudeness or irreverence and was accused of bookishness and lack of humour by some; but it remained fiercely insistent on its national responsibilities at all times. It was cordially loathed by many members of both the National Liberation Council government (1966-69) and the Busia civilian regime of 1969-72.

The *Observer* was taken to court on a charge of contempt in 1968 and fined, was resented but left alone by the Progress Party, and had a succession of its editors summoned before various members of the second and present (1976) military government, the National Redemption Council (converted into the Supreme Military Council in October 1975). Finally it was rendered suddenly and dramatically *hors de combat* by the action of its printers (and previous guardian angels) in withdrawing their services. *This happened one fine and foolish Monday in June 1974, without warning or notice!* The printers declared that they had not acted under any political pressures, only from business considerations, since the recurrent political difficulties of the *Observer* were beginning to threaten to affect the business of the house. . . . At the time of writing the paper had not resumed publication, though it still hoped to do so, if and when the government granted its request for renewal of licence.

Other members of the Ghana press have also had chequered careers. The *Spokesman*, a fierce little anti-Busia clarion from its birth in 1970, favoured the succeeding regime but ceased publication in 1973/74, with the editor becoming a major media figure in the management echelon of one of the two big government owned dailies, the *Graphic*. The *Echo*, educationally, editorially and politically bold though erratic, was started in 1968 as an independant weekend paper, but is now (1976) in suspended animation, like the *Observer*. Nor should one forget the good old *Ashanti Pioneer* (lately simply the *Pioneer*). Both this paper and its various editors have suffered from recurrent political and financial 'Stop-Go' spasms, ever since the evil day in 1962/63 when the CPP blows fell on them.

Various other editors, including those of the government-owned *Graphic* and *Ghanaian Times*, have had their ups and downs too, not excluding the occasions when the authorities (to be fair to them) have caught these media functionaries professionally and otherwise obtuse or errant. . . . All in all, and everywhere, a period of uneven struggle for the West African press, and one also of monumental misconceiving of role and responsibility on the part of fast-changing, mostly authoritarian governments.

The newspaper press as 'prime'—a personal view

In August 1974 I gave a paper to the Historical Society of Ghana at the University of Cape Coast on 'Some Persistent and Peculiar Problems of Press History Research: The Particular Case of the *Accra/West African Herald*, 1857-73,' and prefaced it with an expression of profound regret that so many students and writers of history should so often neglect one of the greatest of primary sources, namely the newspaper of yesterday and all the days before yesterday. I went on to declare that in my studied opinion a newspaper collection or archive was, as a primary source, every bit the equal in importance of official documents, of private correspondence and personal papers, of diaries, oral testimony, archaeological objects, and any other kind of primary material that anyone else—even the historians themselves—could name.

At question time one Ghanaian history lecturer challenged me to resolve a dilemma. How could I declare the newspaper to be equal to the best of all primary sources of history, and then go on to suggest an opposite view? The sycophantic and poor-quality daily press of Ghana today, he repeated, was unreliable for factuality, accuracy and, therefore, truthfulness and good judgment. In the face of this, could one really go to the 1974 files of the Ghana press, say in 1984, for reliable history?

This was all said there in Ghana itself, remember, and the question was a tough, fundamental one not easy to answer, especially if, like me, one is permanently full to overflowing with enthusiasm for this transcendentally wonderful institution called the newspaper press.

I answered the question at the time with more enthusiasm—I suspected afterwards—than concreteness. But in fact there *is* a concrete, adequate answer why, in spite of all the evidence of perversity that one can bring up against the newspaper press, it is still an overwhelmingly important, vital primary source of history. Stated simply, the answer can run something like this: the newspaper leads you directly to a pinpoint in time and place, and the facts and reflections it provides for that point in history and geography can always be confirmed or rejected by cross-reference and contemporaneous checking—that is, as far as simple factuality and reliability are concerned. But a thousand times more important than mere facts and figures is the ability of the historical newspaper publication to recreate and to provide the reader and the researcher with the living atmosphere of a past era teeming with a myriad elements put into it by *the men, women and things involved in that creation.* A newspaper offers 'the clearest reflection of the nature of contemporary society', says the unsigned introduction to one edition of Francis Williams's *Dangerous Estate*[34]; and, in his *The Right to Know*, Williams himself writes:

> Newspapers are unique barometers of their age. They indicate more plainly than anything else the climate of the societies to which they belong.
>
> This is not simply for the obvious reason that they are a source of news about their time but because the conditions in which they operate, the responsibilities they are expected, or allowed, to fulfil, the pressures they have to meet, their circulation and economic base, the status of those who write for them and their relationship to their readers, all provide a direct insight into the nature of their communities.[35]

He adds words of wisdom from Rebecca West, that 'a community needs news for the same reason that a man needs eyes. It has to see where it is going'.

This leads us into a brief consideration of aspects of the sociology of journalism. The principal socio-psychological determinants for the occurrence, or the invention and development, of the newspaper press in world history are—to accept the lead of Lucy Salmon[36]—the following:

i. social man's curiosity about, his basic *need to know*, what is happening to and with the neighbours both near and far—in modern terms, his interest in news about domestic and foreign affairs—since this impinges upon himself in some fashion or other;

ii. his interest in news, or the current information, about the progress of commerce, i.e. trade; in other words his interest in economic affairs, since for man-in-society the economy is a matter of survival and of life itself for the we-group; and

iii. man's desperate concern with the activities of the rulers, that is, with government and government policy, since this is where all the decisions that affect his life are taken (though of course no one can legislate for him whom to marry or how much to spend on beer!).

To these three we can add at least two more:

i. man's obviously compulsive and fundamental need for communication itself; even more: for the communication of *his* views along with the news; and

ii. the urge to instigate individual as well as social change, upward and outward, by the arousing of fellow citizens to a sense of this necessity.

It is possible of course to find another *x* number of more reasons—like the need for entertainment or for other knowledge—why man in society just had to invent and develop the newspaper press and its principal, scientifically inevitable communication companions-in-development, namely telephony, radio and TV. For the purposes of this presentation, however, the above framework satisfies the presenter.

If these postulates are valid—and it is difficult to see how their sociological moorings can be successfully dislodged—then the press can truly claim to be *prime,* to which term in this context I wish to assign the attributes of transcendentalism. The newspaper as an institution is transcendent within itself, self-creating and self-perpetuating; it is, as well, transcendent of all external conditions, positive and negative, expanding or limiting.

Thus it is that the press can survive and *has* survived inherent and *un*repressible conflict with the state—even, to an extent, with a totalitarian state; thus it can live down its 'yellow'-phase history or render irrelevant the existence of its 'yellow' sector; thus it can recover from an almost uniformly disgraceful performance like that on the Nigerian-'Biafra' civil war,[37] and, equally its frightening demonstration of its power to destroy a Richard Nixon. Thus, in the sixty-year period of importance and achievement which this collection of papers is celebrating (and fittingly celebrating, remembering Basil Davidson's courageous, lifelong efforts for the African cause), the press in the Third World has gone in some places from anti-colonial nationalism (with much literary excellence), through Independence exuberance, violent partisanship, and ideological persecutionism to literary mediocrity or to 'gaping sycophancy'[38] under one-man, one-party, or military rule, but in some other places from strength to strength.

The newspaper press is prime: it is essential to free societies, and even to societies for the time being in ideological chains; it transcends all murderous external forces and circumstances, and all suicidal internal tendencies; it is stronger than economics and ideologies. Therefore it will continue to survive, and to play its essential role as an indestructible force for good in human society. . . . It will continue to do and to be so in West Africa no less than anywhere else.

Notes

1   OUP, 1957. Genesis said to have been at Oxford, with General Smuts and the Rhodes Memorial Lecture delivered by him there in 1929. First published 1938, reprinted 1939.
2   New York, Twentieth Century Fund, 1960, vol. II.
3   Washington D.C., International Cooperation Administration; no publication date, but research done in 1960.
4   Of which Professor Ayo Ogunsheye was then Director.

5   Ames, Iowa State University Press, 1971; Madison, University of Wisconsin Centre for International Communication Studies, 1971.

6   Ethiope Publishing Corporation, Benin City. Other works on the West African press include R. Ainslie, *The Press in Africa*, 1968; F. Barton, *The Press in Africa*, 1966; H. U. Behn, *Die Presse in Westafrika*, 1968; E. L. Sommerlad, *The Press in Developing Countries*, 1966; K. A. B. Jones-Quartey, 'Public Opinion in . . . West Africa', in Passin and Jones-Quartey (eds), *Africa: The Dynamics of Change*, 1963.

7   Hailey, *An African Survey*, p. 1235.

8   Now many African countries do have schools or institutes for the study of journalism, though in west Africa only Nigeria and Ghana seem to have established substantial facilities. In Nigeria the University of Nigeria at Nsukka and the University of Lagos carry schools teaching media skills, technical and editorial; the same is true of the University of Ghana's School of Journalism and Communication Studies, established in 1972.

9   Hailey, *op. cit.*, pp. 1236-7.

10   *Ibid.*, p. 1237.

11   George H. T. Kimble, *Tropical Africa*, vol. II, p. 142 (see Note 3).

12   *Ibid.*, p. 143.

13   Hailey, *Survey*, p. 1239.

14   Kimble, *op. cit.*, p. 142.

15   K. A. B. Jones-Quartey, *A Summary History of the Ghana Press*, Accra, Ghana Information Services Department, 1974, p. 4; also *History, Politics and Early Press in Ghana—The Fictions and the Facts*, Accra, 1975, published by the author in association with the School of Journalism and Communication Studies, University of Ghana, ch. 2 and 4.

16   Report on *The Press in West Africa*, Ibadan, 1960, published by the Committee on Inter-African Relations and the Department of Adult Education and Extra-Mural Studies, University of Ibadan, p. *i*.

17   The Seminar was held at the University of Dakar from 31 May to 4 June 1960.

18   William A. Hachten, *Muffled Drums*, pp. 32-3.

19   *Muffled Drums*, p. 33.

20   Two outstanding examples: the Charles de Breteuil chain in French West Africa and the *Mirror Group* in British. For full discussions see Jones-Quartey, *A Summary History*, Part III, 1, adapted from his 'The Ghana Press' in *The Press in West Africa*, 1960; and Hachten, *Muffled Drums*, 1971, pp. 184-5, 186-9. Also Hailey, *op. cit.*, p. 1239.

21   *The Press in West Africa*, p. *iv*.

22   Arno G. Huth, *Communications Media* . . . (Note 4), p. 35.

23   There are now quite a few local book publishing companies owned and run by Africans, particularly in Ghana and Nigeria. Local publishing and book printing is even stronger, naturally, under government in these two countries (Huth, *op. cit.*, p. 43). See *The African Book Publishing Record* (ed. H. Zell), i, 1, 1975.

24   Hachten, *op. cit.*, pp. 36-7.

25   *Ibid.*, p. 40.

26   Jones-Quartey, *Summary History*, p. 24.

27   Hachten, pp. 152, 186-7.

28   The 1971 Legon Seminar was designed to continue the review begun at Dakar in 1960. It is hoped this continuity will be established in the book covering both projects: *The Communication Media in West Africa*, edited by K. A. B. Jones-Quartey and Alfred Opubor (of Lagos University) and expected off the press in 1977.

29   The *Sierra Leone Royal Gazette* did not just 'last about a year' and stop there; that was only the beginning. It stopped and went repeatedly, practically throughout the whole century, as Fyfe shows abundantly. As for the *Royal Gold*

Coast Gazette, it was never 'handwritten'; the *Accra Herald* was, for just a short time in 1857.

30 The records are in fact a terror to the researcher and demand the utmost care and persistence to sort out.

31 There have been several attempts made in Liberia, especially by Mr Henry B. Cole. The present situation there and elsewhere on the coast is unknown to this observer.

32 *The Press in West Africa*, pp. *iv-v*.

33 *Muffled Drums*, p. 39.

34 Francis Williams, *Dangerous Estate: The Anatomy of Newspapers*, London, 1957.

35 Francis Williams, *The Right to Know*, Longman, 1969.

36 Lucy Salmon, *The Newspaper and Authority* and *The Newspaper and the Historian*, OUP, 1923, ch. 1 in each book.

37 The full story of the viciousness and perversity of the international press in covering the Nigerian civil war is told in *Transition*, ix(i), 44, 1974, pp. 30-5, by Adepitan Bamisaiye.

38 The now famous phrase coined by one of Kwame Nkrumah's staunchest former supporters to characterise infamous political behaviour on the part of staunch former supporters of the fallen hero, both *pre* and *post* the fall!

A. H. M. Kirk-Greene

Public Administration and African Studies

For all the verve and versatility of Basil Davidson, in whose honour these papers are collected to celebrate not only his sixtieth birthday but also his twentieth anniversary as an inspiring presence in African Studies, it must be admitted that few of his admirers would readily link his name with the discipline of Public Administration. Pioneer historian and persuasive journalist, sumptuous coffee-table writer, part-time guerilla and full-time advocate—all of these, yes; but associated with the administrators? No! I have searched through a dozen of his books for any apt reference to the context of the administrative framework in which Africa's colonial history and her contemporary politics have been ineluctably set; but in vain.

So, since Basil Davidson may not wish to stand *in loco parentis* to the discipline of public administration in addition to all the other African Studies disciplines to which he has so acted, let us turn the spot-light on one of the most prominent yet least publicised advances of African Studies in the past two decades. This is the Africa-inspired legitimisation of public administration as an academic discipline and its consequent, and considerable, contribution to the expansion of African Studies.

For if it is unarguable that in Anglophone university circles (outside America) public administration was the Cinderella discipline up to the 1960s it is no less demonstrable that, thanks to the magic wand of its African fairy godmother, public administration today rides in a golden coach to glittering assemblies—above all those hosted by African academics—never again to return to the snubbed and despised drudgery of life below academic stairs. In twenty-five years we have, in fact, moved from that curious anomaly of colonial administration (surely a matter of glee to the no-respecter-of-persons-in-high-places Basil Davidson) where the subject of public administration was conspicuous by its absence from the curricula for grooming Britain's imperial administrators, ICS and HMOCS alike, to one where Africa's own administrators may today be expected to top their B.A. with a diploma in public administration merely to be eligible to sit for the administrative grade qualifying examinations.[1] Few new entrants to an African civil service can today avoid exposure, always deliberate and often intense, to instruction in public administration. In modern Africa public administration is no longer an art or a gift: it is a science and a pedigree. In brief, it is Africa that has made public administration respectable; in return public administration has enriched the extent and depth of African Studies.

This paper argues that, as with so many of the older disciplines subsumed under the rubric of African Studies, one of the primary criteria by which to measure the impact of public administration on the growth of African Studies in the period since the Second World War is the quality of its research as reflected in the literature. The paper sets out to demonstrate that, in strong contrast to the pre-war paucity of studies on administration in Africa, there has appeared in the past quarter of a century a literature, of positive Africanist context and content, as remarkable in its range as in its volume. Such a turnabout is attributed to a radical change in thinking, *c.* 1955, on the preparation of Africa's administrators: it became acknowledged that perhaps after all they need not be born but might actually be trained. The catalyst was Africanisation, that natural desire to staff the administrative service, hitherto the preserve of Europeans, with one's own nationals.

The imperative of Africanisation led in the mid-1950s to the creation in Africa of Institutes of Public Administration. In turn, these were to encourage and facilitate the establishment of departments of and degrees in Public Administration at African universities in the 1960s. (The nomenclature needs a word of explanation: since 'Politics' was the prerogative of the political class and 'Government' the privilege of the bureaucratic class during those several First Republics, 'Public Administration' served as an umbrella name that gave offence to few of the bureaucrats and pride to many politicians.) Each of the three stages in the legitimisation of public administration in Africa—that derived from the process of Africanisation, from the creation of Institutes of Public Administration, and from the institutionalisation of university studies—is here illustrated by a reference to some of its prominent contributions to the literature of African Studies.

The contention is that it was the endorsement in Africa and by Africans of public administration as a respectable discipline that helped to bring about its legitimisation and subsequent expansion in Britain, and at the same time paved the way for a substantial strengthening of African Studies. Africa promoted public administration and public administration has enhanced African Studies. The paper concludes with a brief look at what could become a fourth phase in the story of public administration and African Studies, namely the literature generated by the personal experience of the new bureaucratic cadres who have been the end-product of the three antecedent stages, of Africanisation, of Institutes of Public Administration, and of under- and post-graduate study.

In an earlier paper I have reviewed the historiographical data on the growth of Africanist public administration studies in some detail, setting them within a tentative seven-fold periodisation.[2] Since parts of this are relevant to the development of subsequent themes in this paper, a summary will be in order here. Such a periodisation of research into African administrative studies to cover the past fifty years might comprise:

1. Comparative colonial administration, especially after the impetus of Lord

Lugard's proconsular testament, *The Dual Mandate* (1922) and the League of Nations mandate; arguments of moral responsibility and trusteeship; the classic controversies of the merits of indirect as opposed to direct rule (1930s).

2. The period following the 1947 Colonial Office despatch on local government —'the key to success lies in the development of an efficient, democratic [later changed to representative] system of government'; the shift towards the promotion of local government as a prelude to self-government; the failure of the UK model.

3. Africanisation of the civil service in the 1950s; the new role of the African administrator; politicisation of the bureaucracy along the lines of Nyerere's dictum of African states no longer being able to afford the 'luxury of a neutral civil service'.

4. In the 1960s, public administration programmes and training institutions and conferences; the advent of USAID/ODM/IIAS/RIPA/IULA and the Foundations; the consequently accelerated involvement of USA and UK academics in formalised public administration training at university level.

5. Immediately after independence, the reform and strengthening of the administrative infrastructure at independence for inculcated nation-building, with a rationale that variously gave priority to economic, social or political motives.

6. By 1970, review and re-evaluation in Africa of the state of post- independence administration; stock-taking of the achievements of the 1960s, often through an opportunity afforded for political breathing space by the advent of a military regime (e.g., Nti, 1967; Adedeji, 1968).

7. Review and re-evaluation, inside and outside Africa, of the achievements of colonial administration and of its legacy; civil service reform (e.g., Ndegwa, 1971; Wamalwa, 1972; Adebo, 1973; Udoji, 1974).

Projecting this schema forwards, it is possible that by the 1980s the time might conceivably be ripe for a tentative historical interpretation of Africa's European administrators, maybe *à la* Philip Woodruff. Casting the schema backwards, to before the period of colonial administration *qua* public administration, one could usefully add three earlier phases so as to ensure total coverage of administrative studies in their African context:

A. The period 1900-14, when African administration was thought of more in terms of home-centred government (with strong overtones of imperialism) than of formulated in-the-field administrative techniques.

B. The period 1880-1900, which was the heyday of chartered company administration and thus ranks as *sui generis*, however deserving it is of further study.

C. The closer examination of the organisation and administration of pre-colonial empires, kingdoms, chieftaincies and ethnic groups. Quite properly, such studies have principally been the work of social anthropologists (M. G. Smith,1960; Ivor Wilks, 1974); and it is in their care that we may safely leave them in this paper.

For the purposes of this symposium the boundary lines may be drawn a little larger so as to allow for the evaluation of the quality of African public administration studies on either side of the Second World War.

We may start with a question. Up to 1937, what could the District Officer in training have his attention drawn to if he wished to learn something about African administration? On the Tropical African Services Course, inaugurated at Oxford and Cambridge in 1926, he could of course listen to the *ipsissima verba* of the gods themselves. A reading of the minutes of the Cambridge courses and their house journal reveals how Governors by the dozen and Provincial Commissioners by the score were wont to travel up from King's Cross or Liverpool Street to tell the younger generation what they had done in Africa and why and how they had done it; Lord Lugard and the lot.[3] By way of supplement there were a few published reminiscences to learn from, although many of these were of the high-falutin' gubernatorial style ('From the Verandah of Government House' or 'My Darkest Days in Dar') or else of the jungle-and-juju type of lesser mortals ('Up Against it in Matabeleland'). A few again, such as C. L. Temple's *Native Races and their Rulers* (1918), were too intellectual and philosophical to appeal to the griffin: like vintage claret they needed time and taste, a certain maturity of the palate, before one could appreciate their true merit.

There were three important exceptions to this indictment. Raymond L. Buell's *The Native Problem in Africa*, published in 1928, quickly acquired for itself the same encyclopaedic status as Lord Hailey's *An African Survey* was to do ten years later: that is to say, a work of reference, to be marked and learned from rather than a book to be read (2,000 pages do not lend themselves to easy inward digestion). Although Lucy Mair's *Native Policies in Africa* (1936) did come nearer to the actualities of the administrator's trivial round and common task, it was still, as she made clear at the time, the main lines of colonial policy and not administrative practice that were being analysed. Of the two remaining exceptions, one was essentially a retrospective proconsular dissertation on the principles of colonial rule (Lugard's *The Dual Mandate in Tropical Africa*, 1922); while the other, the most explicit and relevant of them all for practising African administrators (Lugard's *Political Memoranda: Instructions to Political Officers on subjects chiefly political and administrative*), remained a confidential and unpublished document from 1906 (1919) until 1970.

In the event, it may be said that the African cadet had to wait until he reached his colony before he could lay his hands on some of the real items of public administration in Africa: the kind of directives prepared by one Secretary for Native Affairs, 'with a view to the guidance of Residents and Senior District Officers in training their junior officers and especially cadets . . . on points of procedure in which it appears that instruction is particularly needed'.[4] This type of basic literature would have included Cameron's *Principles of Native Administration and their Application* (1934) or their Tanganyikan counterpart of 1930, his famous 'little brown books'; Clifford's *Minute* of 1922, 'primarily intended for the guidance and instruction of the junior members of the political service'; and the *Political Memoranda* themselves, colloquially described as 'the DO's Bible' but, as I have suggested elsewhere,[5] only in the limited sense that more often than not it followed the fate of the world's most printed book: not always read after the first obligatory dip-in, left dust-collecting on the shelf, and its precepts frequently taken for granted, knavishly reinterpreted, or simply ignored.

Such was the position until 1937. That year a young researcher, a female treading fearlessly on the hallowed emirate ground where even males (clearly less than angels) from the Lagos Secretariat had hesitated to set foot, published her analysis of what indirect rule was all about at the grassroots and how it operated in daily detail. As the dog-eared, margin-annotated copy in the former Colonial Services Club at Oxford unambiguously demonstrated, Margery Perham's *Native Administration in Nigeria* earned its place as a stimulating and fundamental text. Assuming that the cadet had rejected the 'Sandi the Kingmaker' level of interpretation, there was at this time one further contemporary record of what the life of a neophyte African administrator was really like. This was W. R. Crocker's *Nigeria: a critique of colonial administration* (1936). But it was so depressing and so demoralising that when I rashly read it before sailing to the Coast thirteen years later, I almost resigned my appointment on the spot. It was to take me several more years before I was able to recognise its real worth in the literature.

For all the this-is-the-life realism of Crocker's leaves from a touring officer's journal, it was not until 1943, with the publication of K. G. Bradley's *The Diary of a District Officer*, that the African administrator earned the diarist he deserved. To leapfrog chronology for a moment, since the 1950s the autobiographical element of African administration has shared in the expansion of Africana and there are to hand today revealing memoirs by a host of former district officers—Darrell Bates, Ian Brook, J. C. Cairns, Charles Chenevix-Trench, R. O. Hennings, E. K. Lumley, Robin Short, J. H. Smith and Stanhope White, to name but a few.

But the indictment of the preparation of Britain's African administrators goes further than this chronic lack of literature on what field administration was all about. It has long surprised this writer that, while Britain enjoyed for over a century an enviable reputation for the quality of her imperial administrators, the notion of their being *trained* for administration was, if not unheard of, at least unheeded. The noble tradition of administrator which stretches from those titans of the Punjab like Nicholson and Lawrence, through Milner's brilliant Kindergarten and Cromer's vision of a Sudanese service of 'active young men, endowed with good health, high character and fair abilities' and down to selected individual field administrators in the latter-day Indian, Sudan, Malay and Colonial Services, has this in common: at no time did the topic of public administration ever appear in their education. Even as late as 1949, when the streamlined Devonshire Course 'A' had replaced the Tropical African Services Course at Oxford, Cambridge and London, no administrator in training was taught anything of public administration. (Whether he was a better or worse administrator for this lacuna is not at issue here.) My own notebooks from that year are filled with R. E. Robinson's witty debunking of the theory of indirect rule, but what I learned of the hows rather than the whys of African administration was more germane to the denizens of Government House than to a touring officer in the bush—as on my arrival on the Coast my seniors were quick to remind me! The disbelief that public administration was something that could be taught in the classroom, that administrators could be made and were not necessarily born—the reverse of the classic practice of Britain's corps of imperial administrators—was something that died hard.

Yet if such an idea was an unconscionable time a-dying, it did receive a further—and fatal—dose of insulin from the African experience. This was a by-product of the plans for constitutional advance urged by Creech Jones and Cohen at the Colonial Office and first implemented on the Gold Coast and in Nigeria. The Administrative Service had long been a target of the nationalists: in West Africa, where its commitment to indirect rule was looked on as an infamous device to prop up 'illiterate village yokels'[6] (N.A.s) at the expense of the Western educated élite (B.A.s); in East Africa, for the insensitive authoritarianism of its exercise of control; and in West, East and Central Africa alike, for its immense social aloofness—an hauteur felt as much by departmental and commercial whites as by subject blacks and browns. Condemning the kind of policy advocated in Nigeria, Lord Hailey had warned the colonial governments in a confidential memoir written in 1940,[7] that they were playing with fire in their inflexible handling of recruitment to the Administrative Service (loftily, *never* a Department). But the 'scaffolding' theory, whereby the admission of Africans into the Administrative Service was rejected as pointless since it was assumed that at independence the steel frame would be removed, had won the official colonial mind.[8] For all Hailey's warnings, repeated again in 1942 when he was consulted on the related inclusion of Africans into Executive Councils,[9] it was not until the Gold Coast's Watson Commission declared in 1948 that admission of Africans into the administration was an integral part of constitutional advance that the breakthrough was achieved.[10] Followed in the same year by the Foot Report in Lagos on Nigerianisation of the civil service, by the beginning of the 1950s it was no longer possible to view the upper ranks of the administration as reserved for European officials.

Programmes for scholarships abroad for selected high-fliers followed, yet much of the rationale was based on the old-school conviction that the best kind of administrator was the one with a highly trained brain—and if a Blue or two could be added to the Greats man for good measure so much the better the potential of a first-class administrator.[11] Provided the applicant could prove his intellectual training by having taken a degree, it did not really matter whether it was in chemistry or Chaucer, commerce or crystallography. But the new scholarship programme of schoolboy-into-graduate-into-administrator was, like forest seedlings in the eyes of a quickpenny timber merchant, altogether too slow a process when set beside the pace of constitutional advance in West Africa. Lacking the headstart of the ICS which had been admitting Indians into the competitive entrance examination for half a century before Independence, localisation of the administration in Africa now found itself faced with a crisis of manpower in its higher cadres.

Crises call for crash action; and it was this that brought Africanisation into being as a primary political objective. Short courses at British universities for promising administrators in the making from all over Africa were complemented in 1957 by the pioneer course in Africa designed to train Africans as District Officers. As one of the most distinguished of the first generation of African administrators has observed, it was on this Zaria model that other African countries—Uganda, Kenya, Tanzania, Malaŵi, Zambia, Lesotho—were to base their own programmes for training administrators.[12]

Africanisation reports, many of them today collector's items in African Studies libraries, often led to further research into and reports on the minutiae of central administration. Other African Studies items began to feature among much sought-after acquisitions: reports of public service commissions, salary review bodies, manpower surveys and staff development centres. Public administration data, which before the war had either not been published or had been thrown away by serving officials as yet more dull publications from the Government Printer, now assumed the value—and hence later a rarity status—of basic items of Africana for any serious research on administration in Africa.

The tidal wave of constitutional reform, development plans and Africanisation programmes washed against the portals of the Colonial Office. When the tide receded later, its highwater mark on African studies was clear for all to see. The creation of the African Studies Branch, the launching of the *Journal of African Administration* (its twenty-fifth anniversary issue appeared in 1974), and the inauguration of the annual Cambridge Summer Schools devoted to discussing topics of administrative concern to Africa, all reflected a very new-look Colonial Office image. The full story of the influence of the African Studies Branch on public administration in Africa has still to be assessed,[13] but all three of its agents, and the related *Corona*, house journal of HMOCS, have earned a place of their own in the study of and literature on African administration and have secured a notable niche in African Studies libraries.

Nor was this all. Such training was usually located in an embryo civil service training institute, so that between 1954 and 1964 one found Institutes of Public Administration springing up all over Anglophone Africa. In general, their principal remit was to further the implementation of Africanisation programmes, with special reference to the training of administrators at a number of levels, from district officers and diplomats downward.

This development led in its turn to two more advances in public administration. One was an increase in the number of studies dealing with public administration in Africa. As indirect rule gave way to local government new writing emerged. It is not without significance that among the reforms in colonial service training in the 1950s there now featured the need to give British administrators some practical experience in the kind of local government systems they were expected, *pace* Creech Jones, to promote in Africa. More of it came along too as, besides the writing of teaching texts for African administrators, the emphasis in Institutes of Public Administration was placed on producing case studies of African administration in action. As this kind of research developed and was written up, more and more of the results found their way into the bookshops and on to the bookshelves in Europe and America as staples of African Studies programmes. And as Institutes of Public Administration upgraded their courses in public administration till in some cases postgraduate and staff college levels were obtained, a number of professional journals were launched by them. Prominent among these was Ife's *Quarterly Administration*, today in its eleventh successful year. Later still, as decolonisation passed from promise to realisation, close studies began to appear of the civil service implications of the transfer of power: for example, Kenneth Younger's *The Public Service in New States* (1960), A. L. Adu's *The Civil Service in New African States* (1965) and Richard Symonds' *The British and Their Successors* (1966). At some future date, when the perspective is right, it should be possible to undertake worthwhile studies of the Colonial Administrative Service and build on Robert Heussler's pioneering *Yesterday's Rulers* (1965), *The British in Northern Nigeria* (1968), and *The British in Tanganyika* (1971), and the founding works of Sir Ralph Furse (*Aucuparius*, 1962) and Sir Charles Jeffries, the last of whose publications was the important monograph *Whitehall and the Colonial Service: an administrative memoir 1939-1956* (1973).

The second advance was the acceptance of public administration into university curricula, an event often coincident with the inclusion of the Institute of Public Administration (or parts of it) as a constituent college of the university and the upgrading of its public administration wing into a Department of Public Administration or Government (or of Politics, *sub rosa*). Here another determinant in the legitimisation of public administration deserves special mention. This was the American academic presence in Africa. The history of public administration as a respectable university subject is longer in the USA than in the UK. In the latter, public administration has too long enjoyed (?) a connection with such pedestrian topics as public health and town hall bumbledom. However wrongly, public administration was often thought of as relating to the non-U areas of British public life. The American presence was felt in three ways. First, there was the tie-up between specific African Institutes of Public Administration and selected American Schools of Public Administration, e.g. Kabete and Syracuse, Zaria and Pittsburgh, Lugogo and New York, often with reciprocal teaching facilities. Secondly came the recruitment of American faculty members to the Departments of Public Administration in the new African universities. Lastly, there was the academic output of this collaboration, in the form of research reports, monographs and books. Some of the early contributions by American Africanist scholars have yet to be surpassed for their politico-administrative insights.

In sum, the benefit to African Studies generated by the past twenty-five years of public administration in Africa can be compellingly assessed by the range and quality of its literary expression. Overlapping, as it does, with politics and history on the one hand and with economics and anthropology on the other, public administration today furnishes a distinguished shelf in every African studies library. There can be few books on African politics and modern history that do not need to preface their argument with a description of the administrative context in which the plot is played out.

Casting one's eye along the impressive array of titles, one may think back to the plight of our embryo African administrator of 1950, as much as him of 1940 or of 1930, and imagine what he would have given to have had to hand some of the perceptive studies of public administration that his successor can read today. Virtually every African country is covered. There is Goren Hyden *et al.*, *Development Administration: the Kenyan Experience* (1970); Stanley Dryden's *Local Administration in Tanzania* (1968); W. Tordorff's *Government and Politics in Tanzania* (1967) and *Government and Politics in Zambia* (1974); F. G. Burke's *Local Government and Politics in Uganda* (1964). On the wider scene, we have Hailey's four volumes on *Native Administration in the British African Territories* (1951); Ronald Wraith's *Local Administration in West Africa* (1972); B. H. Sellassie's *The Executive in African Government* (1974); and Bernard Schaffer's forthcoming study of administrative training and development in East Africa and Zambia. Or, to take Nigeria alone, there are D. J. Murray's *The Work of Administration in Nigeria* (1969) and his *Studies in Nigerian Administration* (1970); Adebayo Adedeji's *Nigerian Administration and its Political Setting* (1968); E. O. Awa's *Federal Government in Nigeria* (1964); and L. F. Blitz's *The Politics and Administration of Nigerian Government* (1965). All are very much to the public administration point. Furthermore, a glance at the lists of these in preparation suggests that there is as much again in the pipeline by way of case studies of African administration in action. Nor can one for a moment overlook the relevance of such symposia as the down-to-earth proceedings of the annual Inter-African Public Administration seminar (IAPA), a source too little known because of a regrettable weakness in the matter of publication procedures.[14] For the sake of this paper, strictly theoretical studies of public administration have been omitted. Some of these can, with varying degrees of ease, be applied to the African context: for instance, the models developed by F. W. Riggs or the arguments of Bernard Schaffer. Other works, set squarely within the mainstream of African political history, yet have an important bearing upon the subject of public administration. One thinks at once of studies like those of Anthony Low and Cranford Pratt, Colin Leys, Michael Crowder and Cherry Gertzel, besides the American contributions by David Apter, James Coleman, Lloyd Fallers, Martin Kilson and Gray Cowan, already alluded to. All of these, and many more, have earned an essential place in African studies as well as in the study of public administration.

And so the circle is drawn to a close. Courses for European graduates in African administration, inspired with the doctrine that a first-class Lit. Hum. mind and an on-the-job apprenticeship under a senior officer who had learned most of the ropes and all of the tricks after twenty years in the same post could not fail to produce the *beau idéal* of imperial administrator, gave way first to courses at Africa's own Institutes of Public Administration where African officials were 'trained' to become District Officers, and later to courses at African universities in which public administration was recognised as a proper subject for graduate, and often undergraduate, study. In this abrupt change of direction, the catalyst was the imperative of Africanisation and the agent was the Institute of Public Administration. Thus it is that Africa may be said to have endorsed and promoted the respectability of public administration. In return, public administration has given to African Studies a remarkable richness of literature. A review of the growth of African Studies since the Second World War demonstrates how the status of public administration and of African Studies have been mutually enhanced.

We are left with one foreseeable direction in which public administration may make a further contribution to the reputation of African Studies. This relates to the literature on Africa's bureaucratic cadres. It is not a question of studies of African civil services but of studies by African civil servants. What is needed to complete the picture of public administration in Africa (and what may be expected soon, as the first generation of African bureaucrats approaches retiring age) is the recording and the evaluation of their version of what Africanisation was all about and of their views on what African administration both was, in the colonial period when they were junior officials, and is, in the post-independence period when they have been key civil servants. I have pleaded for this fresh focus of research often enough in the past few years.[15] Let me simply conclude by saying that when African civil servants have written their equivalents of the revealing memoirs of Indian administrators like N. B. Bonarjee, S. K. Chettur, E. N. Mangat Rai, Apa Pant and Navi Rustomji, both public administration and African Studies will be the richer for the record.

Notes

1   E.g., in 1967 the Eastern Region Public Service of Nigeria had sufficient graduate strength for it to demand from applicants for the Administrative Class a Third-class Honours or a First or Second-class General Degree *plus* a Diploma in Public Administration. See the advertisement carried in *West Africa*, 18 February 1967.

2   'An Historiographical Perspective on Administrative Studies in Africa', paper presented to the International Conference on Trends in University Teaching and Research in Public Administration in Africa, held at the University of Ife, February 1970.

3   Nor, of course, was Oxford left out of this. Malcolm Macdonald has recalled, in an unpublished interview, how when he was an undergraduate in the late 1920s, 'great authorities on the Empire', such as Guggisberg and Lugard ('two or three times'), would come up to talk informally to the Raleigh Society. (Interview with Curtis Nordman, graduate student of Linacre College, 8 October 1974; by courtesy of Mr Nordman).

4   SNP Circular (Kaduna) dated 1 July 1928, addressed to all Residents.

5   Introduction to Lugard, *Political Memoranda*, 3rd edition, 1970, pp. xvii-xix.

6   Such was the idiom used by E. F. Gibbons in his unpublished report *African Local Government Reform in Kenya, Uganda and Eastern Nigeria*, 1949, para. 93.

7   Lord Hailey, *Native Administration and Political Development in British Tropical Africa*, 1940 (Confidential), pp. 47-8.

8   This school of thought is usefully set out in Margery Perham, *Native Administration in Nigeria*, 1937, p. 361.

9   Memorandum by F. J. Pedler on a discussion with Lord Hailey at the Colonial Office, in CO 554/131/33702, quoted by Curtis R. Nordman in his forthcoming article 'The decision to admit unofficials to the Executive Councils of British West Africa'.

10   'The constitution and government of the country must be so reshaped as to give every African of ability an opportunity to help to govern the country, so as not

only to gain political experience but also to experience political power'—*Report of the Commision of Enquiry into Disturbances in the Gold Coast* (Watson), 1948, Col. No. 231.

11   Cf. Lord Vansittart's appreciation:
       'I have never wavered in my conviction that the Sudan Civil Service was the finest body in the world. Its members should have proud and abiding recollections. They were all picked men, scholars and athletes. Look at their credentials [Out of an intake of eight, there were] a former Rugby football captain of Oxford and Scotland, an ex-captain of the Cambridge University cricket team, a member of the Oxford University soccer XI, a rowing trials man, a member of the Oxford and Middlesex county cricket teams, and a Somerset county Rugby footballer'—Foreword to H. C. Jackson, *Sudan Days and Ways*, 1954, p. vii.

12   A. L. Adu, *Report of the Localization Committee*, Zomba, 1960.

13   For two preliminary personal recollections, see R. E. Robinson, 'The Journal and the Transfer of Power', and Sir George Cartland, 'Retrospect', *Journal of Administration Overseas*, January 1974, pp. 255-8 and 269-72.

14   For a full discussion of this literature, see 'The New African Administrator', *Journal of Modern African Studies*, x, i, 1972, pp. 93-107.

15   The most recent, and the most detailed, formulation is to be found in 'Administration and Africanisation: an autobiographical approach to an evaluation', *Journal of Administration Overseas*, 25, January 1974, pp. 259-68.

*J. O. Hunwick**

The Study of Muslim Africa: Retrospect and Prospect

When I was originally asked to write this paper it was suggested that I might write on Islamic Studies since the Second World War in relation to Africa. On reflection it became ever more difficult to define exactly what one meant by 'Islamic Studies'. It certainly means the study of Islamic law and theology, Islamic ideologies, mystical and doctrinal movements. Equally certainly, studies in these areas could not be divorced from the study of the introduction and spread of Islam and the wider study of the history of those areas where a significant proportion of the population is Muslim. In turn one becomes involved in the social and political structures and even the languages spoken by Muslims in Africa and the literatures they have produced.

I felt therefore that I could not escape from an attempt (inadequate though it must be) at discussing developments in various interrelated disciplines which have had as their main purport the study of aspects of the history and culture of Muslim societies in Africa. Hence the title of this paper as it now stands. Islamic Studies is, by its very nature, the study of a cultural phenomenon. Just as Islam claims to guide or rule every facet of the believer's life, so in our study of Muslims and Muslim societies we cannot afford to ignore any aspect of the political, social, economic and spiritual lives of the peoples we study.

The paper as presented to the seminar contained a brief review of the study of Islamic Africa before 1945 and a section on post-war developments in north-west Africa. In order to reduce this paper to a length suitable for publication, it has been necessary to omit these sections and concentrate on Africa south of the Sahara. Even so, much has been omitted or referred to only in passing. but it is hoped that it will still be useful as a general guide.[1] At a later date I hope to produce a fuller annotated bibliography and thus provide for Muslim Africa a study guide comparable to that of Sauvaget for the Central Islamic world.[2]

A word must first be said on studies which link the Arabic-speaking Muslim world with sub-Saharan Africa.[3] Some advances have been made in recent years in the study of the political, economic and religious links between north Africa and the western Sudan. The work of the eminent Polish scholar Tadeusz Lewicki spans the pre-war and the post-war period. For the past forty years he has devoted much of his energy to the study of the north African Ibāḍī communities and their trans-Saharan links. His most recent summation is to

* As I was unable to attend the seminar to which this paper was presented I have not been able to benefit from the group discussion. The paper also had to be revised for publication without my seeing other papers presented.

be found in his lengthy paper 'The Ibadites in Arabia and Africa'[4] and his article on the Ibāḍiyya in the new *Encyclopaedia of Islam*. He has also contributed numerous papers on the geography, food, fauna and peoples of the Sahara in mediaeval times drawn from extensive studies of the Arab geographers. His useful account of the contribution of Arab geographers to our knowledge of Africa south of the Sahara written in Polish has now appeared in a rather inadequate English translation under the title *Arabic External Sources for the History of Africa to the south of the Sahara* (1969).

I have myself made one or two excursions into this field and the French scholar Jean Devisse has made some valuable contributions.[5] Some attention has also been given to the relations between the Middle East and West Africa and vice versa. 'Umar al-Naqar published his S.O.A.S. doctoral thesis as *The Pilgrimage Tradition in West Africa* (1972) and Elizabeth Sartain has published a brief but stimulating examination of the relations of the Egyptian scholar Al-Suyūṭī (d. 1505) with the 'people of Takrūr'.[6] A young American scholar, Terence Walz, is completing a study of the economic relations of Egypt with West Africa in the eighteenth and nineteenth centuries and has already published a foretaste in his 'Notes on the organization of the African Trade in Cairo, 1800-1850'.[7] Although much ink has flowed in study of the trans-Atlantic slave-trade, we still await a serious study of the trans-Saharan slave-trade. An equally important and fascinating field waits to be explored by a historian with sociological interests in the dispersal of black African slaves within the Muslim world and their integration into Islamic society.

Two important studies of figures whose activities in the religious and political spheres bridge the Saharan 'gulf' have recently been made by doctoral candidates. The thesis of 'Abd al-'Azīz Baṭrān was concerned with the life and influence of Sīdī al-Mukhtār al-Kuntī (d. 1811) in the southern Saharan peripheries (Birmingham, 1972). That of Charles C. Stewart studied the life and work of Shaykh Sīdiya of southern Mauritania (d. 1868). It has now been published under the title *Islam and Social Order in Mauritania* (1973). Both these studies are important for their recognition of the indebtedness of the leaders of these groups to the rich heritage of Islamic ideas from North Africa and the Middle East and their ability to mould them to the environment and times in which they lived. Both, too, have made use of large quantities of Arabic documents hitherto unknown outside the societies which produced them.

Turning now to West Africa proper, some solid foundations have been laid over the past twenty years which hold out fair promise for the coming decades. University institutions have proliferated, especially in the Anglophone territories; many of these have specialised institutes for African Studies and in some there are teaching departments for Arabic and Islamic Studies, notably the University of Ibadan, the Ahmadu Bello University, Zaria, and its associated Abdullahi Bayero College in Kano and the University of Ghana. At Ibadan a Department of Arabic and Islamic Studies was founded in 1962, in the same year as the Institute of African Studies. Within the latter a project entitled the Centre for Arabic Documentation was initiated in 1964 and a *Research Bulletin* published once or twice annually, having among its objectives to publish brief analyses of the Arabic manuscript materials which were being microfilmed from originals kindly loaned by local Muslim scholars. The Ibadan University Library also had its own collection of Arabic manuscript materials (including many 'originals') dating from the mid-1950s when W. E. N. Kensdale was the Deputy Librarian. This important collection has been constantly added to over the years, but though its present contents total well over 500 items, the only published catalogue is that of Kensdale himself (1955) which lists 165 titles.[8]

Within the Department of History at the University of Ibadan much solid pioneering work was done in the history of Muslim West Africa by Professor Abdullahi (H. F. C.) Smith. Though the students taught and inspired by him, Nigerian and foreign, would make a very long list, special mention deserves to be made of three studies in the Ibadan History Series which reflect the keen interest he helped to focus on the history of Islamic West Africa: D. M. Last's *The Sokoto Caliphate* (1967), R. A. Adeleye's *Power and Diplomacy in Northern Nigeria 1804-1906* (1971) and B. O. Oloruntimehin's *The Segu Tukulor Empire* (1972). Smith's inspiration must also be acknowledged in the editing and translation of two important Arabic texts, both presented as doctoral theses: the *Bayān wujūb al-hijra* of 'Uthmān b. Fūdī prepared by F. H. Elmasri (Ibadan, 1968), a Sudanese scholar working at the time in the Department of Arabic and Islamic Studies and my own work on the Replies of Al-Maghīlī to the Questions of Askia al-ḥājj Muhammad (London, 1974).[9]

We leave Ibadan for Zaria. Here again the debt to Smith, who was appointed Head of the Department of History there in 1964, is considerable. Not only has he worked to train a new generation of northern Nigerian historians, but has laboured with colleagues such as Last and M. A. Al-Hajj to build up another collection of Arabic manuscript materials. Much of this was done under the aegis of the Northern History Research Scheme, a project of collaboration between the Universities of Ibadan and Zaria which still continues.[10] A Sudanese scholar, O. S. A. Ismail is currently working on a catalogue of these Arabic materials, and publication is expected soon. Over the past three years Smith has built up another massive research and documentation project at Arewa House, Kaduna where materials relating to the history of the former Northern Region are being assembled and studied.

The main effort of teaching Arabic and Islamic Studies is concentrated in the Abdullahi Bayero College, Kano. The precursor of this college was the School for Arabic Studies where the combined efforts of its Principal, Shaykh Muḥammad 'Awaḍ and his deputy, Dr M. Hiskett, did much to promote the teaching of these disciplines along modern lines. Several of their graduates went on to read Arabic at SOAS in the 1950s and have since returned to inject new life into the teaching of Arabic in schools and colleges in northern Nigeria.

Of recent research work conducted by members of staff of the Abdullahi Bayero College, mention should be made of the work of the present head of the Department of History, M. A. Al-Hajj, who has worked on Mahdism in northern Nigeria, and its relations with the Mahdiyya of the Sudan, (Ph.D., Zaria, 1973) and has for some years been working at a new critical edition and

English translation of Muḥammad Bello's *Infāq al-Maysūr*. The Provost of the College, H. I. Gwarzo, has presented a doctoral thesis (London, 1972) which includes the text of Al-Maghīlī's treatise on the status and treatment of Jews in Tuwat and his *Risāla* addressed to Muḥammad Rumfa, Sultan of Kano in the 1490s.

There is much else to be said of the work of Nigerian historians of the younger generation such as G. Gbadamosi, S. A. Balogun, Mahdi Adamu, Sa'd Abubakar, M. B. Alkali[11] and of foreign historians with Islamic interests such as Brenner, Low, Paden and Lavers,[12] but considerations of space make nothing more than passing reference possible.

Less work has been done in the field of Islamic law and theology and indeed in the field of Islamic scholarship in general, but mention should be made of I. A. B. Balogun's critical edition of Dan Fodio's major theological treatise the *Iḥyā' al-Sunna* (Ph.D., London 1967), and of the thesis of P. D. Ayagere on the place of 'Abdullahi b. Fūdī in the tradition of Sokoto scholarship (Ibadan, 1970).[13] A major contributor in this field has been M. Hiskett of SOAS. To him we owe a number of important articles[14] and an edition and translation of 'Abdullāh b. Fūdī's *Tazyīn al-waraqāt* (Ibadan, 1963). More recently he has completed a thesis on Hausa Islamic Verse (London, 1969, now in press), and published the first full-length study of the life and times of Dan Fodio, *The Sword of Truth* (1973), which makes use of Hausa poems as source material. The full extent of the Hausa literary tradition is only just beginning to be realised through the collection of manuscripts written in *'ajamī* at centres such as Ibadan, Zaria and Legon. A rich verse literature also exists in Fulfulde; a good deal is preserved in Ibadan, Zaria, IFAN Dakar and in the Bibliothèque Nationale in Paris.[15]

Finally mention must be made of the other important public collections of Arabic and African language manuscript materials in public and private collections in Nigeria. Large collections exist at the National Archives, Kaduna and at the Jos Museum of the Department of Antiquities. The only account of the former is that of D. M. Last who published two articles listing the titles of all items by 'Uthmān b. Fūdī, his brother 'Abdullāh and his son Muḥammad Bello as well as a good deal of other material of Nigerian provenance and some from beyond Nigeria.[16] The collection was built up over many years by gifts or purchase and since the time Last did his work, nearly ten years ago, more has been added and the material reclassified. The collection at Jos was similarly built up over many years, partly by Alhaji Muntaqa Coomassie and by A. D. H. Bivar[17] during the time he was Curator there in the late 1950s. It includes an important collection of Arabic historical materials left by the late Sir Richmond Palmer. A microfilm copy of the entire collection (at least as it stood in 1965) is housed in the University of Ibadan library. A catalogue of the Jos collection and a very small collection at the Lugard Hall Library, Kaduna, was published in 1965 by Drs Arif and Abu Hakima of the University of Jordan, but it is a very inadequate guide.[18]

Many collections of Arabic, Hausa and Fulfulde manuscripts are known to exist in the private collections of Nigerian Muslim scholars and in school and town council libraries, especially in the north. Most of the material microfilmed for the Ibadan Centre of Arabic Documentation came from such sources. The kind and patient collaboration of the 'traditional' scholars of Nigeria in giving access to their manuscript material to institutions and individual research workers has been one of the distinctive and gratifying features of work in Islamic Studies in Nigeria and Ghana. Last's dedication of his book *The Sokoto Caliphate* to the *Waziri* (Mallam Junaidu)[19] was certainly no empty formality and examples of such sincere acknowledgement of this kind of collaboration between Muslim and non-Muslim, traditional and 'Western' scholars could be multiplied.

In Ghana such collaboration was formalised during the period of Thomas Hodgkin's directorship of the Institute of African Studies of the University of Ghana. A local scholar, Alhaji Isaka Boyo of Kintampo was appointed Senior Research Assistant and it was largely due to his efforts under the guidance of Hodgkin and Ivor Wilks that a collection of some 400 items in Arabic, Hausa and some Ghanaian languages was built up. Again the local scholars were generous in lending their manuscripts. These were then xeroxed in multiple copies, of which a number were given to the donors in appreciation of their cooperation. A card index of this material exists at the Institute, but no full account of the Institute's holdings has ever been published.[20]

The early 1960s when Hodgkin, Wilks, Freeman-Grenville, Holden and B. G. Martin were at the Institute were, in effect, the heyday of Islamic Studies in Ghana.[21] Under the M.A. programme introduced at that time, a number of theses on Islamic topics were written, noteworthy among them those of C. C. Stewart and Paulo Farias,[22] both of whom have continued to derive much inspiration from Thomas Hodgkin. Levtzion, whose book *Muslims and Chiefs in West Africa* (1968) is as yet the only extended treatment of Islam in Ghana, also acknowledges his debt to the inspiration of Thomas Hodgkin and I too first had the privilege of his friendship and guidance at this period. The debt of Africanist scholars (not only Islamicists) to Hodgkin is clear from the book of essays, *African Perspectives*, produced in honour of his sixtieth birthday and retirement in 1970.

Wilks too, has been an important contributor to the study of Islam in Ghana with his *Northern Factor in Ashanti History* (1961) and his studies of Dyula scholarship and history. In the latter field he has acknowledged his deep indebtedness to a local Muslim scholar and prolific author, Al-Ḥājj Muḥammad Saghanughu (known as Marḥaba), Mufti of Bobo-Dioulasso as well as to Alhaji Osmanu Isaka Boyo and numerous other traditional scholars of Ghana and the Ivory Coast.[23] In his turn Wilks has inspired a number of other young scholars to turn their attention to problems in West African Islam; of these special mention may be made of Phyllis Ferguson who has completed a study, 'Islamisation in Dagbon' (Ph.D., Cambridge, 1972) and collaborated with Wilks in a number of joint papers.

One Ghanaian writer (of Kebbi-Kano origin), Al-Ḥājj 'Umar of Keti-Krakye (d. 1934), has attracted the interest of a number of scholars, the earliest of whom was the German administrator Mischlich in the first decade of this century.

Al-Ḥājj 'Umar wrote in both Arabic and Hausa and not only on essentially religious topics but also on history and social matters. More recent scholars such as Martin, Wilks, Hodgkin, Sölken, Goody and Ṣalāḥ Ibrāhīm have shown interest in his work and two young Ghanaian scholars, T. M. Mustapha and B. A. R. Braimah are currently working on various aspects of his writings and influence.[24] Two of his Hausa writings have formed subjects for doctoral theses. D. E. Ferguson translated and commented on 'Umar's writings on Hausa history and customs (UCLA, 1972)[25] and S. Pilaszewicz (who has also published a Hausa history of Wala) has translated into Polish with commentary his history of Samori and Babatu[26] and has plans for an English translation of it. The work of one of 'Umar's pupils, Al-Ḥājj Ṣāliḥ of Jenene, has also been investigated by the American scholar Akbar Muḥammad.[27]

We turn now to developments in Francophone West Africa and in Mauritania, the bridge between the Maghrib and West Africa. Higher education has been a much later growth there than in Anglophone West Africa. Whereas the universities of Ghana (Legon) and Ibadan both go back to 1948, it was not until 1957 that the first university in a French territory was founded at Dakar. Universities in the Sahel lands, where the greatest number of Muslims live, are a feature of only the last three years—Chad, 1971, Niger, 1973 and Upper Volta, 1974; Mali still has no university institution. On the other hand, there is a longer history of research institutions concerned with the humanities and social sciences. The Institut Français (now 'Fondamental') d'Afrique Noire was founded in Dakar in 1939 and in the post-war period IFAN centres were created at Bamako, Ouagadougou and Niamey which became national research centres after Independence in 1960.

IFAN Dakar, however, has remained the focus of research work and the preservation of documents and archaeological findings. Islamic Studies received a great impetus there by the appointment of Vincent Monteil who was the Institut's director from 1959 to 1968. Monteil's work has spanned the whole Islamic world from Senegal and Morocco to Soviet central Asia and Indonesia. His extraordinary command of languages (including Arabic, Berber, Wolof and Fulfulde), his affection for the peoples whose cultures he studied and his sheer physical and mental energy have left an indelible mark on the field of Islamic Studies in Africa. To him we owe a wealth of studies on a wide range of topics in this field, including a collection of essays on Islam in Senegal, *Esquisses Sénégalaises* (1966), his fascinating, if controversial *L'Islam Noir* (1964, revised 1971), translations of Al-Bakrī's west African sections,[28] Ibn Baṭṭūṭa's African journeys (with others)[29] and a three-volume French translation of the *Muqaddima* of Ibn Khaldūn. He also edited some of the previously unpublished papers of his father Charles (d. 1949) 'qui m'a appris à aimer l'Afrique' as he says in the dedication of his *L'Islam Noir*.

Under Monteil's direction a new section of the IFAN was created for the study of Islam in 1965. It was also in this year that its rich collection of manuscripts in Arabic and in African languages (especially Fulfulde) was made accessible to the scholarly world through the publication of a catalogue compiled by Senegalese members of the Institut.[30] Since then a number of Senegalese scholars associated with the IFAN have made important contributions to the study of Muslim Senegal: Omar Ba in the field of Fulfulde language and literature, Boubacar Barry in history with his *Le Royaume de Waalo* (1972), Thierno Diallo's *Les Institutions Politiques au Fouta Dyalon au XIXe siècle* (1972) and Amar Samb, now Director of the institute with his *Essai sur la contribution du Sénégal à la littérature d'expression arabe* (1973).[31]

Several English-speaking scholars have worked on Senegal, mostly dealing with the interaction of local Islamic forces with modern political forces: O'Brien on the Murides (1971),[32] Klein's *Islam and Imperialism in Senegal* (1968), Lucy Behrman on various aspects of Wolof religious and political life.[33] Articles on historic Islamic movements in the Senegambia region have come from Curtin and Charlotte Quinn[34] while the American scholar David Robinson has written a thesis on Futa Toro in the second half of the nineteenth century (Columbia, 1971) and the extensive oral material he collected during his research has constituted a new *fonds* at IFAN. A young Gambian scholar, Lamin Sanneh, has also written a doctoral thesis on the Diakhanke using oral materials and written documents (London, 1973).

For Mauritania again we can only sketch some of the more important developments. Special mention must be made of the work of Adam Heymowski, Librarian of the Royal Library of Stockholm. Over the past decade he has made numerous field trips in Mauritania under UNESCO auspices to catalogue the materials held in the numerous private libraries of Mauritania—many of them (like that of Shaykh Sidiya earlier examined by Massignon)[35] in nomadic or semi-nomadic encampments. A *Catalogue provisoire* was published in 1965 and a more complete *recensement* is expected in a year or two. In this work he had the invaluable aid of the 'grand old man' of Mauritanian historical studies, Shaykh Mukhtār ould Ḥamidūn who has been a source of scholarly inspiration and friendly counsel to other foreign scholars such as Norris, in his fascinating *Saharan Myth and Saga* (1972) and other studies of Mauritanian history and Sanhaja scholarship, Paulo Farias, in his study of the early history of the Almoravids, and Charles Stewart in his *Islam and Social Order in Mauritania* (1973). All these European scholars also acknowledge their debt to numerous other Mauritanian learned men who have shown themselves ready to collaborate in the search for historical knowledge with other scholars regardless of race or creed. Only a small part of this rich historical material has yet been published. Norris published two documents in his *Saharan Myth and Saga* and the Mauritanian scholar Aḥmad Bābā Miské has published a part-analysis, part-translation of the important *Kitāb al-Wasīṭ* of Aḥmad al-Amīn al-Shinqīṭī written in 1911.[36] I must accept some reproach here myself as I have long been promising to edit and translate the biographical dictionary *Fatḥ al-Shakūr* of Al-Bartilī (*c.* 1800) and have allowed other research and writing commitments to supervene.

Mauritania has been more fortunate than other West African countries in attracting the attention of archaeologists interested in the Islamic period. A large site at Tegdaoust, thought to be that of the mediaeval caravan town of Awdaghast has been systematically excavated by a French team over a period of twelve years[37] and the first of several projected volumes, *Tegdaoust I*, has been published (1970) giving the geographical background to the area and a lengthy treatment of the material in Arabic literary sources referring to the area.[38] Kumbi Salah, a town of central Ancient Ghana (and perhaps the site of the Muslim merchants' town close to the eleventh-century capital) was also the object of French expeditions between 1948 and 1951,[39] though much remains to be done there and in other nearby sites. Walata and Tchitt, still 'live' towns, have also been thoroughly examined and are the subject of a monograph by D. Jacques-Meunié, *Cités anciennes de Mauritanie* (1961).

Mention must also be made of the archaeological, historical and ethnographic work of three other French scholars: Theodore Monod, among whose numerous outstanding contributions we may mention only his *Majâbat al-Koubra: contribution à l'étude de l'"Empty Quarter" ouest-africain* (1958), Henri Lhote who, apart from his work on the Tassili frescoes, has made enormous contributions to the study of Tuareg history and institutions (see especially his *Les Touaregs du Hoggar*, 1955), and Raymond Mauny, many of whose noteworthy studies in Sahelian archaeology and history are brought together in his *Tableau géographique de l'ouest africain au moyen âge* (1961). These three scholars were also responsible for much of the valuable annotation which appeared in Epaulard's new French translation of Leo Africanus's description of North and West Africa which appeared in 1956.

Mali has been less fortunate in archaeological studies, though the sites there demanding excavation are numerous. The whole Niger Bend right round from Jenne to Gaya and its associated hinterland in the Sahel is littered with ruined towns, villages and cemeteries; a thorough and systematic survey and mapping of these sites in what was one of the major contact zones between North and West Africa is surely one of the most urgent priorities in African archaeology.[40] Nor was it only a zone of culture contact. It was also the home of one of the major mediaeval empires, the Songhay Empire, about which, in spite of the apparent richness of the written source materials, all too little is still known. Sporadic investigations have taken place at a number of sites, including Gao where the extraordinary discovery of twelfth-century 'royal' tombstones inscribed in Arabic was made as far back as 1939 and the results published by Sauvaget in 1950 and Marie-Madeleine Viré in 1958 and 1959.[41] Happily, the University of Birmingham's Centre of West African Studies has now begun to make more systematic investigations at Gao under the direction of Colin Flight, while Paulo Farias and myself are working on the Arabic written sources and the epigraphic side, as further tombstones of the twelfth and thirteenth centuries have now come to light. The only other archaeological problem which has attracted attention is that of the 'capital' of mediaeval Mali. A Polish-Guinean expedition has done extensive work at Niané-sur-Sankarani (just inside the Guinea border) though the results published so far seem unimpressive[42] and I have argued that this was not the site of the capital of the Mali Empire in the first half of the fourteenth century at any rate.[43]

Much of the groundwork for the study of the Mali empire was done by Delafosse and by Charles Monteil (some of whose work was published posthumously). Their studies were built on, and their use of oral tradition extended, by the Guinean scholar Djibril Tamsir Niané in his *Recherches sur l'empire du Mali au moyen âge* (1962). Recently a comprehensive study, *Ancient Ghana and Mali* has been published by Levtzion (1973), bringing together and re-interpreting the abundant but hitherto scattered evidence. The French sociologist Claude Meillassoux has also done valuable work on Malian clans and institutions and their historical origins[44] and Yves Person has made some valuable excursions into the field of Manding history not to speak of his encyclopaedic work on Samori (3 vols., 1968, 1975).[45] Manding culture and history was made the subject of a massive conference held at the School of Oriental and African Studies in 1972; many of the papers presented there are scheduled to be published in the proceedings of the conference.

No study comparable to that of Levtzion yet exists for the Songhay empire, except—for Russian readers—the book published in 1974 by L. Koubbel. Other readers have to rely on the now dated *Contribution à l'histoire des Songhay* by Jean Rouch (1955) or on the relevant chapters in the *History of West Africa* edited by Jacob Ajayi and Michael Crowder (vol. 1, 1971, second edition vol. 2, 1974) which also contains many valuable contributions to the history of Muslim West Africa. Various aspects of the history of the Niger Bend have been investigated by European scholars and a study of the Songhay language has been made by Fr. Prost (1956).[46] Happily, some of the small cadre of young Malian scholars have also turned their attention to the area. Worthy of mention among these are Sekéné-Mody Cissoko, Head of the Department of History at the University of Dakar,[47] and Maḥmūd Zubayr, himself a Songhay, who is working on the life and work of Aḥmad Bābā of Timbuktu,[48] a figure to whom some of my own research has been directed.[49] The period following the collapse of the Songhay Empire has generally been neglected, but an Israeli scholar Michel Abitbol is now preparing a doctoral thesis on the Pashalik of Timbuktu and plans to edit with Levtzion a number of Arabic texts concerning this period.[50]

Three doctoral theses in English have been completed on aspects of nineteenth century Mali (and there are no doubt others in French which have not come to my attention). These are the study of the Caliphate of Hamdullahi by William Brown (Wisconsin, 1969), John R. Willis on the movement and ideas of Al-Ḥājj 'Umar b. Sa'īd (London, 1970) and the thesis of 'Abd al-Qādir Zebadiyya on the life and writings of Al-Bakkā'ī (London, 1974). To these we may also add the work of Oloruntimẹhin, referred to above and now published.[51]

For Malian Studies in general we are fortunate in having a very full *Bibliographie Générale du Mali* of Paule Brasseur (1964) which covers the period down to 1960 and to which supplements are planned. Another fundamental development, though still in its infancy, has also taken place within Mali. This is the establishment of the Centre Ahmad Baba de Documentation et Recherches at Timbuktu. This was set up two years ago with the support of Unesco with the object of collecting and analysing Arabic materials from the Niger Bend and neighbouring areas and of stimulating research into the history and institutions of the region. Poor though Mali is in economic terms, it has an extraordinary richness in terms of cultural heritage and the interest shown in it by foreign scholars bodes well for the advancement of our knowledge of this key area of west Africa.

Of developments in Niger I am less well informed. A Centre Nigérien de Recherches en Sciences Humaines has existed since 1960 at Niamey and it publishes an irregular series of monographs, *Études Nigériennes*, which, like its sister publication in Bamako, *Études Maliennes*, does not seem to have the circulation in the English-speaking world which it ought. An important collection of Arabic manuscript materials exists at Niamey which has been assembled through the energy and foresight of M. Boubou Hama who was, until the military take-over of government in Niger in 1974, Président de l'Assemblée Nationale. The collection, which in January 1973, when I saw it, was housed in the Assemblée Nationale, comprised almost 2,000 items, mostly collected within Niger, though with photocopies of some important works from private collections in Timbuktu. An accessions list is kept, but no catalogue has yet been published.

Some interest has been stirred in the history and peoples of the Air region. In 1950 IFAN devoted an entire volume of its *Mémoires* to *Contributions à l'étude de l'Air* and the Danish anthropologist Nicholaissen has published the massive *Ecology and culture of the Pastoral Tuareg* (1964) which largely concerns this area. Harry Norris of SOAS has also found that studies in Air could throw valuable light on his work in more westerly areas of the Sahara and has thus acquired an independent interest in the sultanate of Agades on which we may soon expect some published contributions.

The southern areas of Niger—those bordering on Nigeria, do not seem yet to have attracted the attention they merit. André Salifou has published a monograph, *Le Damagaram ou sultanat de Zinder au 19e siècle* (*Études Nig.*, No. 27, 1971) and M. G. Smith has written on Maradi[52] and has, I believe, done further work on other Hausa states within Niger. His important study of Zaria administration, *Government in Zazzau 1800-1950* (1960) may also be mentioned here as well as the autobiography of a Hausa woman recorded by his wife Mary in her *Baba of Karo* (1954).

The country round Lake Chad has, like the Niger Bend, been an important area of cultural contact and of attraction and dispersion of peoples and cultures. Because it is shared between four countries, it calls for a great effort of international scholarly cooperation if we are to unravel the ethnic, political and cultural history of this complex zone. On the Anglophone side, a good deal of work has been done or is in progress on the history and culture of Borno. Adeleye has written on Rābiḥ and a major study of him is being undertaken by John Lavers who has also essayed a sketch of the history of Islam in Borno.[53] M. Njeuma has devoted a doctoral thesis to neighbouring Adamawa in the nineteenth century (London, 1969) which investigates the role of the Mahdist adventurer Ḥayātu b. Saʿīd, a figure also studied by M. A. Al-Hajj.[54] A meticulous investigation of the mediaeval history of Kanem-Borno has been presented as a doctoral thesis by Dierk Lange (Sorbonne, 1974) incorporating a critical text of the *Dīwān salāṭīn Bornu* which forms a focus for his analysis.[55]

Mention must also be made of the studies of J.-C. Zeltner on the history of the Arabic-speaking tribes of the L. Chad area.[56] Arlette Roth-Laly has compiled a *Lexique des parlers arabes Tchado-Soudanais* (1969-72) bringing together information previously published by several different scholars on Arabic dialects from Bornu to the Nile valley. We may also mention the new dictionary of the dialectal Arabic of the Republic of the Sudan by 'Awn al-Sharīf Qāsim (Khartoum, 1972) which contains many examples of usage and proverbs.[57]

Other areas of Chad have been less well studied. In the more northerly areas this may well be due to the disturbed conditions which have prevailed there since Independence. There is, however, one important study of the Teda peoples by Chapelle, *Les nomades noirs du Sahara* (1958). The area to the south of Tibesti was the scene of much of the later development of one of the great Islamic movements of modern times, the Sanūsiyya. There are two studies of this movement, one by the eminent anthropologist Evans-Pritchard (1949), which chiefly concentrates on political history, and the other by F. Ziadeh (1958) which is useful on Islamic ideology, but says little of the southern expansion. A new study of the Sanūsiyya in Chad and neighbouring territories would thus offer a fruitful field for an Islamicist with African interests.

On Wadday we now have a study of the sultanate by Mme. M.-J. Tubiana.[58] English readers have cause to be grateful for the new translation of Nachtigal's travels (two out of four volumes published so far) prepared by Humphrey Fisher in collaboration with his father A. G. B. Fisher, with additional notes by Rex O'Fahey. The Fishers, father and son, have also used material from this translation and other sources for a book, *Slavery and Muslim Society in Africa* (1970), which contains valuable raw material on the institution of slavery, particularly in West and Central Africa.[59]

The great area which lies between L. Chad and the Nile has tended to be something of a no-man's land, and not merely for Islamicists. Scholars with West African specialisations generally consider it outside their area while those interested in the Sudan have rarely gone even as far east as Darfur. The whole area is worthy of greater concentration of effort and it is to be hoped that from the one end Sudanese scholars, and from the other those of Nigeria, will collaborate with their Chadian and other Francophone colleagues to study this in-between zone more intensively.

As we move eastwards into Darfur we must make special mention of the work of Rex O'Fahey. He has made Darfur his special area of interest and has presented a study of the Keyra Sultanate as a doctoral thesis at the University of London (1972). More recently, in collaboration with the National Archives of the Sudan, he has undertaken field tours in Darfur microfilming land charters and other primary documents among the private papers of certain families and other such expeditions are planned. In another area of documentation M. I. Abu Salim, the Director of the Sudan National Archives, has published a collection of Funj Land Charters (1967)[60] and an annotated English translation is in preparation with the collaboration of an American scholar J. Spaulding.[61] The text of the so-called Funj Chronicle has been published twice, first edited by Mekki Shibeika (1947) and then again by Shāṭir Buṣaylī (1961), but it has not so far been translated. Another important source for the study of Islam in the Sudan prior to the nineteenth century, the *Ṭabaqāt* of Wad Ḍayf Allāh has been published in a new critical edition (1971) by Yūsuf Faḍl Ḥasan, Director of the Institute of African Studies, University of Khartoum. This supersedes the two earlier editions both of which were published in Cairo in 1930. We should also mention the bibliography of Arabic source materials for the study of the Sudan by J. A. Daagher (1968).[62]

From source materials to specific studies. The only overall study of Islam in the Sudan remains that of Trimingham (1949), his first such regional study and perhaps his best. Arkell, a pioneer of the serious study of Sudanese history has written a *History of the Sudan from earliest times to 1821* (1955) and this is complemented by P. M. Holt's *Modern History of the Sudan* (1963). Yūsuf Ḥasan has ably dealt with the early penetration of Islam into the Sudan in his *The Arabs and the Sudan* (1967) and he gives broader though inevitably more general coverage in his *Introduction to the History of the Islamic Kingdoms of the Sudan* (1971).[63] A study of Islam and the Nuba in the Middle Ages (Cairo, 1960) has come from the pen of Muṣṭafā Muḥammad Mus'ad.[64] There are two studies of the Funj Kingdom of Sennar, one by O. G. S. Crawford (1951) and this year (1974) one by J. J. Spaulding published together with O'Fahey's study of the Keyra Sultanate of Darfur.[65] 'Alī Dīnār, the last independent sultan of Darfur was the subject of a book by A. Theobald (1965) and the political history of Darfur in the preceding period (1882-98) the subject of a thesis written in Arabic by Mūsā al-Mubārak (M.A., Khartoum, 1964).

Special mention must be made of the work of P. M. Holt, Professor of Arab History in the University of London. Over the past twenty-five years he has produced a copious outpouring of articles and books of the very highest standard of scholarship, not only on the Sudan but also on aspects of Egyptian and Middle Eastern history in the period 1500-1900. His book, *The Mahdist State in the Sudan* (1958, revised, 1970) is the standard work on the topic and his annotated bibliography of the subject at the end of the book makes it unnecessary for me to add anything here. Five of his articles on aspects of Sudanese Islamic history are to be found in a volume of collected essays, *Studies in the History of the Near East* (1973), while much of his other writing has appeared in the *Bulletin* of SOAS.

Among other work central to the study of Islam in the Sudan mention must be made of the doctoral thesis of J. O. Voll (Harvard, 1969) on the history of the Khatmiyya *ṭarīqa*. Studies of nomadic Muslim tribes, but with emphasis on kinship and tribal institutions rather than Islam, are I. Cunnison's *Baggara Arabs* (1966) and Talal Asad's *The Kababish Arabs* (1970).

Finally it may be noted that the Sudan is relatively well served by the *Encyclopaedia of Islam* and the *Index Islamicus*. There is a general bibliography of the Sudan to 1937 by R. L. Hill (1939) and a continuation to 1958 published in 1962.

Much less can be said about the study of Islam in Ethiopia, the Horn of Africa and East Africa, for these have been comparatively neglected areas for the Islamicist. Perhaps not surprisingly, Ethiopian studies have been dominated either by studies of Axumite history and culture or by the history and literature of the Christian kingdoms of the central highlands. Two important Arabic texts concerning late mediaeval Ethiopia have been published—but long before the period we are looking at.[66] The only comprehensive account is that of Trimingham, *Islam in Ethiopia* (1952) which includes a little material on Somalia also, but it has failed to stimulate research in the way that his much poorer *History of Islam in West Africa* (1962) has done. Interest in the history and culture of the Muslim peoples of Ethiopia at the country's sole university in Addis Ababa has been slight, though recently Abraham Demoz has devoted an article to 'Moslems and Islam in Ethiopian Literature'.[67] This may herald the beginning of a more serious investigation of the religion which claims the adherence of a major element in the population. Among foreign scholars, work on Ethiopian Islam was done in the pre-war period by such eminent men as René Basset and Enrico Cerulli, though the latter's keener interest in the Horn of Africa is indicated in the title of a volume of his collected papers, *Somalia: scritti vari editi ed inediti* (1957). More recently B. G. Martin, whose interests have become increasingly East African (in the widest sense) in the last few years, has written on 'Mahdism and holy wars in Ethiopia before 1600'[68] and the German scholar Erwald Wagner is investigating the history of the Muslim city of Harar.

Somali studies have been dominated by two British scholars, B. W. Andrezejewski and I. M. Lewis, both of whom have often worked in close collaboration with the veteran Somali scholar Musa Galaal. Andrezejewski's main efforts have been in the field of the Somali language (and more recently Galla), but he has taken a keen interest in Somali Islamic writings, the religious poetry written in Arabic and the oral poetry of the Mahdi Muḥammad b. 'Abdullāh Ḥasan. Lewis is an anthropologist with historical interests and to him we owe a study of Somali nomadic life, *A Pastoral Democracy* (1961) and a *Modern History of Somalia*.[69] He also made a valuable contribution to the more general study of Islam in Africa in the long introductory essay to the papers of an International African Institute seminar which he edited under the title *Islam in Tropical Africa* (1966). The whole field of Islam in the Horn of Africa is ripe for investigation. Useful comparative studies could be made of developments and adaptations of the religion among the nomadic Somali with those which took place among other nomadic Muslim peoples in Africa such as the Fulbe, Tuareg and Moors or the nomadic Arabic-speaking tribes of the Nile-Chad region.

The study of the history and culture of the Muslim peoples of Kenya, Uganda and Tanzania has similarly been somewhat neglected. This is evidenced by the need felt to translate and republish a few years ago an article by the German scholar Becker, which first appeared in 1911.[70] Trimingham has devoted a book to *Islam in East Africa* (1964), but it is the thinnest and weakest of all his regional studies. Its shortcomings were made abundantly clear in a review article by G. S. P. Freeman-Grenville [71] who may be regarded as one of the modern pioneers of East African coastal history. To him we owe a *Mediaeval History of the Coast of Tanganyika* (1962) and a volume of *Select Documents* (1962) on the

East African coast as well as work in the fields of numismatics and epigraphy.[72]

Swahili studies have been through something of a boom period in the last decade, though much of the interest has been centred on the language itself, especially in America. Among those who have worked on Swahili literature mention must be made of Lyndon Harries, J. W. T. Allen, who collected a large number of Swahili manuscripts, now preserved at the University of Dar es Salaam, and Jan Knappert who has recently published and translated several volumes of Swahili literature including poems concerned with Muslim mythology, with the *mi'rāj* (ascension) legend and with praise of the Prophet and celebration of his birthday (*mawlid*).[73] In addition to the rich manuscript literature in Swahili, there is known to be a considerable heritage of Arabic writing on the Kenya coast, but so far little of it has been accessible to the wider world of scholarship.

This, essentially, concludes our examination of the developments in the study of Muslim Africa since the Second World War. Few general overviews have been attempted and the unevenness of the materials, both primary sources and modern studies makes this difficult. Trimingham's regional surveys have been mentioned and he has also produced an overall study, *The Influence of Islam on Africa* (1968), but this has led him into some dangerous generalisations and stereotyping. A volume entitled *Islam in Africa* was produced under the editorship of J. Kritzeck and W. H. Lewis (1969), but this is a disappointing medley by almost a score of contributors, partly thematic and partly regional, which breaks little new ground. There is also one general work of Islamic law, Anderson's *Islamic Law in Africa* (1954), but it deals with Islamic law mainly within the framework of modern national (or colonial) codes of law, rather than with the independent development and institutionalisation of the *sharī'a* in its African context.

At the end of this survey we may perhaps allow ourselves a moment for reflection on what has been achieved over the past three decades and what are the prospects and the problems for the coming decades. Certainly much has been achieved by scholars of many different nationalities and disciplines. Among the encouraging features of this period is the emergence of a cadre of young African scholars dedicated to investigating the history and culture of Muslim Africa and the fact that these and many non-African scholars have succeeded in bridging the gap of generations and of methodology in establishing fruitful collaboration with the fast disappearing class of traditional *'ulamā'*. It is a matter of some urgency that these now ageing repositories of Islamic sciences and history should be encouraged to yield up the treasures of their memories and allow copies of their precious written documentation to be preserved in national collections in the countries concerned.

This latter point brings me to the first of what I see as the immediate priorities in the study of Muslim Africa in the coming decades. That is a further massive effort to collect or microfilm written materials in Arabic and in African languages used by Muslims and to analyse, edit and translate them.[74] The same sort of effort must also be made in regard to the unwritten materials before the generation which now safeguards them in their memories dies out.

The second priority is for more archaeological work on sites dating from the Muslim period. Meroitic, Axumite and Ancient Egyptian archaeology are flourishing and a good deal of work has gone into Iron Age and Neolithic sites. From the Islamist's point of view we need intensive effort on the mediaeval sites of the Niger Bend, the Air region, Hausaland and Borno, as also on Saharan sites and such very important north African trading centres as Sijilmasa, Warghla and Ghadames. More studies of material culture and technology— architecture, weaving, brasswork, calligraphy, to take a random selection—are also needed. Again, traditional knowledge and even actual examples of the objects to be studied are likely to disappear rapidly as the twentieth century marches on.

Thirdly, we need more work on Islamic law which lay at the core of Muslim societies down to this century and still enjoys a vigorous life in some areas. Particular attention should be given to the adaptation of the *sharī'a* to local circumstances and to the collection and analysis of *fatwā* material which can shed valuable light on social and economic conditions in bygone ages. More work should be done on Islamic theology in Africa and on Muslim intellectual trends in both the pre-colonial and the modern periods as well as the popular conceptions and folklore of the non-literate masses.

In regard to areas and periods, some indications have already been given. Additionally I would stress the need for more pre-nineteenth century studies, for this period has tended to be neglected, since the primary documentation is relatively less abundant and the effort required to produce even tentative solutions to problems much greater. Apart from the areas already mentioned, increased attention should be given to the penetration of Islam into the forest regions, a more recent phenomenon and one which is still continuing. There is also ample room for sociological studies of the Muslim populations of such great urban centres as Dakar, Lagos, Mogadishu and Dar es Salaam.

Some practical suggestions may be made. First there is a need for more teaching and study of the Arabic language (and other languages spoken and written by African Muslims), and of Islamic studies, in African universities. Nor should they be regarded as the sole preserve of the Muslims themselves, for in the interests of a balanced view and of fostering greater understanding between Muslim and non-Muslim populations, the dedicated collaboration of non-Muslim scholars is needed.

The second development which might help to advance the study of Islam in Africa would be the creation of a specialised journal to publish material on Islam in sub-Saharan Africa. Recent years have seen an enormous (and often unnecessary) proliferation of general journals of African Studies, yet the need is really for more journals with clearly defined objectives and areas of study. Such a journal could be published by the collaboration of a number of interested African universities and would form a focus of interest and a forum for discussion.

Lastly, there is still a deplorable lack of communication, especially in the research field, between East and West Africa, Arab and non-Arab Africa, Anglophone and Francophone Africa. It is often very difficult, except through protracted personal correspondence, to find out what fields are being investigated by one's teaching colleagues in other African universities or by postgraduate students. There is now the useful *Current Africanist Research* bulletin of the International African Institute in London, but further efforts should be made, perhaps through a body such as the Association of African Universities to keep us informed of developments, not only in the study of Muslim Africa, but of other areas as well. Since Muslim Africa receives so little attention in the enormous gatherings of world Orientalists or Islamicists (or even Africanists), and since the field is highly specialised, thought might also be given to holding periodic congresses for the study of Muslim Africa or at least for the study of Islam in tropical Africa.

Before concluding this paper some sort of *apologia* seems necessary. I have at times bemoaned the unevenness of research and effort in this field and the reader might be excused for complaining that my treatment of the topic too has been uneven. Some of the reasons for this were stated earlier in the paper. My approach has been to look at the subject largely from within Africa and to attempt a more or less country-by-country approach. Even in this I have been unfair to some countries, such as the Ivory Coast, Sierra Leone, Upper Volta and the Cameroon. Not only that, but by concentrating on the universities and research institutions in African countries I have inevitably done less than justice to the many European and American institutions where much research into Muslim Africa has been fostered, and many African scholars trained: in Britain the School of Oriental and African Studies, where Islamic and African interests find a fertile meeting ground, Birmingham with its specialised Centre of West African Studies, and Edinburgh itself where Islamic Studies and African Studies have mutually enriched each other. In America too such universities as Princeton, Harvard, Columbia and UCLA have also combined interests in the Arab and African worlds which have been productive of much good scholarship and scholarly inspiration. In Europe institutions and individuals in Paris, Warsaw, Moscow, Prague, Naples and many other centres have made valuable contributions to the study of Islamic Africa.

I think, however, I may fairly claim that I have done no major injustice to the individual European and American scholars who have made outstanding contributions in this field, unless it be to Basil Davidson himself. His interest in Islamic Africa has been quite as keen as it has been in the non-Muslim areas and his enormous labours in the field of African history, his personal commitment to the peoples of Africa and his 'engagement' in their intellectual, social and political struggles make him—to coin an Arabic phrase—*waḥīd dahrihi wa farīd ʿaṣrihi*— alone in his age and unique in his time'. But this whole paper was written as an expression of my admiration for his work and in thanks for personal friendship.

Notes

1 For an earlier survey, chronologically restricted and dealing mainly with W. Africa, see J. R. Willis, 'The historiography of Islam in Africa: the last decade (1960-1970)', *Afr. Stud. Revue* (E. Lansing), xiv, 3, Dec. 1971, pp. 403-24.

2   See J. Sauvaget *Introduction to the History of the Muslim East*, an English translation, with corrections, of the 2nd edition prepared by Claude Cahen, UCLA Press, Los Angeles, 1965.

3   See also below, pp. 142-3 for a discussion of work concerning Mauritania.

4   *Cahiers d'histoire mondiale*, xiii, 1971, pp. 51-130.

5   See his essay in *Tegdaoust I* (1970), 109-56, and his 'Routes de commerce et échange en Afrique occidentale en relation avec la Méditerranée', *Revue d'histoire économique et sociale*, 1972, pp. 42-73, 357-97.

6   *J. Semitic Stud.*, xvi, 1972, pp. 193-8.

7   *Annales Islamologiques* (Inst. français d'archéologie orientale (Cairo)), xi, 1972, pp. 263-86.

8   The state of the collection in the early 1960s is described by K. Mahmud in *Libri*, xiv, 2, 1964, pp. 97-107.

9   Both of these texts and translations are to be published in the Arabic series of a project entitled *Fontes Historiae Africanae* sponsored by the International Academic Union—Elmasri's in 1975 and my own in 1976. See also below, notes 61 and 74.

10 Two *Interim Reports* have appeared, 1966, 1967.

11 G. O. Gbadamosi, 'The Growth of Islam among the Yoruba, 1841-1908', (Ph.D., Ibadan, 1968); S. A. Balogun, 'Gwandu in the 19th century' (Ph.D., Ibadan, 1971); M. Adamu, 'A Hausa government in decline: Yawuri in the 19th century', (M. A., Zaria, 1968)—he has also just completed a Ph.D. thesis (Birmingham, 1974) on the Hausa diaspora in west Africa; S. Abubakar, 'The Emirate of Fombina, 1809-1903' (Ph.D., Zaria, 1971); M. B. Alkali, 'A Hausa community in crisis: Kebbi in the 19th century' (M.A., Zaria, 1968).

12 L. Brenner, *The Shehus of Kukawa*, 1973; V. Low, *Three Nigerian Emirates* (Gombe, Katagum, Hadejia), 1972; J. N. Paden, *Religion and Political Culture in Kano*, 1973; for Lavers, see below, n. 53.

13 See also fn. 9 above. B. G. Martin has published, on the basis of a single text, Dan Fodio's *Ta'līm al-Ikhwān* (*Middle East Studies*, iv (1967), 50-97) and U. F. Malumfashi has edited Gidado dan Laima's *Rawḍ al-jinān* and *Al-Kashf wa 'l-bayān*—biographies of Dan Fodio and Muḥammad Bello, for an M.A. thesis (Zaria, 1972). S. A. Kamali (University of Ghana) is preparing Dan Fodio's *Naṣā'ih al-ummat al-Muḥammadiyya* for publication.

14 See, for example, *Bulletin of the School of Oriental and African Studies* (*BSOAS*), xix, 1957, pp. 550-78 and xxv, 1962, 577-96 and his joint article with A. D. H. Bivar, 'The Arabic Literature of Nigeria to 1804: a provisional account', *BSOAS*, xxv, 1962, pp. 104-48.

15 There is also a great deal of such material in the Cameroon; see, for example, the articles of Eldridge Mohamadou in *Abbia*, 6, Aug. 1964, pp. 15-158 and 8, Feb.-March 1965, pp. 45-76 (translation of a Fulfulde historical text).

16 *Research Bulletin, Centre of Arabic Documentation* (*RBCAD*), ii, 2, July, 1966, pp. 1-10 and iii, l, Jan. 1967, pp. 1-15.

17 Bivar's paleographical interests led him to a pioneer study of west African Arabic calligraphy, *Afr. Lang. Review*, vii, 1968, pp. 3-15. Earlier (*BSOAS*, xxii (1959), pp, 324-49) he published careful studies of five nineteenth-century official documents from northern Nigeria. B. G. Martin has also published official correspondence between Tripoli and Bornu in the nineteenth century, *Journal of the Historical Society of Nigeria*, (*JHSN*), ii, 2, 1962, pp. 350-72, and more was published by H. I. Gwarzo in *Kano Studies* (old series), i, 4, 1968, pp. 50-67.

18 See the review by Last in *RBCAD*, iv, 1968, pp. 87-91.

19 Waziri Junaidu is also a prolific writer on historical topics in both Arabic and Hausa and some of his works are preserved on microfilm in the Centre of Arabic Documentation.

20 For a survey of Muslim writing in Ghana see T. Hodgkin, 'The Islamic Literary

Tradition in Ghana' in I. M. Lewis (ed.) *Islam in Tropical Africa*, 1966, pp. 442-62. Some early nineteenth-century Arabic manuscripts from Ghana, preserved in the Royal Library, Copenhagen, have been described by Levtzion in *Transactions Hist. Soc. of Ghana*, viii, 1965, pp. 99-119.

21 A mark of this is the Conference on Arabic Documents organised at Legon by Hodgkin in February 1965; see report in *RBCAD*, i, 3, July, 1965, pp. 8-25.

22 C. C. Stewart, 'The Tijaniyya in Ghana,' 1965; P. de M. Farias, 'The Almoravids: some questions concerning the character of the movement during its periods of closest contact with the Western Sudan', 1965, published in *Bulletin de l'Institut français* (later *'fondamental'*) *de l'Afrique noire*, (*BIFAN*), xxix, 1967, pp. 794-878. See also J. P. Dretke, 'The Muslim Community in Accra', 1968.

23 See, for example, his 'The transmission of Islamic learning in the Western Sudan' in J. Goody (ed.), *Literacy in Traditional Societies*, 1968, pp. 161-97.

24 For his works and the state of their preservation and publication see Goody, *op. cit.*, 251-3. He does not cite the History of Kebbi (in Hausa) translated by H. Sölken in *Mitteilungen des Instituts für Orientforschung*, vii, 1959, and ix, 1963.

25 A transliterated text with German translation, but no annotation was published by the German administrator Adam Mischlich in the *Mitteilungen des Seminars für Orientalische Sprachen*, x, xi, xii (1907-1909).

26 Institute of Oriental Studies, University of Warsaw, 1973. For the history of Wala see *Africana Bulletin* (Warsaw), x, 1969, pp. 53-76 and xi, 1970, pp. 59-78, in English.

27 Before leaving Ghana mention should be made of the continuing archaeological work on the Muslim trading terminus at Begho under the direction of Merrick Posnansky and the work on Islamic architecture by Phyllis Ferguson, *Aspects of Muslim architecture in the Dyula regions of the Western Sudan*, Inst. Afr. Stud., Legon, 1968, and Labelle Prussin, *Architecture in Northern Ghana* (1970) and her broader articles on West African architecture in *African Arts*, Los Angeles, i, 2, 1968, pp. 32 ff. and iii, 4, 1970, pp. 64 ff.

28 *BIFAN*, xxx, 1968, 39-116.

29 Publ. de la Fac. des Lettres et Sci. humaines, Univ. de Dakar: Histoire no. 9, with R. Mauny, A. Djenidi, S. Robert and J. Devisse.

30 Thierno Diallo, Mame Bara M'Backé, Boubacar Barry with a non-Senegalese collaborator, Mirjana Trifkovič (*IFAN* Catalogues et Documents no. xx).

31 Samb has also published (*BIFAN*, xxxii, 1970, pp. 44-135, 370-411, 770-818) a translation of a life of Al-Ḥājj 'Umar b. Sa'īd by the important Senegalese Arabist and historian Mūsā Kamara (d. 1943).

32 *The Mourides of Senegal: the political and economic organisation of an Islamic brotherhood.*

33 See her *Muslim Brotherhoods and Politics in Senegal* (1970) and her 'French Muslim policy and the Senegalese brotherhoods' in D. F. McCall and N. Bennet (eds.), *Aspects of West African Islam* (1971), 185-208. This latter volume is a disparate collection of papers of very variable quality.

34 P. Curtin, '*Jihād* in West Africa: early phases and interrelations in Mauritania and Senegal', *Journal of African History*, (*JAH*), xii, 1971, pp. 11-24. C. A. Quinn, 'A Nineteenth century Fulbe state', *JAH*, xii, 1971, pp. 427-40.

35 *Revue du Monde Musulman*, viii, 1909, pp. 409-18.

36 *BIFAN*, xxx, 1968, pp. 117-64. Other chronicles were published before the war: of Tchit by V. Monteil (*BIFAN*, i, 1939, pp. 282-312), of Walāta and Nema by P. Marty (*Rev. des Études Islamiques*, 1927, pp. 355-426, 531-75) and the *Chronique de la Mauritanie Sénégalaise*, 1911, edited and translated by Ismail Hamet, an Algerian scholar who did considerable work on Saharan history.

37 See D. and S. Robert, 'Les fouilles de Tegdaoust', *JAH*, xi, 1970, pp. 471-93 and 'Douze ans de recherches archéologiques en république islamique de Mauritanie', *Ann. Fac. des Lettres et Sci. Humaines* (Univ. de Dakar), ii, 1972, pp. 195-214.

38 See also n. 5 above.

39 R. Mauny and P. Thomassey, 'Campagne de fouilles à Koumbi-Salah', *BIFAN*, xii, 1951, pp. 438-62, and xviii 1956, pp. 117-40.

40 An early survey of sites yielding funeral inscriptions was made by De Gironcourt and published in his mission's *Documents Scientifiques*, 1920, pp. 293-356.

41 *BIFAN*, xii, 1950, pp. 418-40; xx, 1958, pp. 368-76; xxi, 1959, pp. 459-500.

42 W. Filipowiak in *Africana Bulletin*, xi, 1969, pp. 107-17.

43 *JAH*, xiv, 1973, pp. 195-208.

44 E.g. 'Histoire et institutions des *kafo* de Bamako d'après la tradition des Niaré', *Cahiers d'Études Africaines*, iv, 1963, pp. 186-227, and with L. Doucoure and D. Simagha, *Légende de la dispersion des Kusa* (1967).

45 E.g. 'Les ancêtres de Samori', *Cah. d'Ét. Afr.*, iv, 1963, pp. 125-56; 'Nyani Mansa Mamudu et la fin de l'empire du Mali', paper presented to the SOAS Conference on Manding Studies, 1972.

46 *La Langue Sonray et ses dialectes* (Mém. de l'*IFAN* no. 47). He has made many other valuable contributions on the ethnography and languages of the peoples of the inner Niger Bend.

47 E.g. 'L'Intelligentsia de Tombouctou au XVe et XVIe siècles', *Présence Africaine*, lxxxii, 1969, pp. 48-72; 'Famines et épidémies à Tombouctou et dans la boucle du Niger du XVIe au XVIIIe siècle', *BIFAN*, xxx, 1968, pp. 806-21.

48 A doctoral thesis presented at the Sorbonne 1974.

49 See *BSOAS*, xxvii, 1964, pp. 568-93 and *RBCAD*, ii, 2, 1966, pp. 19-31.

50 A *thèse de 3e cycle* was presented at the Sorbonne (1972) by the Ivorian scholar Niamkey Kodjo with the title 'Ishâq II et la fin de l'empire Songaï (1588-1593)'. It is perhaps appropriate to mention here the existence of a sociological study of Timbuktu by H. Miner (1953) based on research in 1940. Its style is inclined to be journalistic and the chapter on 'Islam' leaves us still with everything to be done.

51 Ọlọruntimẹhin has also written on the nineteenth-century Soninke jihadist Muḥamad al-Amīn (*JHSN*, iv, 3 1968, pp. 375-96) and in M. Crowder (ed.) *West African Resistance* (1971), pp. 80-110. Ivan Hrbek, whose work on mediaeval Muslim geographers is well-known, is preparing a full-length study of Muḥammad al-Amīn. There is, as yet, no study in depth of the Hamallist movement founded by Shaykh Ḥamallāh (d. 1943) of Nioro, though a recent survey of it has been given by Pierre Alexandre in I. Rotberg and A. Mazrui (eds.), *Power and Protest in Black Africa* 1970, pp. 497-512.

52 'Maradi under Dan Baskore' in P. Kaberry and D. Forde (eds.), *West African Kingdoms*, 1967, pp. 93-122.

53 See R. Adeleye in *JHSN*, v, 2, 1970, pp. 223-42 and v, 3, 1970, pp. 399-418. For Lavers see *Odu* (new series), v, 1971, pp. 27-53, and also his interesting account of a little-known Nigerian mahdist leader Jibril Gaini in *RBCAD*, iii, 1967, pp. 16-39. He is also editor of a new series of *Kano Studies* (1970-   ), which describes itself as 'a journal of Saharan and Sudanic research'.

54 See his 'Ḥayātū b. Sa'īd, a revolutionary mahdist in the Western Sudan', in Y. F. Hasan (ed.), *The Sudan in Africa*, 1971, pp. 128-41.

55 See also his valuable annotated translation (with S. Berthoud) of the late sixteenth-century account of Bornu etc. by D'Anania in *Cah. d'hist. mondiale*, xiv, 1972, pp. 299-351. B. G. Martin has made two useful contributions to the 'middle period' of Bornu history: 'Kanem, Bornu and the Fezzan: notes on the political history of a trade route', *JAH*, x, 1969, pp. 15-27 and 'Mai Idris of Bornu and the Ottoman Turks, 1576-1578' *Int. J. Middle East Studies*, iii, 1972, pp. 470-90, this latter article containing translations of two official documents.

56 In *Abbia*, xvi, 1967, pp. 129-53 and *Ann. de l'Univ. d'Abidjan* (série F), ii, 2, 1970, pp. 109-237.

57 *Qāmūs all-ahjat al-'āmmiyya fī 'l-Sūdān*, published under the aegis of the Sudan Research Unit (now Inst. of African Studies, Univ. of Khartoum).

58 'Un document inédit sur les sultans de Waddāy', *Cah. d'Ét. Afr.*, ii, 1961, pp. 49-112.

59 Humphrey Fisher has made numerous other important contributions to the study of Muslim West Africa, many of which have appeared in the *Journal of African History*.

60 *Al-Fūnj wa 'l-arḍ.* Land documents of the mahdist period appear in his *Al-Arḍ fī 'l-Mahdiyya* (1970). These two works form Occasional Papers of the Sudan Research Unit nos. 2 and 5 respectively.

61 To be published in the *Fontes Historiae Africanae* Arabic series; see n. 9 above.

62 *Al-Uṣūl al-'arabiyya li 'l-dirāsāt al-Sūdāniyya 1875-1967.*

63 Written in Arabic with the title *Muqaddima fī ta 'rīkh al-mamālik al-islāmiyya fī 'l-Sūdān.*

64 Written in Arabic: *Al-Islām wa 'l-Nūba fī 'l-uṣūr al-wusṭā.*

65 The joint work is entitled *Kingdoms of the Sudan.*

66 Al-Maqrīzī, *Kitāb al-ilmām bi akhbār man bi arḍ al-Ḥabasha min mulūk al-Sūdān*, ed. Jirjī Zaydān, Cairo, 1895 (first published with Latin translation by Rink, Leyden, 1790); Shihāb al-Dīn 'Arabfaqīh, *Futūḥ al-Ḥabasha*, ed. and trans. by R. Basset, 1897.

67 *J. Ethiop. Stud.*, x, 1972, pp. 1-11.

68 *Proceedings of the Seminar for Arabian Studies* (London), iv, 1974, pp. 106-17.

69 See also his 'Sufism in Somaliland: a study in tribal Islam', *BSOAS*, xvii, 1955, pp. 581-602 and xviii, 1956, pp. 145-60. An M.A. thesis on the history of Islam in Somalia is reported in International African Institute: Current Africanist Research (IAICAR) 1972, no. 1879.

70 'Materialen zur Kenntnis des Islam in Deutsch-Ostafrika', edited and translated by B. G. Martin, *Tanzania, Notes and Records*, lxviii, 1968, pp. 31-68.

71 *RBCAD*, i, 3, July, 1965, pp. 35-9.

72 On coins see *JAH*, i, 1960, pp. 31-43; on inscriptions (with B. G. Martin) see *J. Royal Asiatic Soc.* 1973, pp. 98-122. On Muslim architecture in east Africa see P. S. Garlake, *Early Islamic Architecture of the East African Coast*, 1964, J. S. Kirkman, *The Arab City of Gedi*, 1952 and his broader *Men and Monuments of the East African Coast*, 1964.

73 *Swahili Islamic Poetry*, 3 vols., 1971. See also E. Damman 'The tradition of Swahili Islamic Poetry', *RBCAD*, v, 1969. pp. 21-41 with Additional Notes by J. W. T. Allen, pp. 42-6.

74 This, in fact, constitutes the first priority of the *Fontes Historiae Africanae* (see n. 9 above).

Thurstan Shaw

Changes in African Archaeology in the last Forty Years

In writing of African archaeology we must not forget that Egypt is in Africa.
I am no Egyptologist and I am therefore not competent to describe the progress
of Egyptology—in the last forty years or at any time; and as Basil Davidson's
principal contributions have concerned Africa outside Egypt, I shall in this
paper concern myself principally with the same area. However, archaeologists
working outside Egypt have to be aware of what was going on in the Nile valley
both in Predynastic and Dynastic times, and it is unfortunate that the historical
accident whereby Egyptology grew up as a discipline separated both from
European and African prehistory has resulted in too little contact between them.[1]
Of course Egyptologists and Africanist archaeologists have to meet in Meroe;
but apart from this they hardly ever do. If there were more contact, perhaps
there might be more understanding of the African elements in the ancestry of
Egyptian civilisation, or of those elements common to both: the early cultures of
Merimde, the Fayum, Badari and of Naqada I and II are essentially African,
and early African social customs and religious beliefs were the root and foundation
of the ancient Egyptian way of life.[2] With a real knowledge of Egyptology,
perhaps speculators about the African past would have been less subject to what
has been called 'the Egyptian disease'—that is, the tendency to see the hand of
ancient Egypt in every African divine kingship, in every African language
containing superficially resembling syllables, in every burial custom remotely
paralleled in ancient Egypt, and in a host of other heterogeneous manifestations.

Although Egyptian and African parallels have been noted for over 200 years[3]
it was only in the present century that this 'Egyptian disease' became rife. The
infection came from those diffusionists who were so impressed by what they saw
of ancient Egyptian civilisation that they felt it must be the fount and origin of
all civilisation; every country in the world was combed for words, names,
antiquities, customs, religious ideas, social organisations and political
institutions; where there was the slightest analogy with anything Egyptian,
there was found proof of the connection. It did not matter how isolated the
trait was, or how different the rest of the total culture; the ancient Egyptians
were envisaged as explorers, missionaries, traders, colonists and rulers, bringing
the enlightenment of ancient Egypt to a dark world.[4] I sometimes wonder
whether it is no coincidence that this particular theory of diffusionism emerged
out of the heyday of the French and British Empires in Africa, when western
Europeans saw themselves as undertaking a *mission civilisatrice* or what Kipling
called 'the white man's burden', of spreading enlightenment to what he called

'lesser breeds without the law'[5] rather in the manner they pictured the ancient Egyptians. Certainly this particular diffusionist theory greatly appealed to colonial administrators and others, who joined in the hunt for things Egyptian in the territories in which they worked.[6] In defence of the proponents of the theory of diffusion from Egypt one must remember it was much less silly when they were writing than it can now be seen to be, as at the time there was not so much archaeological knowledge about the other ancient civilisations of the Old World and about surrounding areas; chronology was much less securely based and it was not appreciated that the civilisation of Sumer was older than that of Egypt. Nowadays there is much less excuse for holding to the idea, and yet surprisingly enough, the theory is not dead. Perhaps it is its very romanticism which helps to keep it alive.

It is somewhat ironic that the advocacy of Egyptian diffusionism on the part of colonial administrators was accompanied and followed by its enthusiastic espousal by indigenous African writers.[7] Their arguments, however, have been pretty convincingly refuted.[8] The cultural parallels pointed to for some African peoples are no more than can be pointed to for many others in different, and less likely, parts of the world; and there are some areas of culture where there are no parallels at all; the philological arguments are dismissed as entirely unsound by modern linguists; the arguments alleged from physical anthropology are equally unconvincing; and the criteria for political parallels need to be much more carefully specified. There are indeed a few stray pieces of evidence which suggest that sub-Saharan Africa was not completely cut off from Egypt and it behoves archaeologists to be aware of them and to evaluate them. But the emotional attraction of this idea has sometimes outweighed critical judgment, and it dies hard,[9] for ancient Egypt was part of Africa, it had a great and glorious civilisation, and it gives added lustre to African pride to trace cultural or even physical ancestry to ancient Egypt. Critical questions are sidestepped as to the precise date at which different parts of Africa were supposed to have been colonised from ancient Egypt, by what route and whether there is any supporting evidence along the line of this route. What does not seem to have been noticed is that the desire to gain some reflected glory from the splendour that was ancient Egypt is almost a tacit admission that ancient African culture is lacking. But it is not true that ancient African culture is lacking; it has a great deal of ancient culture which arouses the interest and admiration of artists and scholars in all parts of the world. Africa possesses her own glories and needs no borrowed light from other cultures.

Thus one of the changes which has come over archaeological thinking concerning Africa in the last forty years is a much greater caution in attributing African cultural traits to diffusion from Egypt. We are now in a better position to see that both diffusion and independent innovation have been agents of cultural change. Just as this particular shift in thinking is reflected in African archaeology, so it is that other changes in the aims, methods and theory of archaeology are similarly reflected in the modern archaeological approach to the continent.

One of the most notable changes in African archaeology over the last forty years is a purely quantitative one. Outside Egypt and North Africa, by 1934 comparatively little had been done: a number of caves had been excavated in French Guinea around the turn of the century; the Wellcome Expeditions to the Sudan before the First World War, conceived as much in terms of providing employment as in those of archaeological research, had excavated Jebel Moya and Abu Geili, although the reports were not published until after the Second World War[10]; Caton-Thompson had brought some sanity into the investigation of Zimbabwe and confirmed that Randall MacIver[11] was the only previous excavator to be respected. During the 1920s Van Riet Lowe and John Goodwin worked on the problems of the Stone Age in South Africa; Van Riet Lowe was a civil engineer who became interested in stone implements and river terraces as a result of his professional experiences in building bridges, while John Goodwin was one of the earliest students of the Cambridge school of prehistoric archaeology and the first of its many products to open up archaeology in Africa. He was given an appointment in the University of Cape Town in 1923, but Van Riet Lowe did not finally make the switch from professional engineer to professional archaeologist until 1935, when he became the first Director of the newly set up Bureau of Archaeology in the Department of the Interior. With its universities and general level of wealth and education among its white population, it is understandable that South Africa gained a generation's lead in archaeological research over any other part of Africa south of the Tropic of Cancer. By the late 1920s the progress of archaeological research in South Africa had reached a point to attract the interest of leading European prehistorians: Miles Burkitt, John Goodwin's teacher at Cambridge, paid a visit to South Africa; after a conducted tour by Van Riet Lowe and Goodwin and a study of their notes and records, he was able on his return to England to write a book called *South Africa's Past in Stone and Paint*.[12] This was closely followed by Goodwin and Van Riet Lowe's own publication *The Stone Age Cultures of South Africa*.[13] The Abbé Breuil then paid an eleven-week visit in 1929 and in the next two years published his own summaries of the position as he saw it.[14]

Meanwhile, Louis Leakey, a son of the Kenya soil, also trained in Cambridge, was beginning his work in east Africa, and in 1934 the geologist Wayland wrote his famous paper 'Rifts, Rivers, Rains and Early Man in Uganda', in which he adduced evidence from Africa which he interpreted to indicate 'pluvial' periods corresponding to the already well known glacial periods of Europe.[15]

Thus by 1934 important beginnings had been made, enough to suggest the archaeological promise of Africa, but efforts were very sporadic and uncoordinated and the total quantity of archaeological research completed was very small. I estimate that forty years ago there were less than half a dozen archaeologists working in the whole of sub-Saharan Africa; and only the two South Africans were, if you will forgive the archaeological term, *in situ*. Other workers (even including Leakey at this time) were based in Europe and brought archaeological expeditions to Africa; the same was true of Jean Colette, attached to the Tervuren Museum when he carried out his remarkable excavations at Kalina Point in the Belgian Congo[16] The late thirties saw the beginning of an important change in this pattern: in 1937 Desmond Clark was appointed curator of the

Rhodes-Livingstone Museum in Northern Rhodesia and Thurstan Shaw curator of the Anthropology Museum of Achimota College in the Gold Coast; and in 1939 the Institut Français d'Afrique Noire was founded at Dakar, with the eminent archaeologist and polymath Theodore Monod at its head, and later to provide the base for such distinguished archaeologists as Raymond Mauny and Henri Hugot. We can compare the situation forty years ago of less than half a dozen archaeologists working in the whole of sub-Saharan Africa, mostly based outside Africa, with the fact that today there are eighteen archaeologists working in Nigeria alone; what is more, these are all based in Nigeria and paid for by Nigerian funds; and half of them are indigenous Nigerians. Admittedly this is a flowering which has only come about in the last five years. The take-off point in Ghana for the change from isolated efforts to a substantial attack on archaeological problems came in 1951 with the foundation of the Department of Archaeology in the University.[17] Yet as recently as 1959 an American anthropologist was able to write: 'The spade of the archaeologist has thus far lifted perhaps an ounce of earth on the Niger for every ton carefully sifted on the Nile'.[18]

This paucity of accumulated research carries certain consequences. It means that whereas in those parts of the world with a longer history of archaeological research, it is possible to make considerable advances by the analysis of material already published or in museums, and on the basis of established cultural sequences and chronological frameworks, in most parts of Africa these sequences and frameworks are only now being established and the top priority remains to go out into the field and excavate and obtain the necessary primary data. In Europe there was a mass of archaeological material in museums for the twentieth-century archaeologists to get to work on. In Africa there is nothing like that. In the archaeologically older parts of the world, too, interest has moved on from concern with 'What happened', since this is now largely established, to concern with 'How it happened', that is, to the dynamics of cultural change; fieldwork tends to be formulated to discover the answers to questions posed in these terms. In Africa we now have to have both sets of problems in mind in formulating field research programmes, to try, at the same time, to find out both what happened and how and why it happened.

Perhaps I might illustrate this from the examples of Ife and Old Oyo in West Africa, and of Zimbabwe in south Central Africa. In the case of Old Oyo and Ife there are so many questions to which we should like to have the answers, such as what the process was which brought the Yoruba kingdom of Old Oyo into being, what was the relationship with Ife, why was there at Ife such an artistic flowering and why did it disappear. We are unlikely to be able to begin to get the answers to these questions until we have a clearer idea both of the sequence of events at Old Oyo and Ife in relation to each other, and more accurate dating in absolute terms. At long last it looks as if we are beginning to make a breakthrough in Ife in achieving some kind of periodisation as a result of all the work carried out in the last twenty years,[19] but at Old Oyo, logically so much more difficult to work at, it is only now that the University of Ibadan is beginning to follow up Frank Willett's 1956 reconnaissance by conducting its field schools for students there;

it will require many years' work and an expansion of it on to a larger scale than has hitherto been possible to achieve results which can be interpreted in a historical reconstruction capable of answering the sort of questions I formulated above. At the moment we do not know within 300 years when Old Oyo was founded.[20] It can be seen from Figure 1 that we can now at Ife speak of a 'Pre-Pavement' period from the sixth century to about A.D. 1100 and ante-dating the making of potsherd pavements; of a 'Pavement' period from soon after A.D. 1100 to the mid-fifteenth century and which is probably the period of the production of the principal works of art; and of a 'Post-Pavement' period after about A.D. 1450. On present evidence it certainly looks as if some big change occurred at Ife in the first half of the fifteenth century. What is the relationship of such a change to the founding of Old Oyo? How can we reasonably speculate on this when present authorities can differ as to whether this took place about A.D. 1200 or as late as A.D. 1430?

The story of the archaeological investigation of Zimbabwe is somewhat different, as it has been complicated by being a highly emotional bone of contention between white settlers on the one hand, claiming an ancient, Mediterranean origin for it as 'a symbol of the essential rightness and justice of colonization'[21]; and, on the other hand, serious archaeologists who are all agreed upon its indigenous origin not more than a thousand years ago. However, leaving that aside, research at Zimbabwe and in the surrounding territory has not merely established its dates and internal history, but also provided suggestions concerning both the way in which stone wall building came to be practised in the area, and the reasons for Zimbabwe's decline: in the first case it seems that dry stone walls were first built in the area for defensive purposes to link up natural rocky outcrops; and the final decline of Zimbabwe in the mid-fifteenth century seems more likely to have been due to soil impoverishment and an over-exploitation of the local natural resources, than to any external conquest.[22]

Thus, while one change that has come over African archaeology is a greater interest in the causes and mechanisms of cultural change, often it still has to be concerned also with a straightforward establishment of a sequence of events.

Another change in archaeological thinking which has been applied to Africa has been a shift from typology to ecology. This does not mean that typology has been thrown out of the window; but it does mean that much greater attention has been paid to the interaction between prehistoric tool-makers and their environment, in the attempt to reconstruct the life of ancient man. In the early 1950s, under the influence of the Abbé Breuil and the French school of prehistorians, archaeologists of the Stone Age were concerned to establish chronological stages characterised by particular type specimens or type assemblages; a further development of this idea is seen in its being expressed in comparative cumulative-frequency graphs. This way of thinking can be illustrated by Leakey's 1951 volume[23] in which on the basis of material collected at Olduvai he published an evolutionary scheme of stone artifacts set out in eleven stages from Oldowan pebble tools through 'Chellean' to the six stages of Acheulian. Similar stages were published for the Vaal River gravels[24] and for

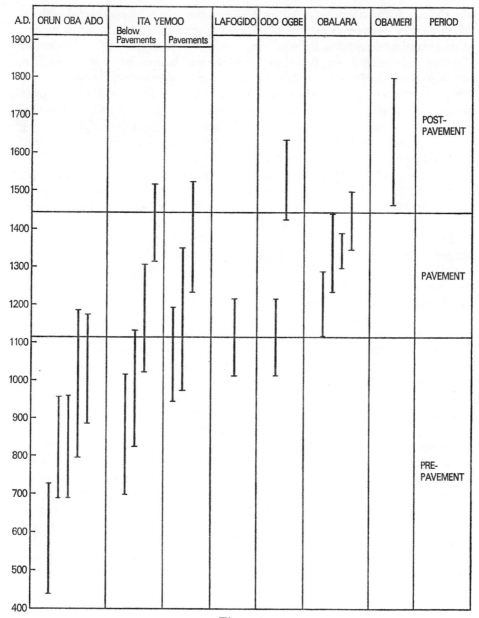

Figure 1

Radiocarbon dates from Ife, corrected by tree-ring calibration (Ralph *et. al.*, 1973).
Laboratory numbers, from left to right, as follows:
Orun Oba Ado: B.M.–265, M–2114, M–2115, M–2116, B.M.–264.
Ita Yemoo, below pavements: M–2121, B.M.–261, B.M.–259, M–2117;
             pavements: B.M.–262, M–2119, M–2120.
Lafogido: I–4911.
Odo Ogbe: I–4670, I–4669.
Obalara: N–1392, N–1393, N–1391, N–1390.
Obameri: M–1686.

the Palaeolithic of north-west Africa.[25] These studies can be contrasted with Mary Leakey's 1971 volume[26] in which are reported the results of much more actual excavation and detailed stratigraphical work; it has thus been possible to distinguish between living floors, kill sites, stream channel infillings, and diffuse sites, to recover complete assemblages from them and to map their details. Similarly, the more recent studies at Olorgesailie have given fresh insights into the nature of Acheulian occupation sites.[27] Another example is provided by the fact that the whole of the first volume of the report on Kalambo Falls is concerned, not with artifacts, but with environmental conditions.[28]

In a later period in the history of man in Africa, archaeology has increasingly turned its attention to the question of the development of agriculture and stock-raising and the way in which the change to food production was effected from a hunting-gathering way of life. Forty years ago Seligman was still propounding the 'Hamitic myth',[29] in which the agricultural Negroes were regarded as inferior to the incoming pastoral Hamites, said to be quicker-witted as well as better armed.[30] Little consideration was given to just how the Negroes had become agricultural and there was no appreciation of the magnitude of the adaptive shift involved in a change from food collection to food production under African tropical conditions. The botanists Vavilov[31] and Roland Portères[32] interested themselves in the origins of African food plants; an economist speculated on the subject,[33] and the question began to be looked at from the archaeological point of view.[34] However, perhaps the biggest shock to conventional thinking on the subject was Murdock's bold theory[35] that there was a major centre of plant domestication in his 'nuclear Mande' area around the headwaters of the Niger some five thousand years ago. Very little of that theory has stood up to the test of further investigation[36] but it stimulated further research, much of which was pooled two years ago at a Wenner-Gren Symposium, at present in course of publication[37] and which makes possible a much clearer picture both of our knowledge and of our ignorance of the subject.[38] It is now appearing that there is a dispersed area along the Sahel zone of Africa in which some seven or eight wild cereals were domesticated, beginning probably not later than the third millennium B.C.; there was almost certainly an area of independent yam and tuber domestication in the south of the eastern part of West Africa, at dates not proven but estimated by some authorities as not less than five thousand years ago.[39] Domesticated cattle appear to have been known in the Saharan highlands from the fifth millennium B.C., perhaps earlier, but for the spread of domesticated animals into sub-Saharan Africa, led apparently by the goat, we have no evidence as yet before the end of the fourth millennium B.C.[40]

Figure 1 also illustrates one of the biggest changes that has come upon African archaeology in the last twenty years—and that is the advent of radiometric dating. In 1963 I think there were no more than six archaeological radiocarbon dates for the whole of Nigeria; now there must be about 150. The importance of radiocarbon dates is also demonstrated by the regularly recurring features of the *Journal of African History* in which the latest dates are tabulated and commented upon. It is Africa, too, which has benefited most from the advent of potassium-argon dating for older ranges of time, since it is this which has made possible the dating of the fossil deposits of Olduvai, the Omo Valley and East Rudolf, and thereby radically altered our whole concept of man's ancestry and the rate and course of human evolution.

Thus radiometric dating has affected the whole dramatic story of the changes which have taken place in our knowledge of man's origins as a result of archaeological work in Africa. Perhaps the most significant find in Africa in the present century was made by a quarryman called De Bruyn at a limeworks near Taung in South Africa in 1924. It consisted of a good part of the fossilised skull of what at first appeared to be an ape. It reached the hands of Raymond Dart, the professor of anatomy in the University of the Witwatersrand, who recognised that this 'ape' skull had certain definitely human characteristics. He named it *Australopithecus* and suggested it might be put in a new family midway between the Pongidae and Hominidae.[41] This was not accepted by the majority of Dart's scientific colleagues, but nevertheless it was the initial find which began a trail leading to the discovery of more australopithecines in South Africa, to others in more easily dated contexts in East Africa, and indirectly to the dethronement of the faked and misleading Piltdown man. It has led ultimately to the recent finding of a veritable harvest of early hominid remains in East Rudolf, one of which, with an age of nearly three million years, appears to have human characteristics not before discovered in specimens more than half a million years old.[42] Since this paper was written, a find has been announced from the central Afar region of eastern Ethiopia taking the figure back to four million years (*The Times*, 26 October 1974). These fossils also establish that it was not 'the brain that led the way' in human evolution, as had been supposed at the time Piltdown was faked, but that the cardinal change was the adoption of a habitually upright posture and the freeing of the hands. Although there has been some suggestion that southern Asia participated[43] in the development of the australopithecines towards *Homo*, there is at present no unequivocal evidence for it, and it really does look as if Africa and not Asia was 'the cradle of mankind'.

I have already referred to Wayland's paper of forty years ago concerning African 'pluvial' periods. Several things have happened since: the geological basis of the East African sequence has been called into question,[44] more geomorphological work has been done in many different parts of Africa[45], and palynological studies have been brought to bear on the situation.[46] As a result it is realised that the climatic changes of the Pleistocene were indeed world-wide, with, almost certainly, simultaneous world-wide fluctuations in temperature but resulting in very different precipitation effects in different parts of the world at the same time, according to the influence of the temperature changes on the weather-systems of the world and the operation of meteorological mechanisms. The result is a much more complicated picture for Africa, in which at one and the same time parts of the continent were more arid and parts more pluvial than at present. As the polar ice-caps advanced and world-wide temperatures dropped, so the climatic zones tended to become compressed towards the equator.

The use of palynology in archaeology is only one example of the battery of scientific aids which has come to assist archaeology in the last thirty yeers. We have seen that it has made a significant beginning in Africa, and it is a tool of great potential usefulness for reconstructing prehistoric environments and vegetational changes in the continent. Similarly, other scientific aids are beginning to be used, although naturally, because these are often expensive and Africa remains a poor continent compared with the industrialised world, not to the same extent as elsewhere. Nevertheless, granulometric analysis served to reveal climatic change at a site in Rhodesia,[47] fission-track dating has been used in Africa,[48] it was the proton magnetometer which revealed the oldest iron-smelting furnaces in sub-Saharan Africa,[49] and spectrographic analysis of 'bronzes' in West Africa has given us a lot of new information concerning differences between different bronze-casting centres—even if we do not yet know how to interpret the significance of these differences.[50] A number of thermoluminescent dates have been published from Africa[51] but in the present state of the technique I do not think any reliance should be placed on thermoluminescent dating; I sincerely hope that the remaining technical difficulties will be overcome, but at present the results of the procedure are not sufficiently validated to give anything like the same level of confidence which we can place in radiocarbon dating.[52] Amino-acid dating of bone is being tried in Africa but is still in the early stages.[53] Flotation techniques for the recovery of organic materials have begun to be used and it is hoped that this will progressively yield information about early agriculture.[54] Some of the more sophisticated techniques, such as site locational analysis, depend upon a density of fieldwork and archaeological knowledge which as yet exists in very few areas of Africa; however, site resource utilisation analysis is beginning to be applied.[55] Statistical techniques are being increasingly applied to the analysis of archaeological material in Africa and I recently organised at Ibadan a computerised analysis of over half a million artifacts from a single site.

Associated with the ecological approach and the use of numerous scientific techniques is the need for planned fieldwork to be carried out by a team of experts in different disciplines, rather than for them to be asked piecemeal to report on particular aspects later. This is something that is usually much more difficult to organise and finance than it is to conceive; it is an approach which may still be more within the resources, both human and financial, of a foreign expedition than of an African country. This is where American participation comes in: before the Second World War, French, Belgian, British and South African efforts had made substantial beginnings in archaeological research in Africa; American involvement is almost entirely a post-war phenomenon. African archaeology has benefited enormously from the funds of American foundations especially the Wenner-Gren Foundation and the National Geographic Society. America has also served to provide a research base for a number of distinguished archaeologists formerly working in Anglophone Africa. Even if more has been achieved in the field of research as a result of the translation of this eminent band to America, in another way America's gain has been Africa's loss. These archaeologists are all engaged in university teaching, and their labours in this field have been devoted overwhelmingly to the teaching and training of Americans, not Africans.

This leads us on to consider another change in African archaeology, in this matter of teaching. In this sphere, if we leave on one side the situation in South Africa, which for reasons already explained is in a rather exceptional position, we find a difference in the history of the development of archaeology in sub-Saharan Africa between east and west. Because of Louis Leakey's early interest and activity, because East Africa was a more favourable habitat for early man, because preservation is better and vegetation cover is less, and because of the founding of the Rhodes-Livingstone Institute in Livingstone and the Coryndon Museum in Nairobi, followed more recently by the Centre for Prehistory and Palaeontology, and the British Institute in East Africa, archaeological research has developed further and faster in East Africa than in West. The only comparable research institution in West Africa is the Institut Fondamental de l'Afrique Noire at Dakar, not exclusively concerned with archaeology, which used to serve the whole of French West Africa but is now mostly confined to Senegal and Mauritania. On the other hand, in West Africa, Nigeria probably has a more effective Government Antiquities Department than most other sub-Saharan African countries, and West Africa has developed the teaching of archaeology and the training of archaeologists further. The University of Ghana has had a Department of Archaeology for over twenty years and the University of Ibadan has one which recently graduated its first Ph.D. and has an establishment of six archaeologists, a palynologist and a curator. By contrast, I think I am right in saying that there is at present only one archaeological post in all the universities of Kenya, Uganda, Tanzania and Zambia put together. So while East Africa will continue to attract outside personnel and outside funds for archaeological research, it looks as if West Africa has itself invested more in archaeology and is better positioned to produce her own indigenous archaeologists.

An index of the maturity and sophistication of the archaeology of an area is provided by its publications. Archaeological excavation is worse than useless, it is destructive, unless its results are properly published. Archaeologists the world over are slow or neglectful in publishing excavation reports, and Africa furnishes no exception,[56] but this matters more in Africa where the total amount of hard evidence is so small. Before the Second World War archaeological reports and articles appeared for the most part in European journals. In 1939 the *Bulletin de l'Institut Français d'Afrique Noire*, published in Dakar, began to carry such papers, and in 1945 the *South African Archaeological Bulletin* was founded; in 1953 a special archaeological journal for prehistoric North Africa and the Sahara was founded with the title *Libyca*; East Africa got its own special journal in 1966 in the form of *Azania*, and West Africa in 1971 with the publication of the *West African Journal of Archaeology*. The publication of regional archaeologies also charts archaeological progress: for South Africa in 1928,[57] 1929[58] 1959[59] and 1965[60]; for North Africa in 1955,[61] 1960[62] and 1974[63]; for East Africa in 1954 and 1964[64]; and for West Africa in 1967.[65]

To sum up then: in the last forty years tremendous changes have come over African archaeology both in its sheer quantity, in its aims and methodology, in its personnel, in its teaching and in its publication. The pace is now accelerating and I have no doubt that in the next forty years these changes will further develop and produce a much greater harvest of knowledge about the African past than has been achieved hitherto.

Notes

1   Jean Leclant, 'Egypte Pharaonique et Afrique Noire', *Revue hist.*, 462, 1962, p. 327; H. W. Fairman, 'Ancient Egypt and Africa', paper presented at the African Studies Association Conference, Birmingham, 1964.

2   E. Naville, 'L'origine africaine de la civilisation égyptienne', *Rev. Archéol.*, 22, 1913, pp. 47-65; Budge, quoted by G. Parrinder, 'The possibility of Egyptian influence on West African religion', *Proc. III Internat. W. Afr. Congr., Ibadan, 1949*, Lagos 1956, pp. 61-7; Fairman, *op. cit.*, pp. 1 and 3.

3   Charles de Brosses, *Du culte des dieux fétiches, ou parallèle de l'ancienne religion de l'Egypte avec la religion actuelle de Nigritia*, 1760; T. E. Bowdich, *Essays on the Superstitions Common to the Ancient Egyptians and Ashantis*, 1824.

4   G. Elliot Smith, *The Migration of Early Culture*, Manchester, 1915, and *The Diffusion of Culture*, London, 1933; W. J. Perry, *Children of the Sun*, London, 1923.

5   Rudyard Kipling, *Verse*, definitive edition, London, 1940, pp. 323, 329.

6   M. Delafosse, 'Sur des traces probables de civilisation égyptienne et d'hommes de race blanche en Côte d'Ivoire', *L'Anthropologie*, 11, 1900, pp. 677-90; Harry Johnston, 'A survey of the ethnography of Africa', *J. Roy. Anthrop. Inst.*, 1913, 43, pp. 375-421; P. A. Talbot, *The Peoples of Southern Nigeria*, London, 1926; C. K. Meek, *A Sudanese Kingdom*, London, 1931; C. G. Seligman, *Races of Africa*, London, 1930; H. R. Palmer, *The Bornu Sahara and Sudan*, London, 1936; G. A. Wainwright, 'Pharaonic survivals between Lake Chad and the West Coast', *J. Egypt. Archaeol.*, 35, 1949, pp. 170-5; M. D. W. Jeffreys, 'Circumcision: its diffusion from Egypt among the Bantu', *Criteria*, Johannesburg, 1, 1949, pp. 73-84, and 'Negro agricultural origins', *S. Afr. J. Sci.*, xlvii, 5, 1950, pp. 127-32; E. L. Meyerowitz, *The Divine Kingship in Ghana and Ancient Egypt*, London, 1960.

7   Samuel Johnson, *History of the Yorubas, London*, 1921; J. O. Lucas, *The Religion of the Yorubas in relation to the Religion of Ancient Egypt*, Lagos 1948, and *Religions in West Africa and Ancient Egypt*, Apapa 1970; Cheikh Anta Diop, *Nations Nègres et Cultures*, Paris 1955, *L'Afrique Noire Précoloniale*, Paris, 1960, and 'Réponse à Quelques Critiques', *Bull. Inst. Franç. Afr. Noire*, 24, sér. B., 1962, pp. 542-74.

8   Roger W. Westcott, 'Did the Yorubas Come from Egypt?' *Odu* 4 (n.d.), pp. 10-15; Parrinder, *op. cit.*; R. Mauny, 'Reviews of Cheikh Anta Diop's *Nations nègres et Cultures* and *L'Afrique Noire Précoloniale*', *Bull. Inst. Franç. Afr. Noire*, 22, sér. B, 1960, pp. 544-55; J. Sainte Fare Garnot, *Revue Historique*, 459, 1961, pp. 99-106; Jack Goody, *Technology, Tradition and the State in Africa*, London, 1971, p. 19; Oladejo Okediji, 'Review of Lucas', *Religions in West Africa and Ancient Egypt*', *Odu*, n.s. 8, 1972, pp. 97-9.

9   T. Obenga, *L'Afrique dans l'Antiquité: Egypte Pharaonique—Afrique Noire*, Paris, 1973.

10   Frank Addison, *Jebel Moya*, London, 1949, and *Saqadi and Dar el Mek*, London, 1951; O. G. S. Crawford and Frank Addison, *Abu Geili*, London, 1951.

11   Randall MacIver, *Mediaeval Rhodesia*, London, 1906.

12   Published in London in 1928.

13   Published in *Ann. S. Afr. Mus.*, 27, 1929.

14   H. Breuil, 'Premières impressions de voyage sur la préhistoire Sud-Africaine', *L'Anthropologie*, 40, 1930, pp. 209-33, and 'L'Afrique préhistorique', *Cahiers d'art*, 1931.

15   E. J. Wayland, 'Rifts, Rivers, Rains and Early Man in Uganda', *J. Roy. Anthrop. Inst.*, 44, 1934, pp. 332-52.

16   Maurice Becquaert, *Les Fouilles de Jean Colette à Kalina*, Brussels, 1938.
17   D. S. Calvocoressi and R. N. York, 'The state of archaeological research in Ghana',
      W. Afr. J. Archaeol., i, 1971, Fig. 1.
18   G. P. Murdock, *Africa: Its Peoples and Their Culture History*, New York, 1959,
      p. 73.
19   Ekpo Okpo Eyo, 'Recent excavations at Ife and Owo and their implications for Ife,
      Owo and Benin studies', unpublished Ph.D. thesis, Ibadan, 1974.
20   A. B. Aderibigbe, 'Peoples of Southern Nigeria' in *A Thousand Years of West
      African History*, ed. J. F. Ade Ajayi and Ian Espie, London, p. 188; Frank Willett,
      'Investigations at Old Oyo 1956-57: an interim report', *J. Hist. Soc. Nigeria*, ii, 1,
      1960, p. 75; Robert Smith, *Kingdoms of the Yoruba*, London, 1969, p. 106.
21   Brian Fagan, 'Review of P. S. Garlake's *Great Zimbabwe*', *Antiquity*, 47, 1973,
      pp. 330-1.
22   P. S. Garlake, *Great Zimbabwe*, London, 1973, p. 198.
23   L. S. B. Leakey, *Olduvai Gorge*, Cambridge, 1951.
24   C. Van Riet Lowe, 'The development of the handaxe culture in South Africa', in
      Proceedings of the Panafrican Congress on Prehistory, Nairobi, 1947, ed. L. S. B.
      Leakey, Oxford, 1952, pp. 167-77.
25   P. Biberson, 'L'évolution du Paléolithique marocain dans le cadre du Pleistocène
      atlantique', *Quaternaria*, 6, 1962, pp. 177-205.
26   Mary Leakey, *Olduvai Gorge Vol. 3 Excavations in Beds I and II, 1960-1963*,
      Cambridge, 1971.
27   G. Ll. Isaac, New evidence from Olorgesailie relating to the character of Acheulian
      occupation sites, *Actas del V Congreso Panafricano de Preistoria y de Estudio del
      Cuaternario*, ed. L. Cuscoy, vol. 2, Tenerife, 1966, pp. 135-45.
28   J. Desmond Clark, *Kalambo Falls Prehistoric Site I*, Cambridge, 1969.
29   St. Clair Drake, 'The responsibility of men of culture for destroying the "Hamitic
      myth" ', *Présence Africaine*, 24-25, 1959, pp. 228-43; Robert G. Armstrong, *The
      Study of West African Languages*, Ibadan, 1964, pp. 3-7.
30   Seligman, *op. cit.*, pp. 100-1.
31   H. Vavilov, 'The origin, variation, immunity and breeding of cultivated plants',
      Chron. Bot., 13, 1951, pp. 1-364.
32   Roland Portères, '*Eleusine coracana* Gaertner', *Bull. Inst. Franç. Afr. Noire*, 13,
      1951, pp. 1-78, and 'Berceaux agricoles primaires sur le continent africain', *J. Afr.
      Hist.*, iii, 1962, pp. 195-210.
33   Christopher Wrigley, 'Speculations on the economic prehistory of Africa', *J. Afr.
      Hist.*, i, 2, 1960, pp. 189-203.
34   J. Desmond Clark, 'The spread of food production in sub-Saharan Africa', *J. Afr.
      Hist.*, iii, 2, 1962, pp. 211-28.
35   Murdock, *op. cit.*
36   H. G. Baker, 'Comments on the thesis that there was a major centre of plant
      domestication near the headwaters of the River Niger', *J. Afr. Hist.*, iii, 2, 1962,
      pp. 229-33.
37   Jack Harlan, *The Origin of African Plant Domesticates*, papers presented at
      Burg-Wartenstein Symposium no. 56 (in press).
38   Thurstan Shaw, 'Early agriculture in Africa', *J. Hist. Soc. Nigeria*, vi, 2, 1972,
      pp. 143-91.
39   D. G. Coursey, *Yams*, London, 1967.
40   Shaw, *op. cit.*
41   R. A. Dart, '*Australopithecus africanus*: the man-ape of South Africa', *Nature*, 115,
      1925, pp. 195-9.
42   Richard Leakey, 'Evidence for an advanced Plio-Pleistocene hominid from East
      Rudolf, Kenya', *Nature*, 242, 1973, pp. 447-50.
43   G. H. R. von Koenigswald, *Meeting Prehistoric Man*, London, 1956, pp. 105-17;
      William Howells, *Mankind in the Making*, London, 1960, p. 15; David Pilbeam,

The Evolution of Man, London, 1970, pp. 170-1; John Napier, *The Roots of Mankind*, London, 1971, p. 215.

44 R. F. Flint, 'On the basis of Pleistocene correlation in East Africa', *Geol. Mag.*, 96, 1959, pp. 265-84.

45 Karl W. Butzer, *Environment and Archaeology*, Chicago, 1971, pp. 312-51.

46 E. M. Van Zinderen Bakker, 'Upper Pleistocene and Holocene stratigraphy and ecology on the basis of vegetation changes in sub-Saharan Africa', in *Background to Evolution in Africa*, ed. W. W. Bishop and J. Desmond Clark, Chicago, 1967, pp. 125-47; J. A. Coatzee, *Palaeoecology of Africa 3*, Cape Town, 1967; Jean Maley, 'Mécanisme des changements climatiques aux basses latitudes', *Palaeography, Palaeoclimatology, Palaeoecology*, 14, 1973, pp. 193-227.

47 Geoffrey Bond, 'The geology of the Khami Stone Age sites, Southern Rhodesia', *Occ. Pap. Nat. Mus. S. Rhodesia*, 3, 1957, pp. 44-55.

48 L. S. B. Leakey, 'Fission track dating of a mesolithic knife', *Nature*, 205m 1965, p. 1138.

49 B. E. B. Fagg, 'Recent work in West Africa: new light on the Nok culture', '*World Archaeol.*, 1, 1969, p. 46.

50 Thurstan Shaw, 'Spectrographic analyses of the Igbo and other Nigerian bronzes', *Archaeometry*, 8, 1965, pp. 86-95; 'Spectrographic analyses of the Igbo and other Nigerian bronzes: postscript, *Archaeometry*, 9, 1966, pp. 148-50, and 'The analysis of West African bronzes', *Ibadan*, 28, 1970, pp. 80-9; Frank Willett, 'Spectrographic analysis of Nigerian bronzes', *Archaeometry*, 8, 1965, pp. 81-3; O. Werner, 'Metallurgische Untersuchungen der Benin-Bronzen', *Baessler-Archiv*, 18, 1970, pp. 71-153; Siegfried Wolf, 'Neue Analysen von Benin-Legierungen in vergleichender Betrachtung', *Abhandlungen und Berichte des staatlichen Museums für Völkerkunde*, 28, 1968, pp. 91-153; O. Werner and F. Willett, 'The composition of brasses from Ife and Benin', *Archaeometry* (in press).

51 Carleton S. Coon, *Yengema Cave Report*, Philadelphia, 1968; B. E. B. Fagg and S. J. Fleming, 'Thermoluminscent dating of a terracotta of the Nok culture, Nigeria,' *Archaeometry*, xii, 1, 1970, pp. 53-5; Frank Willett, 'A survey of recent results in the radiocarbon chronology of Western and Northern Africa', *J. Afr. Hist.*, xii, 3, 1971, p. 367.

52 Glyn Daniel, 'Editorial', *Antiquity*, 48, 1974, p. 5.

53 P. E. Hare, 'Amino-Acid Dating—a history and an evaluation', *Masca Newsletter*, x, 1, 1974, pp. 4-7.

54 Colin Flight, 'Excavations at Kintampo', *W. Afr. Archaeol. Newsl.*, 12, 1970, pp. 71-2; Andrew B. Smith, 'Preliminary report of excavations at Karkarichinkat', *W. Afr. J. Archaeol.*, 4, 1974, p. 51; Bassey Wai-Ogosu, unpublished Ph.D. thesis, University of California, Berkeley, 1973.

55 P. L. Carter, 'Late Stone Age exploitation patterns in southern Natal', *S. Afr. Archaeol. Bull.*, 25, 1970, pp. 55-8.

56 Calvocoressi and York, *op. cit.*, pp. 90-5.

57 Burkitt, *op. cit.*

58 Goodwin and Lowe, *op. cit.*

59 J. Desmond Clark, *The Prehistory of Southern Africa*, Harmondsworth, 1959.

60 Brian Fagan, *Southern Africa, Ancient Peoples and Places*, London, 1965.

61 L. Balout, *Préhistoire de l'Afrique du Nord*, Paris, 1955.

62 C. B. M. McBurney, *The Stone Age of Northern Africa*, Harmondsworth, 1960.

63 G. Camps, *Les Civilisations Préhistoriques de l'Afrique du Nord et du Sahara*, Paris, 1974.

64 Sonia Cole, *The Prehistory of East Africa*, Harmondsworth, 1954; revised edition, London, 1964.

65 Oliver Davies, *West Africa before the Europeans*, London, 1967.

Peter Shinnie

The Development of Meroitic Studies Since 1945

In 1959 Basil Davidson in *Old Africa Rediscovered* made the first serious attempt to bring knowledge of Meroe and its civilisation to the attention of the educated reading public, and also for the first time tried to integrate a description of Meroitic culture into that of Africa as a whole, and to show how perhaps Meroe had played a significant part in wider developments and the spread of techniques. His only partly serious description of the town of Meroe as an 'Athens in Africa' called forth a rebuke from a very distinguished archaeologist, one to whom I am personally deeply indebted for all I know of the techniques of fieldwork. Personal affection and admiration for the two champions of this differing point of view makes it distasteful to make comparisons and to say who was right, but by and large Wheeler's denigration of Meroe has proved rather less close to the truth than Davidson's somewhat exaggerated view of its importance.

An Athens it may not have been in the sense of a world-shaking intellectual centre, but, even though its importance for the development of the African Iron Age still has to be proved, and may be less than some scholars have supposed, of its importance in the development of man in the Nile valley there can be no question. The town of Meroe was the largest urban settlement in Africa south of Egypt at any period before the Middle Ages, perhaps even before the coming of the Europeans. It is difficult to know the size of the main towns of the west African states from ancient Ghana on, but Meroe was a larger town than Kumbi Saleh.

When Davidson wrote he could speak of the 'Mystery of Meroe' and make the point that remarkably little archaeological investigation had been carried out, and that knowledge of the history and culture of the time was minimal. His strong plea for further excavation and research has been met, and though many who have taken part in the development of Meroitic studies over recent years may not have been aware of the remarkably prescient view of Meroitic civilisation given in ten pages or so, and were not directly influenced by it, there is no doubt that the change of intellectual climate which has facilitated the increase of scholarly interest in the first literate African civilisation, outside Egypt, owed much to Davidson's work.

Meroe first came to the knowledge of modern European scholarship in 1772 when Bruce passed by and left a brief and rather uniformative description. He did at least suggest, quite rightly, that he had found the site of the town of Meroe whose existence had been known to European scholars from the writings of the classical authors, Herodotus, Diodorus Siculus, Strabo and Pliny. After

Bruce a number of travellers left descriptions. The most important were the two Frenchmen, Caillaud and Linant who, accompanying the invading Turko-Egyptian army in 1821, made the first accurate studies of sites to the south of Egypt, and also made excellent drawings and plans of the main ancient buildings of the area. Interest in what was at first seen as either an offshoot, or the ancestor, of ancient Egypt, resulted in the Royal Prussian Expedition of the nineteenth century brilliantly led by Lepsius. His massive volumes of illustrations of the monuments of Egypt and the Sudan are still essential to any study of Meroitic culture. Lepsius was also the first to make any large-scale attempt to collect Meroitic inscriptions and to realise that these writings contained a new language, quite different from that of Egypt, already reasonably well known for some years. Lepsius realised that there was an important and difficult problem to be faced in reading these inscriptions, but although he made interesting and intelligent observations he was not able to read them.

During the next half-century a few scholars showed a mild interest in Meroitic inscriptions, but remarkably little in the other material remains of the ancient Sudan. An important change came in 1908 and succeeding years when the excavations in Nubia of the Eckley B. Coxe expedition in the name of the University of Pennsylvania found large cemeteries of late Meroitic times in Lower Nubia, and when the brilliant British Egyptologist F. Ll. Griffith decided to study the large number of funerary inscriptions that were found in the course of the excavations which were under the control of Woolley (later to become famous as the excavator of Ur) and Randall-MacIver. The general chronology of these cemeteries, and of some dwelling sites, became reasonably clear from the presence of imported objects and even at this early stage in the study of Meroe the excavators realised quite clearly that they were dealing with material of the first few centuries A.D.

In two superb studies of the inscriptional material Griffith achieved a breakthrough by establishing the phonetic values of the signs used in the Meroitic writing system. He was helped by an examination of royal names of two rather well known rulers of the beginning of the Christian era, Netekamani and Amantarit, whose names were on a stone pedestal for a sacred boat found at the site of Wad ben Naqa by Lepsius many years before. The good fortune by which these names were written both in Egyptian and Meroitic hieroglyphs enabled Griffith to make the first equation between the signs used in the two different systems and from this start he very soon established the phonetic values of the signs. Although the values attributed to vowels have caused, and still cause, some difficulty, Griffith's work has stood up to subsequent criticism with remarkably little change.

Having established the value of a large number of the Meroitic hieroglyphs (and in view of the alphabetic (or syllabic) manner in which they were used there were only twenty-three different signs), Griffith was able, by the study of 'offering tables' which he assumed, rightly as it turned out, to contain the same formulae in the 'demotic', to establish the values of the cursive signs as well.

At about the same time, 1909 and the years immediately following, Garstang began to excavate at Meroe, the capital city of the Meroitic state, the royal residence and the burial place of many of the rulers. These excavations, which produced a great deal of extremely interesting material, were unfortunately carried out in an unscientific and wholesale way and very little of the work was ever published. The coming of the First World War was one of the main reasons for failure by the excavator to publish, but even the one volume which was produced, containing a report on the first season, leaves a great deal to be desired and raised as many problems as it solved. As a result, the results of the massive excavation carried out in the years 1909 to 1914 are virtually unknown, and the probably important information which could be available from investigation of the royal enclosure in the town at Meroe will never be known.

These activities caused much interest in the whole question of the history and archaeology of the period after the Egyptian New Kingdom occupation of the northern Sudan, but the results did not make it possible to gain a proper understanding of historical development. Though the chronology of the northern sites was clear enough, the evidence from the somewhat different situation at Meroe itself was not, and Garstang's attempts to establish a chronology were not entirely successful, nor was much understanding gained of the processes by which Meroitic civilisation developed and decayed.

The main chronological framework was provided by the next investigations, those of the Harvard/Boston Museum of Fine Arts expedition under the leadership of Reisner. This expedition during the years 1916 to 1923, investigated the whole series of Kushite royal burials dating from before 750 B.C. to c. A.D. 350 at the three main cemeteries of Kurru, Nuri and Meroe, as well as a few associated burials at Gebel Barkal. After excavating these burials Reisner attempted to put them in chronological order on the basis of an analysis of the contents of the tombs, together with a study of architectural style and geographical location. It was already clear that the chronological order was Kurru, Nuri and finally Meroe; but Reisner was now able to take this much further and put each individual burial in order, to identify the burials with names of rulers, and also to make an attempt to establish a precise chronology for them. Although the method of operation is open to criticism, and many would not now try to use the very close dating which Reisner attempted, his work marked a considerable advance in understanding of the chronological problems.

The method by which the dates for individual rulers was arrived at, after arranging the tombs in order by the criteria already described, was to fit the whole list into the period from c. 760 B.C. to shortly before A.D. 350 and to calculate an average length of reign. These average reigns were then weighted in a somewhat arbitrary fashion according to size and splendour of each burial and an approximate date arrived at. A check on this was provided by two fixed points, one being the identification of the king Ergamenes, described by Diodorus Siculus as being contemporary with Ptolemy II, with the Meroitic Arqamani, and the other being a graffito of the reign of Teqerideamani which was dated by a regnal year of the Roman emperor Trebonianus Gallus to A.D. 253. This system provided a date, or rather a statistical statement, for each royal burial, though in a number of cases identification of the one buried was not certain. In spite of the obvious weaknesses of this method, Reisner's list, though now modified by subsequent study, has stood up to fifty years of criticism without being extensively changed.

Reisner's work came to an end in 1923, but the results were not published until 1950 when the first of a series of five volumes appeared, the last one coming out in 1963. This delay in publication meant that for a long time Meroitic studies were severely handicapped, since the few scholars interested were aware that the reports were being worked on, and were hesitant to pursue their own researches until the very rich material known to have been found could be made available. This situation persisted for ten years after the end of the Second World War at a time when there were the first stirrings of a revived interest in the archaeology of the Sudan and in particular of the Meroitic period, and when the Sudan Government was providing for a professionally staffed department to take care of antiquities and to carry out research.

During these years interest in the topic was at a low ebb and research was maintained by a small group of scholars, two of whom, Dunham and Macadam, were primarily concerned with working on the records of pre-Second World War excavations. No new fieldwork was being carried out and attempts by the Sudan Antiquities Service to interest outside organisations in coming to excavate in the Sudan were not successful.

By the middle 1950s the situation began to change and two unrelated but important events played a part in this revival of interest; in 1950 the first volume of Dunham's splendid publication of Reisner's work came out, and in 1956 the Sudan became independent. The importance of the coming to fruition of years of devoted work by Dunham in publishing the results of another man's work cannot be overestimated. These large volumes of the results of the excavation of all the royal burials, together with the large non-royal cemetery known as the West Cemetery at Meroe, came out in regular fashion under the title *Royal Cemeteries of Kush*. The publication dates were, Volume I, Kurru, 1950; II, Nuri, 1955; III, Decorated Chapels of the Pyramids, 1952; IV, Meroe and Barkal, 1957; V, West and South Cemeteries at Meroe, 1963. Somewhat later, in 1970 there was a volume dealing with Barkal temples. Although these volumes are largely catalogues with descriptions of structures and of the artefacts found in the tombs, with minimal discussion, the availability of the material with its at least approximate dates has been of very great assistance to all those studying Meroitic culture.

The independence of the Sudan on 1 January 1956 played a more subtle and less obvious part in the development of Meroitic studies; but the change in the political situation of the Sudan, soon to be followed by other African countries, and the general development of academic interest in Africa in the 1950s are clearly closely connected. All African Studies, particularly historical ones, showed a rapid expansion during these years, and though in other parts of Africa the connection between political and academic developments can be more clearly seen than they can in the Sudan, there is little doubt that foreign scholars were, perhaps unwittingly, so influenced. Those who worked on the archaeology of the Sudan were perhaps less influenced than others, since they had nearly all been trained in the very traditional discipline of Egyptology, well known for its lack of interest in the African element in ancient Egyptian civilisation, and for its remoteness from modern trends in archaeological thinking.

But even from this background those who began to devote themselves to the study of Meroe, and other periods of the ancient Sudan could not help being influenced by other factors. One of these was the rarity of written documents, and of the few, many were in an un-understood language, and this made the excessively text-oriented techniques of conventional Egyptology quite inappropriate. The period also saw the development of 'Sudanology' as almost a separate branch of study and several scholars, some of them with impeccable training and background in Egyptology, began to see themselves as primarily concerned with the Sudan and consequently began to develop and specialise in techniques more appropriate to the problems they were trying to solve.

Another development was the appearance of Sudanese scholars and of an increasing interest by Sudanese in the past of their own country. This change was most striking to those who had worked through the later stages of British rule when it had been a common Sudanese point of view that the earlier cultures and peoples of the country were not ancestral to the modern Arabic-speaking and Islamic northern Sudan, and therefore were not of interest. This attitude began to change in the 1950s with teaching of the history of the Sudan in the University of Khartoum. For a long time only the history of the post-1821 period had been taught, and many arguments were brought forward to suggest, either that no history was known before that date, or that if it was, it was not relevant. This attitude was difficult to shake, but it gradually disappeared until the teaching of the ancient history of the country became firmly based in the curriculum of the University. In this development A. J. Arkell's *History of the Sudan to 1821*, which first came out in 1955, played a very important part. This book has been the main educator for the younger Sudanese historians and archaeologists and although there is much in it that could be questioned, and it over-emphasises some of the author's quirks, there is, as yet, nothing to take its place and it remains an indispensable work for teaching the history of the Sudan.

The building of the high dam at Aswan and the resulting large-scale archaeological surveys on both sides of the Egyptian-Sudanese border which were organised from 1960, focused world attention briefly on the antiquities of Nubia, and though an undue emphasis was placed on the salvage of Abu Simbel and other temples, a large number of excavations were undertaken on sites of all periods. Although a great deal of new material was discovered, very largely from cemeteries, the salvage campaign did not add much to knowledge of the northern part of the Meroitic state. Unlike the mediaeval period, knowledge of which was transformed by the excavation of such sites as Faras, Gebel Adda, Qasr Ibrim and Mainarti, the new Meroitic material in the main reinforced what was already known; that is, that the Meroites were mostly living in a number of agricultural villages and had not inhabited the area in any number, if at all, until the first century B.C. when use of the animal-driven wooden water wheel, the *saquia*, made adequate cultivation possible.

Of far greater significance for Meroitic studies than the salvage operations were the first two investigations, in the post-war period, of sites in the Butana, the traditional 'Island of Meroe'. Here the Humboldt University of Berlin, under the leadership of Hintze, first carried out a detailed survey of the whole area and then started what was to be a ten-year investigation of the virtually unstudied temple site of Musawwarat al Sofra. The complex group of buildings at this place, many of them unencumbered with sand and soil, had presented a problem of interpretation and understanding ever since they were first brought to the notice of scholars by Caillaud and Linant. Devoid of inscriptions as known until recently, only the most vague indications of date could be got from a few architectural features, and the unique nature of this extremely complex site, consisting of a central temple with surrounding corridors, ramps and courtyards, as well as other temples, made it impossible to attempt to understand it by comparison with other known temple buildings.

The work of the Humboldt University expedition, carried out with very considerable professional competence, has now revealed much of the story even though the function of some parts remains unexplained. The general building history, of which the standing monument was only the latest manifestion, can now be reasonably understood from the sixth century B.C. until the fourth century A.D. In one case, that of the famous Lion Temple of Arnekhamani, a building containing important inscriptions in Egyptian, and with portrayals of a known king, was found virtually intact though collapsed. It was restored with skill and imagination so that it is now possible to see exactly what a Meroitic temple, of the special kind dedicated to the lion-headed god Apedemek, looked like.

The other important excavation carried out in the early 1960s was at Wad ben Naqa where first Vercoutter, then Commissioner for Archaeology, and later his successor Thabit Hassan, excavated a large palace complex. Unfortunately the sudden decision to build the high dam meant that this project had to be abandoned in favour of salvage work and it seems unlikely that a full report will ever be available. This is very unfortunate since the site is an unusual one, consisting of a large two-storeyed palace building with store rooms on the ground floor, which as discovered still contained large quantities of pottery, of wood and of ivory. In addition to the palace was a small temple of normal Meroitic type, and a peculiar circular structure whose purpose cannot be identified, since it appears to have been of beehive shape, standing probably some ten metres high. The most likely suggestion is that it was a grain storeage silo—this is entirely speculative but until comparable structures are found elsewhere it must be allowed to stand, failing any more convincing explanation. If indeed it was for grain it suggests some centralisation of storage, and therefore distribution of grain, since it is far larger than required to meet the needs of a royal group living in the Palace.

In addition to these two sites, where work was started before the crisis caused by the building of the dam, since 1965 work has been restarted at the site of the town of Meroe, firstly in the name of the University of Ghana, later of the University of Khartoum, and more recently jointly with the University of Calgary. By now five seasons of work have been carried out and it is anticipated that there will be several more.

In this excavation attention has moved away from study of the monumental and has concentrated on the dwelling areas of the common people and on that part of the site where the now well-known Meroitic skill of iron-working was carried out. Since Meroe is one of the few sites where there seems to be a deposit of occupation material covering a period of some 1,000 years it is likely that when the data are finally available it will be possible to see the development of various classes of artefacts, particularly the ceramics, throughout the whole history of the town. It should also be possible to get information as to the date of the founding of the town, and also to understand something of the process by which it developed from a small settlement of straw huts into a major urban centre with elaborate temples, palaces, and cemeteries as well as ordinary dwelling houses and an 'industrial' area where not only iron-working, but pot-making and perhaps other trades were carried out.

The recent work in the field has enabled a far better understanding of Meroitic culture to be obtained, and more and more thought is being given to the important topics of discussion that now arise. Although it is the fieldwork that has prompted this wider discussion many more scholars with varying skills and interests have entered into these discussions which are not the sole preserve of the excavator. Each new discovery has meant a new series of problems to be solved— but the last fifteen or so years have seen a spectacular increase in knowledge, and an ever growing number of scholars from all parts of the world are involved in the attempt to understand the culture history of the Sudanese Nile valley during the thousand or more years after 750 B.C. The increase in knowledge has been dramatic; far more is known of the nature of the culture. The considerable variations between the northern and southern parts of the state are now well appreciated, even though the reasons for them are not fully understood. The main styles of pottery are an important indicator; for the well-known painted pottery, for so long thought of as *the* Meroitic pottery, is now known to have had a rather short time span in the early centuries A.D.

Attention is now being drawn to a whole range of problems which in earlier years were not considered. Meroe has for some time been the victim of the over-enthusiastic claims made for it as a centre of diffusion of a wide range of technological and ideological traits throughout the African continent. Further study has suggested caution, and archaeology has up to now produced no firm evidence to support these views. The non-Egyptian element in Meroitic culture is still very difficult to analyse, Egyptian influence in the art remained pervasive and though at least in its later stages Meroitic art cannot easily be confused with that of Egypt, in view of the strong local flavour, it still remains unarguable that the main influence came from the north. The other elements, what could be called the African strain in the culture of Meroe, although it comes out in isolated examples—the importance of the queens, and the way in which they are portrayed in sculptured reliefs, the use of an indigenous language, and some of the pottery styles—all attest to non-Egyptian influences. These still remain only hazily understood and much remains to be done before all the strands in Meroitic culture are fully appreciated and their sources identified. That there was an indigenous culture springing from the Late Stone Age people of the central Sudan cannot be doubted—what remains to be done here is to close the large chronological gap of perhaps 1,500 to 2,000 years between the known artefacts so as to see the local roots of Meroe.

Many other important problems have been worked at during this period and results are beginning to appear from the effort expended. Of these one of the most important is the understanding of the language. Very little advance has been made in our ability to understand the meanings of the texts since Griffith's days, but work goes steadily on and a number of distinguished scholars are making important contributions. Failing a bilingual text or the discovery of an existing African language close enough to Meroitic to provide useful information for translation, progress must be slow. Two main trends can be seen at work at the moment, firstly the impressive contribution made by French scholars under the leadership of Leclant in establishing the basic materials for the study of the language, by making files for all Meroitic texts, and organising them in such a way that many questions as to the use and structure of words and grammatical forms can now receive answers in a convenient way and without the need for each individual scholar to search through the complete corpus of texts. As a logical extension of this work all the texts have now been recorded by computer and this very quickly makes accessible all the raw material for Meroitic language studies.

The other recent development in the study of the language has been the detailed study of the linguistic patterns shown in Meroitic texts by Hintze. Basing himself largely on the numerous funerary texts, all of them conforming to a small number of set formulae, Hintze has been able to identify regular patterns in the language, and he has been the protagonist of the view that advances in the understanding of Meroitic are more likely to be made by attempting to establish phonological linguistic identifications.

Although the study of the Meroitic language has made some spectacular advances in the last few years using both these methods, ability to understand the meaning of individual words, and still less to translate whole inscriptions has made little or no progress. Hintze, reverting to suggestions made by Griffith in 1916, has shown that the Meroitic writing system was not alphabetic, as has been assumed, but was a modified syllabic writing in which all consonantal signs represent consonant plus vowel a; when it was desired to indicate a different vowel then the sign for that vowel followed the consonant sign. Priese has made a detailed study of the signs themselves and has shown that the Meroitic 'cursive' signs derive from Egyptian demotic writing, and suggest that the development of a distinctive Meroitic writing system was not a sudden break with past systems in about 200 B.C., but part of an evolutionary process of development from the system used for writing Egyptian, though with increasing use of Meroitic words, in Napatan times (eighth-sixth centuries B.C.).

Lexical studies show almost no development. Suggestions by Trigger that Meroitic belongs with the eastern-Sudanic languages and that therefore a study of those languages might help in establishing the meanings of Meroitic words has met with some scepticism. The geographical and historical considerations suggest that the theory is well grounded, but the small number of words suggested as cognates are not yet sufficient. Earlier attempts to see in Nubian or Beja languages relatives of Meroitic have not been successful; and though Trigger's suggestion may be right, it does not seem that any modern languages of eastern-Sudanic (which may include Nubian) are linguistically close enough to be of much help. One disadvantage in attempting a comparative study to attempt to find cognates is the paucity of information about many eastern-Sudanic languages. Failure to interest scholars concerned with African linguistics in the problem of Meroitic has been a serious hindrance to development of this aspect of the study.

Recent archaeological work has already been described, but reference should be made to the work of Adams in the understanding of the ceramic traditions. Starting with a detailed study of the pottery of the Mediaeval Christian period Adams has now extended his schematic system of analysis back into Meroitic times and is producing what will be the definitive study of the Meroitic pottery of Lower Nubia. Excavations at Meroe and Musawwarat have shown that the ceramic tradition is not identical in the Island of Meroe with that of the sites in the north, and the restriction of Meroitic settlement north of the second cataract to the last few centuries of Meroitic rule means that the earlier pottery styles have not yet been incorporated into Adams' system. The city of Meroe with its deep stratified deposits is particularly suitable for providing information on changes through time in the pottery, and when current studies are published the whole range of Meroitic pottery styles should be known.

Another aspect of research into the Meroitic past is the attention now being paid to material other than artefacts. As part of a change during the last twenty years in the attitudes towards all sources of evidence for understanding the past, excavators are now attempting to provide answers to a wide range of questions concerning Meroitic life. These concern such matters as the nature of Meroitic society, its forms of organisation and administration, the role of the kings and priests, trade patterns, the economy of the state and the presumably changing way in which these operated, since there is no reason to assume that Meroitic society was static. In default of translatable texts it is unlikely that the same detailed evidence for these concerns will be as available as it is for Ancient Egypt, but an emphasis on the excavation of dwelling sites, since much is already known of tombs and temples, should go part of the way to finding answers, as also to providing further information on Meroitic technology.

In addition to these aspects of the life of Meroitic man attention is now being paid to the nature of the ancient environment, its impact on the life of the people, and the way in which it was exploited for human existence. Such evidence as there is suggests that there have been no great changes in environmental factors during the nearly 3,000 years since the beginnings of the Kushite state (Kushite being used to include both of what are usually known as the Napatan and Meroitic periods). There will certainly have been changes in river level—and this to a largely riverain people, heavily dependent on the Nile flood, will have been a matter of importance, and it has been suggested that rainfall was somewhat more abundant during the period. Reasons for this assumption are based on the view that it is not improbable that a town of the size and complexity of Meroe could have flourished, and provided adequate food supplies for its population, under the conditions which prevail today. Firm evidence for such a change is lacking—information on the vegetation of the time would give clues as to rainfall, but attempts to find ancient pollen have been unsuccessful, and arguments recently advanced are erroneous, as the original identification of the seeds was incorrect.

Information on some aspects of ancient diet is now available, at least from Meroe, where examination of animal bones in domestic refuse has shown a heavy dependence on beef. A grain crop, almost certainly sorghum, was used to make the unleavened bread, still a Sudanese staple, and the archaeological evidence—grinding stones and the special flat dish on which the bread was, and is, cooked—is quite clear. As yet few examples of the grain have been found but sorghum is known from both Qasr Ibrim, in Lower Nubia, and from the Island of Meroe. Investigations currently being undertaken will, it is hoped, throw light both on cattle herding and grain growing, and through a study of modern practices an indication of ancient ones may be found.

This brief survey should have shown that Meroitic studies are in a flourishing state, and that knowledge has increased greatly over the last twenty-five years or so. Many more scholars are now involved, and attention is being paid to a wide-ranging study of all aspects of Meroitic culture. Many of the main monuments have now been studied, several expeditions have been in the field, advances in analysing the language have been made, and there is now a firm basis on which to understand the material culture. The founding of a 'Meroitic Newsletter', has been of importance in keeping the scattered community of scholars in contact with each other, and a further decisive advance was made by the organisation of a regular conference of Meroitic studies. The first of these held in Berlin under the auspices of the Humboldt University in 1971, whose proceedings have been published as *Meroitica I—Sudan im Altertum*, marked an extremely significant step in establishing the academic credentials of this branch of learning. A second in this series of conferences was held in Paris in 1973, and a third is planned for Toronto in 1977.

Meroitic studies now takes its place as an integral part of more general African Studies; it has shared in the intellectual development of the last decades and is making its own contribution to the understanding of the continent.

Godfrey Lienhardt

Social Anthropology of Africa[1]

At the first conference of the African Studies Association of the United Kingdom in 1964 the late Professor Daryll Forde's contribution on Social Anthropology and African Studies was followed by a discussion led by Professor Roland Oliver:

> Professor Oliver opened the discussion from the chair by referring to Professor Forde's description of social anthropology as deriving its data and problems from field studies and analyses of communities 'sufficiently small in scale . . . to be comprehended and analysed as total working systems. He wanted to know how anthropologists adapt their research methods to situations where small communities are becoming progressively integrated into nations.

Professor Audrey Richards here said that social anthropologists could also study larger national groupings, to which Professor Oliver replied that he was less concerned with the size of the unit studied 'than with problems raised by the fact that African societies were undergoing rapid social change'. Here, according to the record:

> Dr. Richards declined to draw a hard and fast line between the social anthropologist and the sociologist. A sociologist going straight from England to Lusaka would miss a great deal by not being familiar with the village upbringing, experience and values of the new townsmen. . . .

Professor Oliver 'was still not clear in what direction social anthropology was moving'.[2]

The additional perspective gained in the ten years since that conference does not, I think, enable one to answer Professor Oliver in a much more satisfactory way: but to be required to suggest what has happened in the social anthropological study of Africa *since* 1945 does enable one to see that the Second World War was not, in the academic history of social anthropology, the clear dividing line which it may appear to be in the personal history of those who lived through it, or in the social history of many of the world's peoples since the end of the First World War. Therefore I must begin before 1945. If the account seems to concentrate on the British scene, it is because at that time social anthropology, under that name at least, was most particularly active in Britain and, with Britain's African interests, much of the social anthropology of Africa was written by scholars who had close intellectual contacts with Britain whether themselves British or not. Indeed, one of the main developments in social anthropology since 1945 has been its internationalisation, which may by now make its worthy origins appear somewhat provincial.

The studies of African peoples which produced much of the early theoretical capital of the generation which came into social anthropology after 1945 were made before the Second World War. All the Africanists who moved into academic seniority after the war had been influenced in one way or another by the formulations of Malinowski and Radcliffe-Brown, who themselves had both reacted against and partly assimilated and modified the ideas of their predecessors—Durkheim, Tylor, Frazer and Herbert Spencer, to mention only four important names. Malinowski and Radcliffe-Brown, if in different ways, were both active proponents of the view that social anthropology must and would become an exact science. Their hopes for the subject in this regard produced firm convictions about the way in which social anthropologists should proceed, which could not but suggest that it would be reasonable in time to ask about its scientific progress, methods and adaptation to new experimental conditions, as though it were one steadily developing body of scientific knowledge and theory.

Both Malinowski and Radcliffe-Brown had studied quite small-scale and geographically easily delimited island societies which gave themselves to a concern with the 'total working systems' referred to by Professor Forde earlier quoted. It was considered to be ideally the first duty of a social anthropologist in the field to record every ethnographic fact. Though this ideal has been difficult to achieve, even a superficial survey of the anthropological literature on Africa before and since 1945 shows a major feature of the development of the subject to have been the really *vast* increase in the availability of information, and the critical assessment of its validity.

The second and specifically social anthropological duty was to abstract from all this cultural detail, in the light of comparative knowledge of other societies, basic 'structures' of society and, especially under Malinowski's influence, the 'functions' of its constituent institutions. 'Structure' and 'function' were among the key-words of social anthropological discussion until the sixties at least. They were introduced into anthropology as an attempt to make a break with anthropology as culture-history, which had indeed produced conjectures without either historical or sociological foundation. The history of the use of the words 'function' and 'structure' would itself produce a not-misleading account of the history of social anthropology until quite recently.

From my own personal experience as late as 1945 the evolutionism of the Victorians, with its concern for 'origins' and its interest in 'diffusion' versus 'independent invention' of 'culture traits', was still alive. It was not, on the whole, an intellectual atmosphere in which the indigenous cultures of Africa or elsewhere were best studied in their own right; and although the developments represented by Malinowski and Radcliffe-Brown have proved in turn constricting, they removed some ethnocentric impediments to the anthropological study of Africa, the persistence of which it is now difficult to credit.[3]

It is true, however, that until the 1950s, and as a result of the intellectual directions of an earlier period briefly mentioned above, aspects of African social organisation received more attention from social anthropologists than, say, poetic or religious texts. Here however, one must remember that fieldwork in social anthropology is often carried out a long time before the publication of the results, and the sequence of publication does not necessarily represent the development of particular interests. To take one famous example, Evans-Pritchard's *Witchcraft, Oracles and Magic among the Azande* (1937) is unusual as a first publication on an African people in establishing from the beginning central features of their moral and intellectual assumptions. Books with such titles as *The Dynamics of Clanship among the Tallensi* (Fortes, 1945) or *Schism and Continuity in an African Society* (V. W. Turner, 1957) suggest the focus chosen for earlier works in sequences of publication. The titles of later works by these two social anthropologists alone—*Oedipus and Job in West African Religion* (Fortes, 1959) and *The Forest of Symbols* (Turner, 1967) are of course an indication of post-1945 developments towards some social anthropologists' greater interest in metaphysical questions in African contexts, but far from entirely so. It was almost a dogma of social anthropology (whether or not a mistaken dogma is a different question) that what were regarded as the basic features of societies—forms of kinship and patterns of social control, for example—should be made known before the reader could be expected to understand the complexities of African imagination and morality. To take an analogy from a situation which has often been mentioned to me by African friends, English poetry set for study in African schools in the olden days would have been better understood by them had their teachers realised how much of the social context which they, the teachers, took for granted, was not immediately accessible through personal experience to their pupils.

Here I wish particularly to pay tribute to Basil Davidson's understanding of the place of social anthropology in African Studies, and of the kind of work which social anthropologists attempt to do. He knows as well as any social anthropologist that 'traditional' and 'modern' are terms with limited value for describing African cultural characteristics. His reading in, and grasp of, social anthropologists' African Studies, well represented in *The Africans* (1969), has always commanded my admiration; and in *The Africans* there is a sentence which effectively sums up the efforts of many social anthropologists since 1945:

> And it is in the light of the African moral order that one needs to interpret the specific arrangements of structural abstractions—descent lines, age-sets and the rest—which offer for us the only entry to an understanding of societies so different from our own.

Although he himself published *Witchcraft, Oracles and Magic among the Azande* long before he had given a full account of Zande politics, the late Sir Edward Evans-Pritchard held very firmly that in principle a social anthropologist should start, both in his initial investigations and in his publications, with oecology and material culture, moving thence, as he became more fluent in the language, to political and family relations, and thence to questions requiring still more subtle familiarities with the values and proportions of a people's life. This idea of a *sequence* of monographs, well established by 1945 and put into academic practice by many social anthropologists since that time, was itself an indication that a social anthropologist's knowledge of a people could no longer be represented in one compendious work like, for example, C. G. and B. Z.

Seligman, *Pagan Tribes of the Nilotic Sudan*, published in 1932, but dating in the Seligmans' personal experience from before and just after the First World War. The value of such *compendia* is by no means reduced, for their purposes, by more detailed and theoretically orientated studies. Evans-Pritchard would be accepted as outstanding among social anthropologists of Africa who have influenced the development of the subject both before and after 1945, and the sequence of his publications on the Nuer, whom he made into one of the best-known peoples in anthropological literature, is instructive. From 1933, he began to publish his results in anthropological journals. His first monograph on that people, *The Nuer* (1940) analyses political structure in relation to modes of livelihood, and establishes the paradigm of a segmentary lineage system which has had to be borne in mind, at least, by all students of traditional and modern African politics. *Kinship and Marriage among the Nuer* (1951) is a detailed account of the principles upon which the smaller component units of the Nuer political system are organised. *Nuer Religion* (1956) takes the information and analyses of the other two books for granted, along with numerous articles and publications by himself and others, and raises theological, moral and philosophical questions in a Nuer setting. The discussion of the Nuer statement 'Twins are birds' in his last book became involved in wider philosophical debate, a matter which pleased him. He had thought indeed that one development in post-war social anthropology would and should be the appearance of anthropological information as a point of reference in other disciplines, as R. G. Collingwood many years before, and Michael Polanyi later, had found some aspects of his work on the Azande illuminating in the fields of aesthetics and philosophy respectively. Evans-Pritchard could have claimed, then, to describe and interpret African ways of life and thought so as not only to throw light on other more strictly anthropological concerns, but also on problems arising out of other academic enquiries.

The Nuer was perhaps the single most influential book in the anthropological study of African traditional politics, displaying as it did in an extreme form the segmentary nature of some African political systems, and the complementary tendencies to fission and fusion in political structures more generally. Another work which could not then have been produced without it, was scarcely less influential in establishing some provisional classification and comparison of different political structures in Africa. This was *African Political Systems* (1940). Again, though written before the war, this must be seen in influence as a post-war book.

African Political Systems (with a preface by Radcliffe-Brown) is a series of essays with an introduction by Fortes and Evans-Pritchard designed to show that, on the most general classificatory principle, traditional African politics might be divided into two main types: those with centralised political institutions, characteristically the numerous different forms of African kingship, and those with segmentary systems based primarily upon the segmentary structure of clans and lineages. Much of the later work on African politics since the war has started from the (as all would admit, oversimple) comparative points made by this book, and has been an attempt to redefine them. One may cite, rather than a great body of monographs and articles, a similar series of essays, *Tribes Without Rulers* (ed. Tait and Middleton, 1958) where the uncentralised political structures identified in *African Political Systems* are compared in an attempt to achieve a more precise notion of their similarities and differences among themselves.

African Political Systems provided a model for many other volumes consisting of a series of essays with an introduction seeking to elicit some general principles from the detailed ethnographies of several African societies. The great increase in first-hand information made available after the Second World War demanded such assessments of what particularist studies of African peoples in depth contributed to a broader understanding of African life and thought, and what that in turn added to the theoretical interests of social anthropologists in other fields. Hence *African Systems of Kinship and Marriage* (ed. Radcliffe-Brown and Forde, 1950) attempts to provide some guidelines to the study of that subject not only in Africa but in social anthropology generally. *African Worlds* (ed. Forde, 1954) is a sign of the increasing interest in African religion and cosmology which characterises the whole post-war period. On more specific themes, such collections as *Witchcraft and Sorcery in East Africa* (ed. Middleton and Winter, 1963) and *Spirit Mediumship and Society in Africa* (ed. Beattie and Middleton, 1969) may be cited. Concurrently, the volumes of *The Ethnographic Survey of Africa* which began to be published soon after the war provided a summary, area by area, of what was known about African peoples.

By the very nature of their subject, anthropologists are bound to acquire an intimate knowledge of some few peoples and areas of the world, and so social anthropologists of Africa tend to be real specialists in relatively small fields. This might have led (and to some extent has) to a dividing up of the continent between various groups of regional specialists, each with as much in common with specialists in other subjects working in the same region, as with their colleagues in social anthropology outside that region. But area studies in some respects conflict with the theoretical preoccupations of social anthropology, and in the comparative work which most anthropologists regard as an important part of their subject, studies from outside the area in which they happen to have specialised may suggest, at a given time, more fruitful lines of enquiry than those from the field in which they happen to have worked. Thus, to take an outstanding example, Lévi-Strauss has on the whole preferred to make little reference to Africa in his analytic enquiries, his own anthropological knowledge being primarily derived from elsewhere. Yet the great development of interest in the symbolism and systems of classification of African peoples, and the structuralist analysis of African myth which have been a significant development in recent African studies, owe more to Lévi-Strauss than to earlier writings by African specialists. Similarly, at an earlier period, the writings of Lévy-Bruhl provided much of the stimulus for Evans-Pritchard's study of Zande witchcraft, which in turn affected all subsequent writings on African witchcraft.

A most important post-war development has of course been the great increase in African scholars and students in the subject. Though many, so far, have had to devote their main energies to more practical tasks concerned with the consolidation of their own modern African states, they maintain a most valuable dialogue with others, European or African, who have been able to remain in the academic field. However sympathetic the understanding of African thought and society a non-African social anthropologist may achieve, he cannot aspire to the intimate familiarity with a people of one brought up among them and with the deepest commitments to them. One may hope, from present trends, that more and more of the social anthropology of Africa will be written by Africans themselves.

Connected with this, as a very marked post-war development, is the growth of interest in and knowledge of the indigenous literature of Africa. *The Oxford Library of African Literature*, for example, now in some twenty volumes, presents to the reader as directly as possible authentic expressions of African imagination, and its texts must surely provide valuable source material for future students of African literary culture. The survey of African literary genres by Ruth Finnegan in that series (*Oral Literature in Africa, 1970*) is an outstanding contribution to knowledge of African literature, and represents the potentialities, likely to be increasingly realised, of the marriage of anthropological and literary scholarship.

As by the 1960s the narrow 'structural and functional' obsessions (as they then began to seem) of an earlier period made way for literary and linguistic interests, so the factitious conflict between social anthropologists and historians was soon settled. When Evans-Pritchard first started describing social anthropology as a subject more allied with history and literature than with the physical sciences, there was a certain fluttering in the anthropological roosts. But before long, a symposium on the connections between history and anthropology had been held by the Association of Social Anthropologists. Such historians as Vansina and—a non-Africanist—Keith Thomas made generous assessments of the value of social anthropology. Keith Thomas's study of witchcraft in Britain, *Religion and the decline of magic: studies in popular beliefs in 17th century England* (1917) owes much indirectly to the teachings of non-literate Azande.

There have been so many excellent social anthropological studies of Africa since 1945 that I have tried, in this paper, to avoid singling out authors for special mention. But it is not invidious—since there are as yet so few books of this kind—to mention as of interest in combining history and social anthropology, including that of Lévi-Strauss, Stephen Feierman's *The Shambaa Kingdom: A History*, Wisconsin, 1974.

As what is represented at one end of the social anthropological spectrum by the intellectual constructs associated predominantly with Lévi-Strauss would require another and different paper, so would the works of social anthropologists who, at the other end of the spectrum, continue and are likely to continue studies of a really down-to-earth practical nature, whose theory and methodology must increasingly owe as much to sociology as to traditional social anthropology. These are the kind of studies associated more particularly with societies where abiding non-African rule creates problems of adjustment—such problems as were identified decades ago by terms like 'detribalisation', 'urbanisation' and 'social change'. But social anthropologists have worked and continue to work successfully in urban conditions both in traditional and in modern African towns, while the wider problems of modern nationhood, for the most part seen by the authorities as rooted in economics, have produced a cadre of 'development anthropologists' who live, as it were, in a world between Africa, the World Bank, UNESCO etc. That also, to answer Professor Oliver's question with which I began this paper, is one of the directions in which social anthropology was going, and will undoubtedly continue to go. Eventually, however, as I earlier suggested, social anthropologists either identify themselves with sociologists or return to comparative social anthropology. Areas, however important personally, come second academically. What appear at any time to be disparate interests and aims are constantly reamalgamating, and analyses and insights derived from studies in one part of the world throw light on the nature and meaning of human life in another. Since 1945, as before, but greatly more accumulatively, knowledge of human nature and potentiality which social anthropologists have gained from Africa are introduced into our common moral and imaginative inheritance.

Notes

1   There is inevitably a great deal both partial and personal in a contribution of such brevity to such an occasion. Fortunately, the topic is covered in a balanced, comprehensive and succinct way in Professor P. H. Gulliver's essay on anthropology in *The African World, A Survey of Social Research*, ed. Robert A. Lystad, Pall Mall Press, 1965, up to the date of that publication. Professor Gulliver there more particularly deals with the kinds of concern expressed at the First Conference of the African Studies Association of the United Kingdom in 1964, mentioned in the beginning of this paper.

2   Proceedings of the First Conference of the African Studies Association of the United Kingdom held at Birmingham University in September 1964. 'African Affairs', Spring 1965, pp. 24-5.

3   This very year I noticed the following from Professor George Steiner:
     This is political dynamite, and one gets terribly misunderstood, but let me stick my neck out. I am just not sure what you mean by African civilization, and whether it has ever contributed very much to the store of human possibility.

Shula Marks

South African Studies Since World War Two[*]

Any attempt to analyse the nature of South African studies since the Second World War must be an act of presumption, and selection. The sheer amount of writing on South Africa, good, bad and indifferent, but largely the last, makes even the compilation of a bibliography—in itself somewhat a pointless endeavour —a virtual impossibility. I can in no way claim to have covered all subjects. Inevitably, then, this must not be only an historian's view, but also a somewhat personal and selective account, based on a certain amount of work in the social sciences (archaeology, anthropology, history, sociology, political science and economics), which attempts to analyse the nature of South African society; it cannot take account of the very many empirical studies in these disciplines, although even at the purely empirical level I am aware that there are major gaps in our knowledge which must affect our interpretation of the contemporary situation in South Africa, the questions we ask and the generalisations we make.

In looking at the writing on South Africa since the Second World War from this point of view, I was immediately struck by the apparent dearth of any analytical breakthrough until comparatively recently. Whereas in the immediate pre-war years, in the thirties and forties, it can be argued that South Africa was in the forefront of African Studies—whatever its conceptual and ideological limitations—since the early fifties it would seem that South Africa remained outside the advances being made to the north of the Limpopo, in almost every field. This was not only a view I recorded in a short broadcast in the sixties[1]; it was also the collective view of the one-day symposium held under the auspices of the ASAUK at the beginning of 1969, which expressed concern at the singular lack of research being done on South Africa either in the UK or in South Africa itself, over a very wide range of disciplines.[2] Richard Gray expressed it most strongly in reviewing the *Oxford History of South Africa*, vol. 2, in *Race*, 1972, when he remarked 'that to an extraordinary degree, South African historical research has fallen behind that of other African countries, let alone that of other modern industrial countries'.[3] He may correctly have included with South African historical studies research in all of the allied disciplines outlined above.

The 1950s and 1960s witnessed a general outpouring of books and courses in universities on Africa; South Africa, however, was left out, whether because of a conscious boycott, or because of the feeling that her problems were different

[*] This article was written in 1974; with one or two exceptions it has proved impossible to incorporate the considerable material that has appeared—largely in the form of articles or seminar papers—since that date, or to take account of new work in progress.

from those of the newly independent territories. What Eric Stokes called the 'African historiographical revolution'—and again I think this is true of other disciplines as well—stopped short at the Limpopo.[4] There was probably more debate in the thirties on the nature of South African society than there was in the fifties—debate carried on by both insiders and outsiders. Thus it was essentially in the period before the Second World War through to the forties that the professional standards in a large number of disciplines, and their intellectual assumptions, were laid: in archaeology, with the work of Dart and Broom on early man,[5] and van Riet Lowe and Goodwin on the Stone Age[6]; in history with the work of Walker, de Kiewiet and Macmillan[7]; in social psychology with the work of McCrone which strongly influenced subsequent social scientists[8]; and above all, perhaps, in anthropology where in the thirties South Africa had an outstanding record. Some of the most distinguished disciples of Malinowski reached South Africa, while early chairs were held by Radcliffe-Brown and Meyer Fortes.

It may well be true that in South Africa, as elsewhere in Africa, anthropologists failed adequately to stand outside their own colonial society and criticise the very bounds of their subject; that they tended to present a static picture of African society, failing to take full account of the changes being brought by colonialism, or capitalism. Yet to some extent, these charges are least well directed against the anthropologists of Southern Africa in the thirties—one has but to think here of Godfrey Wilson's *Economics of Detribalization*, which shows a very acute awareness of the impact of the world economy on African societies.[9] Scholars like Isaac Schapera, Monica Hunter, Max Gluckman and the Kupers were well aware of the social changes being wrought in the wake of colonialism and industrialisation.[10] Yet the formative work was done in the thirties, forties and early fifties, and, apart from a small handful of useful studies, I think it can be argued that anthropology in South Africa has since been overtaken by more general changes in the conceptualisation of the discipline. Monica Wilson's chapters in the *Oxford History* are still redolent of a 'timeless past' approach to African societies,[11] and this is even more striking in the recent volume edited by Hammond-Tooke as the second edition of Schapera's *Bantu-speaking Peoples of South Africa*.[12] The latter volume in particular suggests that the work being done from within South Africa at the present time has hardly advanced since the thirties: indeed as John Blacking pointed out in a review in the *Times Literary Supplement* that was perhaps a little overharsh:

> The shape of Schapera's classic work is hard to predict. In some respects it is a museum piece that tells us more about its authors and their society than it does about its subjects . . . it lacks the concern that somehow emerges even now from the pages of the first edition. . . . The first edition was written in the heyday of South African liberalism, while the second edition reflects its failure and collapse. As a work of scholarship it should be a warning to anthropologists who imagine that they can avoid important social issues and still produce good ethnography.[13]

By and large, the intellectual foundations for historians, economists, sociologists and political scientists, if not for archaeologists, in the 1930s and 1940s, were also those of classical liberalism. Deeply concerned, as many of these scholars were, with the tension and conflict arising in the course of industrialisation and urbanisation in twentieth-century South Africa, they saw these as arising essentially from the irrational heritage of the past—much as classical liberal economists, both in South Africa and elsewhere attribute the failure of capitalism to achieve a perfect equilibrium, perfect competition, to extraneous, non-economic—broadly speaking 'political'—factors. Thus the origins of racialism were sought, particularly in the wake of McCrone's influential *Race Attitudes in South Africa*[14] in the formative influence of the frontier, and attention was averted from the way in which forms of racialism may have developed within the capitalist economy and may have been in some ways intrinsically related to it.

At another level, though they were concerned with the position of the black man in South African history, it was still largely with his role as the object of the policies and practices of white South Africans; and although the two-volume *Oxford History of South Africa*, published in 1968 and 1971, sees the black man seemingly taking a more central position in the state, even here the part is seen in static, ahistorical terms. Significantly, even here, the pre-colonial history of the black man has been delegated, if not relegated, to an anthropologist, albeit an outstanding and historically alert one. The result, however, has been to portray African societies as both unchanging and isolated—and this in turn has led to misconceptions which reverberate through the account of the complex relationships of black and white societies, and the way in which pre-capitalist and capitalist modes of production articulated through the nineteenth and twentieth centuries. In this, the *Oxford History* can be seen as the apogee of the liberal tradition. In its attempt to place the African back in South African history, it has, however, opened up a new area of debate and research.

Indeed, in many ways the publication of the *Oxford History* can be seen as a kind of watershed in South African studies—and I say studies advisedly, because in fact both volumes are misleadingly called 'History': in both, eminent practitioners in the disciplines of archaeology, anthropology, history, economics and political science are called on to contribute chapters on some aspect of South Africa's past. This is still a long way from the 'new history', which demands that historians themselves integrate the findings of different disciplines within their own historical, and therefore time-based, account of the past. In part perhaps spurred by the *Oxford History* and the most obvious unanswered questions it laid bare, in part perhaps for rather broader intellectual reasons—and I think largely the latter—the 'backwardness' of South African studies of the fifties and sixties is, in many fields, no longer nearly so obvious, although huge gaps do remain.

As has often been remarked, the end of colonialism was a major reason for the new historiography of Africa—but, of course, the end of colonialism did not happen in South Africa. The transfer of power led historians to look for the continuities before and after the colonial era, the origins of nationalism and its roots in primary resistance. This tended to avert eyes from South Africa—and on the whole white South African scholars were not going to focus their attention. In a sense, South

African studies then have missed out on a great deal of this phase of African historiography. When it came, as in the *Oxford History*, it was grafted on to a strong English-speaking academic 'liberal' tradition, which led to a concentration on the processes of interaction between black and white, rather than of independent development, conflict, subordination or class formation. Now that the first flush of enthusiasm for the nationalist revolution has swung into disillusion with the realities of African poverty and the problems of its economic relationships, however, neo-colonialism and economic imperialism north of the Limpopo have become of central concern to a wide number of scholars: and these are questions which have a more decided resonance in the South African situation. The awareness that independence in the political sphere has in many African countries resolved relatively few problems and has not relieved either economic inequalities or the problems of development, has led to a new set of questions being asked and a turning away from the earlier focus on the purely political aspects of the transfer of power. And here, the South African example becomes acutely relevant.

At the same time, racism in South Africa, which was interpreted largely in ideological terms in the fifties and sixties, is beginning to be re-examined. With the swing towards an exploration of its economic function it can, at least in part, be seen as a device in the unequal allocation of the rewards of society—a role not altogether dissimilar to that of ethnocentricity elsewhere in Africa perhaps. This ties in with the far more sophisticated analyses being made of racialism in relation both to slavery in the United States and contemporary racism in Europe and America. It also reflects the return to the debate about the nature of imperialism.

What then have been the new developments in South African studies in the last five or ten years? Where are the major areas of debate and controversy? Where do we need to go from here?

Probably the first and most obvious area in which South Africa seems to be lagging behind the rest of Africa, and one which it is particularly fitting to refer to in celebrating Basil Davidson's birthday, has been in the field of African archaeology. Despite the vast potential for the subject in the Republic, until the late sixties relatively little attempt had been made either within South Africa, or indeed without, to try to relate advances being made in the understanding of Africa's pre-colonial past elsewhere with the processes within the Republic. Stone Age studies, it is true, had continued to attract a fair amount of scholarly attention, although even here the focus tended to be on typologies of implements rather than on the people who made them, so that dialogue between archaeolgists and social scientists was somewhat limited. Work on the Iron Age was conspicuous by its absence.

In both fields recent years have seen a number of exciting developments. As John Parkington showed recently in an unpublished paper to the seminar on the Societies of Southern Africa in the Nineteenth and Twentieth Centuries at the Institute of Commonwealth Studies, London, there is now a new emphasis among Late Stone Age archaeologists.[15] Archaeologists, perhaps influenced by the developments in their field outside South Africa, are now interested in examining the complex relationship of man to his environment, rather than simply his tool kit, and this opens up the possibility of a far more fruitful exchange between the archaeologist and other social scientists. The recent re-examination of the concepts of the Wilton and Smithfield cultures by Janet Deacon,[16] in particular, should help clear the ground for basic new interpretations of the evidence in terms of how people lived and adapted to their environment, and the nature of ecology and resource utilisation, rather than in terms of the rather stultifying categorisation of tools which we had become accustomed to. At a more detailed level, the latest research on the first appearance of sheep bones and pottery, and the indication that they were present on the coast of the western Cape as early as the beginning of first millennium A.D. and arrived together, has revolutionary implications for our thinking about such questions as the origins of the historic Khoi, and their relationship with both Bantu-speakers and the San: a subject which has been bedevilled in the past by an absence of evidence and an abundance of fantasy.

Whatever its limitations, work on the Stone Age has always been in the forefront of South African archaeological endeavour. Iron Age archaeology has lagged notoriously behind developments north of the Limpopo. Apart from a handful of reports on largely undated surface and cave sites,[17] until the mid-sixties virtually the only works were the two volumes on Mapungubwe,[18] the latter of which was particularly unsatisfactory, and Schofield's pioneering *Primitive Pottery*.[19] The first sign of a change in attitude came with the final section of Revill Mason's *Prehistory of the Transvaal*[20] which, like the very brief outline chapter in Desmond Clark's *Prehistory of Southern Africa*,[21] attempted to synthesise the scattered evidence to date. Notwithstanding the attempts by Brian Fagan and Roger Summers[22] in the mid-sixties to look at the somewhat sparse material on Iron Age excavations in South Africa in relation to the exciting work being done at that time, particularly in Rhodesia, they were clearly hampered by the paucity of actual excavation going on. It is significant that in Basil Davidson's popular accounts of the Iron Age in Africa, he had little to say of South Africa, beyond the broadest of generalisation and an allusion to Mapungubwe.

In the last six to eight years, however, this picture has been changed very considerably. An impressive amount of new work is being done, particularly in the Transvaal, where Revill Mason has been directing far more coordinated research on Iron Age settlement in the province. He has recently claimed to have uncovered probably the most intact Early Iron Age village yet to be excavated in Africa south of the Sahara at Broederstroom, near the Hartbeespoort Dam (Pretoria).[23] The new dates for Early Iron Age sites in the Transvaal, from the third to the fifth century A.D. has significance for our understanding of the spread of the Iron Age in general and its manifestation in South Africa in particular. The beautiful terracotta heads from Lydenburg in the eastern Transvaal and with fifth-century dates, described by Inskeep and Maggs,[24] add an exciting dimension to this picture. According to Mason—in perhaps somewhat euphoric mood: 'the search for more data on the Early Iron Age in South Africa is now on. There is every prospect that a reasonably complete sequence of Iron Age settlements will be discovered, perhaps commencing even before the birth of Christ and continuing to the transformations of the 19th century.'[25]

Apart from the work of Mason and others in the Transvaal, the recent work by Tim Maggs on early farming communities in the Orange Free State, which is based on an analysis of building techniques and architectural patterns, is of the utmost importance for our understanding of the Iron Age all over South Africa. The subject is now moving far beyond the tentative outline first sketched by Professor Inskeep in his cautious opening chapter in the *Oxford History* in 1969.

For the pre-colonial history of South Africa, as for the rest of the continent, archaeology is of the essence, and here the most important developments are taking place. Far less work is, however, being done on the other major areas for our evidence of the pre-colonial past: in historical linguistics, for example, or the analysis of tradition. Here again before the Second World War, it can be argued, South African scholarship was, if no further forward, at least no worse off than elsewhere: indeed in many ways the collection of oral evidence had the lead on many other parts of the continent, with the collection of traditions, albeit in an unsystematic and somewhat haphazard fashion, from the beginning of the nineteenth century in the eastern Cape, and rather later on the highveld. In the 1920s and 1930s a number of vernacular histories were being produced, in addition to the work of N. J. van Warmelo and the massive compilations of tradition by such assiduous amateurs as A. T. Bryant for Zulu, Ellenberger and McGregor on the Sotho, and the Junods on the Tsonga.[26] The re-examination of such collections and the fresh collection of oral evidence which was so marked a development north of the Limpopo in the sixties has not taken place to any large extent in the Republic, except somewhat uncritically in the service of the government's ethnography department.[27]

In historical linguistics, too, despite the fact that important linguistic observation and description goes back to such authorities as Bleek in the mid-nineteenth century, relatively little systematic new work has taken place apart from a couple of pioneering articles by Professor E. J. Westphal in the early sixties on the relationship of the 'Bushman' languages—or lack of it—and by Professor Lanham on their influence on Bantu phonemic systems.[28] Although South Africa has formed part of the concern of linguists such as Guthrie and Greenberg and more recently, and perhaps most controversially of Christopher Ehret,[29] there is as yet no school of historical linguistics directly concerned in detailed fashion with developments within the Republic. Yet South Africa offers an important laboratory for this study with the very different languages spoken within its frontiers: in this field, as in the others, South Africa missed out on an important stage of development which took place elsewhere in the fifties and sixties, and there is little sign at least in this respect that it is being remedied.

At this, critics of African historiography in the fifties and sixties may well retort: 'So what?'. It may well require a leap of the imagination, yet I would argue that our ignorance of the pre-colonial past bedevils our understanding of the more immediate past and of the nature of the colonial experience. We still know far too little about such broad questions as the modes of production of pre-industrial societies, and their articulation—or, in less abstract terms, the precise nature of the relationship between hunting, herding and farming communities in South Africa, the extent of internal and long distance trade, the internal stratification of pre-colonial societies and their increasing linkage with a world economy from the seventeenth century onwards. Until we have a clearer picture of all of this, we will be unable to interpret aright the impact of the Dutch at the Cape, the Voortrekkers on the highveld, or the mining capitalists on the Rand.[30] If I may cite a more recent example of how this ignorance has distorted our understanding of the present: until recently it has been held that labour migration from south Mozambique to the goldfields of South Africa in the late nineteenth century was in large measure to be attributed to the labour policies of the Portuguese Government and the recruiting agency of the Transvaal Chamber of Mines. Yet on closer examination it would appear that the Tsonga were migrating to South Africa in search of work since the 1860s, long before there was any effective Portuguese presence in the area.[31] Until we know more of the social and political organisation of the Tsonga, the ecology of the area, the impact of the nineteenth-century invasions from Zululand, the extent to which by the nineteenth century their economy was already linked to a world trading network, we are unlikely to be able to explain this phenomenon. (This is of course not to argue that labour corvées, Enes's policies, and the WNLA were not of importance, particularly in stimulating the numbers required by the goldfields and channelling the labour to the mines—only that we need a far more precise picture of the different elements involved.) And all this has relevance, I would argue, to the broad question of major concern to the social scientists and historians of South Africa alike: the pattern of domination and subordination for the social scientists, for historians, how and why a handful of white men came to assert their dominance over a territory which has become the most powerful industrial state in Africa today.

The first of these white men to settle in South Africa were, of course, the Dutch in the mid-seventeenth century, and, with their coming, the nature of our sources for the understanding of Southern African societies changes. For the first time we have a large number of written records, and although these mostly relate only to the fairly small area of the Cape Colony itself, and the activities of the white man, they also do shed light on the first peoples they encountered, the Khoisan hunter-gatherers and herders. Even in this field, however, the conventional picture was established back in the thirties and forties and has only relatively recently come under scrutiny. Although J. P. van der Merwe's seminal work on the *trekboer* written at this time, and Neumark's provocative study, *Economic Influences on the Cape Frontier*,[32] existed to disprove many of the stereotypes, essentially the seventeenth and eighteenth century documents were quarried (and I use the term 'quarry' deliberately) by both liberal and Afrikaner nationalist historians to show the evolution of the Afrikaner and his philosophy of racial segregation on the South African 'frontier'.

As Dr Martin Legassick has pointed out, in an important but unfortunately as yet unpublished paper, this 'frontier tradition' which derived much of its sustenance, if not its original inspiration, from Turner's work on the North American frontier, has been used to describe a multitude of facets of South

African life, though 'the influence of the frontier on racial attitudes has been its most persistently argued effect: the frontiersmen regarded the non-white only as a servant or enemy',[33] Yet as Legassick shows, this interpretation of the frontier falls apart when one begins to examine in detail precisely what was happening on the 'so-called frontier'—i.e. the zone of contact between individuals owing allegiance to different sovereign political authorities. A good deal of new work is now beginning to fill in the details of this picture both for the seventeenth and eighteenth century and later. And it is beginning to appear that, far from the frontier being the zone in which philosophies of segregation evolved, this was the area of greatest interaction—an area of violence it is true, which both the liberal historians and Afrikaner found hard to explain, but not necessarily therefore an area of *greater* 'racialism'. Roger Wagner's current work on that flamboyant frontier figure, Coenraad de Buys, is an apposite illustration of this. De Buys, who led the revolt of Boers in Graaff Reinet in 1795 was apparently fully accepted in trekboer society of the time; yet he also consorted with the mother of the Xhosa Chief Ngqika; was bitterly hated by Ngqika's rivals as the source of their woes; was outlawed by the Batavian and British authorities of the Cape; legally married a Thembu wife; gave evidence for Khoi servants against his fellow white burghers to the Black Circuit of 1811; and ultimately fled the Cape colony, landing up in the north eastern Transvaal, having left his mark on the many Sotho-Tswana societies through which he had passed, and leaving behind him a clan of Buys folk of various colours and cultures.[34]

If, however, the frontier can no longer be seen as the *fons et origo* of South African race attitudes, this opens up a number of questions both in relation to the seventeenth and eighteenth centuries, and indeed to the more recent past. If race attitudes are not attributable—in an almost mysterious, or at least a geographical sense—to the 'influence of the frontier'—*à la* McCrone and Walker—where are they to be sought? Do they owe as much to the institution of slavery in the western Cape—to master-servant relations in that part of the Cape which was more labour-intensive and more closely linked with the metropolitan economy and metropolitan norms? Far too little work has been done in this field as yet for the answers to be definitive. The work of Robert Ross at Cambridge on seventeenth and eighteenth century Cape social history and demography, however, and an important thesis by Dr R. Elphick at Yale on the first relationships established between the Dutch and the Khoi at the Cape in the seventeenth century are beginning to reveal some of the clues.[35]

This work on the frontier has further ramifications which are of direct relevance for our understanding of the nineteenth century, and ultimately to our understanding of the processes of capitalist development: the area where most of the more recent debate has centred. If we no longer simplistically trace archetypal colour attitudes to the frontier, what about the colour attitudes supposedly first carried further north by the Voortrekkers, who—again according to the conventional wisdom established before the war and barely questioned since—left the Cape because of the attempt of an alien government, the British, to impose its notions of law and order, and in particular its supposedly more 'liberal' notions of master-servant relations, on the 'frontier'? Here, too, more work needs to be done, but a certain amount of research, as much inspired by an attempt to look at African history and understand the experience for blacks of the coming of the trekkers to the Transvaal as by a desire to pursue the frontier 'hypothesis' *per se*, suggests that white society, even on the highveld, has never been as monolithic in its attitudes to people of colour as the textbooks imply.[36]

This revision of the conventional wisdom on the nature of European rule of the Cape in the seventeenth and eighteenth centuries, and in the interior for much of the nineteenth, has one further aspect: it involves an appreciation of how *weak* white power was in these areas, and not how strong. Both van der Merwe and J. S. Marais in his *Maynier and the First Boer Republics*[37] were aware of this for the Dutch period: and there is much evidence in van Jaarsveld's *The Rise of Afrikaner Nationalism* to support this view of the early republics established in the Transvaal.[38] Yet curiously little attention has been paid to the fact by either the liberal or the imperial school of history in assessing the impact of the Afrikaner on the Africans they encountered in increasing numbers from the end of the eighteenth century. With the new appreciation of the African side of South African history, however, this weakness of white power takes on a new significance and opens again the question—at what point and why and by whom and in whose interest was white supremacy ultimately imposed? This in turn involves a reinterpretation of the impact of the British, first on the Cape and then on the rest of South Africa in the nineteenth century; we need very different terms of analysis to those used even by such historians as de Kiewiet or Macmillan.[39]

And all this leads directly into the area where much of the debate among historians, sociologists, political scientists and economists over the last five years has centred: on the nature of industrialisation in South Africa. Here the conventional wisdom, which was accepted almost without question and interestingly as much by the left as by liberals throughout the fifties and most of the sixties, held that the process of capitalist development in South Africa demanded a rationalisation of the colour attitudes, and that the forces of industrialisation would in and by themselves break down *apartheid*. If, however, one is no longer able to accept the notion that racialism is simply an atavistic carry-over from the eighteenth century which has no place in a modern industrial society, and one looks to the methods of labour repression—which certainly did not first originate in industrialisation, but which were both magnified and systematised in order to maximise the profits of the goldmining industry, as has recently been cogently argued by a number of scholars—this comforting picture no longer obtains.[40]

Despite the tremendous outpouring of literature on contemporary South Africa—perhaps more than on any other part of Africa—one of the major gaps in the study of South Africa, again until the last few years, has been an adequate study of the twentieth century particularly from a socio-economic standpoint. Yet even elementary studies of white politics have been lacking. Much of the work until the late sixties focusing on Afrikaner nationalism, the ideology of *apartheid* and contemporary political developments fails to examine the nature of the South African state, what interests it was mediating, the conflicts within it or the precise function of racism in South African society. Heribert Adam in his *Modernizing Racial Domination*[41] was perhaps the first to depart from the prevalent view of the Afrikaner state as representative of an outmoded colonialism. Work by F. R. Johnston, John Rex Harold Wolpe and Martin Legassick,[42] took this process considerably further in their examination of existing interpretations —largely pluralist—of South African society, and their own analyses of its structure and purpose. Within the last couple of years, further new work has been undertaken, on the structural determinants of white power, the nature of white class interests and of white, especially Afrikaner accumulation, and the implications of this for the regional economy as a whole and for South Africa's internal black majority in particular.[43] Much of this work is still in progress, but clearly in the next few years this approach to South Africa's twentieth-century history is clearly going to be a major growth history.

In part this may well be a reflection of the general move on African studies towards a return to the external constraints on African independence. And from this point of view, South Africa's own role in the economy of the southern African region as a whole has received some, but by no means exhaustive treatment.[44] If there is a danger in these new developments it may be as Terry Ranger pointed out some years ago—of the emerging dichotomy between those who emphasise 'African activity, African adaptation, African choice and African initiative', and what he terms the 'radical pessimist' who in the face of the persistent and persisting poverty of the continent has stressed the international determinants of African powerlessness and who posit salvations only through 'world revolution': those for whom the focal point of African historiography 'should be the process by which African patterns of development became dependent on alien interests'.[45]

By its emphasis on the structure of the white state, and the processes of proletarianisation and impoverishment, there is much in the recent debate which stresses the crucial role of international and white agencies in the control of African destiny and African powerlessness: nevertheless to ignore these determinants in the South African situation would surely be to ignore some of the most fundamental aspects of its historical and contemporary predicament. Nonetheless, in order to understand the ways in which these constraints have operated and the way in which white domination has been imposed and functioned, it is important to be constantly aware, as Basil Davidson himself has always been aware, of the African side of the story. The best of the work in the new field has certainly had this awareness: witness the research of Colin Bundy on African peasant responses,[46] Henry Slater on land relationships in Natal[47] and of Stanley Trapido on the Cape liberal tradition, or more recently on the nature of industrialisation and of slavery in the Transvaal.[48] The work of Charles van Onselen, in particular, on labour on the Rhodesian mines, and more recently on the social history of the Witwatersrand, is rich in insights for the historian of industrialisation in general, and of the mining industry in South Africa in particular.[49] Given the wealth of source material on South Africa's past and present the scope for truly exploring the experience of the black majority is vast and this task has barely begun. It is a task that will be most fruitfully achieved if historians, archaeologists, anthropologists, political scientists, sociologists and economists can find a common language.

Notes

1   'Historians and South Africa' in *Africa Discovers Her Past*, ed. J. D. Fage, OUP, London, 1970, pp. 83-9.
2   *Southern African Studies. Report of a Symposium held at S.O.A.S. London, Sept. 1969*, ed. M. R. Kettle and R. P. Moss. (Special Issue of the Bulletin of the ASAUK, 1970).
3   *Race*, xiv, 1, July 1972, p. 84.
4   'The British Moment in South Africa' (review), *J. Afr. Hist.*, vii, 3, 1966, p. 530.
5   It is virtually impossible to list Dart's many publications here—over fifty articles alone since 1925 when he published his shattering discovery of the Taung skull and strongly argued that man first emerged in Africa—a conclusion amply supported of course by the more recent work, particularly of the Leakeys in east Africa. Although many of his more recent claims, especially those relating to the tool-making abilities of very early man have been controversial, there can be no doubt that his early work and enthusiasm was a tremendous spur to further work. For a recent account of the work over the past fifty years see C. G. Sampson, *The Stone Age Archaeology of Southern Africa*, New York and London, 1974, pp. 16-102. See also pp. 156-68 above.
6   See esp. A. J. H. Goodwin and C. van Riet Lowe, 'The Stone Age Cultures of South Africa' in *Annals of the South African Museum*, 1929. Goodwin was subsequently Professor of Archaeology at Cape Town, van Riet Lowe at the University of Witwatersrand. In 1935 van Riet Lowe became first Director of the South African Archaeological Survey. Neither van Riet Lowe nor members of Dart's school ignored the Iron Age, as many papers in the *S. Afr. Journal of Science* in the thirties and forties attest.
7   E. A. Walker, *Historical Atlas of South Africa*, Cape Town, 1922; *Lord de Villiers and his Times: South Africa, 1824-1914*, London, 1925; *The Frontier Tradition in South Africa*, Oxford, 1930; *The Great Trek*, London, 1938; *A History of South Africa*, London, 1928; C. W. de Kiewiet, *A History of South Africa, Social and Economic*, Oxford, 1941; *British Colonial Policy and the South African Republics, 1848-1872*, London, 1929; *The Imperial Factor in South Africa*, London, 1937; W. M. Macmillan, *Bantu, Boer and Briton*, London, 1929; *The Cape Colour Question*, London, 1927; *Complex South Africa*, London, 1930. Both wrote key chapters in the *Cambridge History of the British Empire*, vol. VIII, *South Africa*, ed. E. Walker, Cambridge, 1937.
8   I. D. McCrone, *Race Attitudes in South Africa: Historical, Experimental and Psychological Studies*, Johannesburg, 1937. Part I of this work is an historical survey of the eighteenth century at the Cape which, it concludes, was 'the formative period of those race attitudes on the part of the European which make an adjustment, satisfactory to both races, the most difficult problem of twentieth century South Africa' (p. 136). We are then led straight into a discussion of attitude measurement and race attitudes in the 1930s.
9   Cf. R. Brown, 'Anthropology and Colonial Rule: the case of Godfrey Wilson and the Rhodes-Livingstone Institute, Northern Rhodesia'. Unpubl. paper, Institute of Commonwealth Studies, London, 1972-73.
10   One has but to think of the title of M. Wilson's (née Hunter) first work—*Reaction to Conquest*, London, 1936—here; cf. also I. Schapera (ed.) *Western Civilization and the Natives of South Africa*, London, 1934, or *Migrant Labour and Tribal Life*, London, 1947; H. Kuper, *The Uniform of Colour*, Johannesburg, 1947;

L. Kuper, H. Watts, K. R. Davis, *Durban, a Study in Racial Ecology*, London, 1958; M. Gluckman, 'Analysis of a Social Situation in Modern Zululand', *Bantu Studies*, xiv, 1940.

11   Especially ch. 2, 3 and 4 in *Oxford History of South Africa I, South Africa to 1870*, ed. M. Wilson and L. Thompson, Oxford, 1969. Given the state of knowledge, this was perhaps inevitable. Nevertheless the absence of a chronological framework severely limits the usefulness of these chapters. See the reviews of the *Oxford History I* in *Race*, xi, July 1969 (Richard Gray), *Bulletin of the School of Oriental and African Studies*, xxx, 1970 (A. Atmore), *J. Afr. Hist.*, xi, 3, 1970 (S. Marks) and A. Atmore and N. Westlake, 'A Liberal Dilemma: A Critique of the Oxford History of South Africa'. *Race*, xiv, 2, 1972, pp. 111-12.

12   London, 1974.

13   *Times Literary Supplement*, 8 November 1974.

14   As N. Westlake and A. Atmore pointed out in 'A Liberal Dilemma'.

15   'Recent Developments in the study of the Prehistory of the Cape', November 1974.

16   J. Deacon, 'Wilton: an assessment after 50 years', *S. Afr. Arch. Bull.*, xxvii, 1972, pp. 10-45. and 'Patterning in the Radiocarbon Dates for the Wilton/Smithfield Complex in Southern Africa', *S. Afr. Arch. Bull.*, xxix, 1974, pp. 3-18. Her articles seem to cut through much of the argument in C. O. Sampson's *The Stone Age in Southern Africa*.

17   E.g. E. C. N. van Hoepen and A. C. Hoffman, 'Die Oorblyfsels van Buispoort en Braklaagte, Noordwes van Zeerust', *Argeologiese Navorsing van die Nasionale Museum, Bloemfontein*, ii, 1, 1935; C. van Riet Lowe and R. A. Dart, 'A Preliminary Report on the Stone Huts of Vechtkop', J.R.A.I., 1927; C. W. Bates, 'Archaeological Sites on the Groot Letaba River', *S.A. Jnl. Sci.*, xliii, 1947. R. A. Pullen, 'Remains from Stone-hut Settlements in the Frankfort District, O.F.S.', *S.A. Jnl. Sci.*, xxxviii, 1941.

18   L. Fouché (ed.) *Mapungubwe I*, Cambridge, 1937; G. A. Gardner, *Mapungubwe II*, Pretoria, 1963. For a scathing critique of the latter, see B. M. Fagan, 'The Greifswald Sequence', *J. Afr. Hist.*, v, 3, 1964.

19   Cape Town, 1948.

20   Johannesburg, 1962, especially pp. 372-453.

21   Penguin, 1959, pp. 281-311.

22   B. Fagan, *Southern Africa during the Iron Age*, London, 1965, pp. 116-19; 153-67. R. Summers, 'Iron Age Industries of Southern Africa', in W. W. Bishop and J. D. Clark, eds., *The Background to Evolution in Africa*, Chicago, 1967. The chapters by David Phillipson on the Early Iron Age and Brian Fagan on the Later Iron Age in L. Thompson (ed.) *African Societies in Southern Africa*, London, 1969, then the best syntheses, have now been overtaken by recent work.

23   'Early Iron Age Settlement of Southern Africa. First Early Iron Age Settlement in South Africa: Broederstroom 24/73 Brits District, Transvaal', *S. Afr. Jnl. Sci.*, lxix, November 1973, p. 324. For the Transvaal see articles by M. Evers, especially 'Recent Iron Age Research' *S.A. Arch. Bull.*, xxx, 1975, pp. 71-83.

24   R. R. Inskeep and T. M. O'C. Maggs, 'Unique Iron Objects', *S.A. Arch. Bull.* xxx, 1975, pp. 114-38.

25   'Early Iron Age Settlement of Southern Africa', p. 325.

26   For the vernacular histories, see e.g. M. M. Fuze, *Abantu Abanyama*, Durban, 1920; W. D. Cingo, *I-Bali Laba Tembu*, Palmerton, 1927; R. T. Kawa, *I-Bali lama Mfengu*, Lovedale, 1929; A. Sekese, *McKhoa le maela a Basotho*, Morija, 1931. Africans were also writing 'traditional' history in English at this time—e.g. J. H. Soga, *The South-Eastern Bantu*, Johannesburg, 1930; S. M. Molema, *The Bantu, Past and Present*, Edinburgh, 1920. For N. J. van Warmelo, see for example, *A Preliminary Survey of the Bantu Tribes of South Africa*, Pretoria, 1935; *The Copper Miners of Musina*, Pretoria, 1940; *A History of Matiwane and the Amangwane Tribe . . .*, Pretoria, 1938 etc. Bryant's major historical works are *Olden Times in*

Zululand and Natal, London, 1929; *A History of the Zulu and Neighbouring Tribes*, Cape Town, 1964—based on articles first published in the thirties. See also D. F. Ellenberger *History of the Basotho, Ancient and Modern*, trans, by J. C. Macgregor, London, 1912; and H. A. Junod, *The Life of a South African Tribe*, 2 vols., London, 1927. Some attempt at analysing the extant collections of oral evidence for the Sotho-Tswana and Natal Nguni respectively was made by M. Legassick and Marks in *African Societies*. For an attempt to synthesise the inadequate evidence see also my contributions to the *Cambridge History of Africa*. The publication of the first volume of the *James Stuart Archive*, C. de B Webb and J. Wright, eds., University of Natal Press, 1976, is welcome.

27   See for example the publications of P. L. Breutz in this series.

28   E. J. Westphal, 'The Linguistic Prehistory of Southern Africa; Bush, Kwadi, Hottentot and Bantu Linguistic Relationships', *Africa*, xxxiii, 3, 1963; 'A Reclassification of Southern African Non-Bantu Languages', *Jnl. of Afr. Lang.*, i, 1, 1962. L. W. Lanham, 'The Proliferation and Extension of Bantu Phonemic Systems influenced by Bushman and Hottentot', *Proc. 9th Annual Cong. of Linguistics, Cambr. Mass. 1962*, The Hague, 1967.

29   See for example his 'Outlining Southern African History 100-1500 A.D.' in *Ufuhamu*, iii, 1, 1972; 'Cattle keeping and milking in Eastern and Southern Africa', *J. Afr. Hist.*, viii, 1, 1967; 'Sheep Central Sudanic People in Southern Africa', *J. Afr. Hist.*, ix, 2, 1968; 'Patterns of Bantu and Central Sudanic Settlement in Central and Southern Africa', *Transafrican Jnl. of Hist.*, iv, 1, 1974.

30   Several scholars are now (1976) working in this area.

31   See M. Newitt, 'Migrant Labour and the Development of Mozambique' in *Collected Seminar Papers no. 17: The Societies of Southern Africa in the 19th and 20th centuries*, vol. 4, ICS, London, 1973, pp. 68-70; also unpublished work by Patrick Harries (SOAS).

32   Stanford, 1957.

33   'The Frontier Tradition in South African Historiography', *C.S.P. no. 12. Societies of Southern Africa*, vol. 2, ICS, London, 1971, p. 2.

34   For preliminary work on de Buys, see R. G. Wagner, 'Coenraad de Buys in Transorangia', *C.S.P. no. 17, Societies of Southern Africa*, vol. 4, pp. 1-9, and 'Zoutpansberg: some notes on the dynamics of a hunting frontier', *C.S.P. Societies of Southern Africa*, vol. 6, 1975.

35   R. Ross 'Some speculations on the Origins of Cape Society' (forthcoming); R. Elphick, 'The Cape Khoi and the First Phase of South African Race Relations', unpubl. Ph.D., Yale, 1972, to be published by Yale University Press; see also forthcoming work by R. Elphick and H. Giliomee on the Cape in the 17th and 18th centuries.

36   See for example P. Bonner 'The Relations between Internal and External Politics in Swaziland and the Eastern Transvaal in the mid-19th century', *C.S.P. no. 12, Societies of Southern Africa*, vol. 2, pp. 34-50.

37   E.g. P. J. van der Merwe, *Die Noordwaartse Beweging van die Boere Voor die Groot Trek*, The Hague, 1937; *Die Trekboer in die Geskiedenis van die Kaapkolonie*, Cape Town ,1938; J. S. Marais, *Maynier and the First Boer Republics*, Cape Town, 1944.

38   Cape Town, 1961, cf. esp. ch. 6.

39   For a preliminary historiographical overview see A. Atmore and S. Marks, 'The Imperial Factor in South Africa, Towards a Re-Assessment', *Journal of Imperial and Commonwealth History*, iii, I, 1974, and E. F. Penrose, ed., *European Imperialism and the Partition of Africa*, London, 1975.

40   D. Yuidelman, 'Industrialization, Race Relations and Change in South Africa', *African Affairs*, lxxiv, 2941, January 1975, pp. 82-96, attempts a summary of this debate.

41   California, 1971.

42   S. Trapido, 'South Africa in a Comparative Study of Industrialization', *Journal*

of Devt. Studies, viii, 3, 1971. F. A. Johnstone, 'Class and Colour in the South African Gold-mining industry, 1910-24', unpubl. D.Phil. Oxford, 1972; 'Class Conflict and Colour Bars in the South African gold-mining industry' *C.S.P. no. 10. Societies of Southern Africa*, vol. I, 1970, pp. 112-27; 'White Prosperity and White Supremacy in South Africa Today', *African Affairs*, lxix, 274, April 1970; M. Legassick, 'Capital Accumulation and Violence in South Africa', *Economy and Society*, iii, 1974; 'Ideology, Legislation and Economy in post-1948 South Africa', *Journal of Southern African Studies*, i, I, 1974; 'South Africa: Forced Labour, Industrialization and Racial Differentiation', in R. Harris, ed., *The Political Economy of Africa*, Boston, 1975; 'Race, Industrialization and Social Change', *African Affairs*, April 1976; H. Wolpe, 'Capitalism and cheap labour power in South Africa: from segregation to apartheid', *Economy and Society*, i, 4, 1972. J. Rex, 'The Plural Society: The South African case', *Race*, xii, 4, 1971.

43   Much of this work is still unpublished see, e.g., B. Bozzoli, 'The role of ideology in the legitimation of South African capitalism', Univ. of Sussex Ph.D thesis, 1975 and from a different vantage point, T. Dunbar Moodie, *The Rise of Afrikanerdom*, Univ. of California, 1975.

44   See for example S. Gervasi, 'The Nature and Consequences of South Africa's Economic Expansion', *C.S.P. no. 12, Societies of Southern Africa*, vol. 2, pp. 140-54; Robert Molteno, *Africa and South Africa*, The Africa Bureau, 1971; J. Barber, *South Africa's Foreign Policy, 1945-70*, OUP, 1973.

45   *Emerging Themes in African History*, London, 1968, xxi.

46   C. Bundy, 'Emergence and Decline of a South African Peasantry', *African Affairs*, lxxi, 285, October 1972, pp. 369-88 and his unpublished Oxford D.Phil. thesis.

47   See for example H. Slater, 'Land and Labour in Natal: the Natal Land Colonization Company, 1860-1948', *J. Afr. Hist.*, xvi, 2, 1975.

48   S. Trapido, 'White conflict and non-white participation in the politics of the Cape of Good Hope, 1853-1910', unpubl. Ph.D., London, 1970; 'Liberalism in the Cape in the 19th and 20th centuries', *C.S.P. no. 17, Societies of Southern Africa*, vol. 4, pp. 53-66; 'The South African Republic: Class formation and the State 1850-1900', *C.S.P. no. 16, Societies*, vol. 3, 1972, pp. 53-64; 'Aspects in the transition from slavery to serfdom', *C.S.P. no. 20, Societies*, vol. 6, pp. 24-32.

49   C. van Onselen, 'African Worker Consciousness in the Rhodesian Gold Mines, 1890-1920', *J. Afr. Hist.*, xiii, 1972; 'The Wankie coal strike, 1912', *J. Afr. Hist.*, xiv. 1973; *Chiboro*, Pluto Press, 1976; 'The Randlords and Rotgut, 1886-1903', *C.S.P. no. 20, Societies*, vol. 6, pp. 52-99 (forthcoming, Past and Present); 'South Africa's lumpenproletariat Army' in *C.S.P., Societies*, vol. 7 (forthcoming), and *History Workshop*, (forthcoming).

Catherine Coquery-Vidrovitch

Changes in African Historical Studies in France

The major influences

As in Great Britain, it was at the beginning of the sixties that the history of Black Africa was finally dignified by recognition as a 'university' discipline. It is not that it had not existed before, but until then it had remained the private domain of the men in the field. Soldiers and administrators were the first to realise the scientific interest of this extra-European domain of which they alone had any knowledge. Their abundant works are far from negligible, but they reflect their times—and their authors' motivations; for these reasons they remain incomplete and biased.

In the field of science, Black Africa remained the domain of a few anthropologists (then more narrowly called ethnologists), and the first of the efforts (1938) to show the historic interest of their work—the thesis by Hubert Deschamps on the 'Ethno-history' of the Antaisakada of Madagascar—was greeted with the indifference still quasi-general among the 'historians'. The only 'recognised' history was that of colonisation. One was either 'colonial'— this was the more usual (and the term then had no hidden pejorative connotation)—or 'anti-colonial'. It was in the latter category that 'Maghreb, Studies' traditionally the closest to the metropolis, made a resounding entry into the university scene with the arrival at the Sorbonne of the great innovator Charles-André Julien, the first occupant, after the Second World War, of the Chair of History of Colonisation. He marked, by his political behaviour as much as by his scientific dynamism, a whole generation of historians whose theses stood out in recent years. He did more, since it was to his obstinacy that we owe the creation at the Sorbonne of the first, and still the only, three chairs dedicated to Black Africa (Medieval History, Modern and Contemporary History and Sociology). True, this was one year after the appearance of a Directorate of Black African Historical Studies (1960) at the École Pratique des Hautes Études (E.P.H.E.) which thus demonstrated its faithfulness to the mission which had devolved upon it, namely to promote advanced research in France.

The early sixties

Establishment in the university was the result of a current which—was it simply by chance?—coincided with the current of 'decolonisation'. The role which fell to Basil Davidson to present (or to expose) to cultivated British opinion the existence of the Black African past, was played in France to some extent by

Jean Suret-Canale, the Marxist geographer, who beginning in 1958 published the first, and for a long time the best, work in the French language on the past of at least a part of the continent[1] (even if today it seems still relatively 'Eurocentric', taking into account the progress which has since been made, in that the great African political formations of the past are still tackled from the point of view of their relationship to the outside world). A little later, another major work— almost equivalent to and simultaneous with the famous Robinson and Gallagher[2]—appeared. This was the work of Henri Brunchswig, *Mythes et Réalités de l'impérialisme français, 1870-1914*[3] which opened up the debate on imperialism. It is undeniable that he contributed *a contrario* to a revision and a deepening of the position of the Marxist historians, who remained conditioned by a certain simplifying schematism since the Stalinist era, by affirming the preponderance of ideological and political motives in economic forces. Nevertheless, as an indication of how much of an innovator he was at that period the author had some difficulty in finding a publisher—who was the first to be surprised by the impact of the work.

The first controversies

Since then, history has asserted itself as a method of learning about Africa but not without hesitation. For in France, perhaps more than elsewhere, the discipline has suffered from ethnocentrism—an anxiety to bring back to itself, that is to say Europe, its object of study. There is nothing surprising in that: slowly elaborated in the nineteenth century with the aid of learned techniques adapted to the analysis of our own civilisation, the science of history remained a prisoner of its own instruments, and the historians of France manifested a tenacious mistrust of peoples without writing, who were supposed for that reason to have no history. This mistrust was dominated by the antagonism, more marked than elsewhere, between 'historians' and 'ethnologists'. The latter saw themselves as being virtually 'dispossessed' of their monopoly of a field of study of which they alone had hitherto revealed the scientific value: the observation of extra-European 'traditional' societies. Conditions were moreover favourable for them to reproach the historians for their inability to adapt themselves to the methodological demands of this new field. It was simply that during this pioneering period, many 'historians' of Black Africa were 'amateurs'. This was in itself quite fortunate since the 'professional' historians refused to take an interest in this field. But it is here that the orientation differs from that in Great Britain: the great merit of Basil Davidson was not only that he made people admit the interest of African history, but that at the same time he sensed how it could enrich the human sciences by the multiplicity of possible approaches (archaeology, sociology, religious science, etc.). Undoubtedly he owed it to his experience as a journalist, trained to grasp each situation immediately in all its complexity.

The first French 'African Historians', mostly ex-French Colonial Service officers, were for that very reason more sensitive to the immediate conditions of the country. They tended to dwell on chronicles of events, thus accentuating the gap between historians and anthropologists. The latter were still at this time captivated by the vogue of structuralism.

The anthropological school, inspired by Claude Lévi-Strauss, only authorised analysis of 'traditional societies' according to the methods of 'La Pensée Sauvage'[4] which reveals a necessary balance between man and nature: that is to say, the study of organic groupings of relationships and interconnections—in short, unvarying social structures, situated for this very reason outside 'dynamic history'.[5] The structuralist influence encouraged the 'professional' historians[6] in their tendency to deny the reality of the African context (an ahistoric field). In acting usefully against this current, the first historians of Black Africa were reduced to giving a rather narrow view of their approach to history which the anthropologists in their turn denounced enthusiastically: they attributed to the inherent weaknesses of history the lack of breadth of certain beginners who were poorly informed about the latest advances in their discipline.

Black Africa, crossroads of the social sciences

In fact these first 'misfires' were of short duration. The specialists in African Studies soon became reconciled in the face of the obvious complexity of their subject. More than any other it involved a 'multidisciplinary' collaboration; no matter which methodological approach was preferred it required a knowledge of all the neighbouring sciences.

Two initiatives decisively resolved the controversy. On one side, that of the sociologist Georges Balandier who resolutely opposed the ahistoric tendency of the structuralists and maintained that the drama which Black Africa had enacted was that of a society in the process of mutation, at one and the same time rooted in the past, but under the constraints of modernism; in short, that the reality of Africa could not be appreciated without recourse in depth to its history.[7]

At the same time, there bloomed on the historians' side what we shall call the École des Annales after the review, where their theses appeared from the 1930s onwards. The current was not in fact new: since 1949 Marc Bloch had been drawing attention to the 'almost infinite' diversity of historic sources ('everything man says or writes, all he makes, all he touches, may, and should, give information about him').[8] But it found new impetus under the driving force of Fernand Braudel who enriched the 'structuralist' contribution by clearly defining the different levels of knowledge possible: not only *the event* itself, immediately ascertainable, but hardly significant in itself, because it appears only as the indicator of all the past which gave rise to it, as a stimulus liable in its turn to influence the future; but also, in the medium term, the social *conjuncture* of which the work inspired by Ernest Labrousse[9] has largely served to underline the importance; finally, the *long term*, 'that of slowness, permanence, inertia, structure',[10] no less fundamental in the Western world than in the so-called 'traditional' societies.

History thus declared itself to be concerned not only to take over time in all its dimensions, but also 'all aspects of social transformation, taken as a whole, without giving special consideration to any particular aspect'.

Concerned with 'reciprocal relationships between economic, social, mental, cultural and political aspects, history is therefore conceived as the crossroads of the human sciences, and as having to serve the progress of these sciences'.[11]

Thus, the different specialists in the human sciences at last find themselves above the quarrels of the different schools of thought. Certainly their points of view are not identical: the sociologist tends to prefer the analysis of social structures at a given moment, resulting from their history: the historian is attached primarily to the evolution which constitutes dynamic forces, or the braking or blocking mechanisms which determine and incessantly modify these social structures. But equally for the one as for the other, 'there are no authorised documents. The written document, which is to begin with produced by the state or by specialised groups (like the traditions set by the Griots), gives ground to documents which reveal the life of the masses, material civilisation, morals and customs, behaviour and attitudes.'[12]

The historian no more limits himself to the event than the anthropologist denies the dynamism of history; and their complementary approaches contribute to the knowledge of the same field of study.

Directions of work and current debates

The present orientation of modern African history is due to these relatively new approaches (note the recent publication date of the two works of reflections on the science of the history given above as references).

Archaeological research inspired by Jean Devisse (Université Paris VIII 'Vincennes') and Raymond Mauny (Université Paris I), despite financial handicaps, seeks not only to illumine their traditional field of study (the mediaeval Sudanese region) but also those centuries of the more recent past reputed to be the 'dark period' of Black Africa in collaboration with other documentary sources written or oral (cf. Campaign undertaken in the Kong region of the Ivory Coast).

'Ethno-history', properly interpreted, which owes so much to Jan Vansina, is carried on round Yves Person and Claude-Hélène Perrot (Paris I), who instruct researchers as experienced in the techniques of investigation and interpretation of oral sources in the modern period (seventeenth to eighteenth centuries) as in the political field up to the present day, under the aspect of the genesis of nationalities from a complex set of ethnic relationships.

The *political history* of the first colonial period remains the special field of Henri Brunschwig's Directorate of Studies at the École des Hautes Études en Sciences Sociales.[13] He contributed to the formation of a team of researchers whose individual works are about to show results, not only on the origins of French Equatorial Africa[14] but also on teaching in French West Africa (Denise Bouche, 1974) or on the contributions of the two Federations to the First World War (Marc Michel). The current emphasis of this effort is on the genesis of a new social category of intermediaries, 'interpreters', born at the beginning of the conquest, the precursor of the modern African élite.

The socio-economic history of the twentieth century is centred on the teams associated with the Universités Paris VII (C. Coquery-Vidrovitch) and Paris XII (H. d'Almeida). Up until the last few years this area remained 'taboo'— in part, due to a certain prudent political reflex, because national susceptibilities remained only skin deep—and also due to the technical difficulties of analysing the galloping inflation of the twentieth century. Numerous paths have to be cleared, to allow a full account of the profound internal social mutations produced by the trauma of colonialism to be taken: the history of work; health policies and demography; differentiation between town and country; 'deculturation' and contamination of political power, from the customary chiefly system to the administrative chiefly system and up to the modern state. Analysis up to now has picked out the major turning points of domination and dependence: mutations crystallised due to the great depression of 1929 to 1936 (this major break from the first colonial era led to a colloquium in April 1976 to bring together all the diverse elements); socio-economic transformations connected with the war effort for the First World War; and structural upheavals sparked off by the Second World War, forerunners in their turn of decolonisation, and the prelude to the emergence of the underdeveloped African 'Third World' (with the recent creation of a Commission d'Histoire de l'Empire français as part of the important Comité d'Histoire de la 2ᵉ Guerre Mondiale).

Though there is no lack of unpublished documentation (administrative and economic archives; systematic compilation of recollections and other evidence; diverse vestiges of the recent past—towns, means of transport, etc.), a proper methodical system of study needs to be set up (how to reconstruct and interpret a series of fragmentary and above all incoherent statistics; how to tackle recent history without recourse to public archives closed after 1940, etc.).

The contribution of anthropological research is vital for ethno-history, as for contemporary socio-economic history. In the forefront the Marxist economic anthropology group must be mentioned, among whom Claude Meillassoux is one of the leading figures. One of their most important fields is 'Pre-capitalist Modes of Production', a study of internal social structures connected with the organisation of production. It means an analysis of 'productive forces' in African societies (rural societies with a low technology level, without ground rent but with a developed trading network, at local level as for long distance trading); an analysis, above all, of the social relationships of production, which exercise control over land, labour or big business and the interactions between control of finance and political power.[15]

These researches have opened up in a dynamic manner the analysis of *slavery*: the institution, use and expansion of internal 'domestic slavery', as opposed to the 'slave trade', which is characteristic of contacts with the Atlantic world.[16] This example illustrates how closely history and anthropology are connected and mutually enriching (the works quoted being applicable equally well to the nineteenth century as to the present day).

A major debate continues between Marxists and non-Marxists, as well as between Marxists themselves, over the relationships between Colonisation and Imperialism. I recalled at the beginning of this article that it appeared with the rebirth of African Studies; since then it has hardly ceased.[17] It allows the relationship between ideology, politics and economics to be put in new terms, not only at the origins of the conquest, but throughout the twentieth century: can Colonisation and Imperialism be assimilated?

Is not the 'falling back on the Empire' of the period between the wars a sign of the crisis of Imperialism? Did not French Imperialism only begin to flourish overseas after the Second World War? What are the connections between the Imperialism of the beginning of the century and that dominating the Third World today? The theme remains on the agenda and enlivens meetings between historians of Black Africa, economic historians and historians of international relations.[18]

Another theme brings together more precisely historians, economists and other specialists of the contemporary world: that of the origins, characteristics and future of 'underdevelopment' and of the place of Black Africa at the heart of the Third World. Here is another occasion to confront the 'take-off' theory with that of 'development of underdevelopment' founded on the historic phenomenon of 'unequal exchange' between the 'centre' and the 'periphery', and to periodise the descent of the African continent into political and or economic dependence from the first contacts to the present day.[19]

From this account emerges simultaneously not only the dynamism—but also the limitations—of present research. The most serious limitation is geographical and cultural. The favourite area of African Studies in France remains French-speaking Africa. This is partly explained by the magnitude of the task to be performed in this area alone, the evidence for which is nearest to us. It is nevertheless regrettable that comparative investigations remain rare, and that specialised research outside these limits is even rarer. It is therefore particularly gratifying to pick up the trails blazed by W. G. Randles (E.H.E.S.S.) on the Bantu world of Central and Southern Africa, by J. P. Chrétien (C.N.R.S.) on Rwanda and East Africa, or by H. Moniot (Université Paris VII) on modern Islam up to the Horn of Africa. Let us hope that the present-day reorganisation of research structures will encourage coordination of their efforts.

The teaching of research

Since the nationwide reform of studies for the 'Troisième Cycle'[20] the universities have organised themselves into vast research groups. This should benefit African Studies.

All the historians are grouped in one 'Formation' entitled 'Histoire des Sociétés de l'Afrique noire' presided over by Yves Person and centred on the Université Paris I, which should ensure the harmonious training of student-researchers and thus promote the development of African history. Moreover, parallel 'Formations' co-ordinate comparative and complementary studies, between disciplines and between neighbouring historic and geographic areas. There are three groups of the Troisième Cycle:

—that led by Jean Devisse centred at the Université Paris VIII on the *comparative study of mediaeval civilisations*;

—that which brings together within the École des Hautes Études en Sciences Sociales (E.H.E.S.S.) a multidisciplinary team centred on Black Africa (history–sociology–ethnology–geography);

—finally that directed by Jean Dresch (Geography) and C. Coquery-Vidrovitch (History), centred on the Université Paris VII, '*Understanding of the contemporary third world*' (nineteenth and twentieth centuries) predominantly history–geography–sociology, divided into comparative subgroups (Black Africa—the Mediterranean Muslim World—Asia and Latin America).

French and foreign students may be streamed to one or other of these centres depending on their educational background and their major leanings, thanks to the cooperation of their directors of research. Well before the reform was under way, the historians had already taken the initiative in holding informal but regular meetings with all the research students, at least in the Paris area, in order to harmonise the organisation of their study which was geographically scattered among various universities.[21]

Where then do the provinces figure in all this? It is well known that the centralist tradition in France concentrates documents and hence specialists around Paris. There are nevertheless several major exceptions:

The University of Aix-en-Provence where J. L. Miège heads a centre of History of Overseas Countries, dedicated to the whole history of colonisation, which is helped by the important local centre of the Overseas Section of the National Archives (ex-Colonial Archives: essentially Algeria, Indochina, Madagascar, Afars and Issas and French Equatorial Africa).[22]

Bordeaux, traditionally looking towards the African continent, and for this reason still receiving a flow of African students, has a centre for contemporary Black African Studies (Institut d'Études Politiques) which is nevertheless hampered by the lack of any large collection of suitable documents. Bordeaux also has a vast and old-established centre of tropical geography (C.E.G.E.T.)

At the other end of the country the University of Lille has just set up a Centre of African Studies (Geography and Sociology). Elsewhere (Tours, Reims, Nancy, Toulouse) researchers remain relatively isolated; more than one specialist in African Studies, who for research can always join one of the 'Formations' already mentioned, is reduced within his own university to teaching general history in the main (history of civilisations, international relations, etc.) and his speciality only peripherally.

One idea which many directors of African Studies in France cherish is that of a national 'House of Black Africa' which would ease the work of researchers by putting at their disposal a vast documentation service for immediate local use (library, bibliography service, microfilms) and direct students through the maze of existing documentation services in the country.[23]

Such an organisation would above all encourage the adoption of a coherent policy, thanks to the influx of young African researchers, who are still increasing, since the university establishments which for several years have been multiplying in their countries mostly cease to cater for students after two or three years' study, that is, when they are on the threshold of research. It is they who make up the great mass of higher-level students in African Studies, the result of their own thirst for knowledge and on the other hand the very limited outlets available to young French researchers in this field.

Nevertheless, let us hope meanwhile that the build-up of the organisations mentioned above will help to strengthen the revival of African Studies in France, through the 'Centres de Formation' as well as more generally through the direction of research.

Notes

1   *Afrique noire occidentale: Geographie, Civilisations, Histoire*, Paris, Editions Sociales, 1968, 3rd edition 1972.
2   *Africa and the Victorians, The Official Mind of Imperialism*, London 1961.
3   Paris 1960. English edition revised and completed: *French Colonialism 1871-1914*, London 1966.
4   Claude Lévi-Strauss, *La Pensée Sauvage*, Paris, 1962.
5   Claude Lévi-Strauss, 'L'Anthropologie Sociale devant l'Histoire', *Annales*, 4, July-August 1960, p. 635.
6   To use the polemic vocabulary of the period.
7   Cf. *Anthropologie politique*, Paris 1967, in addition to numerous articles from *Cahiers Internationaux de Sociologie* of which a number have been recently republished in *Sens et Puissance*, Paris 1971.
8   'Apologie pour l'histoire ou Métier d'historien', *Cahiers des Annales*, 3, Paris, 1949, page 111.
9   In the continuation of his *Esquisse du mouvement des prix et des revenus en France au 18e siècle*, 1933.
10   F. Braudel, 'Histoire et Sciences Sociales: la longue durée', *Annales*, No. 4, October-December 1958.
11   J. Bouvier, 'Tendances actuelles des recherches d'histoire économique et sociale en France', *Aujourd'hui l'histoire*, Éditions Sociales, Paris 1974, p. 135.
12   *Ibid.*, cf. also: *Faire de l'histoire*, J. le Goff and P. Nora (eds.) 3 vols., Paris, Gallimard, 1974.
13   Ex 6th section of the E.P.H.E. (École Pratique des Hautes Études).
14   Publication of documents and commentaries on the first three Brazza missions by H. Brunschwig, (1967 and 1972) and C. Coquery-Vidrovitch (1969); on nineteenth-century Gabon (by M'Bokolo); on the Congolese Administration at the end of the century (by J. C. Nardin).
15   Cf. C. Meillassoux, ed. *The Development of Indigenous Trade and Markets in West Africa*, London, 1971.
16   C. Meillassoux, ed. *L'esclavage en Afrique précoloniale*, Paris, Maspero, 1975. See also E. Terray in *Annales*, September-October, 1973, pp. 1331-8.
17   Cf. Debate of the Centre d'Études et de Recherches Marxistes (C.E.R.M.), Paris, 1970, 2 parts roneo.
18   Cf. in 1974-1975: debate of the Université Paris X (Nanterre) led by R. Girault and J. B. Duroselle; new debate organised by the C.E.R.M. in 1975.
19   Cf. works of Samir Amin, C. Bettelheim, A. Emmanuel, C. Coquery-Vidrovitch.
20   The thesis of the 3rd 'cycle'—in the style of the prestigious 'State Thesis' characteristic of French universities—is carried out in two or three years of study at the end of four years of higher studies, and corresponds to about the same (or lower) level as the British Ph.D.
21   We should point out that at least two centres in Paris use the title 'Centre d'Études Africaines': that of the Université Paris I (Centre de Recherches Africaines) which inherited the ex-Sorbonne Centre and only groups together the old members separated institutionally by the distribution of their original faculty to three

universities (History and Geography at Paris I, Linguistics at Paris III and Sociology at Paris V). The E.H.E.S.S. Centre groups the teaching staff of the School specialising in Black Africa.

22 But a good part of the Madagascar archives remains in Tananarive and the very rich archives of the old French West Africa are kept at Dakar by the government of Senegal and on microfilm at the Archives Nationales in Paris.

23 In the Paris region alone, the Centre d'Analyse et de Recherche Documentaire sur l'Afrique Noire (CARDAN., E.H.E.S.S.) there are at least sixty document centres (archives, libraries, specialist institutes) which may be consulted to advantage.

Imanuel Geiss

The Study of African History in Germany

The development of the study of African history after the Second World War in Germany—both West and East—provides a striking example of the interaction between history and the writing of history. As far as African history was concerned there was a total blank in 1945, *tabula rasa*. The breakdown of Fascism also meant, at least temporarily, the breakdown of the specifically German tradition of writing history. The subsequent attempt to resurrect the tradition of historicism in West Germany and the adoption of Marxism in East Germany corresponded to the political division of Germany into two separate states on the ruins of the German Reich. In both parts of Germany historical scholarship concentrated first on German history, albeit with differing interpretations, echoing also the political and ideological slanging-matches going on in the period of the Cold War.[1]

Since there existed no valid tradition to speak of for the study of African history, in Germany even less than in other societies, it took about two decades for a new generation to come into their own with the advantage of growing up unhampered by the traditional German blinkers—political, ideological and otherwise. The very course of history—Africa's national emancipation in the late fifties and the early sixties, and the national revolts in southern Africa and Guinea-Bissau against the last forms of colonial rule—directed the interest of some, mostly younger, historians to that process which had made possible recent events in Africa. From then onwards African history, as distinguished from colonial history,[2] became increasingly acceptable as an academic subject, if only of marginal relevance on the whole.

Apart from the general course of African history in the last few decades, some more specific factors of academic character influenced the development of interest in African history in Germany, as they also did outside Germany. The general broadening of the approach of social anthropology into a kind of social science of pre-industrial societies in Africa also began to embrace the historical dimension.

Two writers in particular—Basil Davidson writing in English,[3] Jean Suret-Canale in French[4]—helped to stimulate interest by spreading knowledge. Their works were translated into German, one in West Germany, the other in East Germany. Both were writing from a pronounced anti-colonialist and anti-racist point of view. The character of their works differed, and their influence on emerging African historians in both parts of Germany may be hard to measure precisely. But their important contribution to awakening, directing and grounding the new interest of German African historians cannot be denied. Not only for the present writer, but also for younger students of African history in both Germanys, Basil Davidson and/or Suret-Canale provided the first coherent introductions into African history, opened new horizons and gave a more rational sense of purpose to the hitherto vague and ill-articulated general interest in the reasons behind the change on the African scene. Needless to say, this does not mean that German students of African history stopped there, because they gradually developed interests of their own. But few would deny their gratitude for having been initiated into African history by Basil Davidson and Suret-Canale.

So far there are still only a few achievements to record in West and East Germany. This explains why, so far, there is little self-reflection among the few German African historians on what they are doing. They are still groping their own way in a vast neglected field. That is why this volume in honour of Basil Davidson provides such an appropriate chance to present whatever German scholarship has to offer (and is promising to offer in the foreseeable future), just because it is at least partially and indirectly also a fruit of Basil Davidson's seminal pioneer-work in the field.

The dearth of studies on African history in Germany immediately after the Second World War is underlined, paradoxically enough, by the one major publication on African history in the German language to appear in the first decade after 1945—Diedrich Westermann's *Geschichte Afrikas*.[5] Westermann, originally a Protestant missionary in Africa, later one of the greatest African linguists in this century, wrote his book in the old tradition of seeing Africa predominantly from the European point of view. His method of piecing together oral traditions of larger and smaller nations and ethnic units (commonly called 'tribes') confirms the European image of Africa as a chaotic conglomeration of 'tribes'. More general structures brought out by modern research,[6] are still conspicuously absent in Westermann's work, which, of course, will always remain useful as far as it goes and within its very narrow limits. More than a decade later a series of three articles in the Westermann academic tradition appeared in a learned journal predominantly on the history of pre-modern Africa,[7] while the older political tradition is reflected in a history of Africa in two volumes published in 1959.[8]

Apart from Westermann, whose work had in any case been conceived and researched before 1945, there was hardly anything worthwhile to show for more than a decade. There were no specialised African historians in Germany, and general historians were interested only in German colonial history as part of their general policy of producing an apologia for Imperial Germany as a (supposedly favourable) counterfoil against Nazism and the Third Reich. The contribution of the almost all-powerful Gerhard Ritter on the subject, first presented as a lecture in 1937, but published in 1958 (probably, as usual with Ritter, with alterations making due allowance for the changes in political conditions) is a good example.[9] It was whitewash of the German colonial record up to 1945, even if, in 1958, it contained no more demands for German colonies. In his sketch of the origins of European colonialism and imperialism and the first German venture into colonial policy around 1700, executed by the Brandenburgers in West Africa, he managed to do without even the words 'slavery' or 'slave trade'. At least, Ritter conceded in theory the necessity to open up new horizons of global character after the Second World War, which would also include the study of African history. Apart from that theoretical lip service to scholarly internationalism, Ritter, and with him the ruling orthodoxy of historical scholarship in the Federal Republic throughout the sixties, made no constructive contribution whatsoever to the study of African history.

Another illustration of the apparently hopeless situation after 1945 is the case of Wahrhold Drascher. At the height of decolonisation, in 1960, he published a book which purported to present a scholarly balance sheet of colonial rule throughout the Third World. In fact, it was a biased defence of colonialism and imperialism,[10] hardly more than a barely disguised 'modernised' version of his outright racist book on pretty much the same subject, published at the height of Nazi agitation for the return of colonies to Germany.[11] His chapters on Africa, Asia and Latin America are almost devoid of concrete *and* reliable historical information, but offer shallow and superficial statements of his personal views on the achievement of the white man, often based on the authority of some unknown 'authentic' source. Whenever Drascher tried to go into historical detail he did violence to elementary chronology and facts, as in his faulty version of Nkrumah's career.[12] The same kind of ignorance was betrayed by Drascher's enthusiastic reviewer in one of the leading learned journals of the Federal Republic, when the Black Star on the Arch of Independence in Accra was made out to be 'a great Soviet star',[13] apparently as visible proof of wicked communist infiltration in Africa as early as 1957. Garvey's Black Star, it appears, had never been heard of among German scholars.

Drascher and his uncritical follower did not disqualify themselves as scholars by producing such nonsense. On the contrary, they enjoyed a kind of monopoly as reviewers of the few books on African history that appeared in the two most highly regarded learned journals in the Federal Republic, Drascher in the *Historische Zeitschrift*, until his death in 1970, Heinz Lehmann in *Geschichte in Wissenschaft und Unterricht* (GWU) until 1967. Even although by now there have emerged a few younger historians capable of reviewing books on African history, the *Historische Zeitschrift*, perhaps for ideological reasons, does not invite them for continuous reviewing.[14] *Geschichte in Wissenschaft und Unterricht* however has become open since 1967, for major review articles by competent students of African history.[15] The power of the Old Guard as late as the early sixties may be measured by the fact that Drascher was able to drive his first West German critic, N. N. Weiler, then a young political scientist at Freiburg University, into a kind of virtual exile in the USA, because he had dared to publish a scathing review in the *Journal of African History*, in which he also pointed to Drascher's Nazi past.

The little that was produced on African history in the Federal Republic was mainly on the history of South Africa, more or less in sympathy with the racism of apartheid,[16] not surprisingly, as it was (and is) closest to German colonial methods, still defended by Gerhard Ritter, the doyen of West German historical scholarship until his death in 1967. But it was only to be expected that, sooner or later, the new mode of writing African history among the younger generation of historians would react against the racism and imperialism of the older generation, as embodied in South Africa.

The first two serious contributions to the study of African history in the Federal Republic (and West Berlin) came from outside the orbit of traditional historical scholarship in Germany, which was all the better for the study of African history. The first, Franz Ansprenger, a trained historian but a teacher of political science in the Freie Universität (FU) at West Berlin, made an astonishing impact with his first major study of the emergence of modern political parties in French West Africa after 1945—as early as 1961.[17] His easy and slightly flippant style served as an excuse for some professionals not to take him (and African history) seriously. But for almost a decade he acted as a kind of lieutenant for West German scholarship in the field. A few years later, he did a great service to German students of history and to the German reading public by placing Africa's national emancipation into wider historical perspectives in his contribution to a widely read pocketbook world history of the twentieth century.[18] Ansprenger is also educating young political scientists in the field of African Studies, very often with a strong historical dimension.

Freimut Duve, who never completed his academic studies of modern history at Hamburg University and is now a well-known political publicist, is the academic product of a different development that took place within the historical seminar at Hamburg University. There, in the department of Professor Egmont Zechlin, who was mainly interested in imperial and colonial history in the traditional style, Dr Günther Jantzen taught as a modest *chargé de cours* for almost two decades. Although educated as a historian, he was a successful business manager, for many years in charge of the Hamburg Handelskammer, now of a specialised Research Institute on Africa. At Hamburg University he gave lectures and seminars on colonial and later on African history. Over the years he succeeded in raising a small but dedicated group of students interested in African history, who are at present doing much of the research going on in West Germany.

Duve was the first of Jantzen's students to appear in print. In 1965 he edited and contributed to a pocketbook volume on apartheid in South Africa.[19] For the first time in West Germany it expressed such a critical point of view that the book was promptly banned in South Africa.

Duve was followed by his Hamburg colleague Hans Detlef Laß.[20] Although his doctoral thesis is still concerned with white history in South Africa, he has developed interests and knowledge in genuine African history since, which, however, have not yet found their expression in major publications,[21] but mainly in his teaching as lecturer in modern history at Hamburg University.

In a similar vein his colleague, Helmut Bley, also a lecturer in modern history at Hamburg University, produced his doctoral thesis on German colonial rule in South-West Africa, which has meanwhile been translated into English.[22] Bley combined a more systematic approach than was usual in German historical writing with a critical analysis of German colonial rule that, for the first time in West Germany, also saw Africans as active subjects in their history even under colonialism.

At the same time, the study of German colonial rule was placed in a wider context by the appearance of the reader edited by the Swiss historian Rudolf von Albertini, mentioned earlier,[23] and by Hans-Ulrich Wehler. Albertini, who has taught at Heidelberg University for many years, saw German colonial history as part of European colonialism, and he himself contributed an important study on the last phase of colonial rule.[24] As co-editor of a series of monographs on overseas history with Professor Heinz Gollwitzer from Münster University, he also helps to encourage the study of African history. Wehler analysed the beginnings of German colonial policy under Bismarck as part of the history of the German Empire.[25] Both dimensions belong together.

The new turn in historical writing was in line with similar developments in the GDR. There historians enjoyed the great advantage of having ready access to the most important colonial records of Imperial Germany before the first World War, now located at Potsdam. They are also firmly established in academic and university structures.

The first in the field was Fritz Ferdinand Müller with a massive study on the conquest of German East Africa.[26] More polemical in tone than Müller (and more than warranted by the matter as such) were other historians of the GDR, who covered other areas of German colonial rule before 1914.[27] Their writings, however, thanks to their rich documentation, based on official archives, are still colonial history, even if hostile to colonialism. But historians in the GDR are experiencing the same kind of intellectual development as their few colleagues in the Federal Republic.

Developments in the GDR have influenced historians in the Federal Republic, not because of ideological affinities, but because a similar situation gave rise to a similar intellectual process, and also the historians of the GDR were able to make use of archival material, which, because of the division of Germany, West German scholars normally have no chance to see.

Hence some East German studies were followed by studies in West Germany on the same subjects, as in the case of Drechsler and Bley quite independently from each other. Similarly, the collective work on Germany in the Cameroons, edited by Helmuth Stoecker in the GDR, was followed in the Federal Republic by Karin Hauser on German colonial rule in the Cameroons, published in the series edited by Rudolf von Albertini and Heinz Gollwitzer.[28] As a kind of continuation of Müller's study on the establishment of German colonial rule in East Africa can be seen three West German dissertations on German rule in East Africa before 1914.[29]

A different approach to African history was taken by the present writer. Without taking the detour via colonial history, he was led directly to African history by his intellectual curiosity engendered by his political interest in Africa's national emancipation in the late fifties and early sixties. In the search for the historical dimensions behind the spectacular phenomenon of decolonisation, Pan-Africanism emerged as one of the main political and ideological factors.[30] This approach turned out to be particularly rewarding because it meant digesting most of the preceding literature, on the modern history of Africa, with particular emphasis on former British West Africa. Because of the general background provided by the transatlantic slave trade and slavery in the New World, and because of the crucial role of Afro-Americans and Afro-West Indians, the study of Pan-Africanism also gave a lead to the history of Afro-Americans in the United State,[31] and to the importance of racism and imperialism for the making of our modern world.

Such wider perspectives should help to avoid or even overcome one danger latent in much of the present writing on African history—the danger of too narrow a focus on Africa. Looking back, this writer found that many monographs and articles in learned journals on African history make such hard reading, at least for beginners, that they must feel lost at first in a jungle of apparently disconnected facts. The study of Pan-Africanism also made it clear that much of the recent concern with modern African history is part of the effort to reconstruct the history of Africa's modern élites.[32] This is understandable enough, since their rise is largely identical with the rise of African nationalism and thus also of African national emancipation. Also there is more written material on, and produced by, members of the modern élites. However plausible such a comparatively narrow focus may be, students of African history will do well to be fully aware of its inevitable limitations, in order to avoid unnecessary misunderstandings, illusions and frustrations, which may arise subsequently.

One by-product of the study of Pan-Africanism, not intended at the outset, was thus to give a summary of the recent literature on African history for the German-reading public, focused on one important factor in African history itself—the rise of Africa's modern élites and Pan-Africanism as their first political and ideological vehicle. It also led to the publication or instigation of straightforward review articles to give a lead for university and seminar libraries in their purchasing policies, and of articles presenting modest sketches of the history of Ghana and Nigeria for a larger reading public, using the special literature on the subject.[33]

Finally, it proved necessary to keep a critical eye on the writings of social scientists on African history, because their lack of historical training and factual knowledge could, occasionally, lead to rather amateurish treatment of a subject that is complex and bewildering enough even for full-fledged African historians. The works of two particular social scientists on African subjects is full of excellent intentions, but also full of factual mistakes and glaring misunderstandings. Jean Ziegler, a Swiss Social Democrat member of Parliament and a political scientist, is particularly unreliable on the history of Ghana,[34] while Gerhard Grohs, a social scientist in West Berlin and active on international bodies of the Protestant Church, is very weak on the historical aspects of his subject, the formation of the political consciousness of Africa's modern élites.[35]

On the other hand, Heribert Adam has given an excellent example of how fruitful the contribution of political scientists to the study of African history can be.[36] He has warned of too easy expectations of revolution against apartheid in

South Africa. His study provides one of the rare examples of African Studies by social scientists with a valid and competent use of the historical dimension.

One of the symptoms of the new approach to African history is the ousting of the Old Guard from the semi-official *Deutsche Afrika-Gesellschaft* in autumn 1970 in an action of disciplined rebellion from below, rare enough in the history of German society. The new *Deutsche Afrika-Gesellschaft*, with its re-modelled and expanded organ *Afrika heute*, offered such crisp information and comments on developments in Africa, including northern (Arab)Africa, that official subsidies were cancelled in 1974. It was thus strangled financially and liquidated in early 1975. But the critical element will find other outlets of organisational structures and for publications. An older series of monographs on African countries, edited by the old *Deutsche Afrika-Gesellschaft*, was in the process of being rewritten along modern lines, with substantial chapters on the history of the African countries concerned.[37]

Furthermore, for the first time in German history, students of history, without the intention of furthering imperialist or colonialist interests *and* with sufficient time and funds to pursue serious studies on African history, partly in Africa itself, are now coming to the fore, although their works have not yet been completed or published. Since, apparently, they are mostly concentrated at Hamburg University, it becomes possible to give an approximate idea of what is in the offing in the coming years. Apart from Günther Jantzen's teaching colonial and African history, the establishment of a chair for Missiology (*Missionswissenschaften*) under Professor Margull has also helped to focus interest on African history, because of the important role of European missions and African churches in the formation of African nationalism. From Hamburg (and one from Bremen) the following dissertations are expected in the near future:

Werner Ustorf, who studied divinity, history and geography, has finished his doctoral thesis on Simon Kimbangu and the beginnings of Kimbanguism, which will also point to the transformation of social and political protest, couched in religious terms, against colonial rule into a kind of Established Church of the new African bourgeoisie in Zaïre[38] Erhard Kamphausen also has a solid background of divinity with his thesis on Ethiopianism in South Africa, 1884-1910. He had the chance to see Government Archives in South Africa and also taught for a year in one of the 'Bantu' Colleges in South Africa. Günther Rusch at Bremen, but originally from the Jantzen circle at Hamburg University, writes on missions and African churches in Ghana and their impact on the formation of African nationalism, taking the Basle and Scottish missions and, the Presbyterian Church, which resulted from those missions, as his special subject of study. One of the more unexpected by-products of his research was collecting much of the hitherto dispersed material on missions and churches in Ghana in the National Archives in Accra. Wolfgang von Lonski is writing his thesis on the crucial role of national or ethnic minorities in Nigeria in the historical process that led to the Nigerian Civil war of 1966-70. Edgar Mebus is working on the origins and development of the Rassemblement Démocratique Africain (RDA) and thus continues and deepens the pioneer work started by

Franz Ansprenger.[39] Goswin Baumhogger is writing up his thesis on Closer Union in British East Africa, after a period of three years' research mainly in Tanzania. Even before going to Africa he had expanded his massive review article on historical literature on former British East Africa[40] into an independent publication. He also contributed to a new kind of handbook, put out by the *Deutsche Afrika-Gesellschaft*, intended for German travellers and tourists coming to East Africa in order to give them a better idea of the countries they are visiting.[41] Finally, Ingeborg Laß-Westphal, the wife of Hans Dieter Westphal, is writing on European mission and colonialism in ex-Italian east Africa. Another project of H. D. Laß's ought to be mentioned here—African resistance and British colonial policy in Botswana. A critical evaluation of the role of German missions in Africa is being planned by a group centred at Erlangen under Klaus J. Bade. Finally, work on various African subjects with partly an historical approach, is being done by political scientists, mainly in Berlin under the supervision of Franz Ansprenger, but also in Hamburg under Franz Nuscheler.

By German standards this new activity is impressive, by international standards it is just trying to catch up with recent developments outside Germany. The general weakness of all these and other efforts is obvious: so far, there is no institutional basis for them—no institute or chair of African history. The German market for publications, both books and periodicals, on African history is too limited to make possible more than occasional publications based on scholarly research. Interest in African history, so far, has been promoted and sustained mainly by individual scholars, not yet backed by institutions. But a beginning, however modest, has been made, and it is to be hoped that the coming generation of West German students in African history will persist in and broaden their interests enough to avoid the danger of new isolation.

Notes

1   For a first provisional sketch, seen from inside West German historiography, see Imanuel Geiss 'Die westdeutsche Geschichtsschreibung seit 1945', in *Jahrbuch des Instituts für deutsche Geschichte*, Tel Aviv, III, 1974, pp. 417-55.

2   A yardstick for measuring the progress at least of colonial history towards acceptance by academic historians can be seen in the series of readers for students on various subjects, put out by a Cologne publishing firm, Neue Wissenschaftliche Bibliothek, in which one volume appeared on that subject: Rudolf von Albertini (ed.), *Moderne Kolonialgeschichte*, Köln/Berlin, 1970.

3   Basil Davidson, *Urzeit und Geschichte Afrikas*, Reinbek bei Hamburg 1961; also under the title *Alt-Afrika wiederentdeckt* in Berlin (GDR), 1962. Furthermore, *Vom Sklavenhandel zur Kolonisierung. Afrikanisch-europäische Beziehungen zwischen 1500 und 1900*, Reinbek 1966. As documents of Basil Davidson's political involvement in the (by now historical) struggle for Africa's liberation against Portuguese colonial rule see *Die Befreiung Guineas. Aspekte einer afrikanischen Revolution*, Frankfurt, 1970.

4   Jean Suret-Canale, *Schwarzafrika. Geographie, Bevolkerung, Geschichte West- und Zentralafrikas*, Berlin, GDR, 1966.

5   Diedrich Westermann, *Geschichte Afrikas. Staatenbildung südlich der Sahara*, Köln, 1952.

6   Joseph C. Anene and Godfrey N. Brown (eds.), *Africa in the Nineteenth and Twentieth Centuries. A Handbook for Teachers and Students*, Ibadan, London, 1966.

7   Kunz Dittmer, 'Zur Geschichte Afrikas. 1. Die von Europäern miterlebte jüngere Geschichte. 2. Die ältere Geschichte Nordost-und Ostafrikas. 3. Die ältere Geschichte Süd- und Zentralafrikas', in *Saeculum. Jahrbuch für Universalgeschichte*, 14, 1963, pp. 179-93; 15, 1964, pp. 1-17; 17, 1966, pp. 37-89.

8   Otto Zierer, *Ferner Strand Afrika—Geschichte Afrikas von 3000 v. Chr.—1840 n. Chr; Dunkle Schwester Afrika—Geschichte Afrikas von 1840 bis zur Gegenwart*, München, 1959.

9   Gerhard Ritter, 'Geschichtliche Erfahrungen deutscher Kolonialpolitik', in G. Ritter, *Lebendige Vergangenheit. Beiträge zur historisch-politischen Selbstbesinnung*, München, 1958, pp. 126-52.

10   Wahrhold Drascher, *Schuld der Weißen? Die Spätzeit des Kolonialismus*, Tübingen, 1960.

11   W. Drascher, *Die Vorherrschaft der Weißen Rasse*, Stuttgart, Berlin, 1936.

12   W. Drascher, *Schuld der Weißen?*, pp. 184 f. 'Ein selbstbewußter und tatkräftiger Neger, Nkrumah, der aus bescheidenen Bürgerkreisen stammte ... übernahm die Führung einer Unabhängigkeitsbewegung. ... Nach dem Vorbild der Politbüros sammelte er einen kleinen Kreis von Anhängern um sich und organisierte mit ihrer Hilfe eine große Volkspartei, welche die Massen zu mobilisieren verstand. Nach seiner Rückkehr aus Amerika (1949) vermochte er die vorsichtigen konservativen Politiker rasch aus der Gunst der Massen zu verdrängen. .... Als aber ein allgemeiner Aufstand drohte, entließen sie (i.e. the British. I.G.)—wie im Falle Gandhis—den verhafteten Volksführer aus dem Gefängnis und boten ihm selbst die Bildung einer Regierung an. ... Als 1955 Ghana selbständig wurde, trat selbstverständlich Nkrumah an die Spitze des Staates.'

13   Heinz Lehmann, 'Entwicklungsländer, besonders Afrika', in *Geschichte in Wissenschaft und Unterricht*, 9/1964, pp. 580-8, p. 585, in a final remark on the German translation of Nkrumah's autobiography: 'Dem sehr aufschlußreichen Buch sind auch viele gute Photos beigegeben; auf einem sieht man, daß schon bei den Unabhängigkeitsfeiern 1957 in Accra über den Worten Freedom and Justice auf dem Unabhängigkeitsbogen ein großer Sowjetstern angebracht ist.'

14   The miserable coverage of African History by the *Historische Zeitschrift* is just another symptom of how the erstwhile leading historical journal in Germany has lost much of the necessary contact with modern research going on nowadays beyond the classical fields of interest of German historiography.

15   I. Geiss, 'Allgemeine Geschichte Afrikas und Britisch-Westafrika', in *GWU*, 8, 1967, pp. 487-506; Goswin Baumhögger, 'Die Geschichte Ostafrikas im Spiegel der neueren Literatur', in *GWU*, 11, 1971, pp. 678-704.

16   Oskar Hintrager, *Südwestafrika in deutscher Zeit*, München, 1955; *Geschichte von Südafrika*, München, 1952.

17   Franz Ansprenger, *Politik im schwarzen Afrika. Die modernen politischen Bewegungen im Afrika französischer Prägung*, Köln, Opladen, 1961.

18   F. Ansprenger, *Auflösung der Kolonialreiche*. dtv-Weltgeschichte des 20. Jahrhunderts, vol. 13, München, 1966.

19   Freimut Duve, ed., *Kap ohne Hoffnung oder Die Politik der Apartheid*, Rororo aktuell 780, Reinbek bei Hamburg, 1965.

20   Hans Detlef Laß, *Nationale Integration in Südafrika. Die Rolle der Parteien zwischen den Jahren 1922 und 1934*, Hamburg, 1969.

21   H. D. Laß, 'Nationale Befreiung und sozialer Wandel—Dekolonisation und Revolution in Afrika', in: I. Geiss/Rainer Tamchina (eds.), *Ansichten einer künftigen Geschichtswissenschaft*, vol. 2. Revolution—Ein historischer Langsschnitt, München, 1974, pp. 202-24.

22   Helmut Bley, *Kolonialherrschaft und Sozialstruktur in Deutsch-Südwestafrika*

1894-1914, Hamburg, 1968; English edition: *South-West Africa Under German Rule, 1894-1914*, London, 1971.

23 See above, note 2. Rudolf von Albertini (ed.), *Moderne Kolonialgeschichte*. Neue Wissenschaftliche Bibliothek, vol. 39, Köln, 1970.

24 R. v. Albertini, *Dekolonisation. Die Diskussion über Verwaltung und Zukunft der Kolonien 1919-1960*, Köln, Opladen, 1966.

25 Hans-Ulrich Wehler, *Bismarck und der Imperialismus*, Köln, 1969, 3rd ed., 1972.

26 Fritz Ferdinand Müller, *Deutschland—Zanzibar—Ostafrika. Geschichte einer deutschen Kolonialeroberung, 1884-1890*, Berlin, GDR, 1959. This pioneer study was quickly sold out and, unfortunately, never re-published, probably because the author left the GDR in the early sixties. His valuable book has thus become one of the victims of the Cold War, much to the detriment of scholarship in both parts of Germany.

27 Horst Drechsler, *Südwestafrika unter deutscher Kolonialherrschaft. Der Kampf der Herero und Nama gegen den deutschen Imperialismus (1884-1915)*, Berlin, GDR, 1966; Helmuth Stoecker (ed.), *Kamerun unter deutscher Kolonialherrschaft*, 2 vols, Berlin, GDR, 1960, 1968. For an early kind of summary of research on African history in the GDR see *Geschichte und Geschichtsbild Afrikas. Beiträge der Arbeitstagung für neuere und neueste Geschichte Afrikas am 17. und 18. April 1959 in Leipzig*, Berlin, GDR, 1960.

28 Karin Hauser, *Deutsche Kolonialherrschaft in Afrika. Wirtschaftsinteressen und Kolonialverwaltung in Kamerun vor 1914*, Freiburg, 1970.

29 Detlev Bald, *Deutsch-Ostafrika 1900-1914. Eine Studie über Verwaltung, Wirtschaft und Interessengruppen*, Freiburg, 1970; Rainer Tetzlaff, *Koloniale Entwicklung und Ausbeutung. Wirtschafts- und Sozialgeschichte Deutsch-Ostafrikas 1885-1914*, Berlin, 1970; H. J. Niesel, *Kolonialverwaltung und Missionen in Deutsch-Ostafrika 1880-1914*, Bonn, 1972.

30 I. Geiss, *Panafrikanismus. Zur Geschichte der Dekolonisation*, Frankfurt, 1968; English edition, *The Pan-African Movement*, London, New York, 1974.

31 I. Geiss, *Die Afro-Amerikaner*, Frankfurt, 1969. This is a collection of review articles and essays by this author on the development of Afro-Americans in the United States, as provisional by-products of the study of the history of Pan-Africanism.

32 For a first interim summary see this author's paper, presented to the International Congress of Historical Sciences at Moscow, August 1970, published in a slightly expanded version as 'Das Entstehen der modernen Eliten in Afrika seit der Mitte des 18. Jahrhunderts', in *GWU*, 11 1971, pp. 648-67.

33 See above n. 16; also 'Nigeria. Zur Vorgeschichte und Geschichte', in *Beilage zu Das Parlament*, B 8/67; 'Ghana—seine Vorgeschichte und Geschichte', in *Beilage zu Das Parlament*, B 3/69.

34 Jean Ziegler, *Politische Soziologie des neuen Afrika. Ghana, Kongo-Leopoldville, Ägypten*, München, 1966, espec., pp. 47-64; for a detailed critique see this author's review in *Neue Politische Literatur*, 3, 1969, pp. 436-9.

35 Gerhard Grohs, *Stufen afrikanischer Emanzipation. Studien zum Selbstverständnis westafrikanischer Eliten*, Stuttgart, 1967, see also this author's review in *Neue Politische Literatur*, 2, 1970, pp. 284-7.

36 Heribert Adam, *Südafrika. Soziologie einer Rassengesellschaft*, Edition Suhrkamp 343, Frankfurt, 1969.

37 *Deutsche Afrika-Gesellschaft* (ed.), *Die Länder Afrikas*, with volumes on most African countries, appeared from 1958 onwards. Of the new series, so far, only a few volumes appeared or were due to appear shortly.

38 Since published as *Afrikanische Initiative: Das active Leiden des Propheten Simon Kimbangu*. Studies in the Intercultural History of Christianity, vol. v, Frankfurt/Main 1975.

39   See above, n. 18.
40   See above, n. 16, G. Baumhögger, *Grundzüge der Geschichte und politischen Entwicklung Ostafrikas. Eine Einführung an Hand der neueren Literatur*, München, 1971.
41   Baumhögger, Jörn Dargel, Gisela Führing, Rolf Hofmeier, Manfred Schieß, *Ostafrika. Reisehandbuch Kenya und Tanzania*, Bonn, 1973.

Gerald Bender and Allen Isaacman

The Changing Historiography of Angola and Mozambique

In the early 1960s armed struggles erupted in lusophonic Africa which culminated in the independence of Guinea-Bissau in 1974 and Angola and Mozambique in 1975. The decade of the sixties also ushered in a new generation of scholars who sought to liberate the histories of the Mozambican and Angolan peoples from the culturally arrogant and racist myths which had dominated the literature on these two former Portuguese colonies. This study examines the changing patterns in Angolan and Mozambican historiography from the formation of António de Oliveira Salazar's *Estado Novo* in 1932 until Independence in 1975 and concludes with an assessment of those areas which warrant a particularly high research priority.[1]

The impact of the Estado Novo *on the historiography of Angola and Mozambique*

Before Salazar's assumption of power, Portuguese and foreign scholars almost totally ignored Angola and Mozambique. Salazar, however, sought in the great expanses of the African colonies the basis for a national pride which had eluded the small lusitanian nation since the age of explorations. The colonies' importance in this quest for national prestige is captured in a 1935 editorial: 'Africa is for us a moral justification and a reason for being as a power. Without it we would be a small country, with it we are a great nation.[2] Historians were urged to rediscover the glories of Portugal's imperial past and to aggrandise the heroic 'mission' of its imperial present. History, accordingly, became an instrument for consciously instilling national pride. Since few scholars outside Portugal seriously studied the lusophonic colonies, the 'histories' of Angola and Mozambique through the 1950s were essentially state inspired and approved. As a result they suffered from a pervasive Euro-centric bias, a coastal orientation and a lack of rigorous analysis.

With few exceptions, Portuguese historians assumed that events within the European communities constituted the only significant history of the two colonies.[3] Thus, there were numerous accounts of the development of the Portuguese coastal towns of Luanda, Benguela, Mossamedes, Lourenço Marques and Sofala, as well as of Lisbon's attempts to promote European immigration and establish a working administrative system.[4] Military campaigns were especially emphasised.[5] Even the activities of rival Europeans in the colonies (e.g., Dutch, Germans and Boers) merited more discussion than those of the indigenous Africans.[6]

The logical corollary of this assumption was that Africans lacked a history worth studying, only attaining importance in so far as they impinged on the historical development of the settler communities. They were, therefore, depicted as passive beings, reacting to European religious, commercial and military stimuli. In short, they could be moulded by history but could not influence it in a significant way. As the former Portuguese Prime Minister Marcello Caetano noted:

> The blacks in Africa must be directed and moulded by Europeans but they are indispensable as assistants to the latter. . . . The Africans by themselves did not know how to develop the territories they inhabited for millennia, they did not account for a single useful invention nor any useable technical discovery, no conquest that counts in the evolution of Humanity, nothing that can compare to the accomplishments in the areas of culture and technology by Europeans or even by Asians.[7]

The study of the Africans' histories was left to the anthropologists whose ahistorical assumptions about the unchanging nature of 'primitive' societies were rarely questioned by the historians.[8] Most Portuguese anthropological studies before 1960 were unabashedly ethno-centric and racist. Africans were adjudged to be intrinsically inferior to Europeans; indeed, Portugal's self-adulation over her 'civilising mission' was dependent upon that inferiority. Even Portugal's best anthropologists supported this view. Jorge Dias, one of the few Portuguese anthropologists whose work in Africa merited international attention,[9] wrote as late as 1960 that 'Although we may be convinced that our civilisation is superior to that of many indigenous societies of our Overseas Provinces, we never try to impose it. . . . As soon as a native acquires European mentality and customs, he can become a citizen and participate in the civil life of the Portuguese nation.'[10]

Many academics and civil servants also considered *mestiços* to be inherently inferior. José Baptista Barreiros, Norton de Matos, and Vicente Ferreira opposed miscegenation because they were convinced that the offspring would merely constitute a bastardised imitation of the Portuguese and would consequently lower the overall cultural level of the Europeans in the colonies.[11] A. A. Mendes Correia, usually considered to be the father of 'modern' anthropology in Portugal and the first director of the Institute of Higher Overseas Studies (1946-58), argued the improbability of *mestiços*, no matter how brilliant, ever making a complete identification with the Portuguese in terms of temperament, will, feelings, or ideas. He concluded that *mestiços* 'must never hold high posts in the general politics of the country'.[12] Thus, the pseudo-scientific racism of Portuguese anthropology not only contributed to the historians' cultural bias but also provided the *Estado Novo* with the necessary intellectual support for its pre-war *indigenato* system under which all Africans and *mestiços* not judged to have totally affected the (ideal) Portuguese style of life were classified as 'uncivilised' and therefore subject to the brutal system of forced labour and other forms of exploitation and degradation.

The Euro-centric bias of most studies was compounded by their limitation to the coastal ports and towns where the overwhelming majority of Portuguese were located. The vast interior (the *sertão*) was treated as an undifferentiated backland whose inhabitants were generally labelled *gentios*, or heathens. Historians focused on the interior only to describe Portuguese contact situations or to examine the careers of Europeans (*sertanejos*) who permanently resided there. Episodes involving Portuguese missionaries in the Kingdoms of the Kongo and the Muenemutapa were reasonably well documented, as were the activities of European and *mestiço* traders who settled in the Angolan central highlands and the Zambesi Valley.[13] Not surprisingly, those Europeans and their descendants who chose to live among the Africans were depicted as 'half-castes' and 'barbarians' having few redeeming qualities.

A more fundamental deficiency than the Euro-centric and coastal orientations of scholarly studies on Angola and Mozambique was their lack of rigorous analysis. As late as 1960 Charles Boxer, the eminent historian of Portuguese expansion, bemoaned the absence of serious scholarship on the pre-nineteenth-century history of the two colonies.[14] The tendency simply to summarise documents and weave them together in a detailed narrative characterised most of the literature. This failure to go beyond the level of synthesis was a natural extension of the Portuguese educational system which, under Salazar and Caetano, discouraged analysis and independent thinking—especially when it stood on sacred dogmas and myths. The relatively small number of creative scholars were forced either to pursue politically safe subjects or carry out their work in exile.[15] Finally, Portuguese scholars also suffered from most of the handicaps which have plagued foreign researchers such as limited access to archival materials, restricted opportunities for fieldwork and an omnipresent concern over the political ramifications and repercussions of a particular study.

Despite this sterile environment, a few studies of high quality though narrow orientation were published. For example, general works by Magalhães Godinho, António Baião, Hernâni Cidade and Manuel Murias provide important documents and discussion of Portuguese overseas expansion and colonisation.[16] Delgado's *História de Angola* presents an extremely useful account of Portuguese settlement, relations with the Kingdoms of the Kongo and Ndongo, conflicts with the Dutch, and the growth and decline of the slave trade.[17] His work on Benguela and the governorship of Sousa Coutinho also reflects a high standard of scholarship as do the writings of Silva Rego.[18] Lobato's pioneering research not only fills in many gaps in Mozambican coastal history but represents a modest departure from the Euro-centric concerns of his contemporaries.[19] Occasionally, governors and other high officials, such as Norton de Matos and Henrique Galvão, contributed important works which examine the difficulties involved in maintaining a coherent administrative system, settling Portuguese in the hinterlands and enforcing legislation promulgated to protect Africans from the avarice of local Portuguese.[20] Texeira Botelho's military history of Mozambique and Almeida de Eça's study of the nineteenth-century Zambesian wars do provide valuable data on the social and political history of Mozambique, although they are buried in detailed accounts of Portuguese military campaigns.[21]

A small number of foreign scholars also made important contributions to Angolan and Mozambican historiography in the pre-1960 period. Basil Davidson's *The African Awakening* not only transcended the cultural and racial biases prevalent in the literature and exposed the atrocities and immense human cost of the forced labour system, but marked the beginning of his long and important association with lusophonic Africa as an eminent scholar of the area.[22] Axelson published two significant monographs on Portuguese-African relations, albeit from the perspective of the Europeans.[23] His meticulously researched *Portuguese in South East Africa* 1600-1700 remains the major source of information for this time period. Among Boxer's voluminous publications on Portuguese overseas expansion are several important discussions of the relationship of Angola and Mozambique to the larger history of the South Atlantic and Indian Ocean systems, respectively.[24] Haight also presented a very thoughtful discussion of Mozambique within the broader context of Indian Ocean trade and diplomacy during the first half of the nineteenth century.[25]

With the exception of these authors, few non-Portuguese historians made notable contributions to the historiography of Angola and Mozambique through the 1950s. This condition changed dramatically, however, during the succeeding two decades when the struggles for national liberation played an important role in attracting the interests of scores of foreign scholars to the history and contemporary affairs of the two colonies.

Post-1960 Angolan and Mozambican historiography

After 1960 a new generation of non-Portuguese social scientists began to redefine the vital areas of scholarly concern in the historiography of Angola and Mozambique. While many became interested in the colonies because of the struggles for national liberation, virtually all were stimulated intellectually by James Duffy's *Portuguese Africa*.[26] Duffy's pioneering study was soon followed by Boxer's two important monographs on Portuguese expansion and race relations from 1415 to 1825 and Davidson's *Black Mother*.[27] In sharp contrast to their predecessors, this new generation of writers rejected Euro-centrism and treated the Portuguese settlers and traders as only one, often insignificant, element in the historical development of Angola and Mozambique. Furthermore, they challenged the standard Portuguese interpretations and attacked the very soul of Portuguese colonialism—the myth of non-racism.

As part of the effort to redirect Angolan and Mozambican historiography, Africanists have looked to new sources which their predecessors either ignored or dismissed as invalid. Greater attention, for example, has been given to local archives such as the Arquivo Histórico de Moçambique, the Arquivo da Companhia de Moçambique, the Biblioteca da Câmara Municipal de Luanda, the Arquivo Histórico de Angola, the Seminário de Luanda and the Arquivo Quartel Geral. These repositories house important collections of documents which, despite their Euro-centric focus, are requisite for the reconstruction of local history. Publications by Wheeler, Birmingham, Hoppe, Samuels, Christiansen, and Hafkin, among others, suggest their value.[28] Other historians such as Abraham, Alpers, Martin, Newitt and Smith went beyond the traditional archival repositories in Lisbon to discover valuable collections of documents located in such disparate places as Scotland, Holland, France, Goa and the Vatican.[29]

A more significant departure from past historiography has been the recent effort to collect oral data—a task which was complicated by sceptical colonial officials and suspicious secret policemen. Although only a small number of historians received research clearance under the old regime, the oral data which they collected have provided important new insights into the institutions and value of a number of pre-colonial Angolan and Mozambican societies. Abraham's initial work on the kingdom of the Muenemutapa, Isaacman's analysis of the Zambesi *prazos* as an African institution and his work on the Chikunda benefited from such an approach, as did Miller's study of the mythical 'Jaga' and his forthcoming book on the Imbangala.[30] Other historians, most notably Alpers, Birmingham, Randles and Vansina, have used published oral histories collected as early as the seventeenth century to reconstruct important chapters of the pre-colonial history of Angola and Mozambique.[31]

This new orientation has already altered the approach and direction of research. Nevertheless, there is still a considerable need for systematic research to reconstruct the pre-colonial and colonial history of both Angola and Mozambique. At best, the new generation of scholars has filled in only a few of the major gaps. At the highest level of generalisation, the research on Angola and Mozambique since 1960 falls into five thematic categories: (1) origins and state formation, (2) pre-colonial trade and politics, (3) the exploitation of African labour, (4) patterns of African-Portuguese interaction, and (5) resistance to Portuguese rule.

Given the lack of research on pre-colonial African societies, historians were compelled to grapple with the most elementary questions of origins, migrations and state formation. Research on Angola has advanced more rapidly than that on Mozambique, although with both countries attention has been focused primarily on ethnic groups located along the coast and in the immediate hinterland about whom the written documentation is much richer.

The origin and early history of three clusters of Angolan peoples have been studied in some detail. Several scholars, most notably Balandier, Randles and Vansina, have reconstructed the origin and organisation of the kingdom of the Kongo.[32] They all agree that the state was created through a combination of conquest and marriage alliances, although their accounts of the subsequent development of the kingdom are at odds.[33] To the south, the debate between Birmingham and Vansina has shed new light on the Lunda expansion into Angola and the foundation of the kingdom of Imbangala.[34] A provocative article recently published by Miller suggests an earlier arrival for the Lunda immigrants than the dates advanced by Vansina and Birmingham and notes the existence of prior small-scale societies.[35] The early history of the Ovimbundu has been sketched out in several works by Childs.[36] Unfortunately, the original narrative and accompanying king lists are presented without analysis and there is no discussion of the manner in which the data were collected or the somewhat arbitrary temporal designation of the reigns ascertained. Finally, important preliminary work has been published on the origins of the Kissama, the Kasanze, and the Vili, all coastal peoples.[37]

Much less is known about the heritage of the diverse ethnic groups of Mozambique. Only the Shona of the pre-colonial kingdom of the Muenemutapa have been studied in any depth. The principal research on the kingdom of the Muenemutapa was carried out by Abraham who published several suggestive articles in the early sixties as a prelude to a more substantial monograph which, as yet, has not appeared.[38] Abraham's use of oral traditions in conjunction with archaeological reports and scattered Portuguese documents constituted a major methodological breakthrough. Unfortunately, many of his conclusions have been questioned because of discrepancies in his published articles, undemonstrated assertions, and the disproportionate influence he claims for Arab traders at the royal court which is reminiscent of the earlier Euro-centric approach.[39] Beach has recently published several provocative, but tentative, articles which modify and extend Abraham's earlier work,[40] while Randles' cartographic data should prove invaluable to future historians of the Muenemutapa kingdom.[41]

Historians are in general agreement about the origins of a number of offshoots of the Muenemutapa kingdom, including the Barue, Manica, and Rozvi of Changamire.[42] Research on the Malaŵian kingdoms residing to the north of these Shona polities is somewhat less rudimentary. Langworthy has documented the Lunda origins for the kingdom of Undi and Schoffeleers independently arrived at a similar conclusion for the related Manganja kingdom.[43] The most important work on the origins of southern Mozambican peoples is a recent article by Smith in which he analyses the formation of the Tonga, Tsonga and Chopi.[44] In addition, De Mattos has recently published an extremely interesting reconstruction of Chopi history,[45] and Liesegang has examined the Ngoni intrusion.[46] Rita Ferreira's forthcoming history of Ngoni should fill in a major gap in our knowledge of pre-colonial Mozambique.[47]

Despite the flurry of research focusing on origins and pattern of migration, it is distressing how much work remains to be done on this critical subject. For example, systematic research has not been done on such important ethnic groups as the Makua and Lomwe, while our pre-twentieth-century knowledge of the Luchazi, Mbunda and Ambewela is at a rudimentary level.[48] The acceptance and utilisation of ethnic categories which bear no relationship to historical reality is a natural by-product of this gap in historiography. Miller has argued convincingly that the Jaga[49] were a European fabrication and a similar hypothesis might be advanced for the Zimba.[50] Less dramatic, but more prevalent, has been the tendency to create ethnic categories based on very limited evidence. In the Zambesi Valley alone, for example, the Chikunda, Nhungue, Tonga and Nguru have until recently been improperly identified and classified.[51]

In sharp contrast to this lacuna, historians have examined the theme of 'trade and politics' at great length. This subject was quite appealing because it allowed researchers to destroy the lingering myth of 'the African as an uneconomic man' without actual fieldwork. Moreover, the growth of long distance or market-oriented trade[52] was thought to have important implications for the process of state formation and expansion.

Birmingham's book, *Trade and Conflict in Angola*, served as an important model for a number of fine 'trade and politics' studies. He has argued convincingly that trade, primarily in slaves, created commercial and military factors which regulated the growth and decline of such states as the Mbundu kingdom of Ngola and Imbangala state of Kasanje (slave trade),[53] and the Mbundu kingdom of Ndongo (salt trade).[54] A similar explanation has been posited for the expansion of the Vili state of Loango[55] and, indeed, for most of the Central African savanna kingdoms.[56]

The causal relationship between trade and political development has also been a dominant theme in the historiography of pre-colonial Mozambique. Newitt linked the origin of the sultanate of Angoche to its ability to exclude Kilwa from the trade with the kingdom of the Muenemutapa.[57] Hafkin's broader discussion of trade and politics in the major sheikdoms of northern Mozambique demonstrates that their nineteenth-century pre-eminence stemmed from their control of the slave trade, an opinion shared by Newitt.[58] Chanaiwa has recently used the trade and politics approach to explain the expansion of the Muenemutapa empire into the Zambesi Valley. Rejecting Abraham's assertion that the royal family was manipulated by Arab merchants, he argues that their commercial acumen precipitated their northward expansion and explains their subsequent success.[59] Bhila has advanced a similar argument in the case of the kingdom of Manica,[60] and both he and Sutherland contend that trade underpinned the power of the Rozvi dynasty of Changamire.[61] Finally, Smith has suggested that the development of the Zulu kingdom may be linked to commerce with Delegado Bay.[62]

Fortunately, a number of historians have recognised that the causal relationship between trade and political development is somewhat mechanistic and tends to oversimplify a far more complex process. Many of the studies, moreover, ignored such vital internal factors as the organisation of the commercial system, the linkages between commerce and the agricultural sector, and the role of values, focusing instead on the commodities exchanged, trade routes and a variety of other issues external to the society itself. These deficiencies have been remedied to a degree in several more recent studies. Mudenge hypothesises that the redistribution of cattle, rather than the control of the gold trade, underpinned the power base of the Rozvi Changamire.[63] Similarly, Miller has demonstrated that the combination of Chokwe values and their integrative social system facilitated their commercial and political expansion during the nineteenth century.[64]

Historians have also begun to examine the impact of commerce on the system of stratification. Martin's excellent study of the Vili kingdom not only documents the emergence of a new class of commercial brokers linked to the slave trade but suggests how their presence upset the existing hierarchical arrangements and ultimately undercut the position of the king.[65] Similar patterns have been noted in Kasanje, where the matrilineage became the ultimate beneficiary of commerce,[66] and in Undi's Malaŵian kingdom.[67] Hafkin has documented the growth of an élite merchant class of Indians, Swahili and Makua which collectively dominated northern Mozambique.[68]

Alpers' book, *Ivory and Slaves*, represents yet another significant breakthrough in the discussion of the effects of long-distance trade. He skilfully links the economies of the Yao, Malaŵian peoples and the Makua with those of the Portuguese, Indians and French to present a coherent picture of a complex international trading system and identifies the roots of underdevelopment in the former role as a supplier of raw commodities and cheap labour.[69] In a short but very insightful article, Rodney has advanced a similar argument for Angola.[70]

An integral factor in the process of underdevelopment was the mobilisation of forced labour. Several historians have examined some of the demographic and economic implications of the transoceanic slave trade for Angola. Klein's preliminary findings on the source of the exported slaves,[71] which corroborate Vansina's earlier work,[72] should facilitate the efforts of historians to reconstruct the demographic impact of the slave trade—a subject of vital interest for any rigorous analysis of underdevelopment. Davidson's thesis that the slave trade resulted in the stagnation and ultimate decline of local industry has been clearly documented in recent work on the Vilo kingdom.[74] Davidson also traces the roots of the forced labour system (which replaced slavery) to the economic backwardness of metropolitan Portugal.[75] Various authors, including Anderson, Boavida, Mario Pinto de Andrade and Ollivier, Rodney, Sideri, Saul, Minter, Chilcote, Harris and Sousa Ferreira have expanded on this theme to explain the nature of Portuguese colonialism in general as a function of the underdeveloped (and dependent) nature of Portuguese capitalism.[76] Portugal herself was dependent on other European nations (especially England) and therefore lacked the capital and economic infrastructure to exploit appreciably more than the human labour in the colonies.

In contrast with those who have emphasised the economic bases of Portuguese colonialism, Gann, Duignan, Hammond and others have argued that economic considerations were not the main motivations behind Portuguese colonisation in Africa.[77] Frequently citing the same data on Portugal's economic dependency status in the nineteenth and twentieth centuries, they conclude that Portugal was too underdeveloped to effectively exploit the colonies. Noting that neither the metropolitan coffers nor the humble Portuguese settlers in the colonies were enriched by the colonial enterprise, they argue that pride and prestige were the principal motivations behind Portuguese colonialism. These factors have also been emphasised by Henriksen, Wheeler and Bender, although the latter two acknowledge the prominence of the economic dimension.[78] There is no question that until recent decades the colonies were seldom a source of profit for the central government in Lisbon and that the search for pride and prestige in the colonies played an important role in sustaining Portuguese colonisation during the *Estado Novo*. This is not to suggest, however, that massive economic exploitation of Africans did not occur. Portuguese firms and multinational corporations have extracted large fortunes from Angola and Mozambique. If the state shared little in the profits, this was a sign of its weakness and inability to tax the economic oligarchs and not a confirmation of the absence of Portuguese and European imperialism in the colonies.[79]

Many writers strongly castigated the Portuguese government for having continued the use of forced labour into the second half of the twentieth century. Nevinson's *A Modern Slavery* vividly illustrates the scant difference between the systems of slavery and forced labour by 1905, a fact confirmed a few years later by Governor Norton de Matos, who noted that free African labourers in Angola were rare exceptions.[80] The most devastating Portuguese critique of forced labour is contained in Henrique Galvão's famous 'Report on Native Problems in the Portuguese Colonies' presented to a closed session of the Portuguese Parliament in 1947. He confirmed that neither women, children, the sick, nor the aged were spared: 'only the dead are really exempt from forced labour'.[81] Duffy and Davidson have presented the most comprehensive examination in English of the various strategies employed by Portuguese officials and their commercial counterparts to exploit African labour in the post-abolition period. They have detailed with great clarity the repeated Portuguese efforts to circumvent international regulations and world opinion through the Indian Ocean engagé system, the exportation of 'contract labour' to São Tomé, and the recruitment of 'free workers' for Rhodesia and South Africa.[82] A number of other scholars have contributed to the documentation of the obnoxious system of forced labour, which was abolished only after Angolan nationalists initiated the armed struggle in 1961.[83]

The exploitation of African labour is intimately linked to the question of Portuguese race relations in Angola and Mozambique. That Portugal actively participated in the slave trade longer than any other European nation and continued officially to use unpaid African labour until 1961 are incontrovertible facts. The differences among scholars and statesmen over the nature of Portuguese race relations, however, usually transcended questions of fact. Most Portuguese and a number of foreign writers ignored Portuguese dependency and its broader social implications and embraced the ideology of lusotropicalism which holds that because of an historically unique absence of racism among the Portuguese people, their colonisation in tropical territories was characterised by racially egalitarian legislation and human interaction.

The ideology of lusotropicalism was created and popularised by the romantic Brazilian sociologist Gilberto Freyre.[84] Almost immediately, Portuguese officials proclaimed that lusotropicalism represented an accurate description of race relations in the African colonies.[85] The ideology came to dominate most Portuguese scholarly work on Africa.[86] For example, the faculty of the Higher Institute of Social Sciences and Overseas Policy (formerly the Escola Colonial Superior), which included many internationally known African specialists (e.g., Mendes Correia, Silva Cunha, Adriano Moreira, Silva Rego, and Jorge Dias), was responsible for training the élite of the colonial bureaucracy, uncritically subscribed to the idyllic image of harmonious race relations in Angola and Mozambique.[87]

A number of foreign writers accepted the myth of lusotropicalism and simply assumed that race relations in the colonies were generally exemplary. Macmillan, Holder and Harris, Edgerton, Nowell, Gann and Duignan are only some of those who fell into this trap.[88] Many were strongly influenced by the Portuguese experience in Brazil which had given rise to a misleading syllogism: Portuguese colonisers in Brazil created racial harmony, the Portuguese were the colonisers in Angola, therefore racial harmony prevails in Angola and Mozambique. Some writers such as Abshire and Bailey argue, but fail to demonstrate, that the Portuguese in Africa manifested less prejudice than their counterparts in Brazil.[89]

The ideology of lusotropicalism has come under repeated attack from a number of sources. Boxer's important essay on Portuguese race relations throughout their overseas empire demonstrates that the Portuguese frequently manifested racial antipathy and disdain not only toward Africans, Asians and Arabs, but also *mestiços*.[90] Furthermore a number of Brazilian[91] and foreign scholars[92] have rejected Freyre's utopian depiction of Brazilian race relations. Studies by Degler and Skidmore provide voluminous evidence of white prejudice and discriminatory practices in Brazil, historically and contemporaneously, and even suggest that Brazilian blacks and *mestiços* may have suffered more economic and cultural discrimination than their American counterparts.[93] Bender points out that the attitudes and behaviour of the Portuguese in Brazil toward miscegenation and *mestiços* were not appreciably different than the New World Spanish, French, English or Dutch wherever there was a similarity in the demographic composition of the population—especially the proportion of non-whites and the ratio of white women to white men.[94]

African nationalists also strongly condemned lusotropicalism as a cruel myth perpetrated to blind the world to the realities of racial oppression and exploitation.[95] More than two decades ago, Mario Pinto de Andrade declared that lusotropicalism was not a valid explanation of the formation of Brazil and 'is entirely false for the colonial circumstances in Africa'.[96] The late Amílcar Cabral attacked the myth of lusotropicalism in his foreword to Davidson's *The Liberation of Guiné*, ironically suggesting that 'Perhaps unconsciously confusing realities that are biological or necessary with realities that are socio-economic and historical, Gilberto Freyre transformed all of us who live in the colony-provinces of Portugal into the fortunate inhabitants of a Luso-Tropical paradise.'[97]

Documented studies by Portuguese on the interaction between Africans and Europeans living in the same community (especially in the hinterland) are rare because most writers either focused on the goals of government policy or continued to emphasise only the white communities. A content analysis of *Studia*, the most influential Portuguese historical journal on the 'overseas', for the past fifteen years reveals only three articles on Angola and Mozambique which were not Euro-centric in orientation. Of these, two were written by foreigners.[98] Portuguese scholars writing in *Studia* chose to examine such questions as the foundation of Benguela, changing architectural styles in Lourenço Marques, and the vicissitudes of the early Portuguese gold mining operation in the kingdom of the Muenemutapa.[99]

Although Portuguese scholarship remained Euro-centric, important questions about the Europeans in the colonies were ignored. For example, who were the Portuguese that established the 'civilising stations' in the interior and to what extent did they transmit their culture? Hammond concludes that the racial attitudes of both the officials and settlers were antithetical to lusotropical ideals and the goals of the 'civilising mission'.[100] The works of Isaacman and Newitt about the Zambesi Valley demonstrate the Portuguese tendency to become the converts rather than the converters.[101] In Angola nearly all the Portuguese were exiled convicts (*degredados*) before the early decades of the twentieth century. Bender established the failure of Portugal's five centuries of penal colonisation, noting that not only were the *degredados* a major threat to the well-being of Europeans and Africans, but that the system was never able to reform them and not one example of an agricultural settlement founded by *degredados* survived.[102]

Over the last half-century, attempts to establish rural white settlement using free men and women did not greatly improve the social and educational level of the Portuguese in the interior. Bender's statistical analysis of planned rural settlement in Angola documents the expensive failure of the government's rural settlement programmes and, more importantly, its inability to establish racially integrated agricultural settlements.[103] Jundanian's work confirms the same pattern in Mozambique.[104]

There are numerous studies about the failure of the Portuguese to assimilate (or 'civilise' in the colonial lexicon) more than a small percentage of Africans in Angola and Mozambique.[105] Samuels and Wheeler delineate the changes in colonial policies at the turn of the twentieth century which effectively precluded most Africans from entering Portuguese society.[106] Sousa Ferreira's UNESCO study carefully documents the failure of Portuguese post-1961 reforms, to guarantee the presence of a significant number of Africans in the upper levels of the educational system or in skilled occupations.[107] The works by Wheeler and Mario Antonio Fernandes de Oliveira on the assimilado élite in Angola reveal their discontent and extreme sense of alienation from Portuguese society.[108] Assimilation was also inhibited by the presence of large numbers of Portuguese whose background could not be considered 'civilised' by Portuguese standards.[109] Furthermore, many of the whites were overt racists and consequently opposed the upward mobility of Africans.[110]

Studies examining the extent of assimilation and acculturation in Angola and Mozambique provide yet another example of the failure of the Portuguese 'civilising mission'. Heimer's recent work in Angola suggests that official measures exaggerated the level of African acculturation.[111] Using sophisticated survey research techniques and a large random sample of rural Africans, he found that the Portuguese language is rarely used in daily conversation (one per cent of adults and two per cent of children use Portuguese regularly). He also discovered that most Africans had almost no knowledge of Portuguese history or geography. For example, only 6·5 per cent of the rural heads of families in 1970-71 named Salazar, Caetano, or Americo Tomas as the 'Chief of the Portuguese Government' and less than one per cent identified Lisbon as the capital of Portugal. Apparently, in spite of five hundred years of the Portuguese presence, most rural Africans continue to orient themselves within their traditional cultural and geographical context.

The clearest indication of the myth of lusotropicalism was the recurring pattern of resistance to Portuguese rule. Although no detailed analysis of pre-twentieth century opposition to Portuguese rule in Angola has yet been published, a recurring pattern of early resistance to Portuguese encroachments is apparent. Several historians have documented the success of the Kongo, Mbundu, Matamba, Imbangala and Kissama in their early struggles against the Europeans.[112] This strong commitment to remain independent continued until the early part of the twentieth century when the Angolan peoples were forcibly crushed. Pélissier has noted that the Portuguese were compelled to mount more than fifteen major operations between 1885 and 1913 in order to impose their rule in southern Angola.[113] Africans did not constitute the only source of opposition during this latter period. Wheeler carefully documents the growing discontent of *mestiços* and white settlers at the turn of the century.[114]

The theme of resistance has not received as much attention in the historiography of Mozambique. Passing references have been made to the early anti-Portuguese campaigns of the Muenemutapa, Tonga, Manica and Rozvi, but rarely have historians focused on this subject.[115] Similarly, Portuguese conflicts with Angoche and other sultanates have been treated as a chapter in the study of trade and politics.[116] Axelson, Hammond and Warhurst have also noted the role of African resistance in their studies of the European scramble for the Portuguese colonies.[117] Until recently only the opposition of the mulatto *prazero* families, the efforts of Gugunhana, and the Barue rebellion of 1917 have been examined in any detail.[118] Isaacman's forthcoming study of the tradition of African resistance in the Zambesi Valley and adjacent regions of Zimbabwe (Rhodesia) represents the first in-depth analysis on the subject.[119] His book documents the long anti-colonial legacy, examining the symbols, institutions and strategies used to mobilise diverse ethnic groups, and gives special attention to more localised forms of opposition, such as 'day-to-day' resistance and social banditry, which are often ignored by historians focusing on mass movements. The conclusion that class rather than race had become paramount by the first quarter of the century corresponds with the important work Hafkin is doing in northern Mozambique.[120]

Unlike the earlier anti-colonial struggles, the recent wars of liberation in Angola and Mozambique have attracted the attention of a number of writers, most of whom have focused on Angola. Several factors explain this emphasis: (1) the Portuguese and most foreigners have historically been more interested in Angola than in Mozambique; (2) the Angolan war began approximately three years before the armed conflict in Mozambique, and, most importantly, the rivalry among Angola's three major nationalist groups produced a flurry of foreign eye-witness accounts of the war.

The early years of the Angolan war inspired many books by Portuguese writers who concentrated on the 'terrorism' of African nationalists and ignored the basic causes and goals of the liberation movements.[121] In reaction, many foreigners and a few Portuguese published indignant accounts of colonial reprisals and strong attacks on Portuguese policy in general.[122] Subsequently academics of different political persuasions wrote general handbooks which provide background material to the wars and general information on the two colonies.[123]

Although no one matches the depth and scope in Marcum's pioneering work, *The Angolan Revolution*,[124] there have been a number of general studies on the nationalist movements.[125] The considerable controversy among many of the authors who wrote about the Angolan nationalists frequently stemmed from partisan commitments, ideological preferences and strongly held beliefs based upon personal contacts with one or more of the movements. The works by writers favourable to one movement often ignored the others or wrote them off as ineffective organisations or collaborators with the Portuguese. This is especially characteristic of the voluminous literature on the MPLA.[126] Davidson, for example, concluded in the early 1970s that UNITA was 'little more than a distracting side show' while Gibson and Sitte argued that UNITA was the only movement in Angola on the offensive.[127] Rossi and Wastberg disagreed with most, maintaining that the FNLA was the most important nationalist movement in Angola before the end of the war.[128] Others, like Bell, generally dismissed all the Angolan movements as ineffectual and therefore doomed to failure.[129] The doomsday predictions for the prospects of independence usually resulted from analyses which concentrated on each party's internal problems while ignoring the implications of economic and social factors in the colonies and in Portugal which ultimately proved so important in the Portuguese coup and the subsequent resolution of the colonial wars. While FRELIMO was politically and militarily more effective in the 1970s than the Angolan nationalists, there are few detailed studies of the movement or the Mozambican war.[130]

The victory of African nationalists and the Armed Forces Movement not only led to the final dismantling of the Portuguese colonial empire but also made it possible for many scholars to carry out important field work, gain access to previously unavailable archival materials, and to consult data on contemporary social, economic and political phenomena. These new possibilities will undoubtedly stimulate considerable research on Angola and Mozambique and therefore it is useful to explore some of the present basic research needs.

Research needs

Given the immaturity of Angolan and Mozambican historiography, any attempt to detail specific gaps in the literature would necessarily prove futile. Instead, we propose to identify and outline briefly broad methodological approaches and thematic areas which need urgent study. A disproportionate emphasis is placed on the pre-colonial period because the gaps are so substantial and because certain types of material, namely oral traditions and ethnographic data, are likely to become extinct within the next generation.

The reconstruction of Angolan and Mozambican history suffers from the absence of any systematic archaeological research. The efforts in Angola have been localised and limited in scope,[131] while such research in Mozambique is even less developed.[132] As a result of this lacuna the most basic questions about early iron age cultures remain unanswered. The independence of both nations, however, will facilitate serious archaeological research which, in turn, is likely to yield important data about patterns of migration, diffusion of cultures, state formation, and long distance trade.[133]

Despite the research conducted under the auspices of the Instituto Científica de Moçambique, the Museu de Angola and other local institutions, new efforts in social and cultural anthropology are also desperately needed. For the historian such studies would, in the first instance, provide basic information about the core institutions and underlying values which define specific ethnic groups and their cultures. Although historians must avoid the pitfalls of the 'ethnographic present',[134] through careful analysis ethnographic data can be used to reconstruct or, at least, hypothesise significant internal changes.[135]

While new research in both archaeology and anthropology is vital, the systematic collection of oral traditions remains the highest priority. Unless historians move out of the archives and into the 'field' the death of knowledgeable elders combined with the 'modernistic' concerns of the younger generations will destroy the chain of transmission.[136] In short, the overriding responsibility of historians should be to help create an oral archive so that the past will not be lost to posterity. Simultaneously, a serious effort must be made to train Angolan and Mozambican historians in the techniques of oral data collection and analysis, and to establish national oral data archives in both countries.[137] This emphasis on the retrieval of oral data implicitly assumes that the reconstruction of the pre-colonial history of both regions cannot and should not be written exclusively from archival sources and travel accounts.

In addition to methodological concerns, certain areas of historiography have either been treated superficially or ignored completely. Despite the emphasis on political history, there is a marked absence of studies examining the structure and ideology of pre-colonial Angolan and Mozambican states. Similarly, most discussions of commerce still employ such clichés as 'subsistence economies'[138]; and they have failed to link the trading sector with either manufacturing or agriculture. It is particularly important to examine questions relating to agricultural production which had profound implications for the development of Angola and Mozambique. The work of Cruz de Carvalho, Vieira da Silva, Possinger, Morais, Carriço, and others who were associated with the Missão de Inquéritos Agrícolas de Angola and the Angolan Rural Extension Service have provided important data and penetrating analyses on the inner workings and value of historic agricultural pastoral ecosystems.[139] This is only a first step, however, and further research is needed along these lines. There has been no comparable work of this magnitude or quality on Mozambique; however, Mario de Carvalho has published a useful book on the agricultural production.[140] African economic systems also must be placed within a broader regional international context in order to gain new insights into the process of underdevelopment and the exploitation of the rural peasantry.

There is a pressing need for systematic research into the cultural and social history of the two countries. With the exception of Schoffeleers' work on the Mbona cult,[141] there have been no rigorous efforts to analyse the cosmology, symbol system or religious institutions of any Angolan or Mozambican people— a subject which is vital to understanding man's relationship to his universe. Similarly, social historians have as yet failed to analyse the changing patterns of urbanisation and systems of stratification on Angola and Mozambique, and have studiously avoided questions of class formation.[142] In short, while we have become Afro-centric, we remain élitist in orientation.

Finally, it is imperative that scholars of Angola and Mozambique make serious efforts to synthesise their research findings and present them in a broad and intelligible manner to the interested public. One particularly encouraging development has been the recent publication of two general histories of Angola[143] and the history of Mozambique for secondary students written by the Education and Cultural Department of FRELIMO.[144] A thematic study of the Mozambican past will also appear shortly.[145] These works, however, cannot fill in all of the gaps which exist and the need to liberate the past from the culturally arrogant and racist myths continues.

Notes

1   The historiography of Guinea-Bissau falls outside the scope of this article because of the country's unique historical development. From a pre-colonial perspective such themes as the Fulani-sedentary conflict and the penetration of Islam mark Guinea-Bissau as a West African society while Mozambique and Angola fit into the broad sweep of Central African history.

The history of Portuguese colonialism in Guinea-Bissau is also appreciably different from the colonisation carried out in Angola and Mozambique. Guinea-Bissau attracted neither traders nor settlers and thus, near the end of the nineteenth century when Portugal began its wars of 'pacification', there was not a single Portuguese post beyond the coast. As late as 1915 it was considered dangerous for any Portuguese to travel outside the capital of Bissau. Even after the end of the 'pacification' campaigns in 1936 there were still no more than 2,000

Portuguese in the colony, most of whom worked in the administration of urban commerce. Consequently, a history of the peoples of Guinea-Bissau is, for the most part, one which has experienced relatively little Portuguese influence in comparison to the history of the Angolan and Mozambican peoples.

For the purposes of this essay, Guinea differs significantly in yet another way: it received almost no scholarly attention until its recent war of liberation. The most important work on Guinea-Bissau by a Portuguese scholar is the two-volume study of Texeira da Mota, *Guinea Portuguesa*, Lisbon, 1954. Some other useful works by Portuguese are: Honório Pereira Barretto, *Memória sobre o estado actual de Senegambia portugueza, causas de sua decadência, e meios de a fazer prosperar*, Lisbon, 1843; António Augusto Mendes Correa, *Uma jornada científica na Guiné Portuguesa*, Lisbon, 1947; Sociedade de Geografia de Lisboa, *Congresso comemorativo do quinto centenário do descobrimento da Guinea*, 2 vols., Lisbon, 1946; and Manuel Sarmento Rodrigues, *No governo da Guinea: discurso e afirmações*, Lisbon, 1949.

The liberation struggle inspired a number of significant books on Guinea-Bissau. The principal English language publications are: Basil Davidson, *The Liberation of Guiné*, Baltimore, 1969; Gérard Chaliand, *Armed Struggle in Africa*, New York, 1969, originally published in French, *Lutte armée en Afrique*, Paris 1967; Al J. Venter, *Portugal's War in Guinea-Bissau*, Pasadena, 1973; and the recent, comprehensive work by Lars Rudebeck, *Guinea-Bissau: A Study of Political Mobilization*, Uppsala, 1974.

The most penetrating studies of the economy and cultures of Guinea-Bissau have unquestionably been those of the late Amílcar Cabral. His agricultural census published in the mid-1950s still remains the most authoritative study of agricultural production and the ethnic groups in Guinea-Bissau; see *Boletim Cultural da Guiné Portuguesa*, volumes 9-11 (1954-56). Parts of this survey have been translated into English by Ronald Chilcote (in his *Emerging Nationalism in Portuguese Africa: Documents*, Stanford, 1972, pp. 352-5) and Gerald J. Bender and Colleen Hughes Trujillo in *Ufahamu*, iii, 3, Winter, 1973, pp. 31-41. In addition there are various collections of speeches and studies by Amílcar Cabral: *Revolution in Guinea: Selected Texts*, translated and edited by Richard Handyside, New York, 1969; *Our People Are Our Mountains*, London, 1971; *Guinée 'portugaise': le pouvoir des armes*, Paris, 1970; *Alguns princípios do partido*, Lisbon, 1974; and *Guiné-Bissau--nação forjada na luta*, Lisbon, 1974.

In late 1974 the PAIGC published a comprehensive and extremely useful *História da Guinea e Ilhas de Cabo Verde*, Lisbon, 1974. There have been many accounts of the death of Amílcar Cabral but the most exhaustive is by the Soviet journalist Oleg Ignatiev, *Tres tiros da PIDE: quem, porque e como mataram Amílcar Cabral*, Lisbon, 1975.

2   'Editorial' in *O mundo português* 2, July-August 1935, p. 218. The entire editorial is found on pp. 217-19.

3   Among the principal exceptions are the works of two Belgian historians: J. L. Cuvelier, *L'ancien royaume de Congo*, Brussels, 1941; and G. L. Haveaux, *La tradition historique des Bapende orientaux*, Brussels, 1954.

4   See, for example, G. Sousa Dias, *Os portugueses em Angola*, Lisbon, 1959; Alfredo de Albuquerque Felner, *Angola: apontamentos sobre a colonização dos planaltos e litoral do sul de Angola: documentos*, 3 vols., Lisbon, 1940; Alberto de Lemos, *História de Angola*, Lisbon, 1932; Jofre Amaral Nogueira, *A colonização do Huambo*, Nova Lisboa, 1953; Alexandre Lobato, *História da fundação de Lourenço Marques*, Lisbon, 1948; Rocha Martins, *História das colónias portuguesas*, Lisbon, 1933; Caetano Montez, *Descobrimento e fundaçao de Lourenço Marques*, 1500-1800, Lourenço Marques, 1948. *Studia*, the principal journal of the history of the Portuguese overseas, confirms this pattern since almost every article written about the two colonies focuses on the Europeans.

5   For detailed accounts of military activities in Mozambique, for example, see Felipe Gastão de Almeida de Eça, *História das guerras no Zambeze*, 2 vols., Lisbon, 1953-54, and José Justino Texeira Botelho, *História militar e política dos portugueses em Moçambique*, 2 vols., Lisbon, 1934. For Angola, see David Magno, *Guerras angolanas*, Porto, 1934; João de Almeida, *Sul d'Angola: relatório de um governo de distrito*, 2nd ed., Lisbon, 1936; and Lapas de Gusmão, *A querra no sertão*, (sul de Angola), 2nd ed., Lisbon, 1935.

6   While there have been many studies about the Dutch, Germans and Boers in Angola, some of the more prominent works are: A. da Silva Rego, *A dupla restauração de Angola*, Lisbon, 1948; Fran Paxeco, *Angola e os alemais*, Maranhão, 1916; Brito Camacho, *Gente Boer*, Lisbon, 1930; Eric Rosenthal, 'Os Boers de Angola e o seu destino', *Boletim da Sociedade de Geografia de Lisboa*, 52, 1934, pp. 1-14; and Manuel V. Gerreiro, 'Boers de Angola', *Garcia de Orta*, 6, 1958, pp. 11-31.

7   Marcello Caetano, *Os nativos na economia africana*, Coimbra, 1954, p. 16. Some thought that the 'moulding' should be carried out with an iron hand. Carlos Eduardo de Soveral, for example, argued in his sociological study of Angola that an African 'likes to be strongly commanded [by Europeans] and, as all primitive beings, is so close in this aspect to the animal, he wants and loves the vigorous hand rather than the gentle hand. . . .' 'Introdução a um estudo sociológico de Angola', *Boletim da Sociedade de Geografia de Lisboa*, 83, April-June 1952, p. 136.

8   The emphasis of most anthropological studies prior to and during the period under consideration in this paper was on the 'exotic' aspect of African societies, i.e., scarification, craniometry, hair styles, magic, ceremonies, etc. Since African cultures were considered *a priori* to be stagnant and backward, anthropologists were not interested in studying how they functioned or even how they interacted with the environment. See António de Almeida, *Sobre as mutilações étnicas dos aborígenes de Angola*, Lisbon, 1937, and 'Sobre as mutilações étnicas dos Cazamas', *Boletim do Instituto de Angola*, 7, 1955, pp. 43-55; Alexandre Sarmento, *A tatuagem entre as tribos de Angola: Songos*, Porto, 1943; Marieta Cidade Barreto, 'Penteados indigenas de Angola', *Actas do 1.º Congrsso Nacional de Ciêncas Naturais*, vol. 2, Lisbon, 1941, pp. 58-68; J. H. Santos David, *Contribuição para o estudo da antropometria dos indigenas da Lunda e Songo*, 2 vols., Lisbon, 1955.

9   Jorge Dias' work on the Macondes of Mozambique was largely responsible for his being named a fellow at the Institute of Advanced Behavioral Studies in Palo Alto in the late 1960s. See, for example, his five-volume study, *Os Macondes de Moçambique*, Lisbon, 1964.

10   Jorge Dias, 'Convivio entre pretos e brancos nas províncias ultramarinas portuguesas', *Estudos ultramarinos*, no. 3, 1960, pp. 26-7, 29.

11   See José Mendes Ribeiro Norton de Matos, *A Província de Angola*, Porto, 1926, pp. 42-3, 231, and *Memórias e trabalhos da minha vida*, vol. 3, Lisbon, 1944, pp. 148-9; José Baptista Barreiros, *Missão histórica de Portugal: colonização branca da África portuguesa*, Ponta Delgada, 1929, pp. 58-9; Vicente Ferreira, 'Alguns aspectos da política indígena de Angola', originally published in 1934 and reprinted in Vicente Ferreira, *Estudos Ultramarinos*, vol. 3, Lisbon, 1954, pp. 40-1; *ibid.*, 'Colonização étnica da África portuguesa', *Estudos Ultramarinos*, vol. 4, Lisbon, 1955, pp. 202-3.

12   A. A. Mendes Correia, *O mestiçamento nas colónias portuguesas*, Lisbon, 1940, pp. 22-3. It is important to note that neither Mendes Correia nor Jorge Dias (see note 10) nor practically any Portuguese scholar who published pejorative or prejudicial comments about Africans and *mestiços* perceived the racist implications. Mendes Correia, for example, frequently lauded the 'absence of intolerant attitudes or racial prejudices on the part of the Portuguese'. See 'A cultura portuguesa na África e no oriente', *Proceedings of the International*

Colloquium on Luso-Brazilian Studies, Nashville, 1953, p. 50. Also see his *Raças do império*, Porto, 1943.

13   For a discussion of the Portuguese kingdom of the Kongo, see Cuvelier, *L'ancien royaume* and H. Felgas, *História do Congo português*, Carmona, 1958. For descriptions of early Portuguese missionary and commercial efforts in the Kingdom of the Muenemutapa, see Alexandre Lobato, *A expansão portuguesa em Moçambique de 1498 a 1530*, Lisbon, 1954; Eric Axelson, *Southeast Africa 1480-1530*, London, 1940, and *Portuguese in South East Africa 1600-1700*, Johannesburg, 1960. General discussions of Portuguese in the Mozambican interior can be found in: António Alberto de Andrade, *Relações de Moçambique setecentista*, Lisbon, 1955; Botelho, *Historia militar*; Almeida de Eça, *História das guerras*. For Angola see Eduardo de Noronha, *O explorador Serpa Pinto*, Lisbon, 1936; Castro Soromenho, *Sertanejos de Angola*, Lisbon, 1943; António Francisco da Silva Porto, *Viagens e apontamentos de um portuense em África*, Lisbon, 1942.

14   C. R. Boxer, 'S. R. Welch and His History of the Portuguese in Africa, 1495-1806', *Journal of African History*, i, 1960, p. 55.

15   Many Portuguese scholars went underground or into exile, including Oliveira Marques, José Cutileiro, José Capela, Fernando Ganhão and Hermínio Martins. Cutileiro's *A Portuguese Rural Society*, Oxford, 1971, is the most outstanding anthropological study on Portugal ever published by a Portuguese, while A. H. de Oliveira Marques' two-volume *History of Portugal*, New York, 1972, may be the best general history of Portugal written in any language. [Following the 1974 coup Oliveira Marques was named Director of the National Library (Biblioteca Nacional) in Lisbon. Since the independence of Mozambique Fernando Gauhão has been Rector of the University of Maputo.]

16   See V. Magalhaes Godinho, *Documentos sobre a expansao portuguesa*, 3 vols., Lisbon, 1943-56; Antonio Baiao, Hernani Cidade, and Manuel Murias, *Historia da expansão portuguesa no mundo*, 3 vols., Lisbon, 1937-40.

17   Ralph Delgado, *História de Angola*, 4 vols., Benguela, 1948-55.

18   Ralph Delgado, *O reino de Benguela: do descobrimento a criação do governo subalterno*, Lisbon, 1945; *Ao sul do Cuanza: ocupação e aproveitamento do antigo reino de Benguela, 1483-1942*, Lisbon, 1944, and 'O governo de Sousa Coutinho', *Studia*, 8, 1960-62; Silva Rego, *A dupla restauração*. In addition to writing many valuable books, Silva Rego has been actively engaged for decades in restoring, preserving, cataloguing and microfilming documents which would otherwise have been lost.

19   Alexandre Lobato, *Aspectos de Moçambique no antigo regime colonial*, Lisbon, 1953, *A expansão portuguesa em Moçambique*, and *Evolução administrative e económica de Moçambique*, Lisbon, 1957. The latter study is a particularly insightful work which remains a major source of Mozambican history.

20   Some of the more useful works by Norton de Matos are *Memórias e trabalhos da minha vida*, 4 vols., Lisbon, 1944; *África nossa*, Porto, 1953; *A província de Angola*, Porto, 1926. For some important studies by Henrique Galvão see *Angola: para uma nova política*, Lisbon, 1937; *Huila*, Vila Nova de Familiação, 1929; *História do nosso tempo*, Lisbon, 1931; *Por Angola: quatro anos de actividade parlamentar, 1945-49* and *Império ultramarino português*, Lisbon, 1952. The latter book was written with Carlos Selvagem, the pseudonym for Carlos Alfonso dos Santos.

21   Almeida de Eça, *Historia das guerras*; Botelho, *História militar*.

22   Basil Davidson, *The African Awakening*, London, 1955. This book resulted, in part, from a trip which Davidson made through Angola in 1954 at the invitation of *Harpers Magazine*. In 1904 *Harpers* had commissioned Henry A. Nevinson to travel through Angola out of which resulted his classical study of the substitution of forced labour for slavery (*A Modern Slavery*, London, 1906). Harpers marked the fiftieth anniversary of Nevinson's trip by commissioning Davidson to do the same. Just as Nevinson's book set off an international

controversy over Portuguese labour practices, so did Davidson's *African Awakening*. The Portuguese futilely tried to counteract the heavy impact of his charges and even paid another Englishman (Egerton) to follow Davidson's path through Angola to try to counteract his charges. See F. Clement C. Egerton, *Angola Without Prejudice*, Lisbon, 1955 and *Angola in Perspective*, London, 1957.

23 Axelson, *Southeast Africa*, and *Portuguese in Southeast Africa*.

24 Some of C. R. Boxer's pre-1960 works are: *Salvador de Sá and the Struggle for Brazil and Angola, 1602-1686*, London, 1952; 'Mozambique and the "Carreira do India" ', *Studia*, 9, 1961, pp. 99-132; 'The Portuguese in the East, 1500-1800', in *Portugal and Brazil*, ed. H. V. Livermore, Oxford, 1953; and 'The Old Kingdom of Congo', in *The Dawn of African History*, ed. Roland Oliver, London, 1959.

25 M. V. Jackson Haight, *European Powers and South-East Africa*, London, 1942.

26 James Duffy, *Portuguese Africa*, Cambridge, 1959 and the abbreviated but more polemical version of this book, *Portugal in Africa*, Cambridge, 1962. Also see Duffy's *A Question of Slavery*, Cambridge, 1967.

27 See C. R. Boxer, *Four Centuries of Portuguese Expansion: 1415-1825*, Johannesburg, 1961, and *Race Relations in the Portuguese Colonial Empire: 1415-1825*; Basil Davidson, *Black Mother*, London, 1961 which was published later in the US under the title *The African Slave Trade: Precolonial History 1450-1850*, Boston, 1961.

28 See David Birmingham, *Trade and Conflict in Angola*, Oxford, 1966; Douglas L. Wheeler and René Pélissier, *Angola*, New York, 1971; Douglas L. Wheeler and C. Diane Christensen, 'To Rise With One Mind: The Bailundo War of 1902', in *Social Change in Angola*, ed. Franz-Wilhelm Heimer, Munich, 1973; Michael Anthony Samuels, *Education in Angola, 1878-1914*, New York, 1970; Fritz Hoppe, *A África oriental portuguesa no tempo do Marques de Pombal, 1750-1777*, Lisbon, 1970; and Nancy Jane Hafkin, 'Trade, Society and Politics in Northern Mozambique, c. 1753-1913,' Ph.D. dissertation, Boston University, 1973.

29 D. P. Abraham, 'Maramuca: An Exercise in the Combined Use of Portuguese Records and Oral Traditions', *Journal of African History*, ii, 1961, pp. 211-26; Edward A. Alpers, *Ivory and Slaves in East Central Africa*, Berkeley, 1975; Phyllis M. Martin, *The External Trade of the Loango Coast, 1576-1870*, Oxford, 1872; M. D. D. Newitt, *Portuguese Settlement on the Zambesi*, New York, 1973; Alan K. Smith, 'The Peoples of Southern Mozambique: An Historical Survey', *Journal of African History*, xiv, 1973, pp. 565-80, and 'António Salazar and the Reversal of Portuguese Colonial Policy', *Journal of African History*, xv, 1972, pp. 653-67.

30 Abraham, 'Maramuca,' 'The Monomotopa Dynasty', *NADA*, xxxvi, 1959, pp. 59-84, 'The Early Political History of the Mwene Mutapa (850-1589)', *Historians in Tropical Africa*, Proceedings of the Levehulme Inter-Collegiate History Conference, Salisbury, 1962, pp. 61-92, and 'Ethno-History of the Empire of Mutapa—Problems and Methods', in *Historians in Tropical Africa*, ed. Jan Vansina, London, 1964, pp. 104-121; Allen F. Isaacman, *Mozambique: The Africanization of a European Institution, The Zambesi Prazos 1750-1902*, Madison, 1972, and 'The Origin, Formation and Early History of the Chikunda of South Central Africa', *Journal of African History*, xiii, 1972, pp. 443-62; Joseph C. Miller, 'Requiem for the Jaga', *Cahiers d'études africaines*, xlix, 1973, pp. 121-49, and *Kings and Kinsmen: The Imbangala Impact on the Mbundu of Angola* (forthcoming).

31 Alpers, *Ivory and Slaves*; Birmingham, *Trade*; W. G. L. Randles, *L'ancien royaume du Congo des origines à la fin du XIXᵉ siècle*, Paris, 1968; Jan Vansina, *The Kingdoms of the Savanna*, Madison, 1965.

32 Georges Balandier, *Daily Life in the Kingdom of the Kongo*, New York, 1969; Randles, *L'ancien royaume;* Vansina, *Kingdoms*, and, 'Notes sur l'origine du royaume de Kongo', *Journal of African History*, iv, 1963, pp. 33-8; J. L. Vellut,

'Moyen-Kwango et Angola', *Etudes d'histoire africaine*, i, 1970, pp. 75-135;
F. Letour de Veiga Pinto, 'Le Portugal et le Congo au 1e siecle, Paris, 1972;
Filipo Pigafetta and Duarte Lopes, *Description du royaume du Congo et des contrées environnantes*, trans. and ed. Willy Bal, 2nd ed., Louvain, 1965; François Bontinck, *La fondation de la mission des Capucins en royaume du Congo, déscrites par Jean-François de Rome*, O. F. M. CAP, 1648.

33 For a critique of Balandier's work, see Jan Vansina, 'Anthropologists and the Third Dimension', *Africa*, xxxix, 1969, pp. 62-8.

34 Jan Vansina, 'The Foundation of the Kingdom of Kasanje', *Journal of African History*, iv, 1963, pp. 335-74; David Birmingham, 'The Date and Significance of the Imbangala Invasion of Angola', *Journal of African History*, vi, 1965, pp. 143-52; Vansina, 'More on the Invasion of Kongo and Angola by the Jaga and the Lunda', *Journal of African History*, iii, 1966, pp. 421-9.

35 Joseph C. Miller, 'The Imbangala and the Chronology of Early Central African History', *Journal of African History*, xiii, 1972, pp. 549-74.

36 Gladwyn Murray Childs, 'The Chronology of the Ovimbundu Kingdoms', *Journal of African History*, ii, 1970, pp 241-8 and, 'The Kingdom of Wambu (Huambo): A Tentative Chronology', *Journal of African History*, v, 1964, pp. 367-80, and *Umbundu Kinship and Character*, London, 1949.
The most important anthropological and historical works on the Ovimbundu—the most populous ethnic group in Angola—were published by foreign Protestant missionaries. For further information on the Ovimbundu (though not primarily of an historical nature), see A. C. Edwards, *Ovimbundu Under Two Sovereignties*, Oxford, 1962; Wilfred D. Hambly, *The Ovimbundu of Angola*, Chicago, 1934; Merran McCulloch, *The Ovimbundu of Angola*, London, 1952; and Merlin Ennis, *Umbundu Folktales From Angola*, Boston, 1962.

37 Beatrix Heintze, 'Historical Notes on the Kisama of Angola', *Journal of African History*, xiii, 1972, pp. 407-18, and 'Beiträge zur Geschichte und Kultur der Kisama (Angola)', *Paideuma*, xvi, 1970 pp. 159-86; Joseph C. Miller, 'A Note on Kasanze and the Portuguese', *Canadian Journal of African Studies*, vi, 1972, pp 43-56; Martin, *The External Trade*.

38 Abraham, 'Maramuca', 'The Monomotapa Dynasty', 'The Early Political History', 'Ethno-History'; and 'The Role of Chaminuka and the Mhondoro-Cults in Shona Political History', E. Stokes and R. Brown, eds., *The Zambesian Past*, London, 1966, pp. 56-83.

39 A summary of some of the major criticisms of Abraham's work can be found in Edward A. Alpers, 'The Mutapa and Malawi Political Systems', in *Aspects of Central African History*, ed. T. O. Ranger, London, 1968, pp. 7-10; and his 'Dynasties of the Mutapa-Rozwi Complex', *Journal of African History*, xi, 1970 pp. 203-220.

40 D. N. Beach, 'Historians and the Shona Empire', Henderson Seminar Papers No. 19 and No. 20, presented at the University of Rhodesia (n.d.).

41 W. G. L. Randles, 'La fondation de l'empire du Monomotapa', *Cahiers d'études africaines*, liv, 1974, pp. 207-36. See also, his 'South-East Africa and the Empire of Monomotapa as Shown on Selected Printed Maps of the 16th Century', *Studia*, ii, 1958, pp. 103-64.

42 For a brief outline of early Barue history, see Allen Isaacman, 'Madzi-Manga, Mhondoro, and the Use of Oral Traditions—A Chapter in Barue Religious and Political History', *Journal of African History*, xiv, 1973, pp. 395-410. The origins of Manica are discussed in H. H. K. Bhila, 'The Manyika and the Portuguese 1575-1863', Ph.D. dissertation, University of London, 1971. For a discussion of the Rozvi of Changamira, see S. I. Mudenge, 'The Rozvi Empire and the Feira of Zumbo', Ph.D. dissertation, University of London, 1972.

43 Langworthy has treated the origins of the Undi kingdom in some detail in his doctoral dissertation, 'A History of the Undi to 1890', Boston University, 1969.

Also see, Matthew Schoffeleers, 'The History and Political Role of the M'Bona Cult Among the Mang'anja', in *The Historical Study of African Religion*, eds. T. O. Ranger and Isaria Kimambo, Los Angeles, 1972.

44 Alan K. Smith, 'The Peoples of Southern Mozambique: An Historical Survey', *Journal of African History*, xiv, 1973, pp. 565-80.

45 Leonor Correia de Matos, 'Origens do povo Chope segundo a tradição oral', *Memórias do Instituto de Investigação Científica de Moçambique*, Series C, 10, 1973, pp. 3-101.

46 G. Liesegang, *Beiträge zur Geschichte des Reiches der Gaza Nguni im südlichen Moçambique, 1820-1895*. Cologne, 1968.

47 A. Rita Ferreira, *Etno-história cultura tradicional do groupo Angune*, forthcoming.

48 Some background on these ethnic groups can be found in Basil Davidson, *In the Eye of the Storm: Angola's People*, Garden City, 1972. Also see Serpa Pinto, *How I Crossed Africa*, vol. 1, London, 1881, and the diaries of Silva Porto, *Viagens e apontamentos de um portuense em África: excerptos do seu diário*, Lisbon, 1942.

For an interesting summary of the current status of field research in Angola, see David Birmingham, 'Themes and Resources of Angolan History', *African Affairs*, lxxiii, 1974, pp. 188-203. There is no comparable summary for Mozambique.

49 Miller, 'Requiem'.

50 Fieldwork by Isaacman in the Zambesi Valley links the Zimba to contemporary Chewa. This conclusion was reached independently by a prominent Portuguese anthropologist. (See A. Rita Ferreira, 'Os Azimbas', *Boletim da Sociedade de Moçambique*, 84 and 85, 1954).

51 Isaacman, *Mozambique* and, 'Origin and Formation'.

52 For a discussion of the debate among historians as to whether the spatial factor of the distance of the trade or its market orientation is the critical variable, see Jan Vansina, 'Long-Distance Trade Routes in Central Africa', *Journal of African Studies*, iii, 1962, pp. 375-90; Richard Gray and David Birmingham, 'Some Economic and Political Consequences of Trade in Central and East Africa in the Pre-Colonial Period', in *Pre-Colonial African Trade*, eds. Richard Gray and David Birmingham, Oxford, 1970, pp. 1-23.

53 Birmingham, *Trade and Conflict*.

54 David Birmingham, 'Early African Trade in Angola and Its Hinterland' in *Pre-Colonial Trade*, eds. Richard Gray and David Birmingham, pp. 163-74.

55 Martin, *The External Trade*.

56 Vansina, *Kingdoms*, pp. 247-8.

57 M. D. D. Newitt, 'The Early History of the Sultanate of Angoche', *Journal of African History*, xiii, 1973, pp. 397-406 and 'Angoche, the Slave Trade and the Portuguese, ca. 1844-1910', *Journal of African History*, xii, 1972, pp. 659-72.

58 Hafkin, 'Trade, Society and Politics'. A similar example of the interaction between trade and state building can be found in E. A. Alpers, 'Trade, State and Society, among the Yao in the Nineteenth Century', *Journal of African History*, x, 1969, pp. 405, 420; and 'Towards a History of the Expansion of Islam in East Africa: The Matrilineal Peoples of the Southern Interior', in *African Religion*, eds. T. O. Ranger and Isaria Kimambo, pp. 171-201.

59 David Chanaiwa, 'Politics and Long-Distance Trade in the Mwene-Mutapa Empire During the Sixteenth Century', *International Journal of African Historical Studies*, v, 1972, pp. 424-35.

60 Bhila, 'The Manyika and the Portuguese'.

61 *Ibid.*; Nicola Sutherland-Harris, 'Trade and the Rozwi Mambo', in *Pre-Colonial African Trade*, eds. Richard Gray and David Birmingham, pp. 243-64.

62 Alan Smith, 'The Trade of Delagoa Bay as a Factor in Nguni Politics 1750-1835', in *African Societies in Southern Africa*, ed. Leonard Thompson, New York, 1969, pp. 171-89.

63   S. I. Mudenge, 'The Role of Foreign Trade in the Rozvi Empire: A Reappraisal', *Journal of African History*, xv, 1974, pp. 373-91.

64   Joseph C. Miller, 'Cokwe Trade and Conquest in Nineteenth Century', in *Pre-Colonial African Trade*, eds. Richard Gray and David Birmingham, pp. 175-201.

65   Martin, *The External Trade*.

66   Joseph C. Miller, 'Slaves, Slavers and Social Change in Nineteenth Century Kasanje', in *Social Change in Angola*, ed. Franz-Wilhelm Heimer, Munich, 1973, pp. 10-29.

67   Langworthy, 'A History of Undi'.

68   Hafkin, 'Trade, Society and Politics'.

69   Alpers, *Ivory and Slaves*. For a more general discussion of East Africa, see Edward Alpers, 'Rethinking African Economic History', *Ufahamu*, iii, 1973, pp. 97-129, reprinted in *Kenya Historical Review* i, 1973, pp. 163-88.

70   Walter Rodney, 'European Activity and African Reaction in Angola', in *Aspects of Central African History*, ed. T. O. Ranger, Evanston, 1968, pp. 49-70. For a broader discussion of this problem, see Walter Rodney, *How Europe Underdeveloped Africa*, London, 1972.

71   Herbert S. Klein, 'The Trade in African Slaves to Rio de Janeiro, 1795-1911', *Journal of African History*, x, 1969, pp. 533-51, and, 'The Portuguese Slave Trade from Angola in the Eighteenth Century', *Journal of Economic History*, xxxii, December 1972, pp. 894-918.

72   Vansina, 'Long-Distance Trade Routes.'

73   See Basil Davidson's *The African Awakening* and *Black Mother*.

74   Martin, *The External Trade*.

75   See Davidson's *The African Awakening*, *Black Mother* and *In the Eye of the Storm*.

76   See Américo Boavida, *Angola: cinco séculos de exploração portuguesa*, Rio de Janeiro, 1967; Perry Anderson, *Le Portugal et la fin de l'ultra-colonialisme*, Paris, 1963; Mario Pinto de Andrade and Marc Ollivier, *La guerre en Angola: étude socio-économique*, Paris, 1971; Rodney, 'European Activity and African Reaction'; S. Sideri, *Trade and Power: Informal Colonialism in Anglo-Portuguese Relations*, Rotterdam, 1970; William Minter, *Imperial Network and External Dependency: The Case of Angola*, Beverly Hills, 1972; Ronald H. Chilcote, *Portuguese Africa*, Englewood Cliffs, 1967; Marvin Harris, 'Portugal's Contribution to the Underdevelopment of Africa and Brazil', in *Protest and Resistance in Angola and Brazil*, ed. Ronald H. Chilcote, Berkeley, 1972, pp. 210-23; Eduardo de Sousa Ferreira, *Portuguese Colonialism from South Africa to Europe*, Freiburg, 1972, *Aspectos do colonialismo português*, Lisbon, 1974, and 'Ursachen und Formen der Auswanderung und ihre Bedeutung für die Entwicklung Portugals', Ph.D. dissertation, University of Heidelberg, 1974. Also see Ruth First, *Portugal's Wars in Africa*, London, 1971; and Jay O'Brien, 'Portugal and Africa: A Dying Imperialism', *Monthly Review*, xxvi, 1974, pp. 19-36; John S. Saul, 'FRELIMO and the Mozambican Revolution', in *Essays on the Political Economy of Africa*, eds. Giovanni Arrighi and John Saul, New York, 1973, pp. 378-405; and, 'Portugal and the Mozambican Revolution', *Monthly Review*, xxvi, September 1974, pp. 45-64.

77   See L. H. Gann and Peter Duignan, 'Introduction' to *Colonialism in Africa, 1870-1961*, vol. 1, Cambridge, 1969, pp. 1-26; Gann and Duignan, 'Reflections on Imperialism and the Scramble for Africa', in *ibid.*, pp. 100-32; Richard J. Hammond, 'Uneconomic Imperialism: Portugal in Africa before 1910', in *ibid.*, pp. 352-82; and Hammond, *Portugal and Africa: 1815-1910*, Stanford, 1966.

78   Thomas Henriksen, 'Portugal in Africa: A Non-economic Interpretation', *African Studies Review*, xvi, December 1973, pp. 405-16; Wheeler and Pélissier; and Gerald J. Bender, *The Myth and Reality of Portuguese Rule in Angola: A*

Study of Racial Domination, (tentative title), forthcoming, Berkeley and London, 1977.

79 For an extremely cogent statement on the nature of economic exploitation in the colonies and an assessment of who benefited and who lost ('the Portuguese people never gained from the colonies'), see the speech of the then Portuguese Prime Minister, Vasco Gonçalves, made over Portuguese radio and television in late February 1975. Excerpts of this speech can be found in *Portugal Hoje*, 1, 1 March 1975, 1-3.

80 See Nevinson, *A Modern Slavery*, and Norton de Matos, *A Província de Angola*, Porto, 1926.

81 A complete English version of this report can be found in Henrique Galvão, *Santa Maria: My Crusade for Portugal*, trans. William Longfellow, Cleveland, 1961, pp. 57-71. The quote is found on p. 63; the emphasis is in the original. Also see Galvão's *Por Angola: quatro anos de actividade parlamentar, 1945-1949*, Lisbon, 1949.

82 See James Duffy, *A Question of Slavery* and *Portuguese Africa*, and the three works of Davidson cited in note 75.

83 For some examples see Eduardo Mondlane, *The Struggle for Mozambique*, Baltimore, 1969; Rodney, 'European Activity and African Reaction'; Wheeler and Christensen, 'To Rise With One Mind'; Alfredo Diogo Junior, *Angola perante a escravatura*, Luanda, n.d.; José Capela, *Escravatura*, Porto, 1974; Childs, *Umbundu Kinship and Character* and 'Notes on Civil Administration in Angola: Civilizing Words', unpublished manuscript, 11 September 1944; Hammond, 'Uneconomic Imperialism', Orlando Ribeiro, 'Problemas humanos de África', in *Colóquios sobre problemas humanos em regiões tropicais*, Lisbon, 1961, and *Destinos do ultramar*, Lisbon, 1975; Allen Isaacman, *The Tradition of Resistance: Anti-colonial Activity in the Zambesi Valley, 1850-1921*, Berkeley and London, 1976.

84 See the following works of Gilberto Freyre: *The Masters and the Slaves: A Study in the Development of Brazilian Civilization*, 2nd ed., New York, 1964; *Mansions and Shanties: The Making of Modern Brazil*, New York, 1963; *Integração portuguesa nos trópicos*, Lisbon, 1958; *Um brasileiro em terras portuguesas*, Rio de Janeiro, 1953; *O mundo que o português criou*, Rio de Janeiro, 1940; and *The Portuguese and the Tropics*, Lisbon, 1961.

85 See, for example, António de Oliveira Salazar, *Doctrine and Action: Internal and Foreign Policy of the New Portugal, 1928-1939*, trans. Robert Edgar Broughton, London, 1939, *The Decision to Stay*, speech delivered 13 April 1966, Lisbon, 1966 or almost any other speech he made concerning the colonies; Marcello Caetano, *Colonizing Traditions, Principles and Methods of the Portuguese*, Lisbon, 1951, and *Razões da presença de Portugal no Ultramar*, Lisbon, 1973; Franco Nogueira, *The Third World*, London, 1967; J. M. da Silva Cunha, *O sistema português de política indígena, subsídios para o seu estudo*, Coimbra, 1953, and *Problemas actuals de África negra*, Lisbon, 1963; Adriano Moreira, *Administração da justiça aos indígenas*, Lisbon, 1955 and 'The "Elites" of the Portuguese "Tribal" Provinces (Guinea, Angola, Mozambique)', *International Social Science Bulletin*, viii, 1956, pp. 458-81.

86 In addition to the works cited in note 85, see Jorge Dias, 'The Expansion of the Portuguese in the Overseas in the Light of Modern Anthropology', *Estudos de ciências políticas e sociais*, ii, 1957, pp. 237-50, 'Os elementos fundamentais da cultura portuguesa', in *Atlas do colóquio internacional de estudos luso-brasileiros*, Nashville, 1953, pp. 51-65, and '*Convívio entre pretos e brancos*'; Oscar Soares Barata, 'O sentido humano do pluri-racialismo português', *Estudos ultramarinos*, 3, 1961, pp. 57-68, and *A questão racial; introdução*, Lisbon, 1964; A. A. Mendes Correa, 'A cultura portuguesa na África e no Oriente' and *Raças do império*, Porto, 1943; Manuel da Cruz Gaspar, 'Aspectos do multiracialismo em Angola'

(Master's thesis, Instituto Superior de Ciências Sociais e Política Ultramarina, Lisbon, 1966).

87   There were a number of excellent professors at the ISCSPU (e.g., Raquel Soeiro de Brito, Abílio Lima de Carvalho, Narana Sinai Coissoro), but like all teachers and researchers in the country before April 1974, they risked professional, economic and political sanctions if they were too vigorous in their challenges of official orthodoxies.

88   See William M. MacMillan, *Africa Emergent*, rev. ed., London, 1949; B. W. Hodder and D. R. Harris, eds., 'Introduction: The African Scene', in *Africa in Transition: Geographical Essays*, London, 1967; Egerton, *Angola in Perspective* and *Angola Without Prejudice*; Lewis H. Gann and Peter Duignan, *White Settlers in Tropical Africa*, Baltimore, 1962; and Charles E. Nowell, *Portugal*, Englewood Cliffs, 1973.

89   David M. Abshire and Norman A. Bailey, 'Current Race Character', in *Portuguese Africa: A Handbook*, eds. David M. Abshire and Michael A. Samuels, New York, 1969, pp. 202-16. Also see the chapter by Abshire, 'The Portuguese Racial Legacy', in *ibid.*, pp. 91-106. Abshire's conclusions are particularly suspect given the racial prejudice and cultural arrogance which he manifests in these chapters.

90   Boxer, *Race Relations in the Portuguese Colonial Empire*.

91   Some of the Brazilian social scientists who have published important critiques of Gilberto Freyre include Florestan Fernandes, *The Negro in Brazilian Society*, New York, 1969 and 'Immigration and Race Relations in São Paulo', in *Race and Class in Latin America*, ed. Magnus Morner, New York, 1970, pp. 122-42; José Honório Rodrigues, *Brazil and Africa*, Berkeley, 1965; Thales de Azevedo, *Ensaios de antropologia social*, Salvador-Bahia, 1959; Emilio Willems, 'Racial Attitudes in Brazil', in *Readings in Latin American Social Organization and Institutions*, eds. Olen E. Leonard and Charles P. Loomis, East Lansing, 1953, pp. 240-4; Oracy Nogueira, 'Skin Color and Social Class', in *Plantation Systems of the New World*, Washington, D.C., 1959, pp. 166-75. Also see the playwright and artist Abdias do Nascimento's *O negro revoltado*, Rio de Janeiro, 1968, and Eliana Guerreiro Ramos Cooley, 'A Conversation with Abdias do Nascimento', in *Neworld*, Fall 1974, pp. 32-5.

92   For some examples, see Charles Wagley, 'On the concept of Social Race in the Americas', in *Contemporary Cultures and Societies of Latin America*, eds. Dwight B. Heath and Richard N. Adams, New York, 1965, pp. 531-45, *Race and Class in Brazil*, Paris, 1952 and *An Introduction to Brazil*, New York, 1963; Marvin Harris, 'Referential Ambiguity in the Calculus of Brazilian Racial Identity', in *Afro-American Anthropology*, ed. Norman E. Whitten, New York, 1970, pp. 75-86; Charles Wagley and Marvin Harris, *Minorities in the New World*, New York, 1958; Roger Bastide, 'Color, Racism and Christianity', *Daedalus*, 96, Spring 1967, pp. 312-27, and 'Lusotropicology, Race, and Nationalism, and Class Protest and Development in Brazil and Portuguese Africa', in *Protest and Resistance in Angola and Brazil*, ed. Ronald H. Chilcote, Berkeley, 1972, pp. 225-40; E. Bradford Burns, *A History of Brazil*, New York, 1970; Cleveland Donald, Jr., 'Equality in Brazil: Confronting Reality', *Black World*, 22, November 1972, pp. 23-34; and Anani Dzidzienyo, *The Position of Blacks in Brazilian Society*, London, 1971.

93   Carl N. Degler, *Neither Black nor White*, New York, 1971, and Thomas E. Skidmore, *Black into White: Race and Nationality in Brazilian Thought*, New York, 1974.

94   Bender, *The Myth and Reality*, chapter 2.

95   See, for example, the speeches of most of the prominent nationalist leaders found in the valuable collection of nationalist documents published by Ronald H. Chilcote, *Emerging Nationalism in Portuguese Africa: Documents*, Stanford, 1972. Also see Eduardo Mondlane, *The Struggle for Mozambique*, Baltimore, 1969;

Boavida, *Cinco séculos de exploração;* and Domingos António de Mascarenhas Arouca, *Análise social de regime do indigenato,* Lisbon, 1961.

96   Mario Pinto de Andrade (Buanga Fele), 'Qu'est-ce que le "luso tropicalism"?', *Présence africaine,* no. 4, October-November 1955, pp. 24-35. Andrade continued his attack on Gilberto Freyre and lusotropicalism in the preface to the landmark poetry anthology which he edited, *Antologia da poesia negra de expressão portuguesa,* Paris, 1958, pp. vii-xv.

97   Amílcar Cabral, Foreword to *The Liberation of Guiné,* by Basil Davidson, Baltimore, 1969, p. 9.

98   Allen Isaacman, 'The Prazos da Coroa 1752-1830—Functional Analysis of the Political System', *Studia,* 26, 1969, pp. 149-78; Henry H. Keith, 'Masters and Slaves in Portuguese Africa in the Nineteenth Century: First Soundings', *Studia,* 33, 1971, pp. 235-51.

99   António Alberto de Andrade, 'O Regimento do Benguela (1615) e o sentido humano e científico dessa conquista', *Studia,* 33, 1971, pp. 7-91; Alfredo Pereira de Lima, 'Casas que fizeram Lourenço Marques', *Studia,* 24, 1968?, pp. 7-73; Oliveira Boleo, 'Vicissitudes históricas da política de exploração mineira no império de Monomotapa', *Studia,* 32, 1971, pp. 167-210.

100   Richard J. Hammond, 'Race Attitudes and Policies in Portuguese Africa in the Nineteenth and Twentieth Centuries', *Race,* 9, 1967, pp. 205-16.

101   Isaacman, *Mozambique;* Allen Isaacman and Barbara Isaacman, 'The Prazeros as Transfrontiermen: A study in Social and Culture Change', *International Journal of African Historical Studies,* v, 1975; Newitt, *Portuguese Settlement.* Also see Guiseppe Papagano, *Colonialismo feudalismo—la questione del Prazos da Corea nel Mozambico alla fine del secolo XIX,* Torino, 1972.

102   Bender, *The Myth and Reality,* chapter 3.

103   Gerald J. Bender, 'Planned Rural Settlements in Angola, 1900-1968', in *Social Change in Angola,* ed. Franz-Wilhelm Heimer, Munich, 1973, pp. 236-79, and *The Myth and Reality,* chapter 4; Ilidio do Amaral, *Aspectos do povoamento branco de Angola,* Lisbon, 1960.

104   Brendan F. Jundanian, 'Resettlement Programs: Counterinsurgency in Mozambique', *Comparative Politics,* 6, July 1974, pp. 519-40.

105   See, for example, Thomas Okuma, *Angola in Ferment,* Boston, 1962; Sidney Gilchrist, *Angola Awake,* Toronto, 1968; Davidson, *African Awakening* and *In the Eye of the Storm;* Duffy, *Portuguese Africa;* Mondlane, *The Struggle for Mozambique;* Wheeler and Pélissier, *Angola;* Bender, *Myth and Reality;* Chilcote, *Portuguese Africa;* Arouca, *Análise social;* Jim Hoagland, *South Africa: Civilizations in Conflict,* Boston, 1972, pp. 252-310; Mario Pinto de Andrade, 'Colonization, Culture, and Revolution', *Tricontinental,* July-August 1969, pp. 97-106.

106   Michael A. Samuels, 'A Failure of Hope: Education and Changing Opportunities in Angola under the Portuguese Republic', in *Protest and Resistance in Angola and Brazil,* ed. Ronald H. Chilcote, Berkeley, 1972, pp. 53-65; Douglas L. Wheeler, 'Origins of African Nationalism in Angola: Assimilado Protest Writings, 1859-1929', in *Protest and Resistance in Angola and Brazil,* pp. 67-87; Wheeler and Pélissier, *Angola.*

107   Eduardo de Sousa Ferreira, *Portuguese Colonialism in Africa: The End of an Era,* Paris, 1974, with an introduction by Basil Davidson.

108   See the following works by Douglas L. Wheeler: 'Angola is Whose House? Early Stirrings of Angolan Nationalism and Protest, 1822-1910', *International Journal of African Historical Studies,* ii, 1969, pp. 1-23; 'An Early Angolan Protest: The Radical Journalism of José de Fontes Pereira (1823-1891)', in *Protest and Power in Black Africa,* eds. Robert I. Rotberg and Ali A. Mazrui, New York, 1970, pp. 854-74; 'Origins of African Nationalism in Angola: Assimilado Protest Writings, 1859-1929', 'Nineteenth Century African Protest in Angola: Prince Nicolas of

Kongo (1830?-1860)', *African Historical Studies*, i, 1968, pp. 40-59. Also see: Mario António Fernandes de Oliveira, 'Alguns aspectos da administração de Angola em época de reformas (1834-1851)', *Trabalho*, no. 41-44, 1973, and *Para uma perspectiva crioula da literatura angolana*, Guimaraes, 1974.

109 See Bender, 'Planned Settlements' and *Myth and Reality*; and Gerald J. Bender and P. Stanley Yoder, 'Whites in Angola on the Eve of Independence: The Politics of Numbers', *Africa Today*, 21, Fall 1974, pp. 23-37.

110 See Waldir Freitas Oliveira, 'Brancos e pretos em Angola', *Afro-Asia*, December 1965, pp. 33-9; Sousa Ferreira, *Portuguese Colonialism*. The racist behaviour of whites in Angola and Mozambique evoked considerable criticism from the Portuguese military who complained that it seriously undermined their goal to incorporate large numbers of Africans into the European sector. See Bender, *Myth and Reality*, chapters 6 and 7; and IDOC, *Angola: Secret Government Documents on Counter-Subversion*, Rome, 1974.

111 Franz-Wilhelm Heimer, *Educação e sociedade nas áreas rurais de Angola: resultados de um inquérito*, vol. 1, Luanda, 1972 and *Educação e sociedade nas áreas rurais de Angola: análise do universo agrícola*, vol. 2, Luanda, 1974, preliminary draft. No comparable research has been carried out in Mozambique.

112 See, for example, Birmingham, *Trade and Conflict*, 'The African Response'; Heintze, 'Historical Notes'; Rodney, 'European Activity and African Reaction'. In addition, Roy Glascow is completing an interesting book on Queen Nzinga as a resistance leader.

113 René Pélissier, 'Campagnes militaires au Sud-Angola, 1885-1915', *Cahiers d'études africaines*, 33, 1969, pp. 5-53, and 'Etat de la littérature militaire relative à l'Afrique australe portugaise', *Revue française d'études politiques africaines—le mois en Afrique*, February 1972. Pélissier has completed a three-volume, 1700-page study chronicling the major battles between Europeans and Africans during the last one hundred years. Also see Wheeler and Christensen, 'To Rise with One Mind', for an interesting discussion of the Bailundu rebellion of 1902.

114 See Wheeler, 'Angola is Whose House?' and 'An Early Angolan Protest'; Wheeler and Pélissier, *Angola*. Also see Axelson, *Portuguese in South East Africa, 1600-1700*.

115 Bhilia, 'The Manika'; Isaacman, *Mozambique*; Mudenge, 'The Rozvi Empire'; Newitt, *Portuguese Settlement*.

116 Hafkin, 'Trade, Society and Politics'; Newitt, 'Angoche, the Slave Trade and the Portuguese'.

117 Eric Axelson, *Portugal and the Scramble for Africa, 1875-1891*, Johannesburg, 1967, and *Portugal in Southeast Africa: 1488-1600*, Cape Town, 1973; Hammond, *Portugal and Africa*; P. Warhurst, *Anglo-Portuguese Relations in South-Central Africa, 1885-1910*, London, 1962.

118 Isaacman, *Mozambique*; Newitt, *Portuguese Settlement*; M. D. D. Newitt, 'The Massingire Revolt of 1884', *Journal of African History*, ii, 1970, pp. 87-106; Douglas L. Wheeler, 'Gungunhana', in *Leadership in Eastern Africa: Six political Biographies*, ed. Norman P. Bennett, Boston, 1968; and T. O. Ranger, 'Revolt in Portuguese East Africa—The Makombe Rising of 1917,' in *Saint Anthony Papers—African Affairs*, ed. Kenneth Kirkwood, London, 1963, pp. 54-80.

119 Isaacman, *The Tradition of Resistance*.

120 *Ibid.*, Nancy Hafkin, 'Trade, Society and Politics.'

121 For some examples, see: Amândio César, *Angola 1961*, Lisbon, 1962; Artur Maciel, *Angola heróica*, Lisbon, 1963; Eduardo dos Santos, *Maza*, Lisbon, 1965; Bernardo Teixeira, *The Fabric of Terror*, New York, 1965; Hélio Felgas, *Guerra em Angola* Lisbon, 1961 and, *Os movimentos terroristas de Angola, Guiné, Moçambique* Lisbon, 1966; Alfredo Diogo Junior, *Angola perante uma conspiração internacional*, Luanda, 1961.

122 See: Thomas Okuma, *Angola in Ferment: The Background and Prospects of Angolan Nationalism*, Boston, 1962; Len Addicott, *Cry Angola*, London, 1962;

Perry Anderson, *Le Portugal et la fin de l'ultra-colonialisme*, Paris, 1963; Kavalam
M. Panikkar, *Angola in Flames*, New York, 1962; Ander Ehnmark and Per
Wästberg, *Angola and Mozambique: The Case Against Portugal*, London, 1963;
'Angolan Casebook: The Angolan Revolution,' *Présence africaine* 17, 1963, pp.
151-168; Mário Moutinho de Padua, *Guerra em Angola*, São Paulo, 1963;
António de Figueiredo, *Portugal and Its Empire: The Truth*, London, 1961.

123 Ronald H. Chilcote, *Portuguese Africa*; David M. Abshire and Michael A.
Samuels, *Portuguese Africa: A Handbook*, New York, 1969; Wheeler and Pélissier,
Angola; Allison Butler Herrick, *et al.*, *Area Handbook for Angola*, Washington,
D.C., 1967, and *Area Handbook for Mozambique*, Washington, D.C., 1969.
Another useful collection on the early part of the Angolan war is *Angola, A
Symposium: Views of a Revolt*, London, 1962.

124 A few of the many insightful works by John Marcum include: 'The Angolan
Rebellion: Status Report', *Africa Report*, 9, 1964, pp. 3-7; 'Three Revolutions',
Africa Report, 12, November 1967, pp. 8-22; *The Angolan Revolution*, vol. 1: *The
Anatomy of an Explosion* (*1950-1962*), Cambridge, 1969; 'Liberation Movements
of Portuguese Africa', presented to the United Nations Association of the USA,
1 June 1970. (Volume 2 of *The Angolan Revolution* will appear in 1977.)

125 See Ronald H. Chilcote, *Emerging Nationalism in Portuguese Africa*, Stanford,
1969, and *Emerging Nationalism in Portuguese Africa: Documents*, Stanford, 1972;
Kenneth W. Grundy, *Guerilla Struggle in Africa*, New York, 1971, and
Confrontation and Accommodation in Southern Africa, Berkeley, 1973; Richard
Gibson, *African Liberation Movements*, New York, 1972; Frauke Koeppen-
Schomerus, *Angola 1966/67*, Bad Godesberg, 1967; Gérard Chaliand, 'Problèmes
du nationalisme angolais', *Les temps modernes*, no. 231, 1965, pp. 269-88; René
Pelissier, 'Nationalismes en Angola', *Revue française de science politique*, 19, 1969
pp. 1187-215; George Hauser, 'Nationalist Organizations in Angola: Status of the
Revolt', in *Southern Africa in Transition*, eds. J. Davis and J. Baker, New York,
1966, pp. 157-79; Maina D. Kagombe, 'African Nationalism and Guerilla Warfare
in Angola and Mozambique', in *Southern Africa in Perspective*, eds. Christian P.
Potholm and Richard Dale, New York, 1972, pp. 196-204; J. Bowyer Bell, *The
Myth of the Guerilla: Revolutionary Theory and Malpractice*, New York, 1971;
Wheeler and Pélissier, *Angola*; Newton do Espírito Santo, 'Os movimentos
nacionalistas angolanos', *Revista brasileira de política internacional*, 6 September
1963, pp. 457-82; and Michael A. Samuels. 'The Nationalist Parties', in
Portuguese Africa: A Handbook, eds. David M. Abshire and Michael A. Samuels,
New York, 1969, pp. 389-405; Al J. Venter, *The Terror Fighters*, Cape Town, 1969.
For two major articles which assess the strengths and weaknesses of the Angolan
nationalist movements during the period between the end of the war and
independence, see L. H. Gann, 'Portugal, Africa, and the Future', *Journal of
Modern African Studies*, xiii, March 1975, pp. 1-18; and Kenneth L. Adelman,
'Report from Angola', *Foreign Affairs*, 53, April 1975, pp. 558-74. Unfortunately,
both these authors exaggerate and distort the importance of 'Maoism' in UNITA,
'Marxism' in the MPLA and 'lusotropicalism' among the Portuguese.

126 Basil Davidson, *In the Eye of the Storm*, and 'Walking 300 Miles with Guerillas
Through the Bush of Eastern Angola', *Munger Africana Library Notes*, 6 April
1971. For other works on the MPLA see Donald Barnett and Roy Harvey, eds.,
The Revolution in Angola: MPLA Life Histories and Documents, New York, 1972;
Donald Barnett, 'Angola: Report from Hanoi II', *Ramparts*, 7, April 1969, pp.
49-54; Yuliy A. Organisyan, *Natsionalnaya Revolyutsiya v Angole 1961-1966*,
Moscow, 1968; Mario de Andrade and Marc Ollivier, *La guerre en Angola*, Paris,
1971; and Américo Boavida, *Cinco séculos de exploração portuguesa*, Rio de
Janeiro, 1967.

127 See Davidson, *The Eye of the Storm*, and Gibson, *African Liberation Movements*.
Also see the debate between Davidson and Gibson in *West Africa*, 2867, 26 May

1972, p. 657, and 2869, 9 June 1972, p. 727. Fritz Sitte, an Austrian journalist made a film and wrote many articles favourable to UNITA after his trip into Angola with the movement in the early 1970s; see for example, his illustrated article in *The Observer*, London, 9 April 1972. For a study of UNITA during the war by one of the party's leaders see Jorge Valentine, *Qui libère l'Angola*, Brussels, 1969. Also see Leon Dash, *Get Off my Mountain: The Roots of Revolt in Angola*, Howard Univ. Press, 1976. (Title tentative.)

128 Olle Wastberg, *Angola*, Stockholm, 1970 and Pierre-Pascal Rossi, *Pour une guerre oubliée*, Paris, 1969.

129 Bell, *The Myth of the Guerilla*. Also see Gann, 'Portugal, Africa and the Future'.

130 For some examples of studies on FRELIMO see Eduardo C. Mondlane, 'A Document for the History of African Nationalism: A FRELIMO "White Paper" ', *African Historical Studies*, ii, 1969, pp. 319-33, and *The Struggle for Mozambique*; Ronald H. Chilcote, 'Les mouvements de libération au Mozambique', *Le mois en Afrique*, 1, July 1964, pp. 30-42; and Saul, 'FRELIMO and the Mozambique Revolution'; Richard W. Leonard, 'Frelimo's Victories in Mozambique', *Issue*, 4, Summer 1974, pp. 38-46; Glyn Hughes, 'FRELIMO and the Mozambique War of Liberation', *Monthly Review*, 20, December 1968, pp. 7-18; Walter C. Opello, Jr., 'Guerilla War in Portuguese Africa: An Assessment of the Balance of Force in Mozambique', *Issue*, 4, Summer 1974, pp. 29-37.

131 L. S. B. Leakey, *Tentative Study of the Pleistocene Climatic Changes and Stone Age Culture Sequence in North-Eastern Angola*, Museu do Dondo, 1949; J. Desmond Clark, *Prehistoric Cultures of Northeast Angola and their Significance in Tropical Africa*, 2 vols., Lisbon, 1963 and *Further Paleo-Anthropological Studies in Northern Lunda*, Lisbon, 1968.

132 Virtually no systematic archaeological work has been done in Mozambique, although extensive related research has been completed at the Zimbabwe ruins. As early as 1958, Mauny pointed out the need for extensive digs throughout the entire Sofala-Zimbabwe region. Raymond Mauny, 'Notes sur le problème Zimbabwe-Sofala', *Studia*, 1, 1958, pp. 176-84.

133 In addition to filling in the broad outline of many of these processes, archaeological data would provide an approximate chronology necessary to date major changes described in the oral traditions.

134 See Vansina, 'Anthropologists', for an illuminating discussion of the ethnographic present.

135 See Jan Vansina, 'The Use of Ethnographic Data as Sources for History', in *Emerging Themes of African History*, ed. T. O. Ranger, Nairobi, 1968, pp. 97-124.

136 Since 1968, when Isaacman collected oral data in the Zambesi Valley, several of his major informants have died.

137 In his capacity as Director of the Portuguese Africa Project at the University of California, Los Angeles, Bender attempted to establish an oral data programme in conjunction with the Junta de Investigações Científicas do Ultramar in 1972.

138 Recently, a number of economic historians have challenged the uncritical use of the concept 'subsistence economy' when referring to pre-colonial Africa. Among those who have questioned its utility are Professors Paul Lovejoy, Edward Alpers, Margaret Hay, Philip Curtin, Anthony Hopkins and Ralph Austen.

139 For some examples see Eduardo Cruz de Carvalho, ' "Traditional" and "Modern" Patterns of Cattle Raising in South-western Angola: A Critical Evaluation of Change from Pastoralism to Ranching', *Journal of Developing Areas*, 8, January 1974, pp. 199-226; Eduardo Cruz de Carvalho and Jorge Vieira da Silva, 'The Cunene Region: Ecological Analysis of an African Agro-pastoral System', in *Social Change in Angola*, ed. Franz-Wilhelm Heimer, pp. 145-92; Jorge Vieira da Silva and Julio Artur de Morais, 'Ecological Conditions of Social Change in the Central Highlands of Angola', in *ibid.*, pp. 93-110; Hermann

Possinger, 'Interrelations Between Economic and Social Change in Rural Africa: The Case of the Ovimbundu of Angola', in *ibid.*, pp. 31-52; Jacinto dos Santos Carriço and Julio Artur de Morais, *Perspectivás de Desenvolvimento Regional do Huambo*, Nova Lisboa, 1971; Hermann Possinger, *Landwirtschaftliche Entwicklung in Angola und Moçambique*, Munich, 1968.

140   Mario de Carvalho, *A agricultura tradicional de Moçambique*, Lourenço Marques, 1969. Sherilynn Young is currently examining similar problems in southern Mozambique from an historical perspective.

141   See, for example, Matthew Schoffeleers, 'The History and Political Role of the M'bona Cult Among the Maganja', in *The Historical Study of African Religion*, ed. T. O. Ranger and Isaria Kimbano, Berkeley, 1972, pp. 73-94. P. Stanley Yoder is currently doing research in this area among the Chokwe.

142   See Ilídio do Amaral, *Ensaio de um estudo geográfico da rede urbana de Angola*, Lisbon, 1962, and *Luanda: estudo de geográfica urbana*, Lisbon, 1968; José de Sousa Bettencourt, *Subsídio para o estudo sociológico da população de Luanda*, Luanda, 1965; Ramiro Ladeiro Monteiro, *A família nos musseques de Luanda: subsídios para o seu estudo*, Luanda, 1973. Monteiro's comprehensive study of the Luanda slums was awarded a prize as the best study on the 'Ultramar' in 1973. A former officer high in the Angolan army's intelligence service, Monteiro had access to secret military and police data on the slums, much of which appears in the book.

143   MPLA, *História de Angola*, Porto, 1974 and Wheeler and Pélissier, *Angola*.

144   FRELIMO, *História de Moçambique*, Porto, 1974.

145   Edward Alpers, Allen Isaacman and Alan Smith, *A History of Mozambique*, Heinemann, 1977, title tentative.

Index